Instructor's Resource Manual: Cases

Strategic Management

An Integrated Approach

SIXTH EDITION

Charles W. L. Hill

University of Washington

Gareth R. Jones

Texas A&M University

Anu Wadhwa

University of Washington

Houghton Mifflin Company   BOSTON   NEW YORK

Editor-in-Chief: *George T. Hoffman*
Associate Sponsoring Editor: *Susan M. Kahn*
Senior Manufacturing Coordinator: *Marie Barnes*
Marketing Manager: *Steven W. Mikels*

Printed in the U.S.A.

ISBN: 0-618-31820-8

23456789-CRS-07 06 05 04

Contents

INTRODUCTION

Using the Instructor's Resource Manual: Cases

The *Instructor's Resource Manuals* that accompany this edition of *Strategic Management: An Integrated Approach* by Charles W.L. Hill and Gareth R. Jones are designed to present you with a complete teaching package. This volume of the *Instructor's Resource Manual* contains the case teaching notes. A separate volume, *Instructor's Resource Manual with Test Questions* provides teaching support for Chapters 1-13, which cover strategic management theory.

In this section, you will find a brief overview list of the textbook cases; a chart summarizing the topics covered in each case; and sample course outlines, including suggestions on which cases to use at which points in the course.

The case teaching notes in this volume are closely tied to the content of the textbook to drive home the meaning of strategic management and are written in the form of answers to questions. The discussion questions for all of the cases precede the first teaching note. This grouping makes it easy for you to pull out the questions for the cases you decide to use during the course and to put together a student handout. We generally use ten or eleven cases per semester and hand out a list of questions for the selected cases during the first class period. We give out the questions because we have found that with no clues as to what the case is about, students do a poor job of case analysis.

Each teaching note offers comprehensive answers to the discussion questions, bringing out the meaning of each case and the strategic issues facing each corporation. Each case raises fundamental issues and provides a practical illustration of the meaning of the conceptual material given in the textbook chapters.

ABOUT THE CASES

A selection of forty-three cases addressing real-world strategic issues is included in the textbook. The cases are consistently interesting and of high quality. It is important to emphasize that we have completely overhauled the case selection. All but 16 of the 43 cases are new to this edition, and all of the carryovers (Cases 5, 6, 16, 19, 20, 25, 27, 29, 30, 31, 32, 33, 34, 35, 41, 43) have been updated. We wrote nineteen of the cases ourselves, a higher proportion of the total than in competing books. The cases are designed to illustrate major strategic issues, to illuminate the course concepts, and to be integrated with the course material. Too many cases in textbooks are outdated and end just when major strategic problems are confronting the company. We have tried to avoid such cases in this book. Many of these cases emphasize new economy themes, but we continue to carry a good number of old economy cases. As always, we have used a tight screen to weed out poor quality cases and we believe that the selection we offer is the best on the market. A brief sketch of each case is given below, and the case contents are further summarized in the chart that follows.

The quality of the cases is illustrated by the fact that we are able to offer explicit recommendations on which case to use and in which sequence. The course outlines offer alternative tracks of cases that you can use in successive semesters or successive years. The outlines are designed to reinforce an interactive, integrated approach, and we feel that if you use the cases in a generally similar sequence, you will be pleased by the results.

LIST OF CASES

Case 1   **Vail Resorts, Inc.**
Herman L. Boschken, *San Jose State University*
This premier ski resort seeks to maintain its edge and improve performance in a maturing market.

MORE ABOUT THE CASES

The Case Contents chart on the pages that follow provides a general summary of the topics covered in each case. In addition, before each case in the Teaching Notes we offer a more detailed written synopsis that you may wish to consult when deciding which cases to include in your course.

Case Contents

	Strategic Planning	External Environment	Competitive Advantage	Functional Strategy	Business Strategy	Competitive Strategy, Industry Environment	Technology Strategy	Global Strategy	Vertical Integration	Diversification, Acquisitions	New Ventures, Restructuring	Ethics, Governance	Organizational Structure, Control, Culture	Matching structure and Strategy
1. Vail Resorts, Inc.		X	X	X	X	X								
2. Adrenaline Air Sports: Where the Speed Limit Is 120 Miles per Hour…or More			X	X	X									
3. General Aviation: An Industry Note		X												
4. Redlands Municipal Airport	X		X	X	X									
5. Perdue Farms, Inc.: Responding to Twenty-first Century Challenges	X		X	X	X									
6. Wizards of the Coast, 1990-2001	X	X	X		X	X			X	X				
7. Napster			X	X			X							
8. AtomFilms			X	X	X	X								
9. Zoots – The Cleaner Cleaner		X	X	X	X	X								
10. Nike: Sweatshops and Business Ethics								X				X		
11. WestJet Looks East			X	X	X	X								
12. Avon Products, Inc.: The Personal-Care Industry			X	X	X	X		X						
13. The Body Shop International: U.S. Operations	X		X	X	X			X						
14. J.P. Morgan Chase & Co.: The Credit Card Segment of the Financial Services Industry		X	X	X	X	X								
15. Toyota: The Evolution of the Toyota Production System			X	X	X	X		X						
16. Nucor in 2001		X	X	X	X				X				X	X
17. Digital Devices: Current and Future Market Opportunities		X				X	X							

		Strategic Planning	External Environment	Competitive Advantage	Functional Strategy	Business Strategy	Competitive Strategy, Industry Environment	Technology Strategy	Global Strategy	Vertical Integration	Diversification, Acquisitions	New Ventures, Restructuring	Ethics, Governance	Organizational Structure, Control, Culture	Matching structure and Strategy
18.	Treo: Handspring's Last Stand?						X	X							
19.	The Home Video Game Industry: From Pong to X-Box		X	X					X						
20.	Microsoft Windows Versus Linux								X						
21.	IBM Global Services: The Professional Computer Services Industry		X	X		X	X	X							
22.	SAP and the Evolving Web Software ERP Market		X			X	X		X						
23.	Iridium: Communication for the New Millennium			X		X	X	X				X			
24.	A Hundred-Year War: Coke vs. Pepsi, 1890s-1990s		X	X		X	X			X					
25.	Wal-Mart Stores, Inc.: Strategies for Dominance in the New Millennium			X	X	X			X					X	X
26.	Wal-Mart's Mexican Adventure								X						
27.	Kmart Corporation: Seeking Customer Acceptance and Preference			X	X	X	X								
28.	Tosco and the New Millennium		X			X				X	X				
29.	The Evolution of the Air Express Industry, 1973-2002		X			X									
30.	Airborne Express in 2002			X	X	X			X					X	X
31.	Blockbuster in 2002		X	X	X	X								X	
32.	Video Concepts, Inc.		X	X	X	X									
33.	AOL Time Warner: Creating a Colossus			X		X	X	X			X				
34.	The Viacom Empire		X	X		X					X			X	X
35.	Monsanto (A): Building a Life Sciences Company					X	X	X		X	X	X			
36.	Monsanto (B): Merger and Rebirth									X	X				
37.	Eli Lilly & Company: The Global Pharmaceutical Industry		X	X	X	X			X	X	X				

		Strategic Planning	External Environment	Competitive Advantage	Functional Strategy	Business Strategy	Competitive Strategy, Industry Environment	Technology Strategy	Global Strategy	Vertical Integration	Diversification, Acquisitions	New Ventures, Restructuring	Ethics, Governance	Organizational Structure, Control, Culture	Matching structure and Strategy
38.	Kikkoman Corporation in the Mid-1990s: Market Maturity, Diversification, and Globalization								X	X	X				
39.	CenturyTel in a Bear Hug		X			X				X	X				
40.	Whirlpool Corporation's Global Strategy								X						
41.	"You Push the Button, We Do the Rest": From Silver Halide to Infoimaging at Eastman Kodak	X	X	X	X						X	X		X	X
42.	Restructuring Excide								X		X	X	X	X	X
43.	First Greyhound, Then Greyhound Dial, Then Dial: What Will Happen in 2002?									X		X		X	

SUGGESTED COURSE OUTLINES

We offer below three sets of course outlines, each set consisting of two or three alternative tracks: three alternative course outlines for 75- to 80-minute, 30-session classes; three outlines for 50- to 55-minute, 45-session classes; and two outlines for 110-minute, 20-session classes (for a quarter system). As mentioned earlier, the cases fit the lectures and can be used as listed with each lecture sequence. Chapter lectures are often split between days to allow ample time for class discussion after the students have studied each chapter. If group projects are not assigned, then additional cases can be analyzed at the end of the semester.

Course Outline 1

30 Class Meetings of 75 to 80 Minutes

20 Cases and 10 Strategic Management Projects

Session	Course Outline
1	Introduction to course / Analyzing and writing a case study
2	Lecture Chapter 1
3	Cases 3, 4, 5: General Aviation: An Industry Note / Redlands Municipal Airport /Perdue Farms, Inc.
4	Lecture Chapter 2
5	Lecture Chapter 3
6	Cases 11, 29, 30: WestJet Looks East / The Evolution of the Air Express Industry / Airborne Express
7	Exam 1
8	Lecture Chapter 4
9	Cases 9, 15: Zoots – The Cleaner Cleaner / Toyota
10	Lecture Chapter 5
11	Lecture Chapter 6
12	Cases 14, 24: J.P. Morgan Chase & Co. / A Hundred-Year War: Coke vs. Pepsi
13	Cases 25, 27: Wal-Mart Stores, Inc. / Kmart Corporation
14	Lecture Chapter 7
15	Cases 7, 19: Napster / The Home Video Game Industry
16	Lecture Chapter 8
17	Cases 13, 40: The Body Shop International / Whirlpool Corporation's Global Strategy
18	Lecture Chapter 9
19	Lecture Chapter 10
20	Cases 33, 34: AOL Time Warner / The Viacom Empire
21	Exam 2
22	Lecture Chapters 11, 12
23	Lecture Chapter 13
24	Cases 16, 42: Nucor / Restructuring Exide
25	Strategic Management Projects 1, 2
26	Strategic Management Projects 3, 4
27	Strategic Management Projects 5, 6
28	Strategic Management Projects 7, 8
29	Strategic Management Projects 9, 10
30	Final Exam

Course Outline 2

30 Class Meetings of 75 to 80 Minutes

19 Cases and 10 Strategic Management Projects

Session	Course Outline
1	Introduction to course / Analyzing and writing a case study
2	Lecture Chapter 1
3	Cases 2, 6: Adrenaline Air Sports / Wizards of the Coast
4	Lecture Chapter 2
5	Lecture Chapter 3
6	Cases 8, 12: AtomFilms / Avon Products, Inc.
7	Exam 1
8	Lecture Chapter 4
9	Cases 9, 15: Zoots – The Cleaner Cleaner / Toyota
10	Lecture Chapter 5
11	Lecture Chapter 6
12	Cases 18, 21: Treo: Handspring's Last Stand? / IBM Global Services
13	Cases 23, 31: Iridium / Blockbuster
14	Lecture Chapter 7
15	Cases 19, 20: The Home Video Game Industry / Microsoft Windows Versus Linux
16	Lecture Chapter 8
17	Cases 13, 38: The Body Shop International / Kikkoman Corporation
18	Lecture Chapter 9
19	Lecture Chapter 10
20	Cases 28, 35, 36: Tosco and the New Millennium / Monsanto (A) / Monsanto (B)
21	Exam 2
22	Lecture Chapters 11, 12
23	Lecture Chapter 13
24	Cases 16, 37: Nucor / Eli Lilly & Company
25	Strategic Management Projects 1, 2
26	Strategic Management Projects 3, 4
27	Strategic Management Projects 5, 6
28	Strategic Management Projects 7, 8
29	Strategic Management Projects 9, 10
30	Final Exam

Course Outline 3

30 Class Meetings of 75 to 80 Minutes

23 Cases and 10 Strategic Management Projects

Session	Course Outline
1	Introduction to course / Analyzing and writing a case study
2	Lecture Chapter 1
3	Lecture Chapter 2
4	Cases 1, 3: Vail Resorts, Inc. / General Aviation: An Industry Note
5	Cases 8, 9: AtomFilms / Zoots – The Cleaner Cleaner
6	Lecture Chapter 3 / Case 5: Perdue Farms, Inc.
7	Lecture Chapter 4 / Case 25: Wal-Mart Stores, Inc.
8	Lecture Chapter 5 / Case 16: Nucor
9	Cases 15, 13: Toyota / The Body Shop International
10	Exam 1
11	Lecture Chapter 6
12	Cases 31, 32: Blockbuster / Video Concepts, Inc.
13	Lecture Chapter 7 / Case 22: SAP and the Evolving Web Software ERP Market
14	Cases 12, 14: Avon Products, Inc. / J.P. Morgan Case & Co.
15	Lecture Chapter 8 / Case 38: Kikkoman Corporation
16	Lecture Chapter 9 / Case 41: Kodak
17	Lecture Chapter 10
18	Case 34: The Viacom Empire
19	Cases 43, 42: Dial / Restructuring Exide
20	Exam 2
21	Lecture Chapter 11 / Case 10: Nike
22	Lecture Chapter 12 / Case 40: Whirlpool Corporation's Global Strategy
23	Lecture Chapter 13 / Case 27: Kmart Corporation
24	Case 33: AOL Time Warner
25	Strategic Management Projects 1, 2
26	Strategic Management Projects 3, 4
27	Strategic Management Projects 5, 6
28	Strategic Management Projects 7, 8
29	Strategic Management Projects 9, 10
30	Final Exam

Course Outline 4

45 Class Meetings of 50 to 55 Minutes

22 Cases and 10 Strategic Management Projects

Session	Course Outline
1	Introduction to course
2	Analyzing and writing a case study / Case 1: Vail Resorts, Inc.
3	Lecture Chapter 1
4	Cases 3, 4: General Aviation: An Industry Note / Redlands Municipal Airport
5	Lecture Chapter 2
6	Lecture Chapter 2
7	Cases 29, 30: The Evolution of the Air Express Industry / Airborne Express
8	Lecture Chapter 3
9	Lecture Chapter 3
10	Case 11: WestJet Looks East
11	Lecture Chapter 4
12	Lecture Chapter 4
13	Case 9: Zoots – The Cleaner Cleaner
14	Case 15: Toyota
15	Lecture Chapter 5
16	Case 24: A Hundred-Year War: Coke vs. Pepsi
17	Exam 1
18	Lecture Chapter 6
19	Case 14: J.P. Morgan Chase & Co.
20	Case 25: Wal-Mart Stores, Inc.
21	Case 26: Wal-Mart's Mexican Adventure
22	Lecture Chapter 7
23	Case 7: Napster
24	Case 19: The Home Video Game Industry
25	Case 17: Digital Devices
26	Case 18: Treo: Handspring's Last Stand?
27	Lecture Chapter 8
28	Case 13: The Body Shop International
29	Case 40: Whirlpool Corporation's Global Strategy
30	Exam 2
31	Lecture Chapter 9
32	Lecture Chapter 10
33	Case 33: AOL Time Warner
34	Case 34: The Viacom Empire
35	Lecture Chapter 11
36	Lecture Chapter 12
37	Lecture Chapter 13
38	Case 16: Nucor
39	Case 28: Tosco and the New Millennium
40	Strategic Management Projects 1, 2
41	Strategic Management Projects 3, 4
42	Strategic Management Projects 5, 6
43	Strategic Management Projects 7, 8
44	Strategic Management Projects 9, 10
45	Final Exam

Course Outline 5

45 Class Meetings of 50 to 55 Minutes

22 Cases and 10 Strategic Management Projects

Session	Course Outline
1	Introduction to course
2	Analyzing and writing a case study / Case 2: Adrenaline Air Sports
3	Lecture Chapter 1
4	Case 6: Wizards of the Coast
5	Lecture Chapter 2
6	Lecture Chapter 2
7	Case 8: AtomFilms
8	Lecture Chapter 3
9	Lecture Chapter 3
10	Case 12: Avon Products, Inc.
11	Lecture Chapter 4
12	Lecture Chapter 4
13	Case 9: Zoots – The Cleaner Cleaner
14	Case 15: Toyota
15	Lecture Chapter 5
16	Cases 29, 30: The Evolution of the Air Express Industry / Airborne Express
17	Exam 1
18	Lecture Chapter 6
19	Case 24: A Hundred-Year War: Coke vs. Pepsi
20	Case 23: Iridium
21	Case 31: Blockbuster
22	Lecture Chapter 7
23	Case 17: Digital Devices
24	Case 18: Treo: Handspring's Last Stand?
25	Case 19: The Home Video Game Industry
26	Case 20: Microsoft Windows Versus Linux
27	Lecture Chapter 8
28	Case 13: The Body Shop International
29	Case 38: Kikkoman Corporation
30	Exam 2
31	Lecture Chapter 9
32	Lecture Chapter 10
33	Case 28: Tosco and the New Millennium
34	Cases 35, 36: Monsanto (A) / Monsanto (B)
35	Lecture Chapter 11
36	Lecture Chapter 12
37	Lecture Chapter 13
38	Case 16: Nucor
39	Case 37: Eli Lilly & Company
40	Strategic Management Projects 1, 2
41	Strategic Management Projects 3, 4
42	Strategic Management Projects 5, 6
43	Strategic Management Projects 7, 8
44	Strategic Management Projects 9, 10
45	Final Exam

Course Outline 6

45 Class Meetings of 50 to 55 Minutes

27 Cases and 10 Strategic Management Projects

Session	Course Outline
1	Introduction to course / Analyzing and writing a case study
2	Lecture Chapter 2
3	Case 1: Vail Resorts, Inc.
4	Case 3: General Aviation: An Industry Note
5	Lecture Chapter 3
6	Case 28: Tosco and the New Millennium
7	Cases 8, 9: AtomFilms / Zoots – The Cleaner Cleaner
8	Lecture Chapter 4
9	Case 25: Wal-Mart Stores, Inc.
10	Lecture Chapter 5
11	Case 16: Nucor
12	Case 15: Toyota
13	Case 13: The Body Shop International
14	Exam 1
15	Lecture Chapter 6
16	Cases 31, 32: Blockbuster / Video Concepts, Inc.
17	Case 11: WestJet Looks East
18	Case 5: Perdue Farms, Inc.
19	Lecture Chapter 7
20	Case 22: SAP and the Evolving Web Software ERP Market
21	Case 21: IBM Global Services
22	Case 12: Avon Products, Inc.
23	Lecture Chapter 8
24	Case 38: Kikkoman Corporation
25	Case 40: Whirlpool Corporation's Global Strategy
26	Lecture Chapter 9
27	Case 41: Kodak
28	Lecture Chapter 10
29	Case 34: The Viacom Empire
30	Case 43: Dial
31	Exam 2
32	Lecture Chapter 11
33	Case 10: Nike
34	Case 27: Kmart Corporation
35	Lecture Chapter 12
36	Cases 35, 36: Monsanto (A) / Monsanto (B)
37	Lecture Chapter 13
38	Case 37: Eli Lilly & Company
39	Case 33: AOL Time Warner
40	Strategic Management Projects 1, 2
41	Strategic Management Projects 3, 4
42	Strategic Management Projects 5, 6
43	Strategic Management Projects 7, 8
44	Strategic Management Projects 9, 10
45	Final Exam

Course Outline 7

20 Class Meetings of 110 Minutes

18 Cases and 8 Strategic Management Projects

Session	Course Outline
1	Introduction to course / Analyzing and writing a case study / Lecture Chapter 1
2	Cases 3, 4, 5: General Aviation: An Industry Note / Redlands Municipal Airport / Perdue Farms, Inc.
3	Lecture Chapter 2
4	Lecture Chapters 3, 4
5	Cases 11, 29, 30: WestJet Looks East / The Evolution of the Air Express Industry / Airborne Express
6	Cases 9, 15: Zoots – The Cleaner Cleaner / Toyota
7	Lecture Chapters 5, 6
8	Cases 14, 24: J.P. Morgan Chase & Co. / A Hundred-Year War: Coke vs. Pepsi
9	Exam 1
10	Lecture Chapter 7
11	Cases 7, 19: Napster / The Home Video Game Industry
12	Lecture Chapter 8
13	Cases 13, 40: The Body Shop International / Whirlpool Corporation's Global Strategy
14	Lecture Chapters 9, 10
15	Cases 33, 34: AOL Time Warner / The Viacom Empire
16	Lecture Chapters 11, 12, 13
17	Cases 16, 42: Nucor / Restructuring Exide
18	Strategic Management Projects 1–4
19	Strategic Management Projects 5–8
20	Final Exam

Course Outline 8

20 Class Meetings of 110 Minutes

17 Cases and 8 Strategic Management Projects

Session	Course Outline
1	Introduction to course / Analyzing and writing a case study / Lecture Chapter 1
2	Cases 2, 6: Adrenaline Air Sports / Wizards of the Coast
3	Lecture Chapter 2
4	Lecture Chapters 3, 4
5	Cases 8, 12: AtomFilms / Avon Products, Inc.
6	Cases 9, 15: Zoots – The Cleaner Cleaner / Toyota
7	Lecture Chapters 5, 6
8	Cases 21, 31: IBM Global Services/ Blockbuster
9	Exam 1
10	Lecture Chapter 7
11	Cases 19, 20: The Home Video Game Industry / Microsoft Windows Versus Linux
12	Lecture Chapter 8
13	Cases 13, 38: The Body Shop International / Kikkoman Corporation
14	Lecture Chapters 9, 10
15	Cases 28, 35, 36: Tosco and the New Millennium / Monsanto (A) / Monsanto (B)
16	Cases 37, 39: Eli Lilly & Company / CenturyTel in a Bear Hug
17	Lecture Chapters 11, 12, 13
18	Strategic Management Projects 1–4
19	Strategic Management Projects 5–8
20	Final Exam

Case Discussion Questions

DISCUSSION QUESTIONS FOR CASE 1—VAIL RESORTS, INC.

1. Analyze Vail Resorts' competitive environment using Porter's Five Forces Model.

2. What do you see as the internal strengths and weaknesses of Vail Resorts?

3. What is the Business level strategy being pursued by the company?

4. Discuss why Vail Resorts has been successful in their vertical integration and diversification programs? What are some potential risks associated with these strategies?

5. Evaluate the changes made by Vail Resorts to its organizational structure.

DISCUSSION QUESTIONS FOR CASE 2—ADRENALINE AIR SPORTS: WHERE THE SPEED LIMIT IS 120 MILES PER HOUR…OR MORE

1. How do you get first time jumpers to come back for more jumps, when industry wide only 3% attempt a second jump?

2. What can Adrenaline Air Sports do to make its pricing for the first 9 jumps more attractive to new parachute jumpers?

3. What are the most important customer groups that Adrenaline Air Sports should target?

4. What advertising media should Billy Cockrell use to market his Adrenaline Air Sports?

5. What steps will Billy Cockrell have to satisfy in order to go full-time with his Adrenaline Air Sports?

DISCUSSION QUESTIONS FOR CASE 3—GENERAL AVIATION: AN INDUSTRY NOTE

1. What are the benefits to a community of having a general aviation airport?

2. What are some downsides of having a general aviation airport near a community?

3. What do you think has been the impact of the World Trade Center (WTC) tragedy on general aviation airports? How do you think this will influence the future of the General aviation industry?

DISCUSSION QUESTIONS FOR CASE 4—REDLANDS MUNICIPAL AIRPORT

1. Who are the stakeholders in this case, and how do they interact? Specifically, what is the relationship between the public and the tenants at the airport, the City of Redlands and the Airport Advisory Board?

2. Who is responsible for the airport? Who should be in charge of economic growth at the airport: the City or the fixed base operators? Why is the delineation of responsibility so ambiguous?

3. What are the advantages/disadvantages for a city to own an airport? Why not just keep the airport private?

4. What are the problems and opportunities of being a business at or near a small general aviation airport?

5. Why were the forecasts wrong, and why was the Master Plan overly optimistic? Should the government officials rely on forecasts? What variables should be used in creating a forecast? What forecasts would you develop to help the government officials?

6. Why should an airport be concerned about safety and noise issues? How should they be addressed?

7. If you were a management consultant to the City of Redlands, what recommendations would you make to ensure the economic viability of the airport?

DISCUSSION QUESTIONS FOR CASE 5—PERDUE FARMS, INC.: RESPONDING TO TWENTY-FIRST CENTURY CHALLENGES

1. What resource strengths and competitive assets does Perdue Farms have that can help determine realistic strategic directions, i.e., potential goals the company is capable of achieving?

2. What weaknesses and resource deficiencies does Perdue Farms have that put it at a competitive disadvantage, i.e., potential goals they will probably have a difficult time achieving?

3. What industry opportunities exist that are unusually attractive and are a good match with Perdue Farms' strengths, i.e., potential company opportunities?

4. What industry factors threaten Perdue Farms, i.e., pose serious threats to its future growth and profitability?

5. In what ways have Perdue Farms' structure and culture helped or harmed its attempts to implement its strategy?

6. What generic business-level and competitive strategies does Perdue Farms use?

7. What is Perdue Farms' corporate-level strategy, and how does it support its business-level strategy?

DISCUSSION QUESTIONS FOR CASE 6—WIZARDS OF THE COAST, 1990-2001

1. How was Wizards of the Coast able to "re-create" the adventure game market?

2. How important was the early international expansion of Wizards? What strategy did the firm pursue? What are the opportunities and threats in international growth in the future?

3. What were the sources of capital for Wizards of the Coast? What implications does this have for the future strategy of the company?

4. What were some of the challenges Wizards experienced as a result of its tremendous growth?

5. What would you do given the situation in mid-1997 described in the case? If you chose to end the game, how would you go about it? What path would you pursue? Why?

6. What were the reasons that compelled Hasbro to acquire Wizards of the Coast? What do you see as the biggest challenge for Wizards and Hasbro?

7. Why did Wizards acquire TSR (the maker of *Dungeons and Dragons*)?

8. Why did Wizards try to turn Magic into an Intellectual sport by setting up competitions and leagues between Magic players?

9. What lay behind Wizard's move into retail stores? What are the potential problems with this strategy?

DISCUSSION QUESTIONS FOR CASE 7—NAPSTER

1. What are the economics of the music recording business?

2. Do the big five music recording companies have market power? If so, where does this power come from? Was this market power starting to erode prior to the arrival of Napster?

3. Does file-sharing technology over peer-to-peer networks have the characteristics of a disruptive technology? What are the implications of this technology for the market power and growth prospects of established music recording companies? How might this technology, including variations developed by established music companies, "disrupt" the industry?

4.   What are the implications for the music recording business of widespread violation of intellectual property rights? Do new digital technologies increase the potential piracy rate? Why?

5.   How did Fanning come up with the original idea for Napster? What does this tell you, if anything, about the birth of entrepreneurial organizations? Was Shawn Fanning an insightful business thinker or accidental entrepreneur?

6.   Why did peer-to-peer technology suddenly come to the fore in the late 1990s? What explains the extraordinary early growth of Napster?

7.   In retrospect, what mistakes did Napster make? How might things have been done differently?

8.   Do you think the business model proposed by Barry was potentially viable? What flaws can you see in it? How might it be improved?

9.   What are the lessons that Napster holds for the established labels in the music recording businesses?

DISCUSSION QUESTIONS FOR CASE 8—ATOMFILMS

1.   What does the competitive structure of the established film distribution business in the United States look like? What are the implications of this structure for a company looking to get into the film distribution business? Why have these companies not actively pursued opportunities to distribute short films?

2.   Why has "Digital Hollywood" been such a failure?

3.   What is the market opportunity that Mika Salmi is going after with AtomFilms?

4.   What must Atom do to build a company?

5.   Where is the greatest long-term growth potential for AtomFilms—in the B2B market place (off line distribution) or in B2C (online distribution)?

6.   Does the growth of peer-to-peer computing represent an opportunity or threat for AtomFilms?

7.   Which of the three business models suggested at the end of the case do you think AtomFilms should pursue?

DISCUSSION QUESTIONS FOR CASE 9—ZOOTS – THE CLEANER CLEANER

1.   How would you characterize the economic structure of the dry cleaning industry? Do you think the average player in this industry earns anything other than "normal" economic profits?

2.   Why is the dry cleaning industry fragmented?

3.   What is the most important asset of a dry cleaning store? What drives sales?

4.   Describe and evaluate the business model for Zoots. How does Zoots intend to earn a rate of return that exceeds its cost of capital? What are the strengths of this business model? What are the weaknesses and flaws in the model?

5.   How might the hub and spoke system employed by Zoots lead to cost savings? Under what circumstances might it lead to cost increases?

6.   How would you characterize Krasnow's approach to identifying a business opportunity? Can you see a drawback with this approach?

7.   Krasnow and Stemberg and company did not have to raise venture capital to fund the venture. Was it an advantage or a disadvantage?

8.   What do the problems Zoots was having expanding in Portsmouth tell you?

9.   Rethink the strategy pursued by Zoots. Might the company have done things differently?

10. Can you see any flaws in the way Krasnow and his associates developed the Zoots concept?

DISCUSSION QUESTIONS FOR CASE 10—NIKE: SWEATSHOPS AND BUSINESS ETHICS

1. Should Nike be held responsible for working conditions in foreign factories that it does not own, but where sub-contractors make products for Nike?

2. What labor standards regarding safety, working conditions, overtime and the like should Nike hold foreign factories to: those prevailing in that country, or those prevailing in the United States?

3. An income of $2.28 a day, the base pay of Nike factory workers in Indonesia, is double the daily income of about half the working population. Half of all adults in Indonesia are farmers, who receive less than $1 a day. Given this, is it correct to criticize Nike for low pay rates for subcontractors in Indonesia?

4. Could Nike have handled the negative publicity over sweatshops better? What might have been done differently? Not just from the public relations perspective, but also from a policy perspective?

5. Do you think Nike needs to make any changes to its current policy? If so, what? Should Nike make changes even if they hinder the ability of the company to compete in the marketplace?

6. Is the WRC right to argue that the FLA is a tool of industry?

7. If sweatshops are a global problem, what might be a global solution to this problem?

DISCUSSION QUESTIONS FOR CASE 11—WESTJET LOOKS EAST

1. Describe the trends in the Canadian airline industry in the 1990s and how they affected the competitive situation in 1999?

2. Describe the competitive environment for WestJet.

3. Outline the main features of Southwest Airlines' business model that WestJet is trying to emulate. What are the benefits and drawbacks of the model? Why has Southwest Airlines been so successful?

4. What are the external opportunities and threats facing WestJet in expanding to Eastern Canada?

5. In light of the threats and opportunities facing WestJet in 1999, what would you recommend to WestJet regarding expansion plans in eastern Canada?

DISCUSSION QUESTIONS FOR CASE 12—AVON PRODUCTS, INC.: THE PERSONAL-CARE INDUSTRY

1. Describe the structure of the personal-care industry.

2. What are the major industry trends, including opportunities and threats?

3. What are the critical factors affecting success?

4. What are Avon's strengths and weaknesses?

5. What are the strategic alternatives presented in the case? Are there other alternatives Avon can consider?

6. Critically evaluate the above strategies in light of the competitive position of Avon in the industry. What would be your recommendation to Avon?

DISCUSSION QUESTIONS FOR CASE 13—THE BODY SHOP INTERNATIONAL: U.S. OPERATIONS

1. Do you think that Anita Roddick possesses the skills necessary to run a large organization?

2. Anita believes that shareholders should not have more rights than the employees, the community, and the environment. What do you think is the primary responsibility of a business organization? Is it to the shareholders, the employees, customers, or the community? Explain your answer.

3. Anita believed that "business should do more than make money, create decent jobs, or sell good products. Rather, business should help solve major social problems such homelessness, unemployment, and social alienation." Where do you stand on this issue? Do you think that the only goal of business is to increase shareholders' value or to solve social problems as well?

4. Anita was against advertising claiming that "customers were so overmarketed that they became increasingly cynical about advertising which told them half truths or untruths." Critique Anita's philosophy showing why you would agree or disagree with it.

5. Do you agree with Anita that "to the vast majority of employees, profit is boring and that they did not care about it even if they get a piece of the action." Provide your reasoning.

6. Does the composition of the Body Shop's board of directors constitute a strength or a weakness for the company? Why?

7. Evaluate the mission statement of the Body Shop.

8. Evaluate the Body Shop's vision statement.

9. Evaluate the Body Shop's values statement.

10. Evaluate the Body Shop's statement of objectives.

11. What grand strategy did the company use? And what was the rationale behind it?

12. Why did the Body Shop's grand strategy in the U.S. begin to falter?

13. In what way did the Body Shop's failure to understand U.S. consumer behavior contribute to the company's strategic problems?

14. If you were an outside member of the company's board of directors, would you recommend ousting Anita and hiring a new CEO? What are the pros and cons of ousting her?

15. If you were selected as the CEO of the company, what strategies and actions would you take to improve its performance in the U.S?

DISCUSSION QUESTIONS FOR CASE 14—J.P. MORGAN CHASE & CO.: THE CREDIT CARD SEGMENT OF THE FINANCIAL SERVICES INDUSTRY

1. Give an overview of the structure of the credit card industry.

2. What were the opportunities and threats confronting JP Morgan in the credit card industry?

3. What are the key success factors in the credit card industry?

4. Who were the main competitors for JP Morgan? Critically evaluate their strengths and weaknesses.

5. What are the possible strategic options available to CCS for growth? What are the costs of pursuing each one?

6. What are the various alternatives being recommended to CCS? What other alternatives can you suggest? Evaluate each one and recommend which alternative CCS should pursue.

DISCUSSION QUESTIONS FOR CASE 15—TOYOTA: THE EVOLUTION OF THE TOYOTA PRODUCTION SYSTEM

1. Compare and contrast Toyota's manufacturing system with a conventional mass-production system. What are the advantages of Toyota's system?

2. Describe the essential difference between the way supplier relations are managed at Toyota and at the typical U.S. auto manufacturer. What are the consequences of these differences?

3. How does Toyota's approach to customer relations influence its design and production planning process? What are the implications?

4. Do you think that the cooperation that Toyota has achieved with its suppliers and employees in Japan can be replicated in its overseas manufacturing operations?

5. What is the basis of Toyota's competitive advantage? Is it imitable?

6. Will Toyota be able to sustain its competitive advantage into the next century?

7. What markets should Toyota concentrate on in the future? What challenges does it face?

DISCUSSION QUESTIONS FOR CASE 16—NUCOR IN 2001

1. What is the nature of the competitive environments in which Nucor operates? What are the competitive implications?

2. What factors have helped Nucor achieve a low-cost position?

3. How did Nucor's organizational structure help the company achieve a low-cost position?

4. How did Nucor's incentive systems help the company achieve a low-cost position?

5. How did Nucor's management style help the company achieve a low-cost position?

6. Why was Nucor's organizational structure changed in 1999?

7. What strategies should Nucor pursue in the future?

DISCUSSION QUESTIONS FOR CASE 17—DIGITAL DEVICES: CURRENT AND FUTURE MARKET OPPORTUNITIES

1. Why is the emergence of digital devices happening now? To what extent can the rise of digital devices be viewed as a response to unmet customer needs, to evolutionary changes in the personal computer industry and perceived limitations in the nature of the personal computer?

2. Over the next few years, do you think that the way in which people will use digital devices such as the Handspring, Palm, and Windows CE handheld computers will change? How?

3. Where do handheld computers fit into the broader computing and communications industry? What are the implications of this for the rates of return that can be earned in the handheld segment of the broader industry?

4. Does the rise of digital devices represent a potential paradigm shift in the nature of computing? What are the implications of such a paradigm shift for Microsoft?

5. Will standards be important in the digital device arena? Why?

6. Why was Palm so successful? Why did it continue to be successful through to 2000?

7. Why did Palm's competitor, Handspring, license the Palm OS? What are the advantages and disadvantages for Handspring in using the Palm OS?

8. What is Microsoft's strategy for establishing the Windows CE as the de facto operating system standard for digital devices? How successful do you think this may be?

9. What is the business model that Microsoft should use to profit from the spread of Windows CE?

10. If digital devices "grow up" to replace the PC, or at least segments of the PC market such as notebooks, what are the implications for Microsoft's core Windows franchise?

DISCUSSION QUESTIONS FOR CASE 18—TREO: HANDSPRING'S LAST STAND?

1. Why has Handspring decided to move into smartphones?

2.   How is the smartphone industry different from the PDA industry?

3.   What will determine Handspring's success in this new industry? Does it have any sources of sustainable competitive advantage?

4.   Why did Handspring decide to discontinue development of its Visor line? Was this a good decision?

DISCUSSION QUESTIONS FOR CASE 19—THE HOME VIDEO GAME INDUSTRY: FROM *PONG* TO X-BOX

1.   How did Nintendo successfully recreate the home video game business following the Atari-era boom and bust?

2.   How was Nintendo able to capture value from the home video game business?

3.   How was Sega able to gain market share from Nintendo?

4.   Evaluate the competitive strategy of 3DO? Given this strategy, how successful do you think 3DO is likely to be?

5.   Why did the Sony Play Station succeed, while 3DO failed?

6.   What drove Microsoft's decision to enter the industry with its X-box offering?

7.   What lessons can be learned from the history of the home video game industry that could have been used to help launch the Sony PlayStation II and Microsoft's X-Box? Do Microsoft and Sony appear to have learned and applied these lessons?

DISCUSSION QUESTIONS FOR CASE 20—MICROSOFT WINDOWS VERSUS LINUX

1.   Are their economic reasons why the personal computer market has standardized on a Windows operating system?

2.   Is Linux a potentially disruptive technology? What are the advantages of Linux over Microsoft Windows? What are the disadvantages?

3.   What are the switching costs that make it difficult for computer users to switch from Windows to Linux? Are these switching costs the same in all market niches, or are their niches where it is easier for Linux to gain market traction?

4.   What do you think IBM's motives are in championing Linux?

5.   What strategies is IBM pursuing to establish Linux as a viable alternative to Windows in the market place?

6.   What strategies might Microsoft pursue to check the rise of Linux?

DISCUSSION QUESTIONS FOR CASE 21—IBM GLOBAL SERVICES: THE PROFESSIONAL COMPUTER SERVICES INDUSTRY

1.   What explains the prolonged period of rapid growth in the Professional Computer Services industry?

2.   What are the opportunities and threats facing IBM Global Services?

3.   Evaluate the competitive position of IBM Global Services. What are the key factors required for success in the Professional Computer Services industry? Compare IBM Global Services and its competitors on each key success factor.

4.   How would IBM Global Services' competition react to its domination of the market?

5.   What are the alternatives confronting IBM Global Services? Evaluate each alternative.

6.   What would be your recommendation to the executive team at IBM?

DISCUSSION QUESTIONS FOR CASE 22—SAP AND THE EVOLVING WEB SOFTWARE ERP MARKET

1.   What are the main elements of SAP's business-level strategy? What are SAP's main strengths and weaknesses? How did the nature of its culture affect its strategy?

2.   What opportunities and threats did SAP encounter in the 1990s? How did it change its strategy in response to those threats?

3.   What major implementation problems arose in SAP over time? Why do you think it experienced these problems?

4.   Why did competition increase in the ERP industry in the mid-1990s and beyond?

5.   How has SAP responded to the threat of new competition, what is its new strategy? How successful do you think it will be in the future?

6.   Why is Microsoft emerging as a potential threat to SAP?

7.   How did SAP change its structure to help support its changes in strategy?

DISCUSSION QUESTIONS FOR CASE 23—IRIDIUM: COMMUNICATION FOR THE NEW MILLENNIUM

1.   What are the benefits of Iridium's technology? Limitations?

2.   Was Motorola's decision to spin Iridium off as a separate company a good one?

3.   What were Iridium's target markets? Were they appropriate? Was the potential market not big enough, or was it not adequately penetrated? What factors facilitated/hindered the market penetration of the system?

4.   What competitors and substitutes did Iridium face? How did the relevant cost and price factors compare? (e.g., development costs, variable costs, price to consumers, etc.)

5.   What strengths and advantages did Motorola/Iridium have in developing and deploying this technology? Was the relationship/tie-in with Motorola an advantage or constraint?

6.   Was the satellite phone system a bad project choice? Could Iridium have done anything differently?

DISCUSSION QUESTIONS FOR CASE 24—A HUNDRED-YEAR WAR: COKE VS. PEPSI, 1890S-1990S

1.   The soft drink industry evolved with a franchised bottler system. For most of the industry's history the concentrate producers nurtured and preserved this system. Why?

2.   During the 1980s both Coke and Pepsi began to acquire bottlers. Why?

3.   Why did Coca-Cola dominate the soft drink industry by the end of World War II?

4.   How was Pepsi able to come back from near bankruptcy and gain market share at the expense of Coke from the 1950s to 1975?

5.   During the 1950s, 1960s, and early 1970s, being a concentrate producer yielded high returns. Why was this the case?

6.   How did the national launch of the Pepsi challenge in 1977 change the nature of competition in the industry?

7.   In retrospect, did the Pepsi challenge and the competition that followed it benefit or harm Pepsi and Coke?

8.   During the 1990s Coca-Cola gained market share back from Pepsi, and was significantly more profitable. Why?

9.   Why do you think Coca-Cola holds such a dominant position over Pepsi in the international marketplace?

DISCUSSION QUESTIONS FOR CASE 25—WAL-MART STORES, INC.: STRATEGIES FOR DOMINANCE IN THE NEW MILLENNIUM

1. Identify and evaluate the strategies that Wal-Mart pursued to maintain its cost-leadership position.

2. Evaluate Wal-Mart's competitive environment.

3. Discuss the importance of changes in the external environment to an organization like Wal-Mart.

4. What conclusions can be drawn from a review of Wal-Mart's financial performance over the decade of the 1980s? From this review, what can you conclude about the financial future of the firm?

5. Speculate on how much impact the "absence" of Sam Walton had on the forward momentum of the organization. What steps have been or should be taken by management to continue Sam Walton's formula for success?

6. Is Wal-Mart's competitive advantage imitable?

7. What are the challenges facing Wal-Mart in the New Millennium?

8. What recommendations do you have for CEO Lee Scott?

DISCUSSION QUESTIONS FOR CASE 26—WAL-MART'S MEXICAN ADVENTURE

1. Why did Mexico make such a good proving ground for Wal-Mart's foreign expansion strategy?

2. What is the source of Wal-Mart's competitive advantage? What barriers did Wal-Mart have to overcome in transferring its competencies to Mexico?

3. How did Wal-Mart create value in the Mexican market?

4. Despite some early setbacks, Wal-Mart has apparently been successful in Mexico. In contrast, some other United States retailers pulled out of the country in the aftermath of the 1994 peso crisis. What do you think distinguishes Wal-Mart from those companies?

5. "If Wal-Mart can succeed in Mexico, it can probably succeed in most other countries." Discuss this statement. Is it correct?

DISCUSSION QUESTIONS FOR CASE 27—KMART CORPORATION: SEEKING CUSTOMER ACCEPTANCE AND PREFERENCE

1. Evaluate the strategies that Kmart has introduced as part of its renewal program of the 1990s. How much impact did these strategies have in the competitive environment as the firm sought to maintain its position and grow in the future?

2. How much importance is placed on the planning function at Kmart? What are some constraints that are likely to decrease its effect on the development of the organization?

3. Why do you think strategic planning is important to an organization like Kmart?

4. How does strategic planning fit into the management process at Kmart?

5. Discuss the importance of changes in the external environment. How much impact do they have on strategic plans in retail firms like Kmart?

6. What conclusions can be drawn from a review of Kmart's financial performance in the period 1990-1999?

7. What new directions are needed to position Kmart to meet the challenges of the next 20 years? Review the alternative strategies that Kmart might implement in order to be successful.

DISCUSSION QUESTIONS FOR CASE 28—TOSCO AND THE NEW MILLENNIUM

1. Describe the competitive structure of the oil and gas industry in the 1990s.

2. What was the growth strategy followed by Tosco?

3. Critically evaluate Tosco's growth strategy and the inherent risks it represents.

4. What are the future growth prospects for Tosco in this industry?

DISCUSSION QUESTIONS FOR CASE 29—THE EVOLUTION OF THE AIR EXPRESS INDUSTRY, 1973-2002

1. How true is it to say that "Federal Express pulled off one of the greatest marketing scams in the industry by making people believe that they absolutely, positively had to have something right away"? (This comment by an industry observer was made with reference to Federal Express's creation of the industry.)

2. Why, despite rapid growth, was the air express industry characterized by low returns during much of the 1980s?

3. Why did competitive intensity moderate and prices rise during 1988–1989?

4. What do you think will happen in the industry if the U.S. economy enters a deep recession?

5. What form do you think the competitive structure of the global air express industry will take during the next decade?

6. To what degree do first-mover advantages form the basis of Federal Express's competitive position in the air express industry? Given this, how vulnerable is Federal Express to renewed price competition?

7. How vulnerable is UPS to intense price competition?

DISCUSSION QUESTIONS FOR CASE 30—AIRBORNE EXPRESS IN 2002

1. According to Porter's framework, what generic strategy is Airborne Express pursuing? Is this a sound strategy in the context of the air express industry?

2. What are the strengths of Airborne Express? Does it have a distinctive competency? If so, where does it lie? Is this competency imitable?

3. What are Airborne Express's weaknesses?

4. Is Airborne's strategy of using strategic alliances to expand overseas wise? What are the pros and cons of this strategy?

5. Is Airborne's strategy of trying to diversify its product offering to include logistics services for clients wise?

6. If you were CEO of Airborne, what would your strategy be?

DISCUSSION QUESTIONS FOR CASE 31—BLOCKBUSTER IN 2002

1. What gap in the video-rental market did David Cook discover and how did he fill it?

2. What key strengths did David Cook develop in his company that made it so successful?

3. How did these distinctive competencies provide Blockbuster with a competitive advantage?

4. What generic, competitive business-level strategy did Blockbuster use to become the leading competitor in the video-rental business?

5. How did Blockbuster manage the industry environment over time to support and develop its business-level strategy?

6. How did Blockbuster use its strengths at the business level to exploit new opportunities, counter threats, and develop its corporate-level strategy?

7. What structure did Blockbuster use to manage its corporate-level strategy?

8. After Viacom acquired Blockbuster in 1996 what developing problems came together to cause its profitability and stock price to plunge?

9. What steps did Redstone, Field's and Antioco take to turn around Blockbuster's declining performance?

10. How was Blockbuster positioned by 1999 to deal with the future?

DISCUSSION QUESTIONS FOR CASE 32—VIDEO CONCEPTS, INC.

1. What was Chad Brown's original strategy for Video Concepts, and what distinctive competencies did he try to develop?

2. How did Rowan's strategy help Video Concepts manage the competitive industry environment before Blockbuster's arrival?

3. How did the entry of Blockbuster affect Video Concepts' competitive advantage, and what steps did Rowan take to fight back?

4. What problems is Rowan experiencing in the short term, and what strategy would you recommend that he adopt to respond to Blockbuster's challenge?

DISCUSSION QUESTIONS FOR CASE 33—AOL TIME WARNER: CREATING A COLOSSUS

1. Following AOL's decision to move to a flat rate pricing scheme, demand for AOL's service ballooned. What does this tell you about AOL's service, and demand for its product?

2. What business model did AOL move to under Pittman? What were the strategic implications of this model for AOL's strategy?

3. How does AOL's quest for bandwidth fit into the company's strategy?

4. By 2000, who were AOL's primary competitors? What potential advantages, if any, did they have over AOL? What advantages did AOL have over them?

5. What was the primary strategic rationale for the AOL-Time Warner merger? How was it expected to benefit both parties?

6. Evaluate the early experience with the merger? Has it worked? Could it work in the future?

7. What are the main strategic issues that AOL-Time Warner must grapple with in mid-2002?

DISCUSSION QUESTIONS FOR CASE 34—THE VIACOM EMPIRE

1. How did Viacom's business activities evolve until 1996? What business-level strategy(ies) did it use to obtain a competitive advantage?

2. Why did Sumner Redstone take over Viacom?

3. Why did Redstone think that a merger with Paramount could add value to Viacom's core businesses? After the merger with Paramount what corporate-level strategy was Viacom pursuing?

4. Why did Sumner Redstone want to merge with Blockbuster Video Corp.? How did the merger with Blockbuster affect Viacom's corporate-level strategy?

5. What major challenges and problems faced Redstone and his managers as they attempted to manage Viacom's diverse array of businesses to create new value for shareholders in 1996?

6. What kind of structure does Viacom have, why does Viacom use it, and what are the potential problems associated with it for Viacom?

7. What steps did Sumner Redstone take in and after 1996, to turn around the performance of its Blockbuster division?

8. What steps did Redstone take to manage Viacom's problems and achieve the promise of its other extensive entertainment assets?

DISCUSSION QUESTIONS FOR CASE 35—MONSANTO (A): BUILDING A LIFE SCIENCES COMPANY

1. How would you describe the competitive economics of Monsanto's business in the 1970s? What does this description suggest about the outlook for the company at that time?

2. Trace the evolution of technology strategy at Monsanto. Think through the advantages, disadvantages and risks associated with the various approaches that were used to build world class skills in life science research at Monsanto.

3. What decision process did Monsanto go through when considering whether to build a life sciences business?

4. One could argue that scientific talent was the most critical resource that Monsanto needed to access in order to develop its life sciences business. What did Monsanto have on its side in the competition for scarce talent? What factors were working against the company? How did it overcome some of these factors?

5. What was the logic for the Searle acquisition? How did the acquisition add value to Monsanto's life science program?

6. What was Needleman's strategy for drug development at Searle? Does this strategy make sense for a company like Monsanto? Why or why not?

7. What is the value proposition to farmers of Monsanto's Roundup Ready and Bt seeds? Does Monsanto's pricing strategy make sense given this value proposition? What special problems does Monsanto face in trying to sell to farmers?

8. Outline Monsanto's business model for Roundup Ready seeds and its Roundup products. What is the basic strategy here and how might it lead to economic profits?

9. Why has Monsanto been vertically integrating forward into the seed corn industry? What is the strategic rationale for such a move?

10. Evaluate Monsanto's launch strategy for its Cox-2 inhibitor. Does the strategy make sense? Why?

11. Comment on the opposition of groups such as EU consumers and Rifkin's organization to Monsanto's genetically engineered products. Are these groups latter day Luddites, or do they have a point? How should Monsanto deal with the opposition from such groups?

DISCUSSION QUESTIONS FOR CASE 36—MONSANTO (B): MERGER AND REBIRTH

1. What was the rationale behind the merger between Pharmacia and Monsanto?

2. Evaluate Pharmacia's decision to spin-off Monsanto.

3. What are the main challenges that the new Monsanto faces?

4. Why is Monsanto's strategy going forward?

DISCUSSION QUESTIONS FOR CASE 37—ELI LILLY & COMPANY: THE GLOBAL PHARMACEUTICAL INDUSTRY

1. Describe the structure of the pharmaceutical industry.

2. What are the major industry trends, including opportunities and threats?

3.   What are the critical factors affecting success?

4.   Do a comparative evaluation of Eli Lilly and other players in the pharmaceutical industry.

5.   How is Eli Lilly positioned in the pharmaceutical industry?

6.   What are the different alternatives available to the new CEO, Sidney Taurel, in order to provide a strategic direction for Eli Lilly in the new millennium?

7.   Evaluate the strengths and weaknesses of each of the three alternatives and recommend a course of action for Sidney Taurel.

DISCUSSION QUESTIONS FOR CASE 38—KIKKOMAN CORPORATION IN THE MID-1990S: MARKET MATURITY, DIVERSIFICATION, AND GLOBALIZATION

1.   Evaluate Kikkoman's development of key success factors or various competitive advantages. How has the firm managed to remain successful over such an extended period of time?

2.   What factors led to industry consolidation in Japan? How did the company respond to consolidation and in what ways did the company contribute to industry consolidation?

3.   Evaluate the firm's various phases of international activity.

4.   Evaluate the attractiveness of the US market for entry in the mid- and late 1960's.

5.   Evaluate the firm's strategic and operational choices in entering the US market in the post WWII period.

6.   What was the status of Kikkoman's operations in the US, European, and Asian markets in the mid-1990's.

7.   What challenges do you foresee for Kikkoman, especially in the US market, and how should the company respond?

DISCUSSION QUESTIONS FOR CASE 39—CENTURYTEL IN A BEAR HUG

1.   What are the threats and opportunities facing telecommunications service providers?

2.   What is the situation facing CTL? What are the strengths and weaknesses of CTL and of the opposition?

3.   What would be the advantages and disadvantages of the acquisition of the wireless segment or acquisition of the entire firm from CenturyTel's view and from AllTel's perspective?

4.   How successful is the "bear hug" likely to be? Give reasons for your answer. What role does the Board of Directors play in the takeover battle?

DISCUSSION QUESTIONS FOR CASE 40—WHIRLPOOL CORPORATION'S GLOBAL STRATEGY

1.   What was the structure of the home appliances industry in the United States in the 1990s?

2.   How was the appliances industry in Asia, Europe and Latin America different from the United States industry?

3.   Why did Whirlpool choose to expand globally?

4.   What was Whirlpool's global strategy? Was it an appropriate strategy to pursue? Why or why not?

5.   What was Whirlpool's experience in Asia, Europe and Latin America? Why did it fail to generate profits?

DISCUSSION QUESTIONS FOR CASE 41—"YOU PUSH THE BUTTON, WE DO THE REST": FROM SILVER HALIDE TO INFOIMAGING AT EASTMAN KODAK

1. How did Kodak's corporate strategy change over time? How did the strengths and weaknesses of Kodak change as its strategy changed over time?

2. In what ways did the environment affect Kodak during this period?

3. How did Kodak change its strategy to respond to the changes in the photographic imaging market?

4. What other changes in corporate strategy did Kodak make to strengthen its position?

5. How did these changes in strategy affect Kodak's performance?

6. How did Kodak change its structure and control systems to respond to a hostile environmental threats and internal weaknesses?

7. What was George Fisher's new strategy for Kodak? Did he succeed in turning around its performance?

8. How did Kodak's strategy change under Carp?

9. What do you think of Kodak's future prospects? Would you buy shares in this firm? Why or why not?

DISCUSSION QUESTIONS FOR CASE 42—RESTRUCTURING EXIDE

1. What kind of industry environment does Exide operate in? Is it a global industry, a multi-domestic industry, or something in between? What are the pressures for local representatives in the industry? What are the pressures for globalization?

2. How might a structure based on geography (country subsidies) result in inefficiencies at Exide?

3. What are the potential benefits to Exide from moving from a geographic structure based on country organization to a product structure based on global business units? What are the potential drawbacks to such a structure?

4. Following the GNB acquisition, Lutz again changed the structure of Exide, at least on the industrial side of the organization. Why did he do this? Do you think this was a wise move, or might it create additional problems in the future?

DISCUSSION QUESTIONS FOR CASE 43—FIRST GREYHOUND, THEN GREYHOUND DIAL, THEN DIAL: WHAT WILL HAPPEN IN 2002?

1. What were the critical incidents in Greyhound's growth and development over time?

2. What was the underlying corporate strategy behind the development of Greyhound's portfolio of investments up to Teet's appointment as CEO? Was Trautman correct to pursue this strategy? What were the advantages and pitfalls of this strategy?

3. What environmental factors affected Greyhound's businesses? Could anything have been done to control for environmental factors? In what ways did they distort the picture of Greyhound's performance?

4. What did Teets do to change Greyhound's corporate strategy and financial position? Analyze the rationale behind this strategy. Did he succeed?

5. Why did Dial break up into two different companies? Was this good for shareholders? For Teets and his managers?

6. What happened to Dial under its new CEO's Jozoff and then Baum? What strategies did they pursue?

CASE 1

Vail Resorts, Inc.[1]

SYNOPSIS OF THE CASE

Vail Resorts is an upscale vacation resort company specializing in ski and mountain venues. This case outlines the recreation resort industry environment, the challenges facing Vail Resorts in the new millennium and strategies that are being pursued by the management at Vail Resorts to provide a new strategic direction for profitability and growth.

Vail Resorts has been very successful in establishing a reputation for itself as a premier ski resort in the last 40 years and went public in 1997. The company has four world-class destination winter resorts in Colorado and a summer resort in Wyoming, each with a distinct theme and client base.

Vail Resorts is now confronted with a changing recreation industry with a shrinking demand for ski resorts, increased competition in a maturing market and environmental concerns about the negative impact of ski resorts.

Since 1997, in order to maintain its leadership position in the industry, Vail Resorts management has embarked on a growth strategy through vertical integration of resort services and diversification into non-ski resorts. The acquisitions have produced a much larger organization with twice the asset and employee base, and the resultant complexity has prompted the management to revamp the organizational structure. The question is whether the new growth strategy will make a positive impact on the future profitability of Vail Resorts.

TEACHING OBJECTIVES

This case can be used to achieve several teaching objectives:

1.   To illustrate Porter's Five Forces Model and critical issues related to the macroenvironment.

2.   To analyze the internal strengths and weaknesses and examine how different value chain components may be sources of competitive advantage.

3.   To underscore the importance of designing strategies that are consistent with corporate objectives.

4.   To understand different corporate level strategies and different organizational forms that firms can use to implement their strategies.

In addition, a 3-part video documentary involving senior management interviews and visual company descriptions is available for a fee. For information and ordering please email the author at boschken_h@cob.sjsu.edu.

STRATEGIC ISSUES AND DISCUSSION QUESTIONS

1.   **Analyze Vail Resorts' competitive environment using Porter's Five Forces Model.**

Rivalry in the Industry

Vail Resorts is in the "mountain recreation and resort" sub-industry of the giant "entertainment, leisure and recreation" industry. This industry is not only fragmented but the boundaries of its various sub-parts are vague and overlapping. This gives rise to significant and multiple and indirect competition in addition to the direct rivals. Showing the complexity of building distinctive competence in multiple overlapping markets, one might structure a discussion according to a matrix of North American competition.

---

[1] This teaching note is based on a teaching note by Herman L. Boschken.

	MOUNTAIN/ SKI	NON-MOUNTAIN
DESTINATION RESORTS	VAIL RESORTS, INTRAWEST, AM SKI CO, ASPEN	DISNEY, CLUB MED, PRINCESS CRUISES
NON-DESTINATION RESORTS	SQUAW VALLEY, BOOTH CREEK PSHP, NEW ENGLAND PROVIDERS	SIX FLAGS, SEA WORLD

The destination resorts segment of the recreation industry is consolidated with 4 major players and some smaller specialized companies. The consolidation has also resulted in a bifurcation of ski resorts into two types. The smaller specialized players that do not have deep pockets operate "windshield" resorts i.e. resorts that have day-use slopes with few accommodations on-site. The larger players have shifted focus from being ski-resorts to all-season recreation resorts and cater to customers who come to stay for a week or more. They offer accommodations, restaurants and activities other than skiing. The competition in destination resorts has focused on technological development of the resorts-thematic villages, snowmaking equipment, luxurious restaurants and cutting edge ski lift designs.

Threat of Substitutes

Since recreation resorts industry's boundaries are amorphous and ill-defined, there is a possible threat of substitutes from related industries like gaming, sporting events, cruises, amusement parks and the like. This makes it hard to come up with different product-market offerings for customer profiles in the recreation resorts industry that do not overlap with these related industries.

Barriers to Entry by Potential Competitors

The "destination resorts" segment that Vail Resorts operates in has higher capital requirements and hence entry is difficult.

Buyers

The demand in the 1990s has been maturing. The aging baby boomer population fed the demand in the 1960-1985 period, and is now less interested in an expensive, strenuous and singles oriented sport-like skiing. As a result, the growth in skier days has been flat in the last 10 years. This has forced destination ski resorts to modify their offerings to include more luxurious resort venues, more convenient (ski in/ski out) access to recreation, and less strenuous leisure activities. It raises questions about what demographic pressures might be considered (secondary boomlet of young, multi-generational family travel) to move demand forward into new areas like snowboarding.

It is harder to assess which demographic factors determine distinguishable customer profiles. In addition to income, age and family status, there are non-traditional demographic factors including educational level, psychographic characteristics and family make-up that complicates an analysis of customer profiles and demand. Customers seek more value for their money and are willing to pay a premium for exceptional quality and service.

Suppliers

The case does not provide much information on suppliers, but given the market leadership position of Vail Resorts, they do not seem to pose a threat for the company.

Complementors

These are Vail Resorts's "co-producers." In this industry, the "product" is a service and requires the coordination of a lot of individual contributors through the use of strategic alliances and cooperative arrangements. These include airline partnering as well as resort village vendors (hotels, restaurants, shops) and public service providers (police, medical, parks and recreation). VR's success is heavily dependent on integrating its co-producers. Its competition has yet to perfect this coordination, thus giving Vail Resorts a competitive edge.

Macroenvironment

In addition to the 5 (or 6) forces, the case raises significant "macroenvironment" issues, the most important of which are global terrorism and environmental advocacy. Vail Resorts is development-oriented and has accumulated a record for not being as sensitive as it should toward the physical environment. After approval of its massive add-on development at Vail Mountain in 1998 (called Blue Sky Basin), an eco-terrorist group burned the resort's state-of-the-art restaurant and several lift stations, causing $12 million damage. The event received national publicity and VR experienced both scorn and sympathy from a variety of public groups. It also caused the firm to establish an environmental management unit in 2001 (an unintended addition to its strategy).

2.   **What do you see as the internal strengths and weaknesses of Vail Resorts?**

The case describes many strengths and weaknesses (although the firm has few obvious weaknesses) as they relate to an analysis of competitive advantage:

Strengths

- Innovation – Through its innovative ideas, Vail Resorts has been able to derive revenue from non-lift ticket sources at the resorts, generating as much as 50% more revenue from each visitor as compared to competitors. This has been done through up-scaling its onsite restaurants, a redefinition of ski-school, vertically integrating into classy hotels and resort retail, and offering an online system for reservations. They have been the pioneers of the "pedestrian village" concept offering mountain and village activities to consumers without the hassle of an automobile.

- Research and Development – In addition to undertaking innovative development of resorts (described above), Vail Resorts has also invested heavily in mountain technologies such as thematic planned-unit-development villages, luxurious on-mountain restaurants, and state-of-the-art lift designs and snowmaking equipment.

- Marketing – Vail Resorts has built a reputation for quality service and excellence in providing a unique, seamless experience.

- Location of the resorts – All the resorts are easily accessible by both air and ground.

- Vail Resorts has maintained a co-operative administrative control over all the activities at its resorts, including those of companies that operate the accommodations, restaurants, entertainment venues and ground and air transportation.

Weaknesses

- Unorganized environmental management approach that may have caused the eco-terrorist attack on its facility.

- Lack of a global strategy – Although design of the modern ski resort is an American invention, industry demand is a worldwide phenomenon. The World Cup and Winter Olympics draw vastly greater interest worldwide than any other sport (including soccer). For U.S. producers like Vail Resorts, 80 percent of the world's skiing population lives outside of the country. Yet, even before 9/11, VR and its North American competitors have catered mostly to a domestic customer. In VR's case, only about 10 percent of customers reside outside the U.S.

3.   What is the Business level strategy being pursued by the company?

From the beginning, Vail Resorts has pursued a strategy of focused differentiation. It is a provider of upscale "world-class" destination skiing resorts and its product domain strategically emphasizes quality and excellence. The company primarily caters to high income, college-educated, well-traveled professionals and their families. This group of customers has been further segmented into subgroups (blue-chip company executives, families, single and couples, etc.) and each of the resorts owned by the company has a distinct theme and atmosphere to cater to the specific needs of a particular subgroup. Vail Resorts was the first company to recognize emerging psychographic desires among its customers and differentiate its resorts to fulfill those needs (for example, in addition to skiing, customers may also look for a cosmopolitan ambience, friendly gathering places, spiritual renewal or novel adventure). Vail Resorts has distinctive strengths in marketing and research and development and has been able to offer a high quality, seamless experience to its customers.

Over time, Vail Resorts's differentiation advantage over its competitors has earned it the reputation for being the top destination resort according to annual ski magazine surveys.

4.   Discuss why Vail Resorts has been successful in their vertical integration and diversification programs? What are some potential risks associated with these strategies?

In recent years as demand for traditional skiing has waned, VR has looked for new ways to derive revenue. As noted in the case, the firm is the only one in the industry to successfully integrate vertically into non-ski revenue sources at its resorts. It has done this mostly by buying some of its co-producer establishments (especially hotels), by dominating the resort reservation business through an on-line website reservation system, and by providing a comprehensive web server service to its resorts' hotels and condominiums.

In addition to a vertical component, VR has also vigorously pursued related diversification outside ski resorts. In 2000, it purchased the Grand Teton Lodge Co, which is a mountain venue but only has summer operations (an attempt to reduce the effects of seasonal revenue limited to the 5 months of winter). In 2001, it purchased Rock Resorts, a luxury provider of spa resorts located mostly outside ski or mountain resort. As noted in the case, Vail Resorts is diversifying in order to spread its financial risks. Such diversification is expected to allow Vail Resorts to leverage their existing competencies and avoid dependence on a seasonal single source of income.

However, both these strategies are not risk free. Although its vertical integration provides the firm with significantly higher revenue per skier (as shown in Figure 4 of the case), the revenue growth from these non-lift ticket sources occurs from investments that produce lower gross margins (about 35%) than lift tickets, which have gross margins of up to 85% in good years. Moreover, even though the company is diversifying into a related business, the risk of diversification is that it might increase bureaucratic costs of managing and coordinating the new resorts. Similarly vertical integration can also increase the bureaucratic costs of running the company if the company owned suppliers of resort services are not able to lower their operating costs due to technical changes or an uncertain demand for upscale destination resorts.

Vail Resorts has to monitor its costs carefully so that value created by vertical integration and diversification efforts does not vanish.

5.   Evaluate the changes made by Vail Resorts to its organizational structure.

Vail Resorts's organizational structure consists of several forms including functional, divisional, and partial matrix. They are arranged to optimally implement the firm's strategy. For example, in dealing with the simultaneous needs for differentiation and integration, the firm's strategy takes a "brand management" approach. Each resort has its own management and is free to develop programs and market to its defined customer profile. Nevertheless, senior management requires all resorts to conform to a corporate-defined quality image and "world-class" distinction. Hence, while each resort operates as a product division, its marketing programs are managed by a dual authority i.e., division CEO and the corporate VP of Marketing.

While this complex organizational structure might be an optimal way for the company to manage its complex operations, it misses one key aspect. Since environmental management is likely to be an instrumental part of the firm's strategy, the organizational chart should account for resources that will be devoted to this increasingly important area. A part of the company's managerial resources should be allocated to provide a policy driven direction to manage resource sustainability and development planning.

The firm also distributes authority in an unusual manner that can have several downsides. Organizational structures built on dual authority can potentially lead to a lack of coordination, turf wars and inappropriate subordination of one function over another. This can lead to further ambiguity and loss of morale among employees who are already struggling with an impersonal, "survival-of-the-fittest" environment.

POSTSCRIPT

In October 2002, citing continued industry weakness after 9/11, CEO Aron fired his president, Daly, saying the position was redundant and cost cutting required such high-level action. The CEO also removed the COO of the Keystone resort and consolidated the position with the COO of Breckenridge. The corporate VP of public relations was fired and the position eliminated, and the environmental management program was terminated.

CASE 2

Adrenaline Air Sports: Where the Speed Limit Is 120 Miles per Hour…or More (condensed version)[1]

SYNOPSIS OF THE CASE

Billy Cockrell opened Adrenaline Air Sports in November of 1999. His weekend parachute drop zone is open on Saturdays and Sundays from March through October and every weekend during the colder months weather permitting. The buildings and airport space he rented were at Smith Mountain Lake Airport, southeast of Roanoke, Virginia.

Adrenaline Air Sports flight operations work as follows. All jumpers are taken up to 10,000 feet elevation in two four-seater Cessna planes. First time jumpers pay $189 and jump with a coach in a tandem jump after receiving some training and signing release forms. Regular experienced jumpers pay $16 per jump because they typically have their own parachute, helmet, and pack their own chute.

Adrenaline Air Sports is a successful, newer small business even though it relies completely on part-time employees. In fact, even its President Billy Cockrell has a 40-hour full-time job as a technician 80 miles away in Blacksburg where he works Monday through Friday from 8:00 a.m. to 5:00 p.m. or so. Many weekday evenings and all weekend long Billy Cockrell works at his parachute drop zone, weather permitting.

TEACHING OBJECTIVES

The main teaching objectives of the case are:

1.   To gain students' interest and attention by analyzing a high thrill youth oriented sport, parachuting.

2.   To understand the difficulties in starting and running a small business.

3.   To identify and analyze how to address various strategic issues facing Adrenaline Air Sports.

4.   To analyze what it would take for Billy Cockrell to go full-time as owner of Adrenaline Air Sports.

5.   To appreciate the technical details that must be satisfied to be successful in any industry.

STRATEGIC ISSUES AND DISCUSSION QUESTIONS

1.   **How do you get first time jumpers to come back for more jumps, when industry wide only 3% of parachuters ever take a second jump?**

Getting first time jumpers to come back is very difficult. Most say they had a really great experience and that it was a rush. However, after a week or so, the new parachutist may lose interest largely due to a lack of money for more jumps. It may also be that many first time jumpers viewed it as something to do once or a challenge to scratch it off their "to do" list. Thus, it may not be surprising that only 3% of first time jumpers ever take a second jump.

(The partial answers here and to subsequent questions are selected paragraphs from among the best student answers. All comments are from undergraduate business seniors taking the capstone business strategy course at Virginia Tech when this case was first tested, and revised for one year.)

---

[1] This teaching note was prepared by Larry D. Alexander. Copyright © Larry D. Alexander.

Student A – One way to increase second time jumpers is by giving them a coupon after they complete their first jump. This 10% to 25% off coupon should be given to first time jumper before they leave Adrenaline's facility. Adrenaline's staff could even try to schedule a date to jump again before they leave, or they might never return.

Student B – An aggressive ad campaign toward first time jumpers could also be helpful. After their first jump, many jumpers may not be so sure that they want to go through it again. By sending them advertisements and brochures, Adrenaline can keep the idea fresh in their minds. Sending coupons and special offers, may sway jumpers to come back again. A free copy of a parachuting magazine, like the Parachutist, might also help maintain their interest in jumping again.

Student C – A simple way to get customers back for more jumps is to take them up higher, to 12,000 or 13,000 feet. This will give them a bigger thrill because the jumpers will be in freefall for almost a full minute. Obviously, Adrenaline will have to charge some more for the cost of taking jumpers up higher. Jumpers can still opt to jump from just 10,000 in Billy's other plane.

Student D – Still another recommendation to increase second time jumpers would be to offer a free video with the second jump. This way anyone who did not purchase a video the first time would be influenced to jump again and have it taped. These tapes could be great memorabilia for the jumpers. Not only can they show their family and friends their daredevil experience, it might make them consider jumping a third time and beyond.

Comments by United States Parachute Association Officials – Officials at this national organization point out that the worse thing a drop zone can do is to segregate new jumpers from the experienced jumpers. Drop zones should do just the opposite and introduce them to veteran jumpers and get them talking about parachuting.

Lead author's comments – The lead author has observed at some drop zones first time jumpers in separate groups filling out numerous liability waiver forms, paying a couple hundred dollars, to do something they are looking forward to doing but still very nervous about. Comments about changing the pricing schedule to attract second time jumpers are covered as a part of the next discussion question.

2. **What can Adrenaline Air Sports do to make its pricing for the first 9 jumps more attractive to new parachute jumpers?**

Lead author's comments – Billy Cockrell gives the ninth jump free sort of as a graduation present for successfully completing the first series of jumps. The third author, Jonathan Charlton, points out that if a jumper has done eight jumps, he will do the ninth one whether it is given to him free or not. Thus, it might be a great present, but may not be an incentive to come back during the first eight jumps which total a sizeable $1,582.

Perhaps the free jump should be moved forward to the second, third, or fourth jump. Or perhaps two different jumps spaced apart could be given at a 50% discount.

Another way to get new jumpers back for the first nine jumps is to carefully screen them for their financial ability to support this hobby. College students who belong to a Greek society may have more money, college students from rich communities, and men age 25 years old and up who are already established in their career may be good market segments to pursue. For other people wanting to jump with limited funds, helping them realize their dream of taking one parachute jump may be the best a drop zone can realistically expect.

Some more student comments are as follows:

Student E – One approach would be to offer the free jump earlier in the progression of jumps. Right now, because the free jump is not until the ninth jump, it seems very distant from both a time and financial standpoint. By making the free jump on the third jump, this would give students a much more immediate goal. First of all, $478 for three jumps sounds much more doable than $1,582 for 9 jumps. Secondly, the third jump is where students actually get to wear their own parachute. Having made their first solo jump might motivate beginning jumpers to continue with the sport.

Student F – Another approach to reduce the costs of the initial jumps relates to recruiting. Whenever a newer jumper brings in a friend for a first time jump, they would get say 50% off their next jump. Since people new in many activities are very enthusiastic about that activity, including parachuting, they may be telling everyone they know about it and this may get others interested in taking a first jump. In addition, these new parachute customers may be consciously motivated for cheaper jumps to get others to try the sport.

Student G – Billy should change the cost structure for potential new skydivers. He should charge the most for the first jump, but then the price should continue to drop for each consecutive jump. Instead of offering the ninth jump as the free jump, he should make it the fifth jump. This would provide a much greater incentive to pay for the second, third, and fourth jumps, knowing that each one gets cheaper with the fifth one free. Then, after the ninth jump, the student will be paying $16 per jump just like the veteran jumpers plus the cost for renting a parachute and equipment.

Student H – Adrenaline should change its pricing policy, and eliminate the 9th free jump. Instead, the discount should be dispersed between the 3rd, 6th, and 9th jumps. Each of them would be $63, with the additional $100 for ground school before the 3rd jump. This allows new jumpers to consistently reap the benefits of continuing to parachute. A second option would be a "buy 2 in advance, and get 1 free". The first two jumps would be regularly priced, but the third jump would only cost the $100 for ground school.

3. **What are the most important customer groups that Adrenaline Air Sports should target?**

Student I – Adrenaline Air Sports should target college students because these young adults are likely candidates to take a first time jump. College students are always looking for new environments to have exciting experiences, whether from a dare, a bet, or a gift.

Many college students feel that parachuting is death defying and offers a tremendous rush, much more so than the scariest roller coasters. Clearly, peer pressure and wanting to do something that will impress their friends is a big factor that will motivate college students. The many colleges within a few hours drive from Adrenaline Air Sports include Virginia Tech, Radford University, James Madison University, University of Virginia, the University of North Carolina at Greensboro, plus lots of smaller colleges.

Student J – Adrenaline Air Sports should target men between the ages of 30 and 45. These men should be targeted because they need something in their lives to break the monotony of the 9 to 5 work grind, their wives, kids, etc. It is a way for them to prove that "they still got it!" In addition, most of these men probably are financially stable, making them less cost sensitive.

Student K – Another group to target would be sports teams, both varsity and club teams. Skydiving can be offered as a team building experience, making it more attractive to these groups. These groups consist of active people, making them prime candidates for athletic activities like skydiving. Special demonstrations and activities building group cohesiveness and leadership would make the skydiving experience very attractive to team groups.

Student L – Still another customer group to target is extreme sports enthusiasts. Those involved in extreme sports are looking for new challenges or a new risky activity. They often seek out heart stopping, adrenaline rushing activities which Adrenaline Air Sports clearly offers. Enthusiasts involved in rock climbing, bungee jumping, snowboarding, mountain biking, white water rafting, and skiing are likely candidates. This target group is found doing their sport throughout southwest Virginia and the surrounding mountains, lakes, rivers, etc. where these sports flourish.

Student M – College Greek students also present an attractive group to target. They often come from families that have more money, which is needed for parachuting. As it stands now, many of them go on expensive spring break trips, which may be even out of the United States. With their group mentality, it might be possible to plan a parachute jump for many in a sorority or a fraternity on the same Saturday or Sunday.

Authors' note – Billy Cockrell and some loyal customers/part-time employees have tried to identify students at some local colleges that are in various other sports. Then Billy has tried to talk to them at one of their regularly scheduled meetings to make a pitch for skydiving. At Virginia Tech, with 25,000 students, third author and student Jonathan Charleton is President of the Virginia Tech skydiving club that ties in directly to Billy's Adrenaline Air Sports.

4. **What advertising media should Billy Cockrell use to market his Adrenaline Air Sports?**

Authors' note – Here is what several good students had to say about this issue.

Student N – One suggested advertising approach would be to advertise on the radio. Radio would allow Adrenaline Air to reach a large customer base. Radio advertising can target specific customer groups by the time and day that the program is broadcast. Radio's prime advantage over television is its cost, which is relatively cheap. In addition, many radio stations will help Billy develop an ad campaign. If Adrenaline consistently advertises on the radio, sales should increase due to the increased exposure.

Student O – Adrenaline Air Sports T-shirts would be a great way to advertise. They would be distributed to those individuals who successfully complete a jump for about $15.00. The shirt would be brightly colored and have a picture, a phone number, web site, and address on the back. A slogan such as "I got high with Adrenaline Air Sports" would be on the front or back. T-shirts are great because they are highly visible and will suggest that anyone can participate in this type of activity.

Student P – Another advertising medium to use is the 10 to 15 minute video that many first time jumpers purchase. When they get home, they are more than likely to show the tape to some of their friends, which is free publicity for Adrenaline Air. Currently the tape costs $60 a piece. Adrenaline should consider offering the tapes for free by including it in the price of a jump. By including the tape in the price of a first time tandem jump with an instructor, every new parachutist will have a VHS videotape that will probably be shown to everyone that person knows. Even if they never jump again, that video will serve as an effective advertising media to lure other people to come parachute at Adrenaline Air Sports.

Student P and Lead author – Another advertising recommendation would be to invite John Carlin, Roanoke's WSLS-10 television news anchor to Adrenaline's facilities. He could film a segment for television which covers the region and hopefully do a skydive himself. He loves sports, has run a marathon, and helped announce the Tour duPont's 12-day bike ride as it went through the Roanoke and Blacksburg areas. This could provide significant exposure on television simply by offering him a free jump and a challenge.

Lead Author's and Wife Anne's Comment – We feel a unique way to advertise and promote Adrenaline Air Sports is to sponsor an unusual triathlon. First, it would involve white water rafting, probably on the Gauley River in nearby West Virginia. Second, it would involve wild caving at one of several caves in the area, using headlights and crawling for say four hours. Third, it would involve taking a tandem skydive jump at Adrenaline Air Sports. This unique combination of three high adventure sports would be called the "AWEsome triathlon". 'A' in awesome stands for air (skydiving), 'W' stands for water for white water rafting, and 'E' stands for earth for caving. Brochures would be at various rafting, caving, and Adrenaline Air Sports locations helping to promote each other's sports. For anyone doing all three in one calendar year, Adrenaline would give them an "AWEsome Triathlon" t-shirt.

Authors' Comment – Billy Cockrell feels that his tear off poster is one of his most effective advertising media. He puts them up anywhere and everywhere and also given them to his customers to likewise put them wherever they want.

Some other advertising media that the authors and past students have identified for Adrenaline Air Sports (some being done already) are as follows:

- Volunteer to have several jumpers perform at a local Fourth of July celebration, a football game, etc.

- Put signs on roads in and around Smith Mountain Lake to make it easier for customers to find Adrenaline Air Sports.

- Help sponsor skydiving clubs at local colleges and get an Adrenaline customer who goes to school there to lead it.

- Have Billy and other regular customers to talk to various college and non-college groups about parachuting.

- Put ads in the Smith Mountain Lake magazine.

- Improve on Adrenaline's Website, www.air-sports.com.

- Rely on word of mouth advertising among veteran jumpers to attract other veteran and beginning jumpers.

- Tow "Adrenaline Air Sports" banners behind airplanes.

- Bumper stickers for cars.

- Ads in the Parachutist magazine.

- Various flyers to mail or make available at businesses.

- A booth at every college to promote Adrenaline and its affiliated college subsidiary.

- Put an ad on a large billboard near colleges and Smith Mountain Lake.

- Classes and camps for new and experienced skydivers.

- Special parachuting events on holidays.

- Provide a pleasing and comfortable place to hang out and socialize at Adrenaline Air Sports.

- Invite an experienced skydive team to practice at the drop zone for a weekend.

- Put tandem students' pictures on its web site.

5. **What steps will Billy Cockrell have to satisfy in order to go full-time with his Adrenaline Air Sports?**

Student Q – One of the benefits for Billy changing to full-time at Adrenaline is the ability to cutback on his part-time employees. During the week, Billy can be repacking all of the main chutes instead of paying others to do work at the end of the weekend. In addition, he can repack reserve chutes, which must be done every 90 days. He would also have more time to arrange for getting maintenance done on his planes. Finally, he would have more time to promote his business with flyers and talk to various potentially interested groups.

Student R – Billy Cockrell could supplement his revenues by adding parasailing on scenic Smith Mountain Lake. Parasailing is when a person is attached to a speedboat by a large rope. As the boat moves faster and faster, the parasailer (looks like a parachute) is lifted into the sky higher and higher. This is very safe since the person is only 75 feet or so over the water and securely harnessed to the rope. He could run this new operation from the end of the runway where the water starts or more likely from another part of the lake which is more populated. This activity could be done for about six months of the year, without any regard for how cloudy it is, which parachuting always is concerned with.

Student S – Adrenaline Air Sports should increase its weekly operation to three days a week during good weather. We recommend adding Wednesdays to Saturday and Sunday, or an alternative would be Friday through Sunday. This would put Adrenaline Air Sports on a par with some other drop zones that currently are opened more days a week. It would bring in more revenue, keep Billy busy, and generate a customer appeal from a greater distance.

Lead Author – Although Billy's drop zone is located in a most beautiful setting by Smith Mountain Lake, the weather is adverse and unpredictable for many months each year. Thus, one way for Cockrell to go full-time with Adrenaline Air Sport is to move his location to another state. Since there are many well-established drop zones in Florida, perhaps something near Columbia, South Carolina or Charlotte, North Carolina, would work. Columbia is the state capital, located in the center of the state and has a population of 116,278 people. Charlotte is much larger with a population of 540,828 in the city, and nearly one million including the surrounding area.

Lead Author – Many student groups have argued that Adrenaline Air Sports needs to get bigger, more powerful planes. Currently, their two four seater Cessna planes take jumpers only up to 10,000 feet. They avoid going to 12,000 feet because it takes so much longer for their less powerful planes to get up the extra 2,000 feet. If Adrenaline purchased a Twin Otter or a similar plane, they could take approximately 12 customers up to 14,000 feet. This could help Adrenaline differentiate itself from other drop zones that use smaller planes with less power.

CLASSROOM APPROACH TO THE CASE

Lead Author's notes – My usual written assignment is for student groups to answer three of the above five discussion questions. They have one single spaced, typewritten page to answer any three questions of their choosing. We have one or two class discussion days on the case before this written assignment is due.

Ask ahead of time if any students have parachuted in the past or are active parachuters now. They will be good to question in class, and some may have a video to show in class of them parachuting. Find out if your college has an expert who can come to your class, show videos they have, answer student questions, and share their thoughts on the discussion questions. At Virginia Tech I have Jonathan Charlton who is third author of this case (a junior in Engineering) come to my class. He has over 300 jumps to his credit and students love his enthusiasm and willingness to answer questions.

There may be someone at your school—a student, faculty member, or hourly worker—who would love to come to your class because they love this sport so much. Another source for a guest speaker is to contact your local parachute drop zone, or call the U.S. Parachute Association (www.uspa.org). To further illustrate the case, additional exhibits are available to you and your students at the textbook web site.

I have a VHS video of Jonathan coming to answer student questions. I tell my students in the class beforehand that crazy Jonathan is going to skydive onto the campus right before our next class and come to class to answer student questions (he really doesn't). At the next class period I start class with no guest speaker and tell students how upset and disappointed I am that this irresponsible skydiver did not show up. Then about five minutes into class (as is carefully rehearsed), Jonathan barges into class wearing his helmet and jump suit and holding his parachute. He acts as if he is really mad at me because he rented a plane for $100, skipped his class, made an illegal jump onto our campus, had to evade the campus police, and I didn't have my class out on the drill field to see him jump. I have since added a couple of my own students to this role playing skit, which is a great introduction and students just love it.

CONCLUDING NOTE

Any professor using this case can telephone the lead author Larry Alexander to discuss it. His home phone is 540-951-8172 (please call between 6:30 am and 8:30 pm eastern standard time). His phone number is 540-231-7382 at Virginia Tech. For a nominal fee to cover the cost of duplication and mailing, he can also make two short skydiving videos (one showing a sample jump, and one showing a guest speaker Q&A session) available to interested instructors.

CASE 3

General Aviation: An Industry Note[1]

SYNOPSIS OF THE CASE

The case provides details about the General Aviation industry. General Aviation is any "civil aviation activity except that of scheduled air carriers." In addition to the large airports, there are about 334 reliever airports and 2472 general aviation airports throughout the United States that help form the backbone of the air transportation system of the country. The case goes on to outline the requirements for flying as a general aviation pilot, the number of general aviation airports serving various communities and the legislation governing these airports. The case also discusses how communities neighboring general aviation airports are served and/or harmed by the airports. In spite of the downsides discussed, the future of general aviation airports is projected to show some growth in terms of the number of aircraft, and significant growth in terms of the number of pilots and total flight hours logged.

TEACHING OBJECTIVES

This case provides a snapshot of the general aviation industry and should be used together with the case on Redlands Municipal Airport. The main teaching objectives of this case are:

1.   To understand the structure of the General Aviation industry.

2.   To understand the regulations governing the General Aviation industry.

3.   To conduct an industry analysis outlining the opportunities and threats facing General Aviation

STRATEGIC ISSUES AND DISCUSSION QUESTIONS

1.   **What are the benefits to a community of having a general aviation airport?**

     General aviation airports can offer significant benefits to the communities located near it. A general aviation airport can:

     - Create opportunities for family owned operations that sell fuel, provide maintenance, give flying lessons, and offer charter services and hangar rentals at GA airports.

     - May attract other businesses to locate to the area, thus creating jobs and wealth for the communities.

     - Serve as the primary training ground for many pilots that go on to become pilots in scheduled air carriers.

     - Be used for various purposes like agriculture, firefighting, business/corporate/cargo activities, traffic reporting, medical emergency evacuation, charter planes, disaster relief, search and rescue, training, recreational flying, law enforcement and border patrols.

     - Help the economy by creation of manufacturing and other related jobs. The industry is estimated to have created about 638,000 jobs in 1998.

     - May serve as a vital link to communities that are not served by a large airport.

2.   **What are some downsides of having a general aviation airport near a community?**

     The downside to having a general aviation airport near a community is that it may lower the overall quality of life in the community. Specifically, general aviation airports:

---

[1] Parts of this teaching note are based on a teaching note by Harold Dyck.

- Create noise and air pollution.

- May put nearby communities at risk from aircraft accidents.

- May lower property values in the neighbor communities.

3. **What do you think has been the impact of the World Trade Center (WTC) tragedy on general aviation airports? How do you think this will influence the future of the General aviation industry?**

   Among the effects of the WTC tragedy on general aviation airports were the following:

   - Airport closures: Numerous airports shut down nationwide, including a two-week closure of the Redlands Municipal Airport.

   - Airspace changes: Both the FAA and the military upgraded their efforts to create and enforce temporary flight restrictions such as those to protect the President and Vice President of the U.S., nuclear reactors and other facilities of national importance

   - Legislation: Legislators passed a flurry of new legislation, including:

     - A massive victim's compensation and airline bailout bill

     - A major aviation and transportation security act affecting flight schools with increased screening of flight instruction candidates and further enhanced airspace restrictions.

     - A bill making airport security personnel employees of the federal government

     - A GA Industry Reparation Act of 2001 that lobbyists claim small GA businesses were as adversely affected by 9/11 as much as the airlines.

   - Industry Forecasts: While the AOPA predicts gradual growth of student pilots over the next five years, the FAA forecasts 15,000 fewer student pilots.

   The future of the General Aviation industry is likely to be impacted adversely because of the events of September 11, 2001.

   To begin with, the 2-week closure of airports in September 2001 meant lost revenues for GA airports. Since then, there has been a significant decrease in air traffic which is sure to impact the smaller general aviation airports as well as the small businesses that serve the airports. In addition, the restrictions on flying in certain areas have led to an economically unstable situation for GA airports.

   Increased national security considerations may force GA airports to upgrade their security personnel and systems. The resultant increase in costs may make some of the smaller GA airports unviable. Increased screening of candidates at flight schools is expected to lower enrollment in the coming years, leading to lower revenue streams.

   In summary, GA airports are as likely to suffer from the aftermath of September 11, 2001 as large air carriers are. The future is likely to be difficult for the survival of many GA airports and it remains to be seen whether government support will be extended to these airports in the same measure as it is being extended to the major airlines.

CASE 4

Redlands Municipal Airport[1]

SYNOPSIS OF THE CASE

The case begins with Ron Mutter, Director of Public Works for the City of Redlands, contemplating how to make the airport self-supporting. Currently, the $40,000 in lieu property fee makes the airport appear as a loss in the city budget, and most revenues are fixed in long-term 50-year leases. A major issue in this case is: whose responsibility is it to promote economic growth of the airport? Mayor Patricia (Pat) Gilbreath thinks the airport should be run entrepreneurially, as a franchise. But the main leaseholder says, "This is not our airport. We are not running this airport… our business is simply to rent hangars and tiedowns and to sell some fuel, to enjoy flying our own airplanes and we are not really very enthusiastic about politics."

TEACHING OBJECTIVES

The case deals with the operations of a municipally owned airport and describes the interface between businesses and various governmental bodies. It focuses on how responsibility issues complicate the planning process and how forecasts of demand for airport services can be way off base. The objectives are to:

1. Expose students to how government interfaces with businesses at a municipally owned airport.

2. Describe how the planning process at a municipal airport is hampered by a lack of clearly defined responsibility.

3. Have students think about the startup of an enterprise, such as an airport, and why a city would want to own it.

4. Examine the benefits to businesses to locate at or near an airport.

5. Examine how national and local trends are used as inputs in the forecasting process and how various forecasts are reconciled with each other.

6. Consider safety and noise issues at an airport.

7. Review the various options available to the city to ensure its future.

This case is of medium complexity and could be used in the early to middle part of a strategic management course or operations management, or a course on government-business policy.

STRATEGIC ISSUES AND DISCUSSION QUESTIONS

1. **Who are the stakeholders in this case, and how do they interact? Specifically, what is the relationship between the public and the tenants at the airport, the City of Redlands and the Airport Advisory Board?**

   There are many stakeholders in this case: those that appear in Exh. 1 (the mayor, the Airport Advisory Board, the City Council, the Director of Public Works, the Assistant Public Works Director, the main leaseholder, the fixed base operators and the various airport businesses), pilots and small plane owners, the citizens and business community of Redlands. Other major stakeholders include federal and state government agencies, such as the U.S. Department of Transportation, the FAA, and the California Department of Transportation (CalTrans) with its Aeronautics Division.

---

[1] This teaching note was prepared by Harold Dyck. Adapted by permission.

The relationship between the public and the tenants at the airport, the City of Redlands and the Airport Advisory Board is tenuous and not clearly defined. There is a lease arrangement between the City and the main leaseholder. Since the City is not involved in the day-to-day operations of the airport, the City has limited interaction with the public's need of the airport. Not mentioned in the case is the fact that the previous five-member appointed Advisory Board resigned *en masse* due to their lack of decision-making power.

2. **Who is responsible for the airport? Who should be in charge of economic growth at the airport: the City or the fixed base operators? Why is the delineation of responsibility so ambiguous?**

Ultimately, the City has legal responsibility for the airport. The City owns the airport. However they have entrusted the development to their fixed base operators (FBO). The City expects the FBOs to take the initiative to create more activity. For example, Mission Aviation Fellowship (MAF), has created jobs in Redlands, expanded its facilities, and is actively engaged in creating a viable organization at the airport. On the other hand, the main leaseholder, the Jansen family, has a different point of view: they just want to fly their airplanes. Therefore, the City has to either 1) more actively promote the airport itself, or 2) do a better job in screening and selecting their main leaseholder for the airport.

According to the mayor, the FBOs are responsible for the economic growth at the airport, but if they are not sufficiently committed to this, then City Manager and the Director of Public Works need to "pick up the ball" and become more actively involved in running the airport. The delineation of responsibility is so ambiguous because of these differing viewpoints.

3. **What are the advantages/disadvantages for a city to own an airport? Why not just keep the airport private?**

The advantages for the city to own the airport include:

*   Receiving federal funds for expansion and improvements

*   Providing a service to the citizens of Redlands

*   Creating an integrated transportation system controlled by the City

*   Giving the City the ability to control growth and other quality of life aspects

The disadvantages of city ownership include:

*   Expending time and effort to oversee the airport

*   The opportunity cost of losing tax revenues from private development of the area—if a privately owned airport were making a loss, it might be closed and sold

*   Lack of incentives that a private firm might have to become profitable in a timely manner

4. **What are the problems and opportunities of being a business at or near a small general aviation airport?**

The problems of being located at or near a small general aviation airport include:

*   Zoning restrictions that may limit or restrict the type of business, e.g., a school or tall building cannot be located beneath the landing pattern

*   The terms of the leases limit businesses to be aviation related

Opportunities are:

*   Favorable long term leases

*   Zoning that may be favorable to business and at the same time limit competition

5. **Why were the forecasts wrong, and why was the Master Plan overly optimistic? Should the government officials rely on forecasts? What variables should be used in creating a forecast? What forecasts would you develop to help the government officials?**

The Master Plan was needed to apply for federal funds. In order to justify these funds, it was necessary to predict a steady increase in operations at the airport. The case writers suspect that the Master Plan was overly optimistic to meet the outcome required. Federal funds were needed to validate the City's previous decision to purchase the airport. Methods used relied on population growth rather than economic variables. California's recession of the early 90's made it clear that economic variables should have been included in the analysis. Relevant regression variables might be: stock market activity, disposable income, GDP, the inflation rate, interest rates, and the number of pilots. The predicted number of aircraft would need to be modified by other factors such as: the closing of Norton U.S. Air Force Base, competition from surrounding airports, business trends in the aviation industry, and regulatory and legal changes.

6. **Why should an airport be concerned about safety and noise issues? How should they be addressed?**

Regardless of who owns the airport, the city has an obligation to its citizens for safety and other quality of life issues. They are required to provide police and fire protection. The zoning and aviation easements also restrict home building and other development for both safety and noise reasons. This is all part of the democratic process wherein a government listens to and responds to its constituents. City Council and Airport Advisory Board meetings are the proper avenues to address these issues.

7. **If you were a management consultant to the City of Redlands, what recommendations would you make to ensure the economic viability of the airport?**

The following recommendations are appropriate:

*   There needs to be a strategic plan in place when the ten-year renewable options are up on the 50-year leases. The leases need to be renegotiated with terms more favorable to the city and backup businesses need to be lined up to strengthen the hand of the city.

*   The city should raise the rental rate on hangers if provided for in the leases. The hanger rental charge is below market and there is a waiting list for hangers, while tiedown space remains mostly unused.

*   Better forecasts should be made to improve the planning process.

*   The City should choose the major leaseholder more selectively. The main leaseholder should be required to make a commitment to actively develop the airport. The main lease should be rewritten to reflect the desire of the City for a more pro-active management.

*   The City should re-evaluate the $40,000 *in-lieu* property tax to determine if it fairly represents the opportunity cost of lost property tax revenue it might have earned if the airport land had been used in its next best land use. The airport is located next to the Santa Ana Wash, a dry bed that is subject to flash flooding leaving the land without many alternative uses.

*   A comprehensive marketing plan needs to be developed (which the city could contract to do). This could be part of an overall plan for the entire City. Benchmarking of successful airports would be appropriate to generate ideas to better promote the airport. Ideas for a restaurant and an air fair could be included here.

The City should go ahead with the efforts to create the soccer fields just south of the airport. This would be a magnet to attract businesses toward the airport due to the popularity of soccer.

CASE 5

Perdue Farms, Inc.: Responding to Twenty-first Century Challenges[1]

SYNOPSIS OF THE CASE

Perdue Farms, Inc., began in 1920 when Arthur Perdue quit his job with Railway Express and started a table egg business. Arthur Perdue's son, Frank, was born that same year. In 1939, after two years at what was then the State Teacher's College in Salisbury, Frank (who preferred baseball to chickens and played minor league ball) joined his father. In 1940, the company switched from selling eggs to growing broilers. Frank became a full partner in 1944 and took over leadership in 1950. By 1952, annual revenues were $6 million.

In 1967, with sales of $35 million, Frank and his father decided that increased profits would come from processing chickens, rather than just growing them. The firm then became a vertically integrated chicken processor. Because Frank believed that only fresh chicken was of high enough quality to carry the Perdue name, the company's markets were limited to locations that could be serviced overnight by truck. Frank Perdue chose the densely populated cities of the northeast, serviced particularly New York City. During the 1970s, the firm entered the Baltimore, Philadelphia, Boston and Providence markets. When Arthur Perdue died in 1977 at age 91, he left behind a firm worth $200 million.

One of Frank Perdue's greatest contributions to the poultry industry was proving that chicken could be significantly differentiated with quality factors, such as permitting it to be branded. In the early days, chicken was sold to markets in bulk and butchers cut and wrapped it. Perdue realized that Perdue Farms could have the butcher's markup if customers could be influenced to ask for chicken by brand. He began an advertising program, first by radio and later using television that emphasized Perdue chicken's superior quality, broader breast, and healthy golden color.

Using the same advertising firm for more than 20 years and becoming the firm's media spokesperson, Frank Perdue created a consistent, recognizable ad campaign that transformed Perdue chicken into the most recognizable brand in its markets. Frank Perdue believed in focusing on one product and becoming the best at it. He asserted that diversification is the most dangerous word in the English language.

In 1981, Babson College named him the 18th recipient of their Academy of Distinguished Entrepreneurs. In 1990, William Donald Shaeffer, Governor of Maryland, proclaimed Frank Perdue's 50th anniversary with Perdue Farms as "Frank Perdue Day," as did the governors of Delaware and Virginia.

Jim Perdue, Frank's only son became Chairman of the Board in 1991. Jim, who holds a PhD in fisheries from the University of Washington and an MBA from Salisbury University, is a very different personality from his father. While Frank possesses the single-minded dedication of the true entrepreneur, Jim tends to focus on operations, quietly striving to make Perdue Farms the most efficient firm in the industry. This generational leadership change seems to have taken place very smoothly—without the acrimony that sometimes accompanies succession in entrepreneurial firms.

The Perdue Farms Inc. case is about a highly successful privately owned company that has transformed itself from a simple chicken grower into one of the largest, vertically integrated poultry companies in the nation. Its hallmark is unyielding quality, an attribute that Frank Perdue used to differentiate his product and build brand recognition in his ground breaking "entrepreneur/CEO as the spokesperson" marketing program. The key issue is whether the firm can continue adequate growth as a regional poultry producer or whether it must become national/international and begin to diversify in earnest.

---

[1] This teaching note was prepared by George C. Rubenson. Adapted by permission.

TEACHING OBJECTIVES

This case illustrates powerfully the way in which managers can develop a cohesive strategy to give a company a competitive advantage, and it also shows how the structure and culture developed by the founding entrepreneur can be important in implementing the strategy successfully. The principal teaching objectives of the case are as follows:

1. To chart the development of a company from its earliest beginnings.

2. To illustrate how an entrepreneur can develop a successful competitive strategy.

3. To show how vertical integration can help a company pursue a differentiation strategy.

4. To demonstrate the importance of structure and culture in implementing strategy.

5. To illustrate the potential of strong values, consistency of purpose, a commitment to quality and the ability to differentiate the product.

The case can be used for in-class discussion of the above attributes, for in-depth discussion of either external or internal issues, or it can be assigned as an integrative case assignment near the end of the semester to let the students grapple with Jim Perdue's (Frank's son and current Chairman) problem of leading the firm into the 21st century.

STRATEGIC ISSUES AND DISCUSSION QUESTIONS

Because the case is well suited to a traditional SWOT analysis, assignment questions are organized to lead the discussion to issues about possible future directions.

1. **What resource strengths and competitive assets does Perdue Farms have that can help determine realistic strategic directions, i.e., potential goals the company is capable of achieving?**

    Jim Perdue faces numerous challenges. However, he leads a firm that possesses strengths in virtually every basic function and relatively few weaknesses.

    *   The company has been profitable every year since it was founded except for 1988, a loss it blamed on a decentralization program which increased costs, and 1996, a poor year for the entire industry due to high corn prices. Perdue Farms uses conservative financial management. It generally finances replacement projects and normal growth from cash flow and retained earnings. For larger expansions, it utilizes long-term borrowing to a target level of 55% of equity. Growth plans are targeted to return $2 of increased sales for each $1 of capital invested. The company's debt policy, although conservative, has not prevented growth.

    *   Perdue Farms has continued to expand:

        *   It has extended its markets to Pittsburgh, Cleveland, Chicago, Atlanta and Miami.

        *   In the past five years, the company has purchased Showell Farms (an Eastern Shore integrated poultry producer), Deluca Inc. (an independent producer of fully prepared entrees) and Gol-Pak Corporation (products for the food service industry).

        *   International revenues have grown from $20 million to about $140 million during the past five years.

        *   Total revenues in 2000 were more than $2.5 billion and total employees were about 20,000.

    *   Perdue Farms tends to attack environmental issues head-on. Jim Perdue speaks directly to the issue, stating that complying with existing laws is not enough. The firm's Environmental Steering Committee must "...provide all Perdue Farms work sites with vision, direction, and leadership so that they can be good corporate citizens from an environmental perspective today and in the future." Examples of Perdue Farms' commitment include:

        *   Development of a process for pelletizing excess manure so that it can be removed from the growing facilities, sold as fertilizer or fuel, and shipped economically to distant locations;

- Development of a comprehensive network of wellness centers directed at attacking the issue of employee health and safety.

- The firm's marketing program is state of the art. Although not the largest poultry firm in the U.S., Perdue Farms holds the distinction of having "branded" chicken. "Perdue" is arguably the best-recognized name in the industry within its regional markets. The marketing function is responsible for how many chickens and turkeys to grow, what the advertising and promotion pieces should look like, where they should run, how much the company can afford, and which new products the company will pursue.

- The Perdue approach to operations is based on achieving unsurpassed quality and efficiency. Perdue Farms has had an aggressive Total Quality Management (TQM) program in place for many years. The firm believes that efficiency comes from managing the details and closely monitors every step of the production process including genetic research, egg production and hatching, chicken house technology, formulating and manufacturing its own feed, overseeing the care and feeding, operating its own processing plants and distributing via its own trucking fleet.

- Perdue Farms considers management information systems to be a fundamental part of its overall business strategy. For example, in late 1999 the company undertook development of a comprehensive, information systems based supply chain management system. The goal was to solve the complex integration problem of forecasting product requirements, growing the right number of birds at the right time, processing the right amount of each of the more than 400 products the company produces, and delivering the right mix and amount of products to each customer at the right time. Implementation of this system is progressing.

- The firm has long been considered a research leader in the industry, employing specialists in avian science, microbiology, nutrition and veterinary science to ensure that its health and nutrition programs are state of the art.

- Human Resource Management is a mix of traditional but modern systems.

  - Perdue is a family firm and its personnel policies reflect the values of the owners—total loyalty and a penchant for hard work. The company has an unyielding anti-union stance. However, it has a relatively modern view of worker relations, calling all workers "associates" and encouraging everyone—from production line workers to managers—to get involved in suggesting ways to increase efficiency and produce a better product.

  - The firm has a very enlightened benefits program. While it provides the usual paid holidays and vacation, health, accident and life insurance, and saving and pension plans, it also provides several unusual benefits such as leave of absence for up to 12 months for non-job related injury or illness, the birth or adoption of a child, the care of a spouse or other close relative, or other personal situations.

  - The company instituted an aggressive wellness program in 1993 and currently has 10 wellness centers spread across its processing facilities. Providing universal access to covered associates and dependents, the program permits employees to see a health care provider without leaving the work-site or clocking out. The charge is $7 payroll deduction co-pay. A former trauma nurse lured out of retirement to work in the program stated "I don't know of any organized medical program that's as good as this and I've been in nursing 30 years and seen all sorts of programs."

2. **What weaknesses and resource deficiencies does Perdue Farms have that put it at a competitive disadvantage, i.e., potential goals they will probably have a difficult time achieving?**

- Despite its growth and efficiency, the firm's profitability is minimal. Although the firm releases little information regarding its financial situation, its profitability during the period 1994-1999 has ranged between $25 and $58 million and the trend is down. In 1999, profits were only $25 million on sales of $2.5 billion (1%). Although perhaps not as important to a private firm as it would be for a publicly traded firm, profitability is clearly a significant problem (Data from *Forbes* magazine).

- The company's long-standing insistence on selling nothing but the highest quality *fresh* (not frozen) young chickens complicates future growth and product diversification, i.e., retail markets must be within overnight distance by truck. This policy may be archaic. Surveys indicate that the 21st century marketplace values speed and ease of preparation. Additionally, a majority of consumers freeze their meat once they get it home.

- Food service is the fastest growing segment of the market and currently amounts to approximately 50% of revenues across the industry. However, Perdue Farms receives only about 20% of its revenues from food service. Thus, it is clearly behind. This is a difficult area for Perdue Farms because the nature of institutional contracts places limited value on the company's traditional competitive advantage, i.e., superior quality and branding. In addition, institutional contracting leaves little room for profit.

- Perdue Farms is an "Eastern" company and considers itself to be both an important employer and a community resource. Although it has built numerous new facilities in other regions, it is loath to move existing facilities off the shore. Unfortunately, the high density of poultry farms in so small an area creates constant stress between the company and environmental advocates who are concerned that excessive poultry waste is having a serious, negative effect on the Chesapeake Bay. Additionally, resource costs (e.g., labor rates) are above average. Thus, it can be argued that protecting those facilities located on the shore places Perdue Farms at a competitive disadvantage.

3. **What industry opportunities exist that are unusually attractive and are a good match with Perdue Farms' strengths, i.e., potential company opportunities?**

- It is unlikely that Americans will lose their taste for chicken any time soon. The industry has done an exceptional job of developing poultry into a wide variety of products that are considered tasty and healthful. Most of the increases in annual consumption have come at the expense of red meat and pork. Its other major competitor is seafood. While seafood also has an enviable reputation for healthfulness, it suffers from worldwide over fishing and there are concerns regarding contamination from polluted waters. By comparison, there appears to be no real limit to the amount of poultry that can be raised economically and efficiently.

- Lifestyle changes have resulted in increasing demand for meat products that can be prepared quickly. Poultry producers have responded with value added products such as fully cooked and seasoned whole chicken and chicken parts. These products are sold in supermarkets as home meal replacement entrees that are sold with salads and desserts, allowing customers to assemble their own dinners.

- The food service market is growing rapidly. Food service consists of a wide variety of public and private customers including restaurant chains, governments, hospitals, schools, transportation facilities and institutional contractors. Across the domestic poultry industry, food service currently accounts for approximately 50% of total poultry sales.

- A variety of international markets are developing. Asian populations, in particular, like poultry, especially dark meat. This can be an excellent fit with domestic tastes which favor white meat, assuming that the dark meat can be economically transported to the Asian markets.

4. **What industry factors threaten Perdue Farms, i.e., pose serious threats to its future growth and profitability?**

- Poultry is a saturated market that is extremely competitive and produces paper-thin margins. Analysts worry how much growth is possible given that Americans currently eat about 80 pounds of chicken per person per year. Producers must constantly seek ways to reduce costs to generate acceptable profits.

- The industry suffers from overcapacity so that market share increases are hard won and not very profitable. For example, after climbing from 40 cents per pound in 1960 to about 90 cents per pound in 1990, prices have been stagnant and, in real terms, the price of chicken is at an all time low.

- A major problem appears to be too many producers. There are currently about 35 poultry producers in the United States. The top four (Perdue hovers between number three and number four) hold approximately 40% of the market. Consolidation is very slow.

- The poultry industry suffers from a number of serious environmental threats. Raising, slaughtering, and processing poultry is a difficult and tedious process. Detractors argue that the process is dangerous to workers, inhumane to the poultry, hard on the environment and results in food that may not be safe.

- An issue constantly facing the industry is the claim of some poultry plant workers that their work produces a high incidence of injury, in particular repetitive motion disorders. The industry counters that the unions are often behind these charges. A major section in the case discusses various aggressive actions that Perdue Farms has taken to become an industry leader in worker safety and wellness.

- The industry receives a significant amount of bad press from animal rights advocates. Their claim has been that the industry is inhumane, forcing thousands of chickens to live in extremely close quarters and brutally killing them. Poultry growers believe these claims are unfounded, countering that birds that are mistreated would not produce good meat. These concerns seem to have quieted down somewhat.

- Claims that the industry is hard on the environment have been more intractable. Although the industry can claim a long list of innovative solutions to various environmental problems, disposal of dead birds and hatchery waste has continued to create bad press due to release into the soil of excess nitrogen and phosphorus that can leach out into tributaries, possibly infecting fish and other sea-life. This has been particularly troublesome to Perdue Farms because it produces a significant percent of its poultry on the DelMarVa Peninsula (the Eastern Shore of Delaware, Maryland and Virginia), a relatively small land area surrounded by water. Most solutions are very expensive and, given the low profit margins in the industry, could seriously erode profitability.

- Product safety relates to the susceptibility of poultry to infectious diseases. Perhaps the most feared is avian flu, which, while not harmful to humans, is so infectious to chickens that it is sometimes necessary to exterminate an entire flock to eradicate the disease. The poultry industry has done an excellent job of developing procedures to determine very early that avian flu is present. Outbreaks of the disease appear to be less frequent and less devastating than earlier.

5. **In what ways have Perdue Farms' structure and culture helped or harmed its attempts to implement its strategy?**

From the beginning, the company's structure and culture has been managed in a very hands-on manner by the Perdue family. It is still privately held and firmly in the control of the founding family. Until the 1980s it operated very successfully with a centralized, functional structure. However, its structure began to harm the company in the late 1980s when, after Perdue's plunge into turkey raising, a consulting company recommended that the company move to a multidivisional structure and decentralize control of its operations to divisional managers. This resulted in the duplication of many functional activities, such as MIS, and significantly raised operating costs.

To correct this mistake, the company moved back to basics and now uses a product structure in which one set of centralized support functions services the needs of all its different product lines, for example, chicken and turkey products. The company's well-developed MIS allows it to manage its operations efficiently using this simpler structure.

There has also been a big change in the company's culture. The company has moved from a top-down, autocratic management approach to one based on team management and the involvement of employees in many aspects of running the business. Jim's "people first" management style ensures that employees or associates are involved in quality and operational issues of the company. Employees are given opportunities for advancement through training and education programs. In addition to medical benefits given to employees and dependents, an ergonomics committee ensures that employees enjoy a safe and healthy environment.

The company has changed its approach in large part because of its commitment to improving the quality of its product, and all attempts at TQM require the commitment and involvement of employees to improve product quality.

6. **What generic business-level and competitive strategies does Perdue Farms use?**

Perdue Farms pursues a strategy of differentiation based on the high quality and freshness of its products. All its marketing is geared to emphasizing the uniqueness of the product—that it has never been frozen and that it contains no artificial substances such as drugs or steroids. At the same time the company pays attention to costs and seeks to minimize them, but its strategy is clearly focused on putting quality first and cost second. Perdue also charges a premium price for its poultry products, which are generally the highest priced in the grocery store.

In terms of competitive strategy, Perdue Farms is quick to change its strategy to suit changing competitive conditions. For example, the company originally began as an egg producer, but then, as its founder realized that more money could be made in selling chickens, he took the company into the chicken business and sold whole birds. In the 1980s the company extended its activities by raising and selling turkeys and by selling processed chicken and turkey products. The company has continuously broadened its product line ever since. Today its products include different types of chicken products, such as breast nuggets, cutlets, tenders, and even fully cooked whole chickens, in addition to many kinds of turkey products, such as sweet and hot turkey sausages.

The company follows a strategy of product development in offering new products to its existing market, and it also uses market development in packaging its chicken and turkey products in ways that allow it to serve new market segments—for example, fully cooked microwaveable chicken for the market segment that wants ready-cooked meals. At the same time, it pursues a market-penetration strategy, and it has increased its market share to become one of the largest poultry producers in the U.S.

7. **What is Perdue Farms' corporate-level strategy, and how does it support its business-level strategy?**

Perdue Farms has stayed firmly focused in one industry, and it has concentrated its resources in the poultry business to achieve a strong competitive position in this industry. However, as related in the text, to strengthen a company's position in the core business it is sometimes useful also to engage in a strategy of vertical integration. This is what Perdue Farms has done. By 1968 Perdue Farms had become involved in all stages of the value-added chain, except for actually selling the chicken. It breeds its own laying hens, hatches its own eggs in 19 hatcheries, selects its contract growers, builds Perdue engineered chicken houses, formulates and manufactures its own feed, overseas care and feeding of the chicks, processes the broilers in its own processing plants and finally ships them to market in its own fleet of refrigerated trucks. Thus the company is adding value at every stage of the production process. Vertical integration helps Perdue maintain the high quality and freshness of its broilers, and this is the differentiating factor that its customers pay a premium for. Thus, vertical integration helps support its business-level strategy of differentiation.

CASE 6

Wizards of the Coast, 1990-2001

SYNOPSIS OF THE CASE

This case is about the founding, growth and acquisition of Wizards of the Coast, the world's leading adventure gaming company. It describes in detail how the company was founded and how its strategy emerged. An entrepreneurial success story, it follows the company's meteoric growth in revenues to approximately $130 million in less than five years. However, this success brought with it tremendous challenges. Some of the company's founders were unable to make the transition into management, while professional managers brought in from the outside did not fit the creative, artistic culture of Wizards. In the meantime, many original investors began to demand that their paper wealth be transformed into something more concrete, and the sales revenues that had skyrocketed during the first four to five years started to reflect the ups and downs of a roller coaster ride.

As the company struggled to seek new sources of revenue through product development, acquisitions, international expansion and game centers, it struck gold yet again when Nintendo licensed the Magic patent for its Pokemon trading card game in 1998. The success of Wizards led to its acquisition by one of the major players in the toy industry, Hasbro, for $325 Million. The case further outlines the game related and retail strategies pursued by Wizards as a division of Hasbro.

TEACHING OBJECTIVES

The Wizards case highlights many important strategic issues relevant to the success or failure of entrepreneurial firms:

1. The nature and importance of the individual entrepreneur, in this case, Peter Adkison, the founder and CEO of Wizards.

2. Intentional entrepreneurship, as Wizards of the Coast began international expansion early on to achieve about half of its revenues outside the United States.

3. Sources of capital, in that the company was originally funded by the founders and their friends and families, and is now in need of external funding to continue on its growth trajectory and to satisfy the demands of its original investors.

4. Managing early growth and new venture expansion. Wizards grew extremely fast in a short period of time and thus experienced all the challenges that go along with fast growth.

5. Ending the game: the considerations behind the choice made by the top management in being taken over as opposed to going public or continuing independently.

STRATEGIC ISSUES AND DISCUSSION QUESTIONS

1. **How was Wizards of the Coast able to "re-create" the adventure game market?**

    The instant success of Wizards was based on bringing together the idea of highly collectible trading cards, like baseball cards, with a role-playing adventure game. The result was *Magic: The Gathering.* In essence, Wizards did not create an entirely new product with the introduction of *Magic,* but combined two existing ideas/products into a hybrid. This ability to synthesize existing, well-proven ideas into an innovation has been one of the defining activities of the entrepreneur since Schumpeter (1912; "new combinations").

    In particular, the idea of *Magic* came about when Peter Adkison met with Richard Garfield. Each person had a piece of the puzzle. Adkison had the idea that there was a need for a fantasy role-playing game that was portable and could be played anywhere in less than one hour. He thought that maybe it should be a card game. Garfield, a game inventor by heart, was able to transform Adkison's idea into a "real" game through his innovative combination of the trading-card element with the role-playing game envisioned by Adkison.

Interestingly, the two met in an Internet chat room. Even though one could argue that this was purely coincidental, one needs to admit that Peter Adkison was proactive in searching for a "complementary" partner who could help him actualize his idea. Had Adkison not had a strong vision regarding the product of his start-up company, all the luck in the world would not have led him to the perfect partner to help him shape his ideas into a viable product.

2.   **How important was the early international expansion of Wizards? What strategy did the firm pursue? What are the opportunities and threats in international growth in the future?**

Early international expansion was crucial to Wizards' success. In particular, when the firm experienced a dramatic drop in its domestic sales, international sales were still increasing. Thus, one could argue that early international expansion saved Wizards from possible bankruptcy in its very early years. Within four years of its release, *Magic* was sold to over 5 million customers in 52 countries worldwide, with about half of its market outside the United States. In this very short time period, the company had opened offices in Antwerp, London, and Paris, with more offices in Europe and Asia to follow.

Wizards' international strategy was shaped by its desire to retain control over the quality of its product and its distribution channel, both of which are important strategic levers in building brand name and equity. Thus, Wizards chose to open its own offices abroad and directed its international sales through the nearest geographic office. Through one hundred percent ownership in the office and close geographic proximity, Wizards was able to have complete control over its international activities.

The international scene holds very bright prospects for Wizards. There is a tremendous demand for the game worldwide, and the company has just begun to tap into the vast Asian market. It seems likely that *Magic* will do well in this part of the world since strategic games, like Go, have been part of its culture for many thousands of years. In addition, its status in Western markets should serve it well, as popular 'foreign' products tend to be in high demand—particularly among the youth—in economically successful countries like Japan, Korea, Taiwan, and Hong Kong/China. In addition, Wizards has been able to form a global community of players through its international tournaments (World Championships) and ever present rankings on its Web page (www.wizards.com), which are comparable to the rankings issued in tennis by the World Tennis Association.

3.   **What were the sources of capital for Wizards of the Coast? What implications does this have for the future strategy of the company?**

Initially, the company was funded by the three "Fs": founders, families and friends. That implied that the equity of the company was split among those three groups. Although it is relatively easy to obtain funds in small amounts from families and friends, Wizards experienced some of the negative effects of being funded by these groups. Usually, family and friends are more patient with respect to earning a return on their investments. In Wizards' case, however, some early investors demanded that their newly found "paper wealth" be transformed in real wealth. This prompted Wizards' management to take out a $30 million loan to buy back some of its initial shares. As a result, Wizards regained most of its equity, and was thus able to position itself for an IPO or a takeover. Thus, what seemed to be detrimental to the business (a demand for return on investment by original capital providers) turned out to be beneficial for the company, since it enabled it to position itself more attractively for the endgame.

4.   **What were some of the challenges Wizards experienced as a result of its tremendous growth?**

Fast growth can be a mixed blessing for an entrepreneurial start-up. The initial success of *Magic* was phenomenal. The first printing of *Magic* cards, which was believed to last a year, was sold out within six weeks. Initially, demand for the new product could not be satisfied, since only one printer (Carta Mundi in Belgium) was able to offer the sophisticated, high-quality printing and sorting of *Magic* cards. Thus, production was a bottleneck that needed to be overcome quickly at the outset.

The positive side effect of this strong initial growth was tremendous cash flow. Peter Adkison likes to compare his trading cards to software in that the cost of the first unit is high, but it drops to next to nothing for all subsequent units. With this extremely low marginal cost, the immediate popularity of the cards allowed the company to fund future growth internally.

Wizards experienced the greatest challenges of fast growth on the management side. *Magic*'s remarkable sales put stress on the company's weak, and in some instances non-existent, financial controls. The company lacked even a formal payroll system—instead, Peter Adkison wrote paychecks from his personal account. For months the company paid a "volunteer" who was never formally hired. Even more significant were the human resources challenges of transforming Wizards from a start-up into a well-managed business enterprise. Many original founders were unable to make the transition to professional managers and Adkison was forced to make the tough decision to ask them to leave the company. He pointed out in an interview that it was not only painful for him to see original founders leave, but also that he was severely disappointed with some of the highly recommended professional managers that he brought in from the outside. They were unable to mesh with Wizards' culture and eventually they too had to go.

Adkison also admits to experiencing a kind of "identity crisis," where he was not sure if he was "cut out" to be the CEO of a fast growing, international company. He turned to business consultants to bridge the gap in the short term, while returning to school to earn an MBA. For two years he attended the executive program at the University of Washington Business School while continuing the full time job of running Wizards of the Coast. He also chose his board of directors well, surrounding himself with experienced business leaders whom he could trust. All those steps helped the company to make the transition from an entrepreneurial start-up into a well-managed, international company with its original founder at its helm.

5. **What would you do given the situation in mid-1997 described in the case? If you chose to end the game, how would you go about it? What path would you pursue? Why?**

The essential strategic challenge for Wizards' top management in mid-1997 was how to pursue a sustainable growth strategy. One problem the company had was that it lost focus. It introduced more than two hundred new games within a short time period, and all of them flopped. At this point, Wizards was still a one-product company: *Magic* provided more than 90 percent of its revenues. One possible strategy was to refocus the company on *Magic,* and to transform this "fad" into a sustainable game and sport. Peter Adkison is setting the company up to do just that. During an interview, he indicated that the company's decision to refocus on *Magic* was an emergent strategy suggested by George Skaff Elias, Wizards' chief game developer. Thus, the top management team decided to refocus Wizards on *Magic* to provide the sustainable growth strategy demanded by investment bankers.

The company did not consider the option of independent growth. Wizards needed a capital infusion that could only come from the outside via an IPO or a merger—preferably with a larger gaming company like Parker or Hasbro. A takeover would imply that Wizards would face the new challenge of maintaining its creative, free-minded culture as part of a larger enterprise.

6. **What were the reasons that compelled Hasbro to acquire Wizards of the Coast? What do you see as the biggest challenge for Wizards and Hasbro?**

Hasbro acquired Wizards in an attempt to extend its appeal to a broader audience and rejuvenate sales by expanding into the fast growing games sector. In addition to expanding distribution channels and adding popular board games like *Pokemon* and *Magic* to its portfolio, Hasbro would also get a chance to test out new game concepts at the game centers owned by Wizards.

In the short term, the biggest challenge facing Wizards and Hasbro is managing the different cultures of the two companies successfully so as not to lose the creativity and flexibility that made Wizards a success.

Another challenge facing Hasbro comes from the seasonal nature of the gaming industry – a game that is popular in one Christmas season may not yield the same revenue and profits in the next season and the challenge is to continue scanning for the next big hit while continuing to develop older hits into "classics". The key is not only to be at the cutting edge of the gaming industry but to also define its trajectory.

7. **Why did Wizards acquire TSR (the maker of *Dungeons and Dragons*)?**

Wizard's strategy was to consolidate the adventure/hobby game industry, and to become the dominant player in the industry. It made the acquisition to give the company critical mass, which would improve its leverage over distributors. One of the problems with the retail side of the adventure gaming industry was that it was very fragmented and disorganized. Wizards had to work very hard to persuade retailers to carry new games. Wizards believed that if it controlled two of the most popular games in the industry—*Magic* and *Dungeons and Dragons*—it would be better able to persuade retailers to carry its products.

8. **Why did Wizards try to turn *Magic* into an Intellectual sport by setting up competitions and leagues between *Magic* players?**

    Wizards was trying to transform *Magic* from a fad into an established game like chess or scrabble with a loyal following. They saw the organized competitions as a way of increasing the attraction of the game, and hence demand for *Magic* cards. Most *Magic* players were by their nature competitive, and the organized game play fed on this.

9. **What lay behind Wizard's move into retail stores? What are the potential problems with this strategy?**

    As noted, Wizards strategy was to consolidate the fragmented hobby gaming market. As part of this strategy, Wizards wanted to establish a presence in retail so that it could

    - Get to know its customers better

    - Have a channel for displaying and selling its portfolio of game products

    - Have a physical space where organized game play could take place.

    The problem with this strategy is that it takes Wizards into a business that it does not have any experience in retail and that it requires far more capital than the existing business. Adkinson was aware of these problems, but believed that the benefits outweighed the risks.

CASE 7

Napster

SYNOPSIS OF THE CASE

This case discusses the founding, growth and widespread popularity of Napster's file sharing service and its legal battles with the music industry that led not only to the service being shut down but also to Napster's subsequent decline.

In 1999, Shawn Fanning, a college student, developed the code for a peer-to-peer network of computers managed by a central server that allowed computers on the network to share and swap MP3 music files stored on the hard drive of each computer. After Napster's incorporation as a company in May 1999, the music sharing program spread rapidly as music enthusiasts, primarily students in universities with access to high-speed networks, signed onto the free service. Within a year the Napster community had grown to approximately 40 million users. The growing popularity of Napster was seen as a threat by the music industry that has historically been very concerned about the potential that new technology presents for piracy of copyrighted material.

The case describes how Napster became the target of a number of lawsuits, initiated not only by music companies but also by music groups like Metallica. The courts granted an injunction filed by music companies that would eventually shut the service down in 2001.

Despite the fast growth of its file sharing service, Napster was yet to find a sustainable business model. To compound its problems, it also needed an infusion of capital to keep its operations going. Bertelsmann (owner of the music record label, BMG) announced an alliance with Napster to develop a subscription music distribution service based on Napster's technology, but the alliance made slow progress. A subsequent bid by Bertelsmann to buy out Napster for $15 million was foiled by internal strife at Napster. As of early 2002, unable to overcome its legal problems, Napster stands at the brink of bankruptcy.

TEACHING OBJECTIVES

The Napster case highlights the issues facing both incumbents and a new entrant when the latter introduces a novel technology that transforms the way things are traditionally done in an industry. The teaching objectives of this case are:

1. To understand the bases of competition and profit in the music industry. To understand the value added by a disruptive technology like online music sharing and how it changed the structure of the music industry.

2. To evaluate the effect of the file sharing service on consumers and the traditional players in the music industry—music companies, music retailers, and artists.

3. To analyze the challenges faced by an entrepreneurial startup in promoting a disruptive technology.

4. To demonstrate the challenges of managing intellectual property rights.

5. To underscore the importance of a sustainable business model that generates revenues.

6. To analyze the challenges presented to incumbents by a technology that threatens to eat their lunch and critically evaluate possible incumbent responses to the technology.

STRATEGIC ISSUES AND DISCUSSION QUESTIONS

1. **What are the economics of the music recording business?**

    The music recording business is a high-risk high return endeavor. It costs some $1 million to produce and launch a new act, excluding manufacturing and distribution costs. That is, the fixed costs are about $1 million. Some 7,000 new CDs are issued each year by major labels. The success rate is very low with only 10% making a profit.

This suggests that it is very hard to predict what will sell in the market place. Why? Music recording is clearly a fashion driven market place that is difficult for the recording companies to control and predict.

On the other hand, a successful act can be very profitable for the music companies. For a start, the music companies offset upfront production costs against artists' royalties, which lowers their breakeven point on unit sales volume. Second, the marginal costs of producing additional units of a CD are low, a few cents at best, and the packaging and distribution costs are also relatively low as a percentage of total unit price, implying that at high volume the profit per CD is very high. This creates a presumption for volume growth.

In sum, a relatively small number of successful CDs pay for all of the losses the recording labels bear and generate their profits. It is important to emphasize, however, that deducting costs from artists' royalties mitigates the risk facing the music labels.

2.   **Do the big five music recording companies have market power? If so, where does this power come from? Was this market power starting to erode prior to the arrival of Napster?**

With five companies controlling 90% of global music sales, it would seem that the recording companies do have some market power. The power probably comes from two main sources: (1) access to distribution channels, and (2) economies of scale in advertising and marketing.

Distribution is expensive, and most retail establishments probably prefer to deal with a limited number of companies. Moreover, there are probably economies of scale in distribution associated with the ability to spread the fixed costs of maintaining a distribution system over a large number of CDs (or, equivalently, the ability to push more product down an existing channel). The significant ad dollars spent by music companies probably also enables them to get substantial discounts relative to smaller labels for ad space in the press. It also seems likely that large established music companies are better able to get airplay on radio and music TV channels such as MTV than smaller labels.

The fact that music companies can impose some fairly high costs on recording artists—such as offsetting launch costs against royalties—suggests that they enjoy significant bargaining power vis-à-vis this group. The lack of choice drives artists into the hands of the big labels, and the big labels use their power to extract a significant share of the artists' future economic rents. It is not surprising then that many artists dislike the music companies, and some of the most successful try to break contracts and set up their own labels, or move to another label.

On the other hand, the erosion of CD prices during the 1990s suggests that retail establishments may be gaining power over the music labels, whose own power was starting to erode prior to the arrival of Napster. Consolidation in the once fragmented retail sector, and the arrival of large discount superstores such as Wal-Mart and Target, may have enabled the retailers to gain bargaining power over the recording labels. The retailers also control a valuable asset in the industry—access to shelf space. As fewer retailers control more of the shelf space, they are in all probability using that to bargain down the price they must pay recording companies for CDs, and then turning around and passing on that lower price to consumers in accordance with their business model.

Action by anti-trust authorities on both sides of the Atlantic has also reduced the ability of the recording companies to control prices, and allowed retailers to engage in competitive discounting, a practice that apparently is not in the best interest of the music companies. One can speculate the demand for a successful music recording is price inelastic, and that other things being equal the music companies would like to exploit this fact by raising prices for successful recordings and capturing more profits from consumers. Discount retailers, on the other hand, appear to want to offer discounts on popular CD's as a way of generating sales traffic. These two business models conflict with each other.

What was also reducing the market power of the music companies prior to Napster was the rise in piracy rates along with the related development of digital copying technology such as MP3 files. Piracy can be viewed as a means of distribution that the music companies do not control. In effect, the rise of pirated CDs, MP3 files, and so on, reduces the market share of established recording companies, and thus their market power. The price of pirated CDs is typically much lower than the price of regular CDs to account for their variable quality. The music companies have been forced to respond to the rise of pirated music recordings by reducing the prices for legal CDs, thereby limiting the incentive for consumers to purchase pirated products.

3. **Does file-sharing technology over peer-to-peer networks have the characteristics of a disruptive technology? What are the implications of this technology for the market power and growth prospects of established music recording companies? How might this technology, including variations developed by established music companies, "disrupt" the industry?**

Peer to peer technology absolutely has the characteristics of a disruptive technology. It is a new way of distributing music that took root outside of the boundaries of the established music industry's value chain and was pioneered by a small entrepreneurial company. It could potentially disrupt the established industry in a number of ways. Specifically:

- It limits the power of established retailers, since more and more music may be downloaded directly from music companies via the Internet.

- In so far as established retailers have been gaining power relative to the music companies, this is potentially beneficial for established music companies. However, the calculus is not this straightforward. The switch from physical to Internet distribution is unlikely to be immediate, or complete for a long time (if ever) implying that for significant periods both channels would exist side by side. This creates a situation of channel conflict for the established music companies. If they move to Internet distribution, they may lose the support of established retailers whom they will need for a significant period of time.

- Potentially, the advent of peer-to-peer networks changes the economics of the music industry by taking significant costs out of the system—including the costs of producing and distributing CDs. By reducing the marginal costs of selling more CDs to almost trivial levels, electronic distribution would allow recording labels to cut prices, sell more units, and still make greater profits per unit sale. In theory, the lower price should reduce the incentive that consumers have to engage in theft and download pirated recordings.

- Potentially peer-to-peer networks and Internet distribution increases the ability that consumers have to customize music recordings. They can download what they want, ignoring dud songs and album fillers. Indeed, Internet distribution could potentially kill the concept of the album. This is a mixed blessing for music companies. On the one hand, the ability to offer customers a customized product should increase customer satisfaction. On the other, it means that customers would no longer have to pay for filler songs, which would reduce revenues to music companies, (and royalties to recording artists).

- Potentially the technology diminishes the power of the recording labels by allowing artists to self publish. However, artists would still have to produce and promote their recordings, and the established music labels have considerable expertise and economic resources here. It does not follow, therefore, that the advent of peer-to-peer networks dramatically changes the power of established recording companies over new artists. The Internet is an ocean in which any new artist seeking to self-publish could drown, no matter how talented they might be. On the other hand, peer to peer networks do potentially increase the bargaining power of established artists with well known names and a distinct following, although the increase might not be as much as some artists hope due to the importance and costs of marketing. Moreover, the ability of consumers to pick and chose an artist's recordings potentially limits their ability to pass off filler tracks, and garner royalties form those, as part of an album.

- The technology clearly makes it easier to distribute pirated copies of copyrighted music recordings, which is not good for anyone in the established industry—the artists, record labels, or retailers.

In sum, peer-to-peer technology is clearly a mixed bag for the entire industry value chain.

- Retailers lose, because they sell less.

- Recording labels may lose, because the technology increases the bargaining power of successful artists, because it allows consumers to pick and choose tracks, and because it increases the piracy rate. On the other hand, by taking costs out of their system, the technology may allow established companies to lower prices, sell more, still make more profit per unit, and reduce the incentive that consumers have to steal.

- Artists gain some leverage, but probably only if they are already successful. Moreover, they might see their royalties fall as consumers no longer have to purchase dud tracks.

- Consumers are the clear winners. Peer-to-peer technology should lower the price of purchasing music, allow them to pick and chose what tracks they want to buy, and purchase from the comfort of their homes.

4. **What are the implications for the music recording business of widespread violation of intellectual property rights? Do new digital technologies increase the potential piracy rate? Why?**

By 2001, piracy rates in music were 30% or more globally, representing $10 billion in lost revenues. Sales of new CDs fell in 2000 and 2001, and it is hard to escape the conclusion that piracy rates had something to do with this. Piracy of music recording has always been with us, but there is little doubt that the rise of digital technologies, including MP3 and peer-to-peer networks, made it much easier to illegally copy and distribute music recordings. The essential problem is that peer-to-peer networks are so distributed that it is difficult to know exactly who to go after for violation of copyright. A solution might be found in encryption technology and/or digital watermarks for digitalized intellectual property, but so far no compelling technology of this kind is available.

The impact of piracy goes beyond lost revenues and profits to music companies. Lower record sales also imply lower royalties for artists. This means that fewer artists will be able to make a living from music recording, which will lower the supply of music. In the end, consumers will see less choice than would otherwise have been the case.

5. **How did Fanning come up with the original idea for Napster? What does this tell you, if anything, about the birth of entrepreneurial organizations? Was Shawn Fanning an insightful business thinker or accidental entrepreneur?**

Fanning's idea for Napster came from an attempt to solve a problem his roommate was having—how to find decent quality MP3 recordings on the Internet. Of course, Fanning's roommate was not the only one experiencing this problem. Many other people were probably also experiencing it—and so there was unmet demand for the kind of central index that Fanning developed.

In taking this route toward the establishment of a business, Fanning was following the footsteps of many successful entrepreneurs. Solving problems by developing new technologies or products is a time-honored way of establishing a new company. For example, when women started to work in large numbers, this created a problem—who would look after pre-school children? The problem was solved when entrepreneurs started opening day care establishments for pre-school children.

Having said this, there is little doubt that Fanning was an accidental entrepreneur. He seemed to lack business savvy and indeed any real interest in business. His passion was to write the code that would solve his roommate's problem, and prove to skeptics that he could do it. He was driven by ego gratification, not a desire for profit. It was his uncle, John Fanning, who saw the commercial potential and established a business enterprise to try and exploit Shawn's idea.

6. **Why did peer-to-peer technology suddenly come to the fore in the late 1990s? What explains the extraordinary early growth of Napster?**

The fusion of a number of technologies, including the spread of high speed Internet connections on college campuses, MP3 technology, the advent of CD read write drives in personal computers, and technology for burning CDs, all paved the way for Napster.

Nevertheless, the growth of Napster was extraordinary and owns much to the ability of the Internet to accelerate the diffusion of new digital technologies, and to the compelling features of the technology and the service Fanning put together. Of note, Napster allowed customers to (a) pick and chose music, (b) to get immediate gratification by downloading and playing music, (c) to find music that they would not normally listen to (by browsing through the play lists of others), and (d) to get music for free. What a great value proposition—enhanced functionality for getting music at zero cost! No wonder the service grew rapidly.

Network effects also helped propel the rapid growth of Napster's service. Specifically, the more people who connected to the service and listed play lists, the greater the value of connecting to the service to access recordings, and the more people who signed on, which set up a positive feedback loop.

7. **In retrospect, what mistakes did Napster make? How might things have been done differently?**

Napster made a number of critical mistakes:

- First, the company hired a CEO with no management experience and no real music industry experience.

- Second, the company was started with no clear plan for making profits—no business model in mind.

- Third, the company took a confrontational approach to the established industry. In particular, the CEO was abrasive.

- Fourth, the company made no effort to deal with the piracy problem, which Napster clearly facilitated. They claimed that the piracy problem was the recording industry's problem, not theirs.

- The principle players deluded themselves into believing that because Internet technology was so revolutionary, it somehow stood above or apart from existing laws.

- There was a failure to foresee that its technology would hurt recording artists and lead to significant opposition from this source.

A different approach might have included the following elements:

- Hire a CEO with industry experience.

- Develop a business model early on.

- Adopt a conciliatory approach toward established industry players.

- Develop a plan for dealing with piracy. Hire good legal council from the start.

- Accentuate the positive aspects of the service—Napster could actually help record companies sell more by offering free samples.

- Sell off stock early on to record companies, or alternatively offer to sell the entire company.

It is not clear that Napster would have been able to survive even if it had done these things. From the start, the company was on a collision course with the music recording industry, precisely because it was trying to make money by starting a service that facilitated piracy, but it is at least possible that had things been done differently, Napster would have been able to strike a deal with music industry that would have enabled the company to avoid its subsequent problems.

8. **Do you think the business model proposed by Barry was potentially viable? What flaws can you see in it? How might it be improved?**

Barry proposed a subscription based business model. The established music companies have begun to experiment with such models, so the idea may have some value. Napster was to license the rights to distribute music recording from the music companies. Subscribers would pay a fee, and in return be allowed to download music. The exact fee, and the number of downloads permitted, was not ironed out. Revenues were to come from the subscriptions and from advertising revenues.

To align incentives, the recording companies would take a stake in Napster. The recording companies would also be given a share of Napster's revenues (although whether this was to be in addition to the licensing fee was never worked out).

Although potentially viable, there are several problems with this model. First, it might be difficult to get users to sign on for something they had been getting for free, particularly since free alternatives to Napster were beginning to spring up such as Gnutella. Second, why would the record labels want to contract with Napster when in theory they get into the electronic distribution business themselves? Third, Barry had no compelling plan for limiting piracy. Once a song had been downloaded from Napster, what was to stop it from being replicated across the Internet using peer-to-peer technology such as Gnutella?

Despite these problems, the business model could potentially have worked had it been developed and pushed sooner, and had Napster tried to cooperate with the music industry from the beginning. Unfortunately, by the time Barry came along much of the music industry perceived Napster as the enemy and cooperation was highly unlikely.

9. **What are the lessons that Napster holds for the established labels in the music recording businesses?**

The rapid growth of Napster and its imitators strongly suggests that the digital distribution of technology over the Internet delivers more value to consumers than traditional distribution systems. At the very least, digital distribution will be an important complement to existing physical distribution systems (indeed, it already is). Ultimately it may replace the established system, either in part or entirely. Somehow the established music companies need to harness the power of this disruptive technology, while limiting its adverse impacts.

The technology clearly presents established companies with some difficult problems. How are they going to manage channel conflict? How will they deal with the piracy issue? What will happen to industry revenues and artists royalties once consumers no longer have to download (and "pay") for filler tracks? What business model will work best with digital distribution? How should music distributed digitally be priced? Will a low price stimulate sales and limit piracy? These and other questions must be answered, for the technological genie is out of the bottle and no amount of lawsuits will put it back in.

POSTSCRIPT

Napster's file sharing service has been shut down since July 2001 and the company filed for bankruptcy protection in June 2002. Bertelsmann's most recent offer for Napster was for $9 million, but record companies and music publishers filed motions against the buyout, and a judge blocked the sale of Napster in early September 2002. In the absence of a buyer, Napster is likely to go ahead with the bankruptcy proceedings.

CASE 8

AtomFilms

SYNOPSIS OF THE CASE

The case documents the genesis and evolution of AtomFilms, which is a short-film distribution company. AtomFilms has grown from an idea to a company with a strong brand identity affiliated with short, independent filmmaking. The company has built a profitable offline business-to-business (B2B) film distribution business to license short films to a large number of companies. AtomFilms's public relations strategies have helped establish a reputation for its films resulting in increased submissions of short films and animations from amateur and professional filmmakers. AtomFilms also operates in the online business-to-consumer (B2C) segment with their consumer website aimed at generating public interest in short-form entertainment and creating a community of short-film makers. The website has been immensely popular generating a traffic of 15 million visitors and 1.8 million registered users who viewed 31 million films in 2000.

In order to finance and grow the company, in 2001, AtomFilms merged with Shockwave, an entertainment content company that also distributes a free media player.

The task facing Mika Salmi, the founder of AtomFilms, is to try and grow the market for short-form entertainment in the United States. Consolidating this fragmented niche market is likely to be a formidable challenge. Salmi has to make critical strategic decisions to ensure sustainable future growth for AtomFilms. First, Salmi needs to decide the appropriate allocation of precious internal resources of the company between the offline B2B business or the online B2C business. Second, he has to evaluate the potential problems associated with licensing AtomFilms content via wireless devices for the European market. Third, he had to evaluate whether distributing AtomFilms content using the emerging peer-to-peer technology presented a threat or an opportunity. In addition, Salmi has to choose an appropriate business model for AtomFilms that is sustainable in the long term.

TEACHING OBJECTIVES

This case illustrates the challenges of growing a start-up company in a niche market. The case pursues the following teaching objectives:

1. To understand the structure of the film distribution industry.

2. To demonstrate the challenges faced by a start-up company in generating demand in a poorly developed and fragmented niche market.

3. To critically evaluate the sustainability of different business models being considered.

STRATEGIC ISSUES AND DISCUSSION QUESTIONS

1. **What does the competitive structure of the established film distribution business in the United States look like? What are the implications of this structure for a company looking to get into the film distribution business? Why have these companies not actively pursued opportunities to distribute short films?**

    Six content distribution companies that collectively account for 80% of box office revenues dominate the film distribution business in the U.S. These companies provide most of the financing for studio films, and in addition, have in the last decade moved into the independent film businesses, setting up divisions to acquire and distribute full length independent films—that is, films not made specifically for, and financed by one of the established studios.

    Given the scale and scope of the established companies, and their relationships with existing players in the industry, it is unlikely that new entrants would be able to break into the industry unless they focus on a small out of the way market niche that has no appeal to the established companies. This is exactly what the short film business is. Given the scale of the industry (annual revenues in excess of $20 billion when film and DVD/tape sales are considered), there is almost no financial incentive for large companies to get involved in short-film distribution. There is simply nothing in it for them—this makes it attractive to startups like AtomFilms.

2.   **Why has "Digital Hollywood" been such a failure?**

Digital Hollywood is the name given to the online entertainment industry, and refers specifically to attempts by established movie companies to set up online ventures. Most of these are no longer functioning. They failed because they had no compelling value proposition to offer consumers, and no business model that would enable them to make money out of their offerings.

As Salmi notes in the case, the problem was that many companies were simply taking existing entertainment offerings and shoehorning them into the category of Internet entertainment without understanding what that meant, and the constraints of Internet.

These constraints of the Internet that prevented Digital Hollywood from becoming a success are twofold; a lack of bandwidth, which seriously limits the ability of people to watch filmed entertainment online, and the short attention span of people browsing the Internet. The bandwidth problem will probably ultimately be solved, but it is going to take a while. Currently only 10% of US households have access to high bandwidth connections (DSL or cable modems) and the rollout is slower than most people hoped.

As for the short attention span of people online, it is unclear how this will be solved. People view computers and TVs differently. The computer is placed in the home office, the TV in the living room. The PC is for interactive work or play (e.g. video games), but not for passive viewing. This is both a deep cultural reality, and an ergonomic fact of home office and living room design (home offices are not designed for passive viewing). Given this, it is questionable as to whether people will ever watch clips of more than a few minutes on their PC?

3.   **What is the market opportunity that Mika Salmi is going after with AtomFilms?**

The market for short films in the United States is very poorly developed. Although many short films are made every year by directors hoping to showcase their talent, very few achieve any commercial success, in part because the opportunities for showing short films are very limited, and in part because there is limited demand for the films from viewers. Of course, there is something of a chicken and egg situation here—having not had much exposure to the short film format, the American viewers are not acculturated into this mode of entertainment. Cinemas in the United States do not typically show shorts before a feature film, and there are no TV channels devoted to the short format.

The situation is less dire in Europe, where Salmi is originally from. There short films are still shown in movie theaters prior to full-length features, more short films are shown on TV, and there are even TV channels, such as M6 in France, which specialize in showing films in the short format.

Because the U.S. market is poorly developed, the distribution system for the short feature is also poorly developed. It appears to be something of a fragmented cottage industry with several hundred very small companies trying to distribute shorts.

Against this background, Salmi's goal is to try and create a market for short films in the United States. Although the short-film market is a niche, it is a niche that is being ignored by established companies. AtomFilms could potentially do quite well by becoming the player in the niche and consolidating the market.

4.   **What must Atom do to build a company?**

Salmi's goal is to try and create a market for short films in the United States. To do this, AtomFilms has to do three things:

- Acquire compelling content—AtomFilms can establish a reputation among independent filmmakers as a premier distributor of shorts. If Atom can do this, this will give Atom the right of first refusal on short features. Independent filmmakers will come to Atom first. In fact, Atom already seems to have moved someway down this road both by establishing a highly visible presence at film festivals, and by developing some distribution deals that have established credibility for the company.

- Develop distribution channels for that content—AtomFilms seems to be doing this. One strategy it might try is to go into partnership with established movie distributors. If it can persuade established companies that short films have compelling entertainment value—and if screenings before audiences confirm this—Atom can bundle its content with feature length movies and DVD's, and/or videos that are rented or sold. AtomFilms can also enter into partnerships with airlines, cinemas and cable TV stations in order to promote and distribute short films. Apart from these business-to-business distribution channels, AtomFilms can also concentrate on business to consumer channels and make short films available on video-on-demand over digital cable TV, as well as on the Internet (to be accessed currently by PCs, but also potentially by mobile digital devices like PDAs and smart phones).

- Foster demand for short films among film viewers—Cinema format in the U.S. is not attuned to short-film format and there is no consumer demand for short films in the U.S. They have been used primarily to showcase talent. Changing consumer expectations and tastes may prove to be the hardest goal to achieve. Salmi can try to win over an audience for shorts by screenings in one or more of the above distribution channels.

These goals are not unrelated. If AtomFilms can develop distribution channels and successfully market some short films, it may start to build an appreciation for the format among film watchers, and in turn, such success will enable the company to attract more content at favorable rates.

5. **Where is the greatest long-term growth potential for AtomFilms—in the B2B market place (off line distribution) or in B2C (online distribution)?**

B2B (offline distribution) seems to be the primary channel through which AtomFilms can hope to generate stable revenues in the long term. While the potential size of the B2B market is expected to be relatively small, it may increase as demand for shorts is established in the U.S.

The purpose of B2B (online distribution) appears to be to showcase films and establish an identity, which helps to attract compelling content, which in turn can be licensed to other businesses. B2C's contribution seems limited to serving as an advertising and marketing tool even though the B2C website generates significant traffic.

6. **Does the growth of peer-to-peer computing represent an opportunity or threat for AtomFilms?**

Peer-to-peer (P2P) technology is a disruptive technology that allows computers to share digital music or video files. Flycode, a P2P company, has offered to license AtomFilms' content in exchange for space on its website. In the short term this presents an opportunity for AtomFilms by providing a channel for distribution of short films. However, the experience of the music industry with Napster's online peer-to-peer music sharing service illustrates the problems that peer-to-peer technology may present for AtomFilms—there would be no way for the company to prevent the illegal copying of content. Flycode's goal is to use new encryption technologies and/or digital watermarks for digitalized intellectual property, but so far, no compelling technology of this kind is available. AtomFilms might instead consider using the Flycode service purely as a promotional tool in order to generate awareness about short films.

In the long run, the growth of peer-to-peer computing is more likely to represent a threat rather than an opportunity for AtomFilms, since it is not clear how AtomFilms can benefit by encouraging players like Flycode. Once Flycode becomes a well-known company, and if it is able to resolve the security issues of P2P technology, there is no reason for artists to continue to license their shorts to AtomFilms—they can go directly to Flycode and cut AtomFilms out of the picture.

7. **Which of the three business models suggested at the end of the case do you think AtomFilms should pursue?**

The three models that Mika Salmi has to choose from are:

- The current business model of the company, which includes offline distribution as well as online distribution. The offline distribution business acquires content from artists and generates revenue through advertising, sponsorship and syndication of content to companies. The B2C side of the business is a website that shows AtomFilms' shorts.

- A subscription/pay per view fee for its website.

- Leverage relationship with filmmakers, talent agencies and movie studios for offline entertainment. The idea is to help them find talent and get revenue in the process.

The above business models are not mutually exclusive. Offline and online distribution are complementary and Mika Salmi should supplement the current business model of the company by charging a fee for content on its website and by offering the talent search service to its existing offline consumers. Chances of success of the subscription model for AtomFilms' website are very slim because consumers do not like to pay for content on the Internet. The offline business shows more promise for the future.

Ultimately, success of AtomFilms depends on whether Mika Salmi is able to interest the general public in shorts and stimulate a demand for short films in the United States.

CASE 9

Zoots – The Cleaner Cleaner

SYNOPSIS OF THE CASE

Krasnow was an HBS graduate, and one of the founding management team at Staples, where he became Executive Vice President. He was at Staples for 10 very successful years before he began to think about starting his own venture.

The new venture, a dry cleaning business, was intended to leverage his skill base and experience in retail. Krasnow did extensive research on the dry cleaning industry, talking to both suppliers of the service as well as to customers in order to build a database of usage, product mix, cleaning requirements of different demographics, operational details and competition. Since the dry cleaning industry is a low capital, low skill business, it was extremely fragmented with very few large operators. Krasnow wanted to make convenience and reliability the hallmarks of his new venture. Using his research as a basis, Krasnow began to put his plans into action by raising capital primarily from family and friends. He hired consultants to develop a brand that would convey the value proposition of his venture to the customer through the name of the stores, the store design and marketing campaigns. He modeled the distribution and operational aspects of his venture based on the Hub and Spoke model for efficiency, and differentiated his offerings from the competition by providing extended store hours, drive-through, drop-off and pick-up facilities, a 24-hour pick-up service, and web-based order tracking.

The first Zoots dry cleaning store was tested in affluent Boston suburbs in order to fine-tune the operating model. Krasnow's team was able to solve the initial quality and efficiency related problems, but only at a single store level. As soon as multiple stores were opened, the spike in volume exacerbated all the problems demonstrating the complexity of running a large-scale dry cleaning business and how different this service intensive industry was from running a retail operation. In two years, Krasnow had opened 3 stores in Boston that were performing well and the management and investors felt that Zoots needed to grow into as many geographical markets as possible to gain first mover advantage. The challenge before Krasnow was to manage the fast pace of growth as well as try to iron out the operational wrinkles in the dry-cleaning venture.

TEACHING OBJECTIVES

The teaching objectives of this case are:

1. Understand the dynamics involved in starting a new venture.

2. Illustrate the issues involved in managing a new company with respect to operational effectiveness.

3. Demonstrate the process involved in development of an entirely new business model and brand identity.

4. Understand the pitfalls involved in trying to transfer skills gained from one sector to a related one without making an attempt to learn about the operational aspects of the new business.

STRATEGIC ISSUES AND DISCUSSION QUESTIONS

1. **How would you characterize the economic structure of the dry cleaning industry? Do you think the average player in this industry earns anything other than "normal" economic profits?**

    The fragmented nature of the dry cleaning industry was evident from the large number of small players (45,000 stores in the United States) where 50 of the largest operators had no more than 5% share of the market and 97% of all operators had fewer than five stores. The industry was further characterized by a commodity type product, low skill and capital requirements (commodity type inputs), easy availability of pricing information, and low barriers to entry and exit. All of these suggest that dry cleaning has a structure that approximates toward perfect competition.

This implies that the opportunities for earning profits in excess of the cost of capital is very difficult. It is very unlikely that the average player makes more than "normal profits" i.e. profits that are just enough to cover costs plus pay a salary to the entrepreneur that reflects his or her opportunity cost.

The inability for the average player to earn more than "normal profits" also implies that the entrepreneur has to somehow alter one or more of the basic parameters of the industry. This can be done by adding value to the product (differentiation), create barriers to entry, or find a unique source of lower cost inputs.

2.   Why is the dry cleaning industry fragmented?

Dry Cleaning is a fragmented business because of the absence of any obvious economies of scale. Due to the local nature of demand, each store has to compete locally with other dry cleaning establishments within a 3-minute radius. Thus, a store that was part of a larger dry cleaning chain and close to its central cleaning plant had no advantage vis-à-vis a mom-and-pop operation in its local market. This also makes it difficult to build a brand in each of the distinctive local markets.

3.   What is the most important asset of a dry cleaning store? What drives sales?

The following assets of a store drive sales in the dry cleaning business: location, location and location. Having a retail store that is in a convenient and accessible location is critically important.

4.   Describe and evaluate the business model for Zoots. How does Zoots intend to earn a rate of return that exceeds its cost of capital? What are the strengths of this business model? What are the weaknesses and flaws in the model?

Goal and Unique Value Proposition

Krasnow's goal was to build a nationwide dry cleaning store that focused on customer experience. The unique value proposition that the new venture intended offering was to "get the customer's cleaning done right, reliably and conveniently." Krasnow believed that an emphasis on convenience, uncompromising quality, drop off and pickup anytime of day or night, and fixing errors for free would deliver unique value to the customers. The idea was to increase volume, and presumably, revenues, thereby covering fixed costs and generating higher store sales per square foot than competing dry cleaners.

Operational Aspects – Strengths and Weaknesses

Krasnow wanted to structure the operations of the dry cleaning business around the Hub & Spoke system i.e. have 7-10 retail stores served from a single central dry cleaning facility. He was applying the same distribution system that he knew so well from his experience in retailing to minimize inventory costs. The rationale behind using the Hub and Spoke system was to get economies of scale by using a centralized cleaning facility instead of dry cleaning in each retail store. Another advantage of the system is smaller retail stores that potentially translate into lower retail costs.

The Hub and Spoke idea that works so well in retailing presents a few problems when applied to the dry cleaning business. Specifically:

- There are cost disadvantages of transporting dry cleaning to and from the cleaning hubs.

- Communications between store and hub creates possibility of errors. The need for inspectors at the hubs raises costs.

- Since the store manager is not the person who does the cleaning, extra steps are needed to communicate needs to cleaners at hub. This additional communications complexity creates opportunities for errors.

- The tags that were used to solve the communications problems between stores and hub would fall off and this increased the error rate.

- New problems, such as identification of the store that an article belonged to, cropped up. This problem of orphaned garments would not occur in a mom and pop dry cleaning establishments.

- The Information Systems did not match the needs of the business. Store based information system did not allow for splitting orders.

- Lack of experienced personnel in the central cleaning facility initially led to a lack of productivity. This lack of tacit knowledge (experience) resulted in high costs.

- Operations at a service intensive business are different from operations in a self-service setting. All of the above problems were magnified when Zoots started to open additional stores.

Site Concept and Customer Service

In order to fulfill his promise of convenience to the customer, Krasnow offered a self- service drive-through facility where the lobby area was stocked with clothes lockers that customers could access 24 hours a day. This implies a changeover from the service concept to the self-service concept.

The *advantages* of the self-service drive-through were:

- Convenience for the customer.

- Possibly, lower costs because the retail store would not need many employees.

The idea can have *drawbacks* in the context of dry-cleaning because:

- People do not value a drive-through very highly. Instead, they prefer to talk to store owner to point out spots on clothes.

- The drive-through requirement limits location and points to larger footprint, which raises costs. Moreover, the move away from strip mall locations may be an inconvenience.

Customer set and location

The targeted customers belonged to densely populated affluent areas that place a high value on convenience and quality.

5. **How might the hub and spoke system employed by Zoots lead to cost savings? Under what circumstances might it lead to cost increases?**

    To answer this question, please refer to the discussion on the operational aspects in the previous question.

6. **How would you characterize Krasnow's approach to identifying a business opportunity? Can you see a drawback with this approach?**

    Krasnow's skill set, based on his experience in the office supplies retail business, was in high volume, large footprint, low cost retailing. Hence his basic approach was to leverage his existing skills in supermarket retailing to dry cleaning, a new market context within retailing.

    He chose dry cleaning because obvious opportunities for large footprint stores were already occupied and he decided to focus on smaller units.

    Krasnow's analysis of the opportunity was data driven. He asked family and friends about their experiences with dry cleaning, but seemed to rely primarily upon demographic data about market and sales cycles.

    Some drawbacks of the approach were:

    - The opportunity set was now constrained because the obvious opportunities for large footprint stores had already been exploited.

    - Krasnow decided to focus on smaller operating units (i.e. no obvious scale economies at the store level) that performed a service rather than sold a product. The assumption that his skill set gained from Staples and Jewels may be transferable may be false.

    - He made the choice of business first – dry cleaning – and then did an analysis to justify the choice.

    - His reliance on demographic data raises questions as to whether he and his team understood the operational aspects of dry cleaning. Staples applied supermarket concepts to office supplies, but dry cleaning – a service business – is different from office supplies and supermarkets.

- Although customers were unsatisfied with the dry cleaning services offered but they still accepted the status quo. This was perhaps not as compelling an opportunity as the one presented to them in the office retailing business.

- Krasnow and his team made an implicit assumption that there were significant scale economies to be captured, but the dry cleaning industry shows no evidence of this.

7. **Krasnow, Stemberg and company did not have to raise venture capital to fund the venture. Was it an advantage or a disadvantage?**

Not having to raise venture capital was an advantage in that there would be no dilution of equity. It was a disadvantage in that Zoots missed an opportunity to be reviewed critically by outsiders. A venture capital firm investing in Zoots may have forced them to question some of their assumptions. The Zoots management belonged to an in-group with the same corporate background who first decided to enter dry cleaning, and then used data to backup their prior hypothesis. This tendency may have been reinforced by groupthink. They did not have a devil's advocate to test the robustness of their business plan.

8. **What do the problems Zoots was having expanding in Portsmouth tell you?**

The first problem that Zoots was facing in Portsmouth was finding enough locations since all the drive-through and good retail locations were already taken. The other problem was that Zoots was getting only two-thirds of the volume from Zoots' original stores. The volume projections for these original stores had been made based on data driven analysis of 13 dry cleaners and the same projections were used to calculate an estimated volume for the Portsmouth market. Since actual volumes from the original stores fell short of the projections then that meant that Zoots was not likely to get enough volume in the Portsmouth market either. The Zoots concept did not seem to be working well in Portsmouth.

9. **Rethink the strategy pursued by Zoots. Might the company have done things differently?**

In retrospect, the Hub and Spoke system created more problems than it solved. Instead of simply transferring their knowledge about the office supplies business over to the dry cleaning industry, the management of Zoots could have learnt the business by buying out existing businesses or chains. This would have given Zoots an opportunity to learn first hand about the unique skills and capabilities involved. The fragmented dry market could have been consolidated through acquisitions. Giving franchises to small stores was another option that could have been developed.

Zoots offered a number of novel services, but they could have gone a step further and delivered a way to offer home delivery, a more compelling value proposition. However, the question here is whether the customers are willing to pay for the extra cost incurred in hiring trucks and drivers.

10. **Can you see any flaws in the way Krasnow and his associates developed the Zoots concept?**

As noted in the earlier questions, there were many decision-making biases that led to a faulty development of the Zoots concept by the management. To recapitulate:

- Reasoning by analogy – the management assumed that the dry cleaning business was similar to the office supplies business that they were so familiar with.

- Prior hypothesis bias – Krasnow was guilty of mining the data collected from other dry cleaners to validate his choice of entering the business.

- Hubris – Success with Staples may have made the management team overconfident – they did not stop to consider how different and more complex the dry cleaning business could be.

- Groupthink – The main investors in the company were all from the same background and the absence of outsiders early on in the venture did not allow for a critical questioning of the choices made. A timely recognition of the flawed assumptions on which Zoots' strategies were based could have led to deployment of alternate measures.

CASE 10

Nike: Sweatshops and Business Ethics

SYNOPSIS OF THE CASE

Nike is a worldwide global corporation that has its shoes manufactured on a contract basis in places like Asia, China, and Vietnam. Although it does not actually own any of the manufacturing locations, it has long been accused of having its products manufactured in facilities that exploit workers. Although Nike admits some wrongdoing in the manufacturing facilities of its contractors, it claims to have started a commitment to improve working conditions in those facilities.

Nike has suffered attacks from a number of agencies and organizations throughout the world that claim that the workers who manufacture Nike shoes are denied the basic essentials of living—a fair wage and decent benefits. All that occurs while several sports managers are reaping in multimillion dollar contracts to promote Nike shoes. Over the years, Nike formulated tactics to deal with the problems of working conditions and compensation in subcontractors it hired. A strong consultant (Andrew Young), commissioned an independent audit of its subcontractors, and spelled out initiatives to improve those working conditions. Still, Nike's critics were not satisfied. They protested on university campuses and accused Nike of continuing to hide the conditions of the workers.

TEACHING OBJECTIVES

The main teaching objectives of this case are:

1. Provide an understanding of pressures that can affect an international company accused of worker exploitation.

2. Indicate how a firm must be responsible for its subcontractors, even though they appear to be acting lawfully in a foreign country.

3. Show that aggressive public relations campaigns may still be ineffective when the actions of contractors receive widespread attention and intensive media coverage.

STRATEGIC ISSUES AND DISCUSSION QUESTIONS

1. **Should Nike be held responsible for working conditions in foreign factories that it does not own, but where sub-contractors make products for Nike?**

    Although Nike may be technically removed from responsibility in some areas, it clearly has the obligation to be certain that exploitation by subcontractors do not occur. Certainly the pay and working conditions that the workers of subcontractors receive is due in large part to the contract that has been negotiated by Nike. If Nike had chosen to make improved working conditions a part of the arrangement, then those benefits may have been passed on to the workers. Still, Nike is a publicly owned firm whose goal is to improve the wealth of its shareholders. The workers in these Asian countries were happy, even eager, to accept the conditions that were provided as a manufacturer of Nike. If Nike were to leave the country because of the pressures placed upon it, the workers would undoubtedly suffer greatly.

2. **What labor standards regarding safety, working conditions, overtime and the like should Nike hold foreign factories to: those prevailing in that country, or those prevailing in the United States?**

    Clearly, Nike has the responsibility to hold suppliers to those conditions that prevail only in the supplying country. If it insisted on prevailing conditions in the United States, there would be little reason for Nike to seek contractors from outside countries. However, through pressure or contractual concessions, it is possible for Nike to seek ways to improve the condition of workers in supplying countries. In doing so, Nike may find that it receives some public relations benefit rather than undergoing the effort and cost of developing defensive public relation strategies.

3. **An income of $2.28 a day, the base pay of Nike factory workers in Indonesia, is double the daily income of about half the working population. Half of all adults in Indonesia are farmers, who receive less than $1 a day. Given this, is it correct to criticize Nike for low pay rates for subcontractors in Indonesia?**

   Although student answers will vary according to their sensitivity on this issue, Nike probably should not be held responsible for the pay rates of Indonesian subcontractors. The worker pay and the resulting low cost of goods is a major reason why Nike has contracted with these subcontractors. The result has been to give jobs to Indonesians who might not otherwise have them. It is also not clear to what degree Nike can influence the pay that subcontractors pay to workers. Therefore, it is not fair to be continually critical of Nike in that regard.

4. **Could Nike have handled the negative publicity over sweatshops better? What might have been done differently? Not just from the public relations perspective, but also from a policy perspective?**

   There is certainly a lot of room for Nike to improve its handling of the negative publicity. A defensive policy of denial is always more poorly received than an open admission of fault with constructive strategies for improvement. Part of Nike's problem was that it did not address the total criticisms, and chose to answer the age issue rather than the issue of total inferior working conditions. Its strategy to announce policy change at large public relations functions appeared insensitive, than addressing the criticism directly, on the spot, and with corrective action strategy in hand. From a policy perspective, it would be better to suggest programs for training of workers, changes in suppliers and a general improvement of the plight of the worker. The development of advisory boards and the involvement of interested agencies and outside organizations to achieve a consensus for the improvement of working conditions might be more effective, both from a public relations as well as a policy perspective than to continue with its own inward looking policies.

5. **Do you think Nike needs to make any changes to its current policy? If so, what? Should Nike make changes even if they hinder the ability of the company to compete in the marketplace?**

   Nike does need to make a change in its policy, if only because its current policy has served it so poorly. One strategy would be to involve international agencies to assist with policy adjustments that will help to correct the problem. Another change might be abandoning a defensive, "it's not too broke" strategy and admitting the problem, while outlining strategies for improvement. But Nike's major obligation is to its shareholders and to continuing to operate in an increasingly competitive marketplace. It does not do the plight of the worker any good to have Nike adopt policies that eventually cause its business to go under. The question of changes that make the company uncompetitive is a real one—one that is addressed by international business managers all the time. Clearly, Nike has the formidable challenge of remaining competitive while improving working conditions for its workers.

6. **Is the WRC right to argue that the FLA is a tool of industry?**

   Perhaps no more than to argue that the WRC is a tool of organized labor. If the FLA is incapable of conducting independent units of international workshops, then the charge may be partially true. But the WRC funded and backed by labor unions, refuses to meet with companies because it would "jeopardize its independence." With that kind of posturing and intransigence, both sides appear to be as culpable with a highly emotional issue.

7. **If sweatshops are a global problem, what might be a global solution to this problem?**

   Sweatshops are a global problem in that companies the world over can seek low cost manufacture in every corner of the globe. When these low costs are a result of inferior, and even illegal working conditions, then sweatshops are a major global problem. A possible solution would be to change, or at least modify, the conditions under which sweatshops continue to function. Universal worker's rights with minimum wage and minimum age could be a solution. Still, some countries will always have the advantage of low cost labor and will exploit that advantage in the international marketplace. However, the disparity between the great differences in labor cost can be lessened, but it can best be done by continuing to promote free world trade and continuing to improve the quality of life in developing nations, where low cost labor is most abundant.

CASE 11

WestJet Looks East

SYNOPSIS OF THE CASE

This case reviews Canada's domestic airline industry and the competitive response of West Jet airlines to developments in the industry. After a fierce takeover battle, Air Canada and Canadian Airlines are expected to announce a merger that would create a near monopoly with 80% share of the domestic market.

WestJet is a Calgary based, low-cost, discount airline, which has built a successful business serving cities in Western Canada. It has been profitable since it started operations in 1996 and has recently completed a $25 million IPO. Its business model is based on the low fare, low cost business model pioneered by Southwest Airlines, the most successful airline in the United States. The airline has been focusing on building a presence in Western Canada and is now looking at further expansion.

This case illustrates the challenges facing WestJet as it considers its future strategy. The issues that the WestJet management is grappling with relate to the speed and extent of expansion, whether it should expand into Eastern Canada, and how it should connect its Eastern and Western operations.

TEACHING OBJECTIVES

The main teaching objectives of the case are:

1. To understand how a company can develop a successful strategy in an industry mired by overcapacity and price pressures.

2. To illustrate how companies in the same industry can adopt more than one strategy.

3. To understand the basis of competition in the airline industry to develop a future strategy for WestJet.

STRATEGIC ISSUES AND DISCUSSION QUESTIONS

1. **Describe the trends in the Canadian airline industry in the 1990s and how they affected the competitive situation in 1999?**

    The main elements characterizing the Canadian airline industry in the 1990's are:

    *   The number of passengers traveling by domestic airlines in Canada stood peaked in 1990 to reach 36.8 million. In the period between 1990-1995, this figure decreased by 15%, but strong growth in the next three years has increased passenger count to 45.4 million. Around 70% of the demand for air travel was satisfied by the two largest Canadian carriers, Air Canada and Canadian Airlines.

    *   International and Transborder travel (United States) has grown much more than domestic air travel in Canada. Over the 8-year period, international, transborder and domestic travel grew by 53%, 39% and 14% respectively.

    *   Air travel in Canada is concentrated to a few airports—primarily on the East and West Coasts with fewer airports elsewhere. The 7 largest airports in Canada account for most of the air travel.

    *   The industry environment was characterized by intense competition fueled by overcapacity and heavy price-cutting among the two largest carriers, Air Canada and Canadian airlines. Both the airlines sustained heavy losses in this period although Air Canada was financially more stable than Canadian Airlines.

    *   Government policy has played an important role in the airline industry in Canada. Although the industry was deregulated and Canadian airlines was privatized in 1980s, the Canadian government

intervened by allowing Air Canada to enter into merger negotiations with Canadian Airlines when the latter was threatened by a takeover by Onyx. The government is also likely to impose conditions on the merged company in order to sustain competition in the industry.

- Several smaller airlines also compete in the industry. These niche players have managed to sustain growth in the highly competitive market.

1999 was a year of significant change and restructuring in the Canadian airline industry. In 1999, Canadian airline and Air Canada faced a hostile takeover from Onyx Corporation. Air Canada made a counter offer for Canadian airlines and after a long takeover battle, Air Canada and Canadian Airline got approval to merge into Canada's largest domestic carrier. On one hand, the presence of a dominant carrier accounting for about 80% market share is likely to make it very hard for other companies to compete, but on the other hand, the government's stand on competition in the industry might create opportunities for players other than Air Canada.

2.   **Describe the competitive environment for WestJet.**

The main competitors for WestJet are the newly merged company, Air Canada, and a number of smaller niche players.

- Air Canada is the largest company by far in the industry with about 80% market share. Although Air Canada will have its hands full with the post merger restructuring and rationalization of capacity, it is likely to pose a threat to WestJet if it follows through on its announcement to start a low fare airline.

- The charter carriers like SkyService, Royal Airlines, Canada 3000 and AirTransAt do not compete in the same segment as WestJet does. They are niche players in the long-haul segments and are not likely to compete in the short-haul point-to-point space. However, if WestJet ever enters the long-haul market, it is likely to face stiff price-based competition from these players.

- CanJet's plans for a low-fare discount airline may be a more central concern for WestJet. Although, by 1999, the venture existed only on paper, once it does become a reality, it will cut into WestJet's share. (Note: In fact CanJet did begin serving the Canadian East Coast in Fall 2000 and is now a competitor to WestJet. Source: www.canjet.com).

3.   **Outline the main features of Southwest Airlines' business model that WestJet is trying to emulate. What are the benefits and drawbacks of the model? Why has Southwest Airlines been so successful?**

WestJet is trying to imitate the business model pioneered by Southwest Airlines. Southwest promotes its business model as a complement to the hub and spoke system followed by the traditional airlines. The low-fare discount business model has the following elements:

- Focus on price sensitive passengers
- Fly on short-haul point-to-point routes
- Run a low-cost no-frills operation

More specifically, the customer profile for Southwest is expected to be the budget conscious traveler (as opposed to the business traveler), who travels for personal reasons and might use alternate modes of travel like train, bus or car.

The value proposition of the business model is the low fares offered with few restrictions for travel between secondary airports instead of the metropolitan hubs.

The costs are trimmed by offering fewer services than the traditional airlines. The focus is on only 1 aircraft type, passengers are responsible for checking-in and picking up their baggage, no seat assignments are made, a single class of service is offered, and there are no in-flight meals.

The advantage of this model is that it allows the carrier to operate on a much lower cost structure so that they can compete with the traditional airlines based on price and still make a profit. The system is relatively simpler to set up than the Hub and Spoke model and since there is no transfer of baggage involved and very few interconnecting passengers, the delay for planes is minimized.

The primary disadvantage is that the customers, who pay less for their ticket, but have to contend with frequent stops, and fewer services.

The main reason why Southwest has been so successful over time is that they have maintained a disciplined approach to running their business by carefully segmenting the market to zero-in on a customer segment that works for their model, and by consistently and correctly applying their business model without any deviations.

4.　**What are the external opportunities and threats facing WestJet in expanding to Eastern Canada?**

Opportunities

- Eastern Canada does not have a low-fare discount airline. WestJet can gain significant first mover advantage by offering a low-fare service in Eastern Canada. This allows WestJet to build a reputation in Eastern Canada and gain market share before CanJet and Air Canada follow suit.

- Within the airline industry, the traditional air carriers like Air Canada, have high cost structures that make it hard for them to successfully operate subsidiaries offering discounted fares. In the past, other traditional carriers such as Continental Airlines, United Airlines and Delta Airlines, who have tried to imitate the Southwest Airlines' model, have not been able to operate these subsidiaries profitably. Such barriers to mobility may protect WestJet from being priced out of the market by stronger, larger rivals.

- The Canadian government has made it clear that it will monitor the airlines industry to prevent any abuse of monopoly power by Air Canada. This position of the government is likely to help WestJet and other small carriers from Air Canada's domination tactics.

- If WestJet is able to expand successfully into Eastern Canada, there may be a potential for further growth through expansion into central Canada on a small scale as a low cost point-to-point operator.

Threats

- Air Canada has announced that it will operate a low-fare subsidiary out of Hamilton in Eastern Canada. This presents a competitive threat that is likely to impact WestJet's expansion plans. Air Canada may eventually exit the low-fare space because of its high cost structure, but in the short term it has the potential to make a dent in WestJet's profits.

- Air Canada is also in a position to counter WestJet's expansion by cutting prices on the routes that are serviced by WestJet in order to drive it out of the market. This strategy of predatory pricing cannot be sustained over a long term but it has the potential to weaken WestJet's margins in the short term.

- Start-ups like CanJet, who are planning to enter the airlines industry as a low-fare airline, can also limit the gains that WestJet can expect from expansion into Eastern Canada.

- The domestic market is the slowest growing segment in the airline industry and focusing on the domestic point-to-point short-haul service is not a viable long-term growth strategy.

- Canada's geography presents a barrier to growth of the point-to-point routes beyond a certain point. If WestJet deviates from this model to operate as a hub-and-spoke carrier, it is not clear if it will continue to be as competitive and profitable.

5.　**In light of the threats and opportunities facing WestJet in 1999, what would you recommend to WestJet regarding expansion plans in eastern Canada?**

WestJet has so far adopted a conservative growth policy. It has resisted stretching itself out too thin and is financially very stable with low debt. It has reliably followed the low-fare/low-cost model so far and has opened a new demand segment for the airline industry.

There exists a clear market opportunity in Eastern Canada for a low-fare discount airline. WestJet should take advantage of this opportunity as soon as possible and gain first mover advantages before other players such as Air Canada and CanJet or other start-up companies move into this niche. However, the pace of expansion in Eastern Canada should be consistent with the model it has adopted. It should start small and build operations after testing the waters in the new market.

The experience of Southwest Airline has shown that it is very important that the purity of the model is not compromised and that WestJet does not try to leverage its success in the low-fare discount market to compete directly against Air Canada.

POSTSCRIPT

WestJet started operating in Eastern Canada in January 2001 with Hamilton as its base. In the last two years it has increased the number of flights operating in eastern Canada as well as those connecting the east with its operations in the west. In the year 2002, it has increased profits, lowered costs and increased its capacity significantly (Source: WestJet press releases). Air Canada started a low-fare service called Tango in December 2001. CanJet also entered eastern Canada but was not able to withstand competition from Air Canada and in March 2001, it was acquired by Canada 3000.

CASE 12

Avon Products, Inc.: The Personal-Care Industry[1]

SYNOPSIS OF THE CASE

This case reviews the personal-care industry. In 1999, the global market for personal-care products was valued at $171.39 billion and was expected to increase steadily in the future.

Avon Products, Inc., is the world's leading direct seller of beauty and related personal-care products to women. Avon operates in 137 countries via three million independent sales representatives who generate approximately $5.1 billion in annual revenues. The company's earnings have risen in the low-single digits in the past few years, but more disturbingly, the growth rate has shrunk each year.

Management at Avon needs to make significant strategic decisions in growing the company in lieu of its stagnant sales, limited distribution capabilities, and shifts in personal-care preferences and spending habits in the rapidly changing industry. There is considerable debate within the company regarding Avon's future target markets and product mix. The CEO, Andrea Jung, is looking at alternatives strategic plans and needs to decide which one is the most appropriate one for the company.

TEACHING OBJECTIVES

The main teaching objectives of the case are:

1. To understand the structure of the personal-care industry and the key factors affecting success in the industry.

2. To identify the opportunities and threats facing companies in the industry.

3. To evaluate the different approaches an established and well-known company may utilize in increasing growth and promoting a fresh image to the public.

4. To illustrate how a company can develop alternative strategies to react to changing market conditions such as a shift in consumer groups and preferences.

5. Specifically, the case study demands decisions regarding sales and distribution outlets, Internet development, product line extension or divestiture, and market opportunities in regards to emerging consumer groups.

STRATEGIC ISSUES AND DISCUSSION QUESTIONS

1. **Describe the structure of the personal-care industry.**

    In 1999, the global market for personal-care products was valued at $171.39 billion and is expected to increase steadily in the future. Personal-care products are defined as articles intended to be applied to the human body for cleansing, beautifying, promoting attractiveness, or altering the appearance without affecting the body's structure or functions. The products in the personal-care industry are divided into skin care, makeup/color cosmetics, hair care, personal hygiene products, perfumes/fragrances, spa services, and other related items. The customers in the industry are segmented according to their age (senior citizens, baby boomers, Generation X, Generation Y), by sex (male, female) and by ethnic origin (AfricanAmerican, Asian American, Latin American). Direct selling, retail selling, and online selling are the primary means of

---

[1] This teaching note is based on a teaching note by Robert J. Mockler.

distribution and sales and competition stems mainly from direct sellers of personal-care products and retailers offering either mass merchandise brand products or prestige brand products.

2.   What are the major industry trends, including opportunities and threats?

Overall, the market for personal-care products is expected to increase steadily in the future reaching $197.97 in 2003. Segments such as baby sun care, hair colorants, lip products, self-tanning products, cream deodorants, and facial moisturizers are considered exceptionally high growth areas, while women's fragrances, hand care, baby hair care, face masks, bath additives, styling agents, home perms, and conditioners are expected to see low growth rates.

Products and Services

- Skin care – Approximately 39% of households purchased facial cleansers and lotions at least once a year in 1999. Customers are sensitive to perceived price savings and deals and product claims of "anti-aging, wrinkle reduction, and improves fine lines" dominate this segment.

- Makeup/Color Cosmetics – Growth in the overall color cosmetic/makeup segment, which is heavily influenced by prevalent fashion trends, is expected to remain strong in the future, especially as new products hit the market. Consumers consider cosmetics to be basic necessities and are likely to purchase these regardless of the health of the economy.

- Hair Care – The hair color category had grown 12% over 1998 but is getting saturated due to a proliferation of brands.

- Personal Hygiene – In 1999, the total global market value of personal hygiene was $22.4 billion. Personal-hygiene products do not always follow the same trends as other personal-care markets, since many personal hygiene products are considered staples, as opposed to luxuries. Due to increased competition and number of products offered, consumers now look for value-added products.

- Perfumes/Fragrances – Sales of men's prestige fragrances rose by 6% in 1999, while those of women's fragrances decreased by 1%. Unisex fragrances are likely to drive the market globally. The fragrance market is highly sensitive to the marketing strategies of major fragrance houses and the association with clothing and sports drives the market. Future trends include invisible scents (those that only reach the brain), microencapsulation (these allow scents to remain on the skin for days), and natural "aromatherapeutic" scents (these are mood stimulators that reduce stress). Overall, companies participating in the fragrance industry are subjected to rising price competition, price transparency, with limited future growth prospects.

- Spa Services – Many spas sell a variety of prestigious premium priced personal-care products, and are becoming more commonplace for both men and women.

Customers

- Senior Citizens – This segment, comprising of individuals aged 54 and over, tend to reduce their purchases of personal-care products. The preferred channels of distribution are drugstores, mass merchandisers, and most importantly, direct selling.

- Baby Boomers – The baby boomer segment is comprised of individuals aged 35-53 years old and is the largest demographic segment (30% of the population). This segment tends to have the highest net worth and median income as compared to other segments, and their spending power is expected to grow 16% over the next five years, representing an area of opportunity.

- Generation X – This age segment is expected to have increasing disposable income to spend in the coming years on luxury goods. In the future, they are expected to be loyal to the companies/brands from where they have made purchases in the past, and to companies who demonstrate pro-activeness to women's issues.

- Generation Y – Generation Y is expected to reach 33.6 million by 2005, making for the largest teen population in U.S. history. Generation Y purchases what they perceive to be quality yet affordable personal care products. Most informed of all the populations, they use the Internet for all of their needs, including product information and purchasing and are heavily influenced by the fashion and music industries.

- Women and Men – Females influence about 90% of all household purchase decisions and are the main personal-care product consumers. In addition, male consumers are increasingly purchasing personal-care products, especially hair colorants and fragrances.

- Ethnic origin – By the year 2050, nearly half of all Americans will be non-Caucasian. African-American growth figures have been fairly constant while there has been tremendous growth in the Asian and Latin American segments. The Asian American population, at approximately 7 million and encompassing 3% of the population, is the fastest-growing minority in the United States. Latin Americans represent about 9% of the United States population with a combined buying power of $205 billion. This group is projected to surpass African Americans within 20 years as the largest American ethnic group. Ethnic consumers spend more on personal-care products than any other consumer group and represent a significant growth area.

Sales and Distribution

The direct selling segment caters to the customers with limited mobility and represents lower overhead costs for companies. However, in recent times, sales have been rising at a slow pace due to an increase in workingwomen, a lack of salespersons, and low receptiveness of most consumers to this mode of sales. Sales growth of traditional department stores has been behind that of the full-line discount stores because traditional department stores no longer have brand exclusivity for the items they sell and consumers are becoming increasingly price-conscious and were attracted to discount retailers. The growth in most of the personal-care categories was stronger in full-line discount stores since they were able to attract some of the drug store customers.

Specialty stores have increased in popularity in the 1990s due to their strong consumer focus and image. Drug store sales increased steadily in 2000 with strong growth expected in the near future due to strong marketing and merchandising initiatives. There are opportunities to utilize kiosks as a strategic tool to build up sales per square foot since they are becoming more computerized due to increased technology and offer video, audio, and interactivity, making for a friendly and accessible experience.

Retail sales on the Internet are another growth area. This growth trend is expected to continue as more consumers experiment with online access and e-commerce shopping. At the end of 1999, more than 17 million households were shopping online, purchasing $20.2 billion over the Internet during the year. However, online consumers are extremely brand conscious and consumers may not buy personal-care products or services from the Internet since it is difficult to purchase cosmetics without a trial or sample.

Geographic Markets

Increasing globalization of the world's economy presents significant opportunities for consumer goods manufacturers with decreasing barriers to investment in emerging markets, and increasing disposable income in these regions. The global personal-care industry is expected to experience continued growth in the future, as levels of consumption in undeveloped markets are still significantly inferior to those in Western Europe and North America. Overall, the largest continental market in the personal-care industry in 1999 was North and South America. Asia and Latin America are considered to have huge growth potential even though they are subject to economic downturns.

3.   **What are the critical factors affecting success?**

Products/Service – Keys to success in the different segments of personal-care industry are given below:

- Skin care segment – Products tailored to various needs; frequent new product introductions; strong company research in order to introduce successful new skin-care products; strong brand loyalty and strong brand image in order to make viable product claims.

- Color cosmetics - Developing products according to fashion trends; having a wide range of selection in each subcategory; creating products according to needs; developing color cosmetic product awareness and recognition among young consumers; strong quality control was needed, since color cosmetics can be used in very sensitive areas of the body.

- Hair-care products – Products tailored to needs; use of natural ingredients; a complete line of value-added products; brand loyalty with existing consumers and brand awareness and recognition for new younger consumers.

- Personal hygiene products – Developing all-in-one products and utilize aromatherapeutic ingredients; strong brand name and brand loyalty; developing good relations with storeowners in order to obtain premium shelf space and increase sales.

- Fragrances – New product introductions with an emphasis on mental well being; increased brand awareness through the increased distribution of samples and strong brand loyalty.

- Spa services – Offer samples of products used during the service; develop a strong brand image; develop and sell prestigious high priced products; create products tailored to needs.

Customers: Keys to success for different consumer segments are:

- Senior citizens – convenient channels of distribution, preferably direct selling.

- Men and women baby boomers – High quality and high value products, selling products through numerous distribution channels, providing product information and education, strong brand loyalty and creating products according to needs.

- Generation X – A strong brand image, strong brand loyalty, sponsorship to women's issues.

- Generation Y – Quality products at affordable prices, products tailored to their specific needs, trendy fashionable youth oriented products, creating a brand awareness and recognition, subtle marketing techniques, promotions targeted specifically to them, and the ability to distribute products through various distribution channels.

- Women – Utilizing various distribution channels.

- Men – Promotions targeted specifically to them, creating brand awareness through trials, utilizing masculine packaging for products, having a retail presence and providing services to influence decisions.

- African Americans are sensitive to premium brand name, products targeted to needs, specialized promotions, building relationships, and developing brand loyalty. Asian Americans were sensitive to products targeted to needs, high quality products, and developing brand awareness. Keys to success with Latin Americans are brand recognition, price reductions/discounts, and foreign language advertisements.

Sales and Distribution and Geographic markets

- Direct selling requires recruiting and maintaining quality and enthusiastic sales representatives, for which a company needs to offer incentives and have strong internal relations.

- Drug stores – A wide assortment of products in each category, and products geared toward affluent or non-affluent customers. Kiosks demand exciting new products, enthusiastic and knowledgeable sales staff, strong brand image, and samples and trials to increase brand awareness and trial.

- Online selling requires offering a convenient and easy-to-navigate site, having online selling capabilities, providing coupons and price incentives to shop online, providing community and enhanced features on the website such as product information, articles, etc., offering samples and trials, generating supplemental revenue, and advertising to get consumer to the website. A strong brand name to generate traffic and customer loyalty and developing an early, deep, and loyal customer base are also important factors.

- Keys to success in the international market are products tailored to needs, utilizing various distribution outlets, and having a presence in emerging countries.

4.   **What are Avon's strengths and weaknesses?**

Strengths

- Avon has significant strengths in direct selling, which has been the principle distribution channel for the company.

- A globally recognized brand image as the supplier of high quality beauty products at affordable prices.

- Strength in research and development. Avon pioneered several innovations in personal-care industry, particularly the anti-aging line of products.

- A 3,000,000 strong base of enthusiastic and knowledgeable sales force.

Weaknesses

- Limited distribution channels preclude Avon from reaching all its potential customers.

- A lack of strong relationships in the retail market.

- Weak website and online presence.

5.   **What are the strategic alternatives presented in the case? Are there other alternatives Avon can consider?**

Alternative 1

Alternative 1, initiated by the CEO, Andrea Jung, proposes that in addition to direct and online selling, Avon Products, Inc. expand into retail distribution, specifically in traditional department stores like Sears and JC Penney. According to this alternative, the company would not extend its beauty kiosks in the near future until sales and productivity could be determined, its target markets will include women and baby boomers, and it would develop a higher priced Avon brand to be sold exclusively in the traditional department stores in an attempt to gain more affluent personal-care product consumers. The exclusive brand will focus on skin-care products with an emphasis on cosmeceuticals.

Alternative 2

Avon hired consultants who came up with alternative 2, which proposes that Avon Products, Inc. expand its distribution to include three specific outlets — distribute its current high quality and high priced spa product line in specialty stores, distribute a trendier and more affordable youth inspired product line to be sold in full-line discount stores and extend kiosks in the domestic market.

Alternative 3

Another alternative is for Avon to expand its distribution in two retail areas, namely traditional department stores and beauty kiosks. The company should distribute an exclusive product line in traditional discount stores, specifically in Bloomingdale's and Macys. In this outlet, the company can sell high quality high priced men's skin fragrances and personal-care products and women skin care, color cosmetic, and fragrance products. Avon should also continue to expand its beauty kiosks in the domestic market. The company's target markets should include women, men, baby boomers, and Generation X.

In addition students can be encouraged to think of other strategic plans for Avon.

6.   **Critically evaluate the above strategies in light of the competitive position of Avon in the industry. What would be your recommendation to Avon?**

Students can be encouraged to look at the benefits and downsides of each plan and offer their own recommendations as to which one is more appealing.

Alternative 1

Alternative 1 proposes that Avon Products, Inc. expand its current sales distribution to include retail outlets, specifically in traditional department stores like Sears and JC Penney.

The benefits of expanding into retail distribution are that Avon can potentially benefit from increased profits, sales, and nationwide exposure while attracting the baby boomer segment that was looking for alternative channels to direct selling.

Feasibility of the strategy rests on an increase in retail sales due to higher customer traffic in virtually all the traditional department stores and the growing spending power of baby boomers. An exclusive skin-care line with an emphasis on cosmeceuticals is likely to work because of the increase in anti-aging concerns, Avon's high brand loyalty and brand image with such products, and baby boomers' demand for products to reverse or halt the aging process.

Continuing direct selling makes sense since personal care products are the second most popular product group sold via this channel and Avon already has a huge base of sales representatives.

Avon's Internet strategy is practicable in light of market conditions and the company's internal structure. At the end of 1999, more than 17 million households were shopping online, purchasing $20.2 billion over the Internet during the year and a surge in average online spending per household was expected to increase threefold, taking the Unites States total to $184 billion. By diversifying into online selling, Avon would satisfy baby boomer, generation Y, and women in general's need for alternative channels of distribution and increasing brand recognition and awareness among these customer segments. By expanding its Internet strategy and allowing representatives to create their own web page, Avon stands to profit from the growth and popularity of online selling while maintaining enthusiastic and motivated sales representatives.

The strategy is also realistic in light of Avon's competitive situation. Avon can hope to win against Mary Kay by diversifying its distribution channels into retail traditional department stores, where Mary Kay is weak, thereby increasing its baby boomer customer base. Also, unlike Mary Kay, Avon will have online selling capabilities. The strategy could also win against L'Oreal. L'Oreal has a strong market position in traditional department stores due to its medium to highly priced quality products, a wide assortment in its product mix, relationships with store managers for optimal displays and space, and qualified sales representatives for point of purchase assistance. However, traditional department stores are still seeking new products to add to their mix as well as high turnover personal-care merchandise - exactly the qualities that Avon's new traditional department store product line offers. Avon's cosmeceuticals line has the potential to win against L'Oreal in attracting the baby boomers and generation X by increasing use of samples and trials, product information and awareness. The strategy also gives Avon an advantage against competing brands in leading traditional department stores. Avon's competitive advantage in a globally recognized brand name and image and its known history of exceptional face-to-face selling capabilities and influencing product decisions will go a long way in helping Avon compete successfully.

The plan is financially appropriate since the company would only invest $15-20 million to launch the products in these locations and a bulk of the expenses, such as advertising, overhead, and employee salary, would be carried by the stated department stores.

This alternative presents a number of drawbacks. In implementing such a plan, the company runs the risk of brand name erosion and sending mixed messages to consumers. If the retail products sold in stores are exclusive, consumers might deduce it to mean that the products sold in the brochure are of lesser quality. Sears and J.C. Penney comprise the weak portion of the retail market and tend to lack cosmetic consumers and the selling cosmetic infrastructure such as beauty advisors. This retail expansion plan could also alienate the sales representatives, who may fear job security.

Alternative 2

Alternative 2 proposes that Avon Products, Inc. expand its distribution to include three specific outlets - distribute its current high quality and high priced spa product line in specialty stores, distribute a trendier and more affordable line in full-line discount stores, and extend kiosks in the domestic market.

Specialty stores, which are increasing in customer popularity and growth, sell superior quality and high priced items to a selective market, namely medium to highly affluent baby boomers. Selling via this channel is viable since Avon currently has a prestigious high priced spa line with a strong brand image. Thus synergies exist between the type of products typically sold in specialty stores and Avon's current product mix.

Full-line discount stores with their high customer traffic, are leaders in introducing new products, and attract a less affluent personal-care customer segment, namely Generation Y. As a result, Avon would be a good fit for full-line discount stores since it would create a new and more affordable product line sold in an alternate selling channel, which would appeal to younger personal-care customers.

Although there is not yet enough information to evaluate the performance of kiosks, expanding the structures is viable since their current performance has shown strengths in increasing product knowledge and education and introducing new products to the general public. A realistic start up cost and a team of knowledgeable representatives is likely to give Avon a competitive advantage.

The plan can potentially help Avon gain competitive advantage over Mary Kay since Avon will target Generation Y in areas where Mary Kay is weak, through quality products at affordable prices, products tailored to meet needs, trendy and fashionable youth oriented products, subtle marketing, targeted promotions, various distribution outlets, and increased brand awareness and recognition. Mary Kay does not have unique and prestigious cosmetic collections, which could be sold via specialty stores, does not have a trendy and fashionable product line, which was imperative in full-line discount stores, and does not utilize kiosks as a channel of distribution.

The strategy can also help Avon prevail over L'Oreal. Although Avon plans to compete parallel to L'Oreal in specialty stores and full line discount stores, the company is likely to continue to have the distinct competitive advantage from its kiosks, which can be used to introduce its exciting new products, increase product knowledge and education, and increase brand image through samples and trials. Avon can also win against competing brands in its retail outlets especially in regards to its new ethnic product line. Avon has the distinct competitive advantage of a premium brand name, quality products, price reductions and discounts, and specialized promotions.

Alternative 2 is a financially feasible alternative only if it is carried out in stages. The costs would be tremendous to expand in all three channels simultaneously. The proposed retail strategy could be done in stages beginning with the specialty stores and kiosks and followed by the full-line discount store expansion. The time between the stages could be determined based on the success and profitability of the first stage. Also, the costs of the increased samples and the sponsorship of events directly related to women will be offset by the increased revenues generated from generation X, generation Y, and ethnic customers.

There are significant drawbacks to the solution. First, the plan is not currently financially feasible. The costs would be tremendous to expand in all three channels simultaneously. Second, Avon does not yet have strong relations in the retail market, which are necessary to gain placement in both the specialty stores and full-line discount stores. Third, with regard to the expansion of the kiosks, with 500,000 sales representatives in the United States, there would not be enough urban upscale retail space to accommodate that many kiosks.

Alternative 3

Alternative 3 proposes that Avon Products, Inc. expand its distribution in two retail areas, namely traditional department stores and beauty kiosks while continuing only its direct selling channel.

This alternative proposes numerous benefits to the company. In venturing into retail outlets, Avon can benefit from increased sales and attract new customer groups as well as tap into the male market, which has been virtually ignored by many personal-care companies. By advertising more aggressively the company will further establish a strong brand image, which will be consistent and well known both domestically and internationally.

The proposed retail initiatives are viable in light of the opportunities and threats presented in the personal care industry and the company's present situation. The growth in retail selling in traditional stores and the increasing spending power of baby boomers makes this initiative attractive. Direct selling makes sense for the same reasons as mentioned for Alternative 1.

To overcome its weakness in retail selling, Avon can introduce two new high quality and highly priced product lines in order to successfully launch itself in traditional department stores. In selling the new product lines in these outlets simultaneously, the company is likely to develop a strong retail presence and appeal to both baby boomers, generation X, women in general, and male consumers. Choosing higher end traditional department stores such as Bloomingdale's and Macy's is practical since Avon's new male and female product lines would match both Macy's strategy aimed at middle class shoppers interested in a wide assortment of moderately priced products and Bloomingdale's strategy aimed at upscale customers through more trendy higher priced personal care products.

The additional expansion of retail kiosks is also a feasible alternative. Mall owners are increasingly utilizing kiosks as a strategic tool to build up sales per square foot. Avon has experience in operating kiosks successfully in order to introduce new personal-care products. The kiosks also serve as tools for increasing product knowledge and educating the consumers. The company already has the sales team required for successful kiosk operations.

Alternative 3 is viable in light of the competition Avon Products faces. Avon can get ahead of Mary Kay with respect to its retail strategy. Mary Kay does not and will not distribute its products in retail outlets in the near, intermediate, and long term future. Avon will have the distinct advantage of distributing an exclusive, prestigious, and high quality product line in traditional department stores thereby gaining more loyalty and stronger brand image from baby boomers, generation X and male customers. Avon's advantage against L'Oreal would be the same as that discussed in Alternative 1.

This strategy is also financially feasible. The cost of the beauty certification programs can be offset by the increased sales from the expanded kiosks. The expansion of kiosks is financially viable since the start up cost for a freestanding kiosk is reported to be approximately $6,000. Also, the company can enjoy decreased expenses from the elimination of online selling costs.

Although this alternative is feasible, it presents some serious drawbacks. During the past decade, sales growth of traditional department stores has been behind that of full-line discount stores. Also, by expanding its existing product lines to appeal to older male and female consumers, the company risks ignoring the relative size and buying power importance of Generation Y. This alternative ignores the option of online retailing and seems to suggest that Avon's website will be for informational purposes only. In doing so, Avon is missing an opportunity.

The Body Shop International: U.S. Operations[1]

SYNOPSIS OF THE CASE

The Body Shop International was started in 1976 by Anita Roddick, a 33-year old housewife, in Brighton, England. The store carried 25 naturally based skin-care and hair-care products. Because the store proved to be highly successful, Anita opened another store within a year.

In the 1980s, the company experienced explosive growth. Sales and profits grew by 50% a year. In 1984, the company went public as it opened 138 new stores, 87 of which were located outside the United Kingdom. By the end of the decade, pretax profits climbed to an estimated $23 million on sales of $141 million. In 1994, franchises accounted for 89% of the company's stores.

In 1988, the first Body Shop opened in the United States. All stores were owned by the company as franchising was not permitted until 1990. However, in subsequent years the number of franchises grew to 149 out of a total number of 287 stores. The future looked so bright that Anita and her husband Gorden planned to increase the number of stores to 500 by the year 2000.

The planned expansion in the U.S., however, began to hit some serious road bumps. A host of imitators, notably the Bath and Body Works, invaded the company's market niche. As a result, the company's U.S. division lost 1.3 million pounds in 1996 and 3 million pounds in 1997. In addition, the company's share price, which stood at 365 pence in 1993, dropped to 121 pence in 1997.

The company was also challenged on an ethical level. Its critics alleged that the company, which prided itself on putting principles before profits, had misled the public about its stand against animal testing. Even though the company denied the allegation, the bad publicity had tarnished its image as one of the most glamorous growth stocks.

TEACHING OBJECTIVES

The teaching objectives of this case are as follows:

1. Illustrate the difficulties entrepreneurs such as Anita Roddick face as they shift from running a small business to managing a large organization.

2. Show the problems a company experiences as it operates in a different cultural setting.

3. Demonstrate the dilemma of reconciling the need to make profit while adhering to high and strict ethical standards.

4. Point out how success can lead to complacency, which can result in the loss of profitability.

STRATEGIC ISSUES AND DISCUSSION QUESTIONS

1. **Do you think that Anita Roddick possesses the skills necessary to run a large organization?**

    Anita Roddick is an entrepreneur. As such, she excels at running a small organization that does not require a great deal of formal plans and policies.

    Anita was not able to reconcile herself with the idea of having to run a big business. One almost gets the impression that growth was imposed on her because it was the thing to do. She did not want her company to become another McDonald's where customer's relationship would be lost. She was even uncomfortable

---

[1] This teaching note was prepared by A. J. Almaney. Adapted by permission.

with the language (such as three-year plans, net income, and average sales) used in big organization. She was also uncomfortable with meetings where people deliberate endlessly before making decisions.

For many years Anita ran her company without a formal business plan and without job descriptions. In describing her highly informal management style, she said, "You'd bury your head with laughter if you saw how unprofessional we were." And according to a former employee, "working for Anita was like being in a circus parade. Your job is to follow behind the elephants and scoop up the dung."

One consequence of Anita's highly informal managerial style was the company's difficulty in retaining managers. One manager, for example, left complaining about the Body Shop's unstructured environment and lack of a strategic plan. Another manager, who quit after only one year, said, "They were clueless about what they wanted."

2.   **Anita believes that shareholders should not have more rights than the employees, the community, and the environment. What do you think is the primary responsibility of a business organization? Is it to the shareholders, the employees, customers, or the community? Explain your answer.**

In their values statements, companies differ in how they view their relative responsibilities toward their stakeholders. Starbucks, for example, places the emphasis on its employees. According to its CEO, Howard Schultz, Starbucks is primarily responsible to its employees, then to the customers, then to the shareholders, and lastly to the community. His reasoning is that if the company takes care of its employees, they will take care of the customers. Moreover, if the customers are taken care of, the shareholder's interest would be served. And when the shareholders' interests are served, the community would benefit.

In its values statement, Johnson and Johnson views itself as being primarily responsible to its customers, that is, the patients, the doctors, and nurses who use its product. Like Starbucks, Johnson and Johnson places shareholders' interest at the end of its value statement. Other companies might list shareholders at the top of the list of their responsibilities.

Anita seems to consider all stakeholders as having equal importance to the company. In its mission statement, the Body Shop International proclaims: "To creatively balance the financial and human needs of our stakeholders: employees, customers, franchisees, suppliers, and shareholders." Notice how "shareholders," whether intentionally or not, are listed at the end.

3.   **Anita believed that "business should do more than make money, create decent jobs, or sell good products. Rather, business should help solve major social problems such as homelessness, unemployment, and social alienation." Where do you stand on this issue? Do you think that the only goal of business is to increase shareholders' value or to solve social problems as well?**

This question is likely to generate a considerable amount of discussion among students. Some would argue that the only goal of business is to increase shareholders' value because that is why shareholders invested their money in the company. And the company has no right to spend shareholders' money on causes they might not approve of.

Other students might say that a business organization should serve as a good corporate citizen and, like any other citizen, should act in a socially responsible manner. This includes solving social problems. For just as the company take something from the community in the form of profits, it should also give something back to the community.

4.   **Anita was against advertising claiming that "customers were so overmarketed that they became increasingly cynical about advertising which told them half truths or untruths." Critique Anita's philosophy showing why you would agree or disagree with it.**

It is likely that most students would disagree with Anita's position on advertising effectiveness. Being inundated themselves with advertising on a daily basis, they would be hard pressed to conceive how advertising can be ineffective if it is so widely used.

Anita's philosophy on advertising may be attributed to a significant event that took place early in the life of her business. When her first store was threatened with a lawsuit by two neighboring funeral parlors which objected to having a nearby store named the Body Shop, Anita, after informing the press of the sad story of a mother trying to make an honest living, received enormous amount of free publicity in the local press.

This experience seemed to have had an indelible impact on her, as she continued to use the press freely to promote her business.

To continue receiving press coverage, Anita hired two public-relations firms to make sure she would keep a high profile in both the general and beauty press.

Is such free publicity enough for a company that is facing many agile competitors? Not likely. When aggressive competitors such as the Body and Bath Works launch heavy marketing campaigns coupled with a steady stream of new products, occasional press interviews or TV appearances by Anita are not likely to be sufficient in countering her competitors.

5. **Do you agree with Anita that "to the vast majority of employees, profit is boring and that they did not care about it even if they get a piece of the action." Provide your reasoning.**

Anita is a maverick and an idealist, with a higher calling. And she assumes that other people are, or can be, like her. This may not always be the case.

The above statement represents one of those philosophical positions with which not too many people would agree. Perhaps what Anita means by "profit is boring to the majority of employees," is that employees respond to more than financial incentives. Just as important, they are also motivated by nonfinancial incentives.

That explains why Anita relied heavily on non-monetary tools to motivate her employees. For example, all employees are allowed to attend the company's training school; they are encouraged to spend half a day each month volunteering in a community project—time for which they are paid; and they are allowed a six-month sabbatical after five-years of employment to travel or volunteer at company-sponsored orphanages in Romania and Albania.

In an effort to identify employees' needs and concerns and deal with them promptly, the company periodically conducts employee-opinion surveys and holds frequent focus groups.

This explains why the majority of employees are highly motivated and loyal to the company.

6. **Does the composition of the Body Shop's board of directors constitute a strength or a weakness for the company? Why?**

The board of directors is weighted too heavily with insiders. Eight of the eleven members of the board are company officers. Two of these are Anita Roddick (the CEO) and her husband, Gordon, who serves as the chairman of the board.

Only three members of the board are outsiders. Considering that insiders tend to go along with decisions made by the CEO and the chairman, it is highly likely that in case of disagreement between the outsiders and the insiders, the insiders would prevail.

It should be noted that research studies clearly show that companies whose boards are composed predominantly with outsiders tend to outperform companies whose boards are controlled by insiders.

In view of the above, the board is a weakness. As a result, the company needs to tip the balance in favor of knowledgeable and experienced outsiders who are able to provide Anita and her husband with objective advice and counsel.

7. **Evaluate the mission statement of the Body Shop.**

The mission statement sounds more like a values statement than a mission statement. It articulates the company's responsibilities to its stakeholders but fails to identify what the company's business is. A primary question that a mission statement should answer is: What business are we in? Another important element a mission statement should include is a description of the products or services the company offers. In this respect, the Body Shop's mission statement is very poor.

8. **Evaluate the Body Shop's vision statement.**

A vision statement is designed to describe what the company aspires to become in the future. The Body Shop does a fairly good job in doing so. The company's vision statement identifies a few aspirations that management seeks to accomplish, for example, trading ethically, being committed to global responsibility and empowering employees.

9.   Evaluate the Body Shop's values statement.

The Body Shop's values statement is clearer and more precise than the mission and the values statement. It clearly spells out the company's responsibilities toward human and civil rights in general and workers' rights in particular. It also addresses such issues as discrimination, relationship with the community, the environment, and animal protection. Just as important, the statement emphasizes the company's resolve to institute appropriate monitoring, auditing, and disclosure mechanism to ensure the company's accountability and demonstrate its compliance with these principles.

10.   Evaluate the Body Shop's statement of objectives.

The Body Shop set three objectives for itself:

- To manage the business with the aim of maximizing shareholder interests, while also balancing the needs of other stakeholder groups.

- To develop and build relationships with shareholder and prospective shareholders, with the aim of creating a base of well-informed investors who fully understand the company's aims and objectives.

- To operate a progressive dividend policy.

The above statement of objectives is poor as it fails to meet two of the minimal requirements of a good statement of objectives. That is, the objectives should be measurable and time-bound.

The three objectives sound more like goals in that they are open ended. They are expectation targets that the company continuously seeks to accomplish as long as it stays in business. Such a statement of objectives does not provide the company with any standards that determine whether the company is getting close to achieving what it seeks to accomplish.

11.   What grand strategy did the company use? And what was the rationale behind it?

The Body Shop used a grand strategy of market development. This strategy aims, among other things, at increasing the company's growth rate by expanding into new markets.

The company's push into the U.S. market was part of its global market development grand strategy. By 1997, the global expansion stretched the company's operations to 46 countries with a total of 1,491 stores.

The company's entry into the U.S. market in 1988 was prompted by the saturated market in the United Kingdom. Anita Roddick hoped that the U.S. huge market would more than offset the stagnated business in the U.K.

12.   Why did the Body Shop's grand strategy in the U.S. begin to falter?

Initially, the company's grand strategy in the U.S. was a huge success. When the company decided to franchise in 1990, it received more than 2,000 applicants.

This was caused by the exceedingly positive image that the company enjoyed in the U.S. even prior to its entry into this market. The company's counter-culture approach to cosmetics appealed to a large number of women. It aroused in them a feeling of enthusiasm, commitment, and loyalty more common to political movement than a corporation.

In subsequent years, however, the company's image began to fizzle and its business started to decline. Several reasons contributed to that:

- Many American customers began to be turned off by the company's excessive emphasis on its politically correct message. After a while, the message not only lost its impact on many customers, it also became a liability.

- Although the Body Shop pioneered the specialty bath-products concept, several copycat retailers began to steal its market share with aggressive discounting.

- As the company opened stores in malls, it was burdened by high real estate as well as promotion costs.

- The appearance of the stores began to deteriorate with their shelves too cluttered with shoddy-looking products. The stores were also full of cards with stories about the products as well as pamphlets on animal testing and natural ingredients.

- In the early 1990s, the company failed to introduce any significant new products. Top management paid more attention to launching environmental products than to revamping the aging product line. Although the company attempted in subsequent years to introduce new products, the number of such products fell below the industry average and had mixed results.

- Anita's relationship with the franchisees began to suffer for the following reasons:

  - Some of them did not share her enthusiasm about certain causes. They were fearful that Anita's radical ideas drove some customers away.

  - They were concerned that the company's rapid expansion had a cannibalizing effect on them by taking sales away from them and turning the company into another McDonald's.

  - Some franchisees were upset for having to pay $40,000 purchase fee, something that their counterparts in the U.K. were exempted from.

  - The company's communication with its franchisees worsened. For example, 48% of them did not think the company's long-term strategy was clearly communicated to them.

- Anita's tendency to micromanage coupled with her lack of managerial skills contributed in some measure to the company's ability to implement its U.S. strategy.

- Anita's refusal to use advertising to promote her business. She relied exclusively on press interviews and TV appearances, which proved to be insufficient in countering the assault mounted by several aggressive competitors.

13. **In what way did the Body Shop's failure to understand U.S. consumer behavior contribute to the company's strategic problems?**

- The American consumers no longer bought into the company's political message even though such a message continued to be popular in Europe. The American consumer got tired of hearing the same political message repeated incessantly.

- The American consumers are not as brand-loyal as the Europeans. More than European customers, Americans' purchasing decisions were influenced not only by product quality but also by price.

- Americans are used to shopping in malls where relationships with the community are not as strong as the relationship of a stand-alone store with the community, as is the case in Europe.

14. **If you were an outside member of the company's board of directors, would you recommend ousting Anita and hiring a new CEO? What are the pros and cons of ousting her?**

The Pros

Anita lacks the managerial skills to run a global company. Like many entrepreneurs, the skills that enabled her to succeed at the early stages of business are not suitable for a large company. Anita also acts more like a social crusader than a businessperson, devoting more time and attention to environmental and human problems than to her business. Further, she does not appreciate the importance of having an independent board of directors capable of standing up to her when the need arises. She stacked up her board with insiders who either heartily agree with her philosophy or are afraid of voicing their objections as to how to run the business in a more professional manner.

The Cons

Anita Roddick is a smart entrepreneurial woman. She is passionate about her business and is able to generate enthusiasm in her employees and customers for her business and the social values it stands for. She is also an accomplished communicator preferring to engage in face-to-face communication with all her stakeholders.

The Decision

It would be best for the Body Shop International and perhaps even for Anita to bring in a new CEO with the skills necessary to run a retail company more effectively. Anita can continue to play a role as a member of the board or as a spokeswoman for the company.

15. **If you were selected as the CEO of the company, what strategies and actions would you take to improve its performance in the U.S?**

- Use a retrenchment strategy. The company should slow its torrid expansion to concentrate on improving the performance of its current stores.

- Improve the appearance of the stores. The current stores have a cluttered, confusing look with too many brochures carrying political messages. The stores should be redesigned to improve product displays.

- Introduce new products. Currently, the company's new products comprised 15% of the product mix, which is below the industry average of 25%.

- Improve customer service. Unlike the Body and Bath Works, employees of the Body Shop are not aggressive in providing service to customers; they, in essence, use a "hands-off" approach.

  The company also needs to implement an "after-sale-service" policy in which a beauty advisor calls the customer to see if she is happy with the product.

  To add value through service, the company should also consider giving free gifts with purchase.

  Such service-oriented actions can help not only in retaining current customers but also in winning new ones.

- Hire a vice-president in charge of advertising. Currently, marketing plays a negligible role in the business. Having a vice president should change that. It is very difficult for a retail business to cultivate awareness and familiarity among consumers without media advertising. With her negative views of traditional advertising, Anita is not likely to change her style.

- Target ethnic market with greater force. Efforts should be made to target such groups as Hispanic and African American who are growing at a rapid pace and are becoming a significant economic force.

CASE 14

JP Morgan Chase & Co.: The Credit Card Segment of the Financial Services Industry[1]

SYNOPSIS OF THE CASE

This case reviews the credit card segment of the much broader financial services industry including the structure of the industry, the players and the nature of competition.

Chase Cardmember Services (CCS) made up 29% of the earnings of JP Morgan Chase's commercial banking sector. The majority of the CCS portfolio consisted of standard credit cards, including Platinum and Gold cards, all of which were associated with either MasterCard or Visa. CCS also derived revenues from co-branded cards, agent-banking cards and had a growing presence in the business and corporate credit card market.

Although CCS was the industry's 5th largest card issuer, it was having problems acquiring and retaining profitable customers. In order to avoid being sold-off by JP Morgan Chase, CCS had 24 months to implement a successful growth strategy that would differentiate its offering from the competition and ensure short term as well as long term success. The executives of the company are looking at some alternatives that would achieve the goals they had set for CCS.

TEACHING OBJECTIVES

The teaching objectives of this case are as follows:

1. To understand the credit card segment of the Financial Services industry and how it functions.

2. To understand how to research and assess the competitive landscape of an industry.

3. To enable students to analyze trends that will affect the industry.

4. To develop different strategic objectives and the keys to success that will make the company better than the competition.

STRATEGIC ISSUES AND DISCUSSION QUESTIONS

1. **Give an overview of the structure of the credit card industry.**

    The financial services industry consists of investment banks, insurance companies, broker/dealers, asset managers, venture capitalists and commercial banks. Commercial banks include the traditional branch banking functions of deposit taking, lending and cash management. It also includes mortgage banking, small business and middle market banking activities and the credit card segment.

    Functions of the Credit Card Segment

    The credit card segment of the industry serves two major functions for its customers: payment mechanism and debt access mechanism. Credit cards serve as a payment mechanism when cardholders use them as a means of paying for goods and services. The advantages to this payment method are that the customer can make purchases without having to physically interact with a merchant and it allows cardholders to keep track of all of their purchases with one monthly statement. The credit card issuer earns revenue by charging annual fees for providing this service. Credit cards function as a debt access mechanism when cardholders make purchases of goods and services, accumulating a debt to the credit card issuer, and then make

---

[1] Parts of this teaching note were prepared by Robert J. Mockler. Adapted by permission.

payments periodically when funds are available. The credit card issuers earned revenue primarily from interest charged on debt outstanding.

Customers

The customers in the industry can be divided into three general categories. The individual consumer market is the largest of the three and is fiercely competitive. Individual customers can be divided further into three categories: prime, low prime and sub prime customers. Prime customers are those with the best credit history and competition for these customers is fierce. Low and sub prime customers are those with less appealing credit histories or those with serious past credit problems.

The business card market consists of small businesses and merchants. This market is less competitive and smaller than the individual consumer market.

The corporate market focuses mainly on the payment function of credit cards. Corporate employees are able to submit expenses such as travel and entertainment to the corporation and the corporation in turn pays the credit card bill. American Express is the dominant player in this market.

Products

Products in the credit card segment consist of Visa or MasterCard associated cards, co-branded cards, affinity cards, agent bank cards and secured cards.

Visa and MasterCard are associations on whose networks most credit card transactions are cleared. American Express and Discover do not issue Visa or Master Card and have proprietary networks.

Co-branded cards partner with large corporations such as airlines, hotel chains, long-distance telephone companies, retailers and gasoline companies, and offer cardholders rebates or rewards each time the card is used.

Affinity cards are cards that partner with companies or organizations and are offered to customers that are affiliated with or want to be identified as being affiliated with the card's partner. Most universities, professional athletic teams and professional organizations can be in affinity partner relationships with card issuers.

In an agent bank relationship, a smaller bank's customers are issued a card in the name of their bank, but the cards are owned and serviced by a larger card issuer. The advantage for the smaller company is it could continue to meet the needs of its clientele, and the advantage for the issuing company is the additional loans. Since customers tend to be loyal to the bank where they had their accounts, the issuing firm is able to obtain loans from a population to which it would otherwise not have access. Also, customers are less likely to default on loans to banks in which they have their other accounts. Thus, agent-banking cards generally have lower loan loss rates.

Secured cards are offered to customers with poor credit quality. They require customers to keep cash on deposit with the card issuer. The customer is given a card with a credit limit equal to the amount of their deposit.

Customer Services

Customer services include the creation of convenience and value for the customer, which can be used to generate and maintain customer loyalty, generally comes from offering distinctive features in addition to providing payment and debt access mechanisms. Additional services that create value include extending warranties for goods bought with the card, offering cash back or insurance for goods bought with the card that were stolen or damaged and co-branding cards with stores, restaurants and airlines to give customers discounts.

Technology

Technological developments have dramatically changed the credit card segment of the payment methods industry. Two new technologies, the Internet and smart card technology, have the potential to bring about sweeping changes in the industry. The popularity of the Internet has significantly changed the credit card segment of the financial services industry. About 90-95% of all purchases made online are made by credit card and purchases over the Internet are expected to top $1 trillion by 2004. However, there are widespread security concerns among consumers about using credit cards online. Merchants are wary of accepting credit cards as payment over the Internet for fear of fraud. The smart card, which contains a computer chip that holds up to one hundred times more information about the user than a normal credit card, offers a solution to minimize these concerns.

Regulation

In November 1999, the Financial Services Modernization Act was passed. The law repealed the Glass-Steagall Act, in effect since the 1930s, and allowed new types of relations between the banking, securities and insurance industries. The effect of the law led to unprecedented consolidation in the industry and the creation of huge multi-dimensional one-stop-shopping financial services conglomerates. The spate of mergers and acquisitions transformed the credit card segment of many commercial banks from top moneymakers into marginalized segments of a large conglomerate organization.

2. **What were the opportunities and threats confronting JP Morgan in the credit card industry?**

Opportunities

- Greater Internet use and gradual change in buying habits of Americans had spawned greater use of credit cards and created an opportunity for increasing market share.

- Upward trend for the desire for debt access mechanism increased credit card usage and created opportunity for greater profits in the industry.

- Track record of profitability in the sub-prime market by companies like Cap One and Providian created new opportunities in the sub-prime market whereas before credit issuers tended to deny this group credit.

- The number of businesses that had created web sites on the Internet to extend their market share and generate greater sales had created an opportunity for the payment methods industry and the credit card industry, particularly because most purchases over the Internet involved credit cards.

- The evolution of Internet networking technologies had created opportunities for credit card companies because of the convenience created by online billing, reconciliation of accounts and approval.

- The existence of co-branded cards provided an opportunity for credit card companies to create brand loyalty in credit card holders and create value for the merchants in the sense that return business could be created.

- The existence of affinity cards created an opportunity for credit card companies to establish brand loyalty by providing convenience and creating value for card holders by partnering with various merchants where the cardholders would get discounts and special offers from companies partnered with.

- Agent banking created opportunities for credit card companies to gain market share by partnering with smaller banks that cannot carry a portfolio of credit card debt, but use the larger commercial banks so that it can still issue cards to its customers.

- Secured cards also created opportunity for credit card companies by enabling them to issue credit cards to less credit worthy customers without taking on as much risk.

- The creation of value for cardholders through different programs was another opportunity for credit card companies.

- Technology created opportunity for credit card companies by providing greater security for online purchasers through smart cards.

- Opportunity exists in the corporate card market for issuers that can use technology to add value for corporate clients by providing electronic statements and settlement.

Threats

- Consolidation in the financial services industry had made many credit card companies a smaller part of large financial services conglomerates. This meant that they could be getting less attention and less funding to carry out operations.

- Lack of security and fraud over the Internet made many consumers wary of using their credit card for purchases over the Internet. Additionally, merchants lose billions of dollars every year due to fraud. This impeded growth of credit card use in this area.

- Lack of consumer loyalty due to the wealth of competition. Many credit card companies offered very low introductory rates to encourage consumers to come on board. This type of marketing caused many consumers to jump from one card brand to another and diminished card brand loyalty.

- A number of payment methods that have appeared during the 1990s, such as debit cards, payment by phone and stored value cards, have the convenience that a credit card has. This evolution of payment methods has detracted from the credit card companies' business.

- A downturn in economy could increase the number of personal bankruptcies, which would have a negative impact on the credit card industry.

3. **What are the key success factors in the credit card industry?**

- Create value for and increase usage from cardholders by providing value-added services and giving special discounts and promotions for using a credit card. In addition, increase customer use through value added services such as rebates, rewards and extended warranties.

- Create value for merchants accepting issuer's card by driving consumer traffic to the merchant.

- Attract new and profitable customers through lucrative rewards programs and aggressive advertising.

- Create cardholder loyalty through affinity or depth of relationship (i.e. providing full range of financial services) and by offering discounts and promotions on cardholders' favorite products and services.

- Attract and maintain debt by offering competitive rates.

- Limit loan losses through strong credit and collections policies.

- Create convenience for cardholder's by using the association with Visa or MasterCard to create wider acceptance of issuing bank's card. Continuously develop technologies that will create convenience and value such as smart cards that offer greater security over the Internet.

- Maintain strong brand name to attract customers and generate customer loyalty.

- Gain market share by partnering with large well known national brands, through affinity cards by maintaining flexible processes to allow for many different types of cards, by maintaining a sales force to sign up new partners and by maintaining a strong marketing team to identify new segments.

- Access to capital required in order to acquire portfolios and participate in the consolidation of the industry.

4. **Who were the main competitors for JP Morgan? Critically evaluate their strengths and weaknesses.**

The main competitors of Chase Cardmember Services (CCS) were providers of payment methods or debt access mechanisms. The principal providers of these services were credit card companies such as Citibank, MBNA, and American Express. Banks like Bank One and other mono-lines like Cap One and Discover were also competitors.

Citibank has historically been the largest player in the credit card market, pioneering many of the innovations that exist in the industry. Citibank's cards featured value added services such as rebates and rewards. The globally recognized Citibank brand name enjoyed consumer loyalty throughout the world through its aggressive advertising. Although Citibank was a major player in the prime market, it did not focus its attention in the low and sub-prime markets and consequently was not strong in this area. Citibank, however, maintained a substantial presence with businesses by offering promotions, leveraging its commercial banking presence and offering competitive rates and flexible payment arrangements. Citibank did not strongly leverage its investment banking relationships in the corporate sector in order to generate business, nor did it use Internet technology to create convenience for corporate customers nor maintained an aggressive sales force to attract and sign up new corporate customers. Citibank did create value for its cardholders through co-branding, but did little in terms of developing affinity cards. One area where Citibank was strong and able to expand its market share was in agent banking due to its large capital capacity to acquire new portfolios.

Other bank card issuers were players in the credit card industry. The largest other than Citibank was Bank One, which had become a well-known issuer by using aggressive direct mail campaigns and very low introductory rates. Bank One also had an extensive affinity relationship program with over 2000 partners. Smaller banks, although lacking the scale of the larger competitors, managed to stay in the market by offering competitive rates and providing promotional incentives to customers. Although these smaller banks did not participate in the affinity market, co-branding had been a method of attracting new customers and maintaining customer loyalty. With regard to agent banking, these smaller banks were more likely to be the targets of larger banks like Citibank and CCS. Many smaller banks were exiting the credit card business but entering agent bank arrangements in order to continue to serve their customers. Additionally, because of their small size these banks were not likely to make capital-intensive technology a large part of their strategy for customer acquisition or retention.

MBNA had become one of the largest credit card issuers in the United States and well known for its affinity relationships with over 4000 organizations. These affinity relationships proved to be one of the most effective ways of maintaining customer loyalty. They were also able to attract new customers by maintaining competitive rates and offering value added promotions through direct mail. One of MBNA's strengths was the aggressive sales force that it maintained in order to establish the many affinity relationships that it had and to identify new small segments in the market that it wished to find affinity partners to serve.

American Express provided a different type of service to its customers because its primary business was a charge card or non-revolving debt card where cardholders pay their full balance each month. However, it remained a key competitor because of its Blue card, which incorporated smart card technology and allowed cardholders to revolve (not pay their full balance every month). Amex had strong worldwide brand name recognition. This translated into greater consumer loyalty for Amex and consequently greater market share. Amex was very strong in the prime market and the corporate card sector, and was effective in attracting customers by creating greater value for them by offering special sales, promotions and driving consumer traffic to merchants accepting the American Express card.

Discover, another mono-line bank, had gained brand name recognition through the development of a strong marketing campaign and the use of a cash back rewards program. Capital One grabbed market share by issuing cards across the credit spectrum. This would include prime (most creditworthy) and sub-prime (least creditworthy) borrowers as well as offering secured cards to the sub-prime market. Cap One's use of technology allowed it to explore the low and sub-prime markets profitably. The great strength of the mono-lines had been their sales and promotions used to attract new customers such as direct mail campaigns, partnering with highly trafficked web sites and offering online instant credit approval. However, these banks could not compete on the international level or in the capital-intensive market for portfolio acquisition.

The strengths of these issuers varied. For example, Citibank's strength was in its widely known brand name, its worldwide presence and the array of services that it offers consumers along with its tremendous access to capital. MBNA was very strong in the affinity market and developing relationships with numerous organizations that create durable brand loyalty. Bank One's strength was in its considerable presence in the credit card market, established through its aggressive campaign of direct mail and low introductory rates. Capital One's strength was its ability to use technology to issue cards across the credit spectrum and remain profitable, even in the sub-prime market. American Express had a strong brand name and was very strong in the corporate sector because it allowed companies to keep track of all their purchases with one monthly statement. American Express had also been an innovator in its use of technology with its use of the smart card in its recently issued Blue.

The weaknesses of these issuers also varied according to the company. For example, Bank One ran into considerable financial trouble because of its profit strategy. Bank One was forced to take large write-offs because of the poor credit quality of its portfolio and continued to struggle to remain profitable. American Express had difficulty in moving from a charge-card business model to the traditional credit card model of revolving debt. Conversely many of the other cards, such as Discover, were weak in the corporate area and had not established themselves as a strong competitor in this market segment. Additionally, all of the cards were unsuccessful in creating a greater environment of security to allay Internet users' fear of theft and the merchants' fear of fraud. Not enough was done in the area of security over the Internet and as a result merchants lost millions of dollars a year due to fraudulent use of credit cards. Also the lack of a worldwide presence of many of the credit card issuers had been an inhibitor to their success in both Internet purchases and international credit card issuance.

The future of the credit card segment was expected to remain highly competitive. The continuous battle for market share would continue to include low introductory rates, aggressive advertising and direct mail campaigns. Additionally, the competitive strategies to develop new technologies for convenience, value creation and ease and secure use over the Internet were expected to multiply with the use of Internet as a shopping tool.

5.   **What are the possible strategic options available to CCS for growth? What are the costs of pursuing each one?**

The strategic alternatives for CCS include maintaining the status quo, expanding into the low and sub-prime markets, co-branding, moving into new technologies, establishing a larger business and corporate card presence, offering value added services and expanding the agent banking program. An analysis of the benefits and costs involved in pursuing each option is given below:

- Maintaining the status quo - The advantage of maintaining the status quo is a high level of comfort and confidence in running the business. The biggest opportunity cost of maintaining status quo would include losing market share by not taking advantage of the available opportunities before competitors.

- Expanding into low and sub-prime markets - This area was proven to be profitable by Capital One and it can be expected that competitors will move into this area with a model for doing business that is similar to Cap One. However, the risk of an economic downturn and the possibility that an increasing number of personal bankruptcies will threaten profitability must be taken into consideration. The costs of expanding into the low and sub-prime markets involve an allowance for delinquencies and maintaining strong customer service and collection centers.

- Co-branding with other companies can enhance value and impede delinquencies, thus creating value-added services for customers, such as rebates and discounts, and at the same time driving customer traffic to merchants co-branding with CCS. Co-branding is already a widely used tool to establish greater use of cards and brand loyalty and that partnering can only be expected to expand with well-known brands, especially with widely known and highly trafficked Internet web sites. However, co-brands tend to attract less profitable "transactors" that do not incur finance charges.

- The addition of new technologies to a strategic plan would include use of smart technology and creation of Internet platforms that would bring cardholders and merchants together. The smart card would be a great benefit to CCS because customers would see it as added convenience and security. Additionally, establishing an Internet platform where merchants accepting CCS cards could advertise their goods and services would be a great value enhancer for both consumer and merchant. This would create greater traffic on the chase.com website, enhance use of the card, create value and convenience for all involved and create greater market share for CCS. The cost of investment in new technology could initially be considerable. However, these new technologies are more likely than not to become the norm. This is an area where opportunity costs will far outweigh the costs of establishing a greater presence on the Internet and the issuance of smart cards.

- Establishing a greater presence in the business and corporate markets will be of great importance in terms of profits for CCS. The corporate market, presently dominated by American Express, is growing rapidly and CCS cannot afford to not concentrate on this market. Strategies would include leveraging the present relationships that JP Morgan Chase now has with its business and corporate customers. The costs of such a strategy would not be as extensive as going out into the market and trying to establish completely new relationships with clients.

- Agent banking, which has largely been an untapped market is one attractive way of gaining greater market share. Citibank has been a major portfolio acquirer, but issuer has been dominant in this area. The firm that is able to establish itself as the primary player will have an advantage in future agent bank transactions and will be able to earn higher returns than its competitors due to the agent bank portfolio's lower loan losses and higher customer loyalty. However, agent banking as a means of acquiring market share would incur new costs for CCS due to the capital required to purchase these portfolios and the manpower needed to research which portfolios were worth acquiring.

6. **What are the various alternatives being recommended to CCS? What other alternatives can you suggest? Evaluate each one and recommend which alternative CCS should pursue.**

Alternative 1

This alternative proposes that CCS maintain the status quo, which involves having customers such as prime individuals with a limited business and corporate presence, driving a customer acquisition strategy through internal growth and using co-branding with some agent banking. Under this alternative, the geographic market will be strictly domestic and technology will be limited to the use of the magnetic stripe.

There are elements of comfort as well as a danger in pursuing this strategy. CCS would have a high comfort level with the strategy because till now this is the way it has run its successful business. However, the payment methods industry is evolving rapidly and new developments and methods for attracting customers are being initiated constantly. The danger, therefore, in maintaining the status quo is that CCS will eventually lag behind in the industry, lose customers and eventually lose market share.

The benefits of this strategy are that CCS is likely to limit its losses by targeting customers that have sound credit. The company would be working in areas that are familiar to it. Hence, not moving outside the domestic market would keep expenses for growth to a minimum and no new expenses would be incurred in new technologies.

The drawbacks to this strategy are that with a limited business and corporate presence CCS will be giving up a large part of the potential market, thus leading to a stagnant market share and customer growth. Limiting technology to magnetic stripe cards will eventually limit the use of CCS services due to the expansion of Internet use and the use of new technologies like the smart card.

Alternative 2

In this alternative, CCS should expand its customer base to include prime, low prime and sub-prime customers along with business and corporate customers. The growth strategies under this plan include aggressive targeting to all credit levels with intensive co-branding domestically as well as internationally, and using direct mail, Internet and television advertising as the principal methods of promotion in both domestic and international markets. Movement into international markets where the JP Morgan name is widely recognized while continuing to service the domestic markets is key to this alternative. Technologies developed should include magnetic stripe and smart cards as well as a strong Internet presence by partnering with other Internet companies to attract new customers and create convenience platforms for existing customers.

The benefits of this alternative are that CCS will be able to capture a greater market share by offering customers both payment and lending features. The growth strategy of aggressive targeting of all credit levels and co-branding would allow CCS to draw from a much larger target market and offer a substantially greater number of services. Moving into the international market would also allow CCS to offer its customers services world wide as well as domestically and draw from a much larger market base than its present one. Using new technologies would facilitate Internet use and address security issues that presently inhibit many customers from making greater use of the Internet.

This strategy is a viable one because the payment and lending features are services that CCS already offers. The below prime markets have also been proven to be a highly profitable area for many competitors and

Co-branding has been proven to improve customer loyalty. The move into new technologies will be necessary to remain competitive as use of smart cards and Internet purchasing expands. Although JP Morgan Chase did not have an international commercial banking presence, it did have international name recognition from its investment banking presence. It could leverage this brand name recognition to expand its credit card business into international markets. It also could expand internationally via acquisition since it had the capital needed to acquire portfolios.

The drawbacks of this strategy are that moving into the below prime market will cause CCS to incur greater risks and losses in its portfolio. The aggressive targeting of these markets will also increase the costs of acquiring new customers that have a higher probability of defaulting on the credit and loans extended. Additionally, the lack of an Internet strategy, such as collaborating with high traffic web sites and developing web sites that would drive traffic to merchants accepting the CCS card is a significant drawback because the competition is implementing these strategies and creating this kind of value for cardholders and merchants. Also, CCS did not have the international commercial banking presence to leverage for international expansion and Citibank had a competitive advantage over CCS in the international credit cards issuance market.

Alternative 3

The third alternative has been designed to allow CCS to remain a leader in both the payments and lending functions of the credit card industry and focus on individual customers, particularly prime customers, and corporate customers. CCS could seek to grow via an aggressive portfolio acquisition campaign. In addition to focusing on co-branded cards and value-added service, CCS would also expand significantly into the agent-banking business using portfolio acquisitions to acquire new agent banking relationships. In terms of geographic markets, CCS would focus primarily on the US market. Finally, CCS would increase its focus on technology, incorporating smart card technology into all of its customers.

Alternative 3 would allow CCS to use its competitive strengths to its advantage and to continue to be a winner in the payments and lending functions of the credit card industry. The benefits of expanding into the Low Prime segment of individual customers are that CCS will be able to increase its profitability by lending to a group of customers more likely to revolve and incur interest charges. Also, by taking advantage of this opportunity, CCS would not expand into the Sub-prime segment, which has very high loan losses that would only increase if there were a downtrend in the economy. This strategy allows CCS to reap the benefits of lending to lower credit quality customers while mitigating the potential risk of lending in this arena. Another benefit to this strategy would be for CCS to diversify its earnings stream by competing aggressively for corporate card business. This would help insulate CCS in case of a recession since loan losses are negligible for corporate customers.

A major benefit of this approach is that it will allow CCS to capitalize on the consolidation of the credit card issuer market by being an aggressive acquirer of portfolios as they come up for sale. It can use this approach not only to build up its corporate card business, but also its agent banking business. For focusing on agent banking, CCS can acquire customers likely to be loyal to their bank, and thus to CCS as the owner of the agent banking relationship. By beginning to offer dual cards that incorporate smart card technology, CCS will be positioned to take advantage of increases in web based purchasing.

The feasibility of this alternative rests on CCS' access to capital required to grow via portfolio acquisition. CCS also has the investment banking presence required to attract new corporate card customers and a growing experience in managing agent baking relationships. Finally, the low prime market is still not saturated and there is room for CCS to expand into this arena.

CCS can be competitive in pursuing this strategy because CCS has access to capital that some of its major competitors, in particular the mono-line issuers, do not have. While bank-card issuers do have access to capital, only Citibank has proven the ability to effectively integrate acquired portfolios but it is focused on growing its international credit card business. As a result, CCS can compete for, win and integrate agent bank portfolios better than its competitors going forward. CCS can win against the competition in the corporate card business by leveraging its recently acquired technology platform for servicing corporate card customers, which is better than any of its competitors. By using this platform, along with JP Morgan Chase's investment banking relationships with many corporations, CCS can effectively win new corporate card business. Since the trend toward smart card is still developing, CCS can win against the competition by taking a proactive approach toward converting its current credit card customers to dual cards that incorporate smart card technology but still can be used in the current US infrastructure. By doing this, CCS can offset the attracting that its customers might have toward Amex's Blue card. It would eliminate the attracting of Blue by making smart cards a common reality as opposed to a novelty.

The drawbacks to this alternative revolve around the potential competitor responses to CCS' actions. By focusing on portfolio acquisitions and agent banking, the industry leader Citibank could switch its focus from growing its international business to focusing on a similar strategy to CCS. Another drawback related to competition is the possibility that American Express, the primary corporate card issuer could develop comparable or better technology platform for servicing corporate clients. An internal drawback is that if CCS does not deliver high return on investment, its access to capital from JP Morgan Chase could become limited.

DECISION CHART

Kinds of Decisions	Alternatives		
	1 (Status Quo)	2 (Aggressive Internal Growth)	3 (Aggressive Portfolio Acquisition)
Function	Payments & Lending	Payments & Lending	Payments & Lending
Customers	Prime individual consumer focus with some business & corporate presence	CCS will lend across the credit spectrum (Prime, Low Prime and Sub Prime individuals) as well as to businesses & corporations	CCS will expand aggressively into the Corporate card markets and will also expand into the lower credit quality individual segment
Customer Acquisition Strategy	Limited Internal growth through direct marketing	CCS will pursue a strategy of aggressive internal growth by targeting cardholders through direct mail and Internet advertising	CCS will pursue a strategy of aggressive portfolio acquisitions for Corporate Card and Agent Bank portfolios
Products	Some co-brands and value-added products with limited agent banks	CCS will aggressively pursue new co-brand partners (large national firms or firms with strong Internet presence) and use them to attract new customers	CCS will seek out new Agent Banking Partners
Geographic Markets	Domestic Issuance only	CCS will expand into International Markets where the JP Morgan name may be recognized from its Investment Bank presence (Canada, UK, Japan)	CCS will continue to focus solely on the US domestic market
Sales & Promotion	Direct Mail, Internet, TV, Print Media	Creative Direct Mail, TV and Internet advertising campaigns	Promotion will focus on retaining current and acquired customer through cross-selling other JP Morgan products
Technology	Magnetic Stripe Cards	CCS will focus on building its Internet presence and attempt to partner with other Internet companies to create online B2C exchanges	CCS will focus on converting its current card portfolio to Dual cards that incorporate Smart Card technology along with integrating Internet technology to create value for customers

Keys to Success	Relative Weight	Competitors						Compare Weight				
		CCS	Citibank	Banks	MBNA	Amex	Mono-Lines	Citibank	Banks	MBNA	Amex	Mono-Lines
A. Function												
Payments												
1 Universal acceptance required to become cardholder's first choice payment vehicle	1	++	++	++	++	+	+	0	0	0	+	+
2 Create value for and increase usage from cardholders by providing value-added services or rebates/rewards	2	+	+	+	0	++	+	0	0	+	−	0
3 Cardholder loyalty through affinity or depth of relationship needed to retain customers	1	++	++	+	++	++	0	0	0	0	0	++
4 Aggressive advertising needed to attract new customers	2	0	+	−	+	++	++	−	+	0	0	++
5 Develop relationships and trust among consumers by leveraging strong commercial bank presence	1	++	++	+	+	0	−	+	+	++++	++	++++
Lending												
6 Attract and maintain debt by offering competitive rates	2	+	+	+	+	+	+	0	0	0	0	0
7 Cardholder loyalty through affinity or depth of relationship needed to retain customers	1	++	++	+	++	++	0	0	+	0	0	++
8 Aggressive advertising needed to attract new customers	2	0	+	−	+	++	++	−	+	+	−	−
9 Limit loan losses through strong credit and collections policies	1	++	+	−	+	+	−	+	+++	+	+	++++
B. Customers												
Individuals												
Prime												
1 Increase customer's use through Value added services or rebates / rewards	2	+	+	+	0	++	+	0	0	+	−	0
2 Aggressive advertising needed to attract new customers	2	0	+	−	++	++	++	−	+	+	−	−
3 Cardholder loyalty through affinity or depth of relationship needed to maintain customers	1	++	++	+	++	++	0	0	0	0	0	++
Low Prime & Sub Prime												
4 Limit loan losses through strong credit policies	1	+	0	−	+	0	−	+	0	0	0	+++
5 Aggressive advertising needed to attract new customers	2	0	+	−	+	++	++	−	+	−	−	−
6 Limit losses by maintaining strong collections department	1	++	0	−	++	++	+	+	++	0	0	+++
Businesses												
7 Increase profitability by selling charged off accounts	3	+	+	+	++	+	+	+	0	0	0	0
8 Maintain merchant loyalty by offering loyalty programs and promotions	2	+	+	0	0	0	0	0	+	+	0	+

Keys to Success	Relative Weight	Competitors						Compare Weight				
		CCS	Citibank	Banks	MBNA	Amex	Mono-Lines	Citibank	Banks	MBNA	Amex	Mono-Lines
9 Leverage relationships from strong commercial bank presence	1	++	++	+	+	+	--	0	0	0	0	++++
10 Attract and maintain debt by offering competitive rates	2	+	+	+	+	+	+	0	0	0	0	0
11 Create convenience from business cardholders through flexible payment arrangements	3	+	+	+	+	+	+	0	++	0	0	0
Corporate												
12 Leverage strong Investment bank presence to develop relationships	1	++	+	0	--	0	--	+	++	++++	++	++++
13 Create convenience for corporate clients through the creation of Intranet platform that allow online billing and reconciliation and approval of charges within the corporate structure	1	++	--	--	--	+	--	++++	++++	++++	+	++++
14 Maintain aggressive sales force to attract and sign-up clients	1	0	--	--	--	++	--	++	++	++	--	++
C. Products												
Generic Visa / MasterCard Cards												
1 Create convenience for the cardholder by using the association with Visa or MasterCard to create wider acceptance of issuing bank's card.	1	++	++	++	++	0	0	++	0	0	++	++
Co-branded Cards												
2 Create value for cardholders and brand loyalty by offering discounts and promotions on products and services	1	+	+	+	0	++	+	0	0	+	-	0
3 Increase card usage by offering targeted special offers or sales	1	+	+	+	0	++	+	0	0	+	-	0
4 Create value for merchants by driving consumer traffic to merchant	1	+	+	+	0	++	+	0	0	+	-	0
5 Gain market share by partnering with large well known national brands	1	+	+	+	0	++	+	0	0	+	-	0
6 Attract profitable customers through lucrative rewards programs	3	+	+	+	0	++	+	0	0	+	-	0
Affinity Cards												
7 Flexible processes to allow for many different types of cards	1	--	--	0	++	--	--	0	--	--	0	0
8 Effective sales force to sign up large numbers of partners	3	--	--	+	++	--	--	0	--	--	0	0
9 Strong marketing team to identify new, small segments	2	--	--	0	++	--	--	0	--	--	0	0
Agent Bank Cards												
10 Capital needed for purchase of agent bank portfolios from bank card issuers	1	++	++	+	0	0	0	0	+	++	++	++

Keys to Success	Relative Weight	CCS	Competitors					Compare Weight				
			Citibank	Banks	MBNA	Amex	Mono-Lines	Citibank	Banks	MBNA	Amex	Mono-Lines
11 Develop partnerships with agent banks to provide value for customers to give an incentive for the bank to acquire new customers	1	++	++	+	0	0	0	0	+	++	++	++
12 Maintain an experienced agent bank team to service the portfolios and management the relationship with the agent bank	2	++	++	+	0	0	0	0	+	++	++	++
13 Ability to effectively integrate new portfolios into current business to maximize efficiency and return	1	++	++	+	0	0	0	0	+	++	++	++
Secured Cards												
14 Aggressive advertising to targeted customers or regions to attract sub-prime customers	1	--	-	--	-	--	++	-	0	-	0	--
D. Customer Acquisition Strategy												
Portfolio Acquisition												
1 Access to capital to fund acquisitions including agent bank and corporate card portfolios	1	++	++	+	0	0	0	0	+	++	++	++
2 Ability to effectively integrate new portfolios into current business to maximize efficiency and return	1	++	++	+	0	0	0	0	+	++	++	++
3 Maintain an experienced and aggressive acquisitions team to seek out portfolios to acquire	2	++	++	+	0	0	0	0	+	++	++	++
Internal Growth												
4 Develop effective sales & promotion strategy through direct mail, and other forms or media	1	-	0	--	++	++	++	-	+	--	--	--
5 Use technology to segment potential customers and create targeted offers	1	0	0	0	+	0	++	0	0	-	0	-
6 Create value by partnering with merchants to provide value for cardholders and increased traffic to merchants	2	+	+	+	0	++	+	0	0	+	++	0
E. Globalization												
Usage												
1 Leverage the Visa/MasterCard international network, or build a proprietary network to allow cardholders ability to use card worldwide	1	++	++	++	++	+	0	0	+	0	+	++
Issuance												
2 Leverage a strong international consumer banking presence to attract customers	1	--	++	--	--	+	--	--	0	0	0	0
3 Build the international operational and legal infrastructure to support issuing in foreign counties	2	-	++	--	--	+	--	--	+	+	--	+
4 Leverage international brand name recognition to attract new customers	1	++	++	0	0	++	+	0	++	++	0	++

Keys to Success	Relative Weight	Competitors						Compare Weight				
		CCS	Citibank	Banks	MBNA	Amex	Mono-Lines	Citibank	Banks	MBNA	Amex	Mono-Lines
5 Access to capital needed to acquire international credit card portfolios	1	++	++	+	0	0	0	0	+	++	++	++
F. Sales & Promotions												
Direct Mail												
1 Develop creative direct mail campaigns to attract customers	1	0	0	--	++	++	0	0	++	--	--	--
2 Use technology to segment potential customers and send targeted offers	2	0	0	0	+	0	++	0	0	-	0	--
Internet												
3 Partner with highly trafficked websites to attract potential customers	2	0	0	0	+	+	++	0	0	+	+	--
4 Online instant credit approval decisions to allow cardholders immediate access to their lines of credit	2	+	+	0	+	+	+	0	0	+	0	0
G. Technology												
Internet												
1 Partner with highly trafficked websites to attract potential customers	2	0	0	0	+	+	++	0	0	-	-	-
2 Create value for merchants and customers by develop web-based B2C platforms to bring customers and merchants together	2	+	0	--	-	+	-	+	+++	++	0	++
3 Create value for cardholders by adding services like online purchase protection or rebates for online purchases	3	+	+	+	+	+	+	0	0	0	0	0
4 Maintain aggressive advertising targeted to online shoppers to attract new cardholders	1	+	+	0	+	++	+	0	+	0	-	0
5 Create a secure Internet environment through development of high security systems for online credit card transactions	2	+	+	+	+	+	+	0	0	0	0	0
Payment Methods												
6 Develop dual cards incorporating smart card technology as well as traditional magnetic strip cards.	1	0	0	0	0	++	0	0	0	0	++	0
7 Continuously develop new technology	2	0	0	0	0	0	0	0	0	0	0	0
8 Maintain strong advertising to inform customers of new technology and its uses	2	0	0	0	0	++	0	0	0	0	--	0
9 Maintain an aggressive sales force to bring new payment systems to customers & merchants	3	0	0	0	0	0	0	0	0	0	0	0

Key: Relative Weight: 1=High, 2=Med, 3=Low   KTS: ++, +, 0, -, -- reflect firm's ability with regards to key success factor.

CASE 15

Toyota: The Evolution of the Toyota Production System

SYNOPSIS OF THE CASE

The case describes the evolution of Toyota's manufacturing system from its early days until the present day. The central theme is that distinctive competencies in manufacturing and materials management can form the bedrock of a company's competitive advantage. Toyota's distinctive competency in manufacturing and materials management developed over a thirty-year period through a process of experimentation and innovation.

The case opens with a discussion of the early days of Toyota. Its survival was precarious in the 1930s and 1940s. Indeed, had it not been for the persistence of a handful of key executives and a good measure of luck, Toyota might never have gotten off the ground. The case then moves on to describe the evolution of Toyota's manufacturing system. Referred to as lean production or flexible production, this system includes reduced set-up times, organization, improved quality control, and the kanban system of having parts delivered just in time. The consequences of this system include high labor productivity, high quality, low costs, and an ability to produce a wide model range at no cost penalty. The case then discusses how Toyota has tried to bring its customers into the design and production planning process by building lifetime relationships with individual customers. It closes with a discussion of Toyota's expansion overseas and its product strategy. As the severe recession in Japan harms Toyota's domestic sales, and the rise in the value of the yen puts a break upon Toyota's exports, Toyota needs to make strategic choices regarding its expansion plans outside Japan.

TEACHING OBJECTIVES

The main teaching objectives of this case are as follows:

1. To illustrate the role of operations strategy in the creation of a competitive advantage.

2. To discuss the concepts of distinctive competencies and barriers to imitation as they apply to Toyota.

3. To illustrate the advantages of long-term contracts with suppliers as opposed to vertical integration or competitive bidding as alternative ways of managing the supply process.

STRATEGIC ISSUES AND DISCUSSION QUESTIONS

1. **Compare and contrast Toyota's manufacturing system with a conventional mass-production system. What are the advantages of Toyota's system?**

    One of the best ways to tackle this question is to map out the characteristics and drawbacks of the mass-production system. Then one can move on to discuss the characteristics and advantages of the Toyota system. The comparison is very revealing.

    Mass-Production System

    A conventional mass-production system has two main characteristics:

    a. The fixed costs involved in setting up specialized equipment are spread over long production runs to gain the maximum economies of scale.

    b. There is extensive division of labor so that each worker performs only a single task. The original belief was that as a worker became familiar with a single task he or she could perform it much faster, thereby increasing labor productivity.

Although the initial introduction of mass production at Ford in the 1920s did result in enormous economies of scale and productivity gains relative to the prior techniques of craft production, the system does have a number of *drawbacks*:

a.   Long production runs create large inventories that have to be stored. This is costly.

b.   If initial machine settings are incorrect, long production runs result in the production of large numbers of defects, which is wasteful.

c.   The extreme division of labor results in worker apathy and a corresponding reduction in productivity.

d.   The extreme division of labor creates a need for large numbers of specialists (foremen, quality inspectors, tooling specialists) whose jobs could logically be performed by assembly-line workers. This results in excess employment and decreased productivity.

e.   Since quality control is typically the job of specialists, assembly-line workers have no incentive to be concerned about quality.

f.   Because stopping the production line to fix defects is expensive, the prevailing practice is to fix defects at the end of the line in a rework area. Again, this reduces the incentive of assembly-line workers to be concerned about quality. They know things will be fixed at the end of the line.

g.   The mass-production system is not very good at accommodating consumer demands for diversity.

In short, there were a number of weaknesses in the conventional mass-production system that led to real inefficiency. Most seriously, quality control was lax and worker productivity was far below what it might have been. However, as long as the mass-production system was the only available system, this did not matter.

Toyota's System

Toyota's manufacturing system has four main characteristics:

- Set-up times for specialized equipment are reduced from days or hours to minutes, through a number of simple innovations. This obviates the need for long production runs to cover fixed costs and makes shorter production runs economical.

- The work force is grouped into teams. Team members are given a set of tasks to perform. Each team member is trained to perform all relevant tasks, including housekeeping, tool repair, and quality control. The team leader is also an assembly-line worker.

- Each assembly-line worker is able to stop the line if he or she encounters a problem that can't be fixed. It is then the responsibility of the whole team to fix the problem.

- The kanban system was developed so that parts were delivered to the assembly line just in time and so that only those parts that were to be used immediately (that day) were produced.

This system resulted in a number of *major advantages relative to mass production*. Specifically:

- Product quality improved dramatically, for several reasons:

  - Teams were given the responsibility for quality inspection and control. Thus, assembly-line workers had an incentive to be concerned about quality.

  - Shorter production runs meant that not as many defective parts were produced if initial machine settings were wrong.

  - The just-in-time (kanban) system of production meant that defects showed up immediately in the production process.

  - The practice of stopping the line to fix defects reduced the need for an extensive rework area and created an incentive for assembly-line workers to be concerned with quality.

  - Workers were taught to trace defects back to their source and ensure that the problem never occurred again.

- Productivity was also much higher than in a mass production plant, for two main reasons:

  - The improvements in quality discussed above meant that far less time was wasted fixing defects and producing defective parts. This boosted labor productivity.

  - The creation of teams reduced the need for employing specialists. Getting excess manpower out of the system boosted productivity.

- By making short production runs economical, the system was capable of handling much greater product variety than a mass-production system. This enabled Toyota to better serve consumer demands for product diversity.

- The reduction in inventory with the kanban system reduced inventory holding costs and freed up capital for investment elsewhere.

2. **Describe the essential difference between the way supplier relations are managed at Toyota and at the typical U.S. auto manufacturer. What are the consequences of these differences?**

The U.S. System

Historically, U.S. companies have adopted a twofold strategy with regard to managing the supply of component parts:

- Vertical integration to gain control over supply sources. The belief was that vertical integration

  - Allowed for the efficient hierarchical coordination of the supply process and

  - Reduced dependence on powerful suppliers.

- Competitive bidding to reduce remaining procurement costs. This essentially involves playing suppliers off against each other in order to get the lowest price.

In practice, both of these strategies gave rise to *substantial problems*:

- Vertical integration, by creating a captive market for in-house suppliers, reduced suppliers' incentive to minimize costs. They knew they could always pass on cost increases downstream in the form of higher transfer prices. The result was a failure to control costs in in-house suppliers.

- Hierarchical coordination of the supply process in vertically integrated organizations creates a need for management personnel to oversee the process. This can be costly.

- The practice of competitive bidding did not guarantee stable supplies, high-quality inputs, or cooperation beyond existing contracts to solve design or engineering problems. It created resentment on the part of suppliers, who were accordingly hesitant to cooperate with automakers to improve quality or design or to introduce just-in-time systems.

The result is that both strategies have raised supply costs above those achieved by Toyota.

Toyota's Strategy

Toyota has deliberately chosen a middle position between vertical integration and competitive bidding to manage its suppliers. It recognized early on that vertical integration could be costly, whereas competitive bidding would make it hard to achieve cooperation with suppliers. Instead, Toyota's strategy had the following elements:

- Toyota established a two-tier system of suppliers. First-tier suppliers were responsible for the design and assembly of major components. They contracted out the job of fabricating individual parts to second-tier suppliers.

- Toyota took a minority holding in many of its first-tier suppliers (typically 20 to 40 percent).

- Toyota worked closely with first-tier suppliers on the design process for components.

- All suppliers were encouraged to adopt the kanban system.

- The contract for a component had a life of four to five years, with the price being agreed on in advance. If by joint effort Toyota and a supplier succeeded in reducing manufacturing costs during the lifetime of a contract, the additional profit was shared between the two. If the supplier reduced costs on its own, it kept the additional profit for the lifetime of the contract.

- Toyota dispatched some of its managers and engineers to work in its suppliers for extended periods of time.

- First- and second-tier suppliers were grouped into supplier associations. A major function of these associations was to share information regarding new management or manufacturing techniques.

This system has several *advantages*:

- The guaranteed long-term contracts give suppliers an incentive to cooperate closely with Toyota on design problems.

- The terms of the long-term contracts give suppliers an incentive to look for ways of reducing costs (since they keep the gains).

- The extension of the kanban system to outside suppliers has resulted in the same quality and cost gains as it did with Toyota's in-house suppliers. The kanban system is also a low-cost device for coordinating the supply process. It does away with the need for hierarchical coordination (and hence for management to oversee the process).

- The fact that contracts are subject to renewal every four or five years injects an important element of market discipline into the process. Suppliers know they must be efficient and cooperative or their contracts won't be renewed after five years.

- The supplier associations ensure that new management techniques are quickly diffused among all suppliers.

- By taking a minority holding in key suppliers, Toyota provides its suppliers with capital and gives itself a means to exercise some control over supplier operations without having to bear the full costs of vertical integration.

Taken together, these factors have resulted in a reduction in costs and increases in the quality of component parts relative to those that U.S. auto companies have to bear.

3. **How does Toyota's approach to customer relations influence its design and production planning process? What are the implications?**

Toyota uses its dealers to build long-term ties with its customers. The basic objective is to ensure that once a customer purchases a Toyota car, he or she will never purchase the car of another company. This goes beyond providing high-quality cars and excellent after-sales service and support to trying to include customers in the design and production planning process.

With regard to design, Toyota has assembled a huge database on customer preferences, which comes from regular surveys by dealers. It uses these surveys to help design new models and modifications to existing models. As for production planning, Toyota has developed a system whereby customer orders determine short-term production planning. This enables Toyota to serve individual customer needs better than perhaps any other auto company in the world. So flexible is Toyota's production system that it can virtually customize products for individual consumers.

The implications of this should be fairly obvious. Toyota is very responsive to customer needs and so is able to build substantial brand loyalty. This clearly gives it a competitive advantage over other auto companies in the United States, which, historically at least, have lacked the same customer orientation.

4. **Do you think that the cooperation that Toyota has achieved with its suppliers and employees in Japan can be replicated in its overseas manufacturing operations?**

This question is intended to help shatter the myth that the success of Japanese companies is culturally bound and due to some inherent ability of the Japanese to achieve greater cooperation than Westerners. Reflecting this myth, the initial response of students to this question might well be no! They will talk about the problems of managing unionized workers, the adversarial history of management-labor relations in the West, uncooperative suppliers, and the like. At this point the instructor should make three points:

- The cooperative long-term relationships that Toyota has fostered with its suppliers were born of necessity rather than design. Like its U.S. counterparts, Toyota originally undertook substantial vertical integration. However, after World War II it lacked the capital to implement this policy on a large scale, so it opted for quasi-vertical integration in the form of long-term contracts. It was only later that it realized that this was actually a very efficient way of managing supplier relations.

- Team production at Toyota only emerged in the 1950s after a lengthy strike. The union agreed to team production in exchange for guarantees of lifetime employment and pay graded by seniority. Prior to this time, the history of management-labor relations at Toyota was no less disruptive than at many Western plants. The system as it subsequently evolved became the model for many other Japanese operations.

- Toyota's production facilities in the United States, including its joint venture with GM, have productivity and quality records that are close to those achieved by its best-run Japanese plants. This suggests that the company can replicate its domestic success overseas. It also suggests that the success of Japanese companies is not culturally bound.

5.   **What is the basis of Toyota's competitive advantage? Is it imitable?**

Toyota's competitive advantage clearly does not lie in any one element of its production and marketing system. It is not the kanban system on its own, nor is it the organization of the workplace into teams, nor the close ties with consumers, nor shortened set-up times for specialized equipment. Although all of these things are very important, other companies have recently adopted these techniques (such as GM at its Saturn subsidiary), but none have yet replicated Toyota's performance. Evidence of this can be found in the fact that in J. D. Power's 2001 quality survey seven of the top sixteen places went to Toyota cars.

Toyota's competitive advantage derives at least in part from the manner in which all of the various elements of its production system fit together into a smoothly functioning whole. It is the company's capability to manage this whole process that forms part of the basis of its competitive advantage.

A second factor that underlies Toyota's competitive advantage is an organization-wide commitment to quality control. By now it should be apparent that the kanban system, the team organization, the ability of individual workers to stop the assembly line, and so on are all a reflection of the company's obsession with quality. An organization-wide obsession with quality is the theme that runs through much of what Toyota does. What is particularly notable is that unlike many Western companies, Toyota sees improving product quality as a means of enhancing productivity and lowering costs. Many Western companies have traditionally seen these as contradictory goals.

A third factor that historically has been of considerable importance at Toyota has been the company's willingness to experiment with process innovations, or with new ways of doing things. Had Toyota not experimented, it might have become just another mass-production company. Instead, through a trial-and-error process it succeeded in creating a whole new type of production system.

In sum, it can be argued that Toyota's competitive advantage is based on its organization-wide commitment to quality, its willingness to experiment, and its capability to manage the different parts of the production process in a holistic manner.

This competitive advantage also presents high barriers to imitation by competitors. Although competitors can and have copied many of Toyota's process innovations, such as the kanban system and team production, they are finding it much more difficult to replicate Toyota's organization-wide commitment to quality, its capability of managing different elements of its production process, and its ability to innovate. This is because these factors are not visible to outsiders. Rather, they are embedded deep within Toyota's organizational culture in employee attitudes and behaviors. Culture, because it is intangible, is much more difficult to imitate than are the different elements of Toyota's production process.

This does not mean that Toyota is invulnerable. Although it clearly has an advantage for now, it is possible that companies such as GM, in attempting to replicate Toyota's success, may come up with a better way of building cars.

6. **Will Toyota be able to sustain its competitive advantage into the next century?**

    If rivals succeed in imitating not just the elements of Toyota's lean-production system, but also the totality of that system, Toyota's advantage will be eroded. However, as pointed out above, the barriers to imitating Toyota's culture are high, so imitation might not be the cause of Toyota demise (if that should occur). However, there are other challenges facing Toyota right now that require strategic adaptation. If Toyota cannot adapt to meet these challenges, it may well see its competitive advantage decay. Specifically:

    - The rise in the value of the yen has made Japan a high cost production location and requires Toyota to move more production offshore to remain competitive. Although the company has shown that it can do this and still replicate its impressive efficiency and quality performance (e.g., as in Kentucky) any such move leaves it with excess capacity at home.

    - Toyota's success is in part based on its commitment to lifetime employment for its employees. They work hard precisely because they are guaranteed lifetime employment and steady pay increases with seniority. If excess capacity persists in Japan, this gives Toyota a significant problem, how to reduce capacity without breaking its lifetime employment commitment. Because there is already a labor shortage, this is not a great problem with regard to blue-collar workers. It is a problem with regard to the company's many white-collar workers, though. Like many U.S. companies ten years ago, Toyota has to deal with a bloated and relatively unproductive middle-management bureaucracy.

    - The move toward the globalization of markets requires that Toyota, in common with other auto manufacturers, become more of a global company. While companies such as Honda and Ford have already moved toward becoming truly global companies, with an increasingly international management cadre, Toyota has remained very much a Japanese company, and critics question whether Toyota can make the transition. However, there is evidence that Toyota's Japanese leadership has allowed increased local hiring and operational autonomy in the United States.

7. **What markets should Toyota concentrate on in the future? What challenges does it face?**

    The United States seems to be emerging as the biggest opportunity for Toyota. Specifically,

    - In 2001, Toyota sold more vehicles in the United States (1.74 million) than in Japan (1.71 million). More of the company's operating profit comes from the United States than from Japan.

    - Toyota has big hits in the United States - the Camry sedan, Tundra pickup, and Sequoia SUV.

    - With its 10% U.S. market share, Toyota is close to overtaking DaimlerChrylser's 14.5% for a place among the Big Three.

    Toyota needs to capitalize on this opportunity especially since it faces a shrinking market, low margins and intense competition in Japan. Its strategy for the United States seems to be to Americanize design, production and marketing. Some of the challenges that it may face in the American markets are:

    - Replicating the strengths of Toyota (for example, establishing the "Toyota Way" culture) in the United States may not work as well as it did in Japan.

    - Establishing networks with suppliers in the United States in the same fashion as in Japan is a challenge—the number of defects in the parts produced by Toyotas suppliers in the United States has been much higher than that of suppliers in Japan. Toyota has introduced supplier education plans for its suppliers in the United States to lower this defect rate with encouraging results.

    - Increasing market share in the United States in a slow economy will be another challenge. On one hand is an aging customer base (average age of the Toyota customer is 45) and attempts to reduce the age through introduction of Celica coupe and MR2 Spyder roadster have not worked, and on the other hand, newer models like Echo targeted at youth are not doing well. Success may depend on how well its new models (Scion and Matrix) sell in the market.

    Following a strategy similar to that in the United States, Toyota is trying to expand in the European market, which can be significant ($400 Million including Eastern Europe). Toyota has been a small player in Europe with 4% market share. It has put into place a plant in France as well as a factory jointly owned with PSA Peugeot near Prague to begin making Minivans by 2005. The company seems to be on the right track in

Europe, but as with the United States it faces stiff competitions from smaller Asian car manufacturers as well as European car manufacturers (*Source: Business Week, International Edition,* April 2002).

Nucor in 2001

SYNOPSIS OF THE CASE

Nucor is a vertically integrated company that manufactures steel, steel joists, and steel fasteners. The company has a reputation as one of the most efficient steel companies in the world. A "mini-mill" producer, Nucor is the brightest star in the U.S. steel industry. It was ranked second in terms of output per employee in *Iron Age*'s 1986 survey of world steel producers. The case gives a detailed overview of Nucor's steel-making and steel joist operations. It also describes the nature of competition in these industries. Throughout the case, particular attention is paid to Nucor's organizational structure, management style, and employee incentive systems. All of these have played a major role in turning Nucor into one of the lowest-cost firms in the global marketplace.

By 2001, the company, which began making steel in 1969 using new mini-mill technology, was the second largest steel producer in the U.S. and is expected to pass U.S. Steel as the largest producer within the next few years. A culture that rewarded hard work and cooperation with high pay, job security and commitment by the company, solid business decisions, and a willingness to take risks had made Nucor one of the Fortune 500's most respected U.S. corporations.

However, Nucor also faced a number of challenges. The company's increased size had recently forced structural changes that had increased bureaucratic costs in an effort to provide better integration and coordination of the company's many plants. This need for change appeared to have been a major stimulus for the board's replacement of the top management, the very management that has developed the company over the past 30 years. The steel industry was in an extremely unprofitable and volatile phase. Overcapacity, cheap imports, escalating energy prices and decreasing demand led to most of the United States steel companies reporting losses in 2001 with many filing for bankruptcy protection. In 2001, with its earnings, sales and profits showing a downward trend, Nucor had to decide how and whether it would expand into the production of steel outside the U.S. and whether it would diversify further into related businesses that were less cyclical in order to provide stockholders with a higher return.

TEACHING OBJECTIVES

The main teaching objectives of this case are as follows:

1. To explore the role played by organizational structure and management style in implementing a low-cost leadership strategy.

2. To explore the role played by incentive systems and labor relations in implementing a low-cost leadership strategy.

3. To demonstrate the link between industry competitive structure and the strategic options open to a firm.

4. To consider how continuing growth and diversification might affect Nucor's low-cost position.

This case is an excellent vehicle for demonstrating how to successfully implement a low-cost leadership strategy. The case works well both as a subject for a written report and as the basis for classroom discussion. We suggest that the case be positioned late in the course to coincide with the lectures on strategy implementation. At the same time, the case also touches on issues of vertical integration, diversification, and competitive strategy within a hostile environment. Thus, it has general applicability.

STRATEGIC ISSUES AND DISCUSSION QUESTIONS

We have found that the best way of opening this case is to discuss the nature of the competitive environments in which Nucor operates. The instructor should emphasize that in its three main business areas, there is really only one viable strategy: cost minimization. That is, the strategic options open to Nucor are to a large degree environmentally determined. The company has very little choice in the matter. Like other steel companies, in order to succeed, the company has to minimize its costs. Differentiation is not an option. Having discussed this, turn to identifying how the company has achieved this low-cost position. Many factors should be drawn out at this stage (modern mini-mill technology, non-union company, good labor relations, management style, incentive systems). In the forefront, however, are organizational and management factors. With this in mind, focus on identifying what it is about Nucor's organization, management style, and incentive structure that help the firm minimize its costs. At this stage, it is worth stressing the potential disadvantages as well as advantages of its organization. Finally, discussion might close with a review of how continuing growth and diversification might jeopardize the company's competitive position.

1.   **What is the nature of the competitive environment in which Nucor operates? What are the competitive implications?**

Answering this question calls for an analysis based on Porter's Five-Forces Model and a discussion on how the steel industry can be defined as far as Nucor is concerned.

Entry Barriers

Entry barriers, which were traditionally high for the integrated steel mills, are now falling due to technological change and new competitors can easily enter the steel industry by building mini-mills. Steel is a commodity product and low switching costs for buyers further ensure easy entry by new competition. In addition, falling trade barriers under GATT have led to foreign entry into U.S. market. New technologies like electric arc furnaces, thin slab continuous casting, and direct strip continuous casting, have lowered scale economies.

Substitutes

Materials like aluminum, plastics, glass and synthetics have substituted for some uses of steel and have led to declining demand for steel and placed downward pressure on prices. However, the substitutability of steel may be limited because few materials have the same strength as steel does.

Buyers

There exist several large buyers (auto companies, service centers) that order steel in large quantities. While many industries (construction, automobile, farm equipment) use steel as a raw material in their production, they have low switching costs. This implies that buyers have power over steel producers and can bargain down prices of steel.

Suppliers

The primary suppliers for integrated and mini-mills are iron ore and scrap producers. Equipment manufacturers, power companies, and shippers can also be considered suppliers.

Rivalry

Mini-mill technology has lead to a mostly fragmented industry structure, large as well as small steel companies using either integrated mills or mini-mills exist. The steel industry is in the maturity stage of its life cycle and suffers from excess capacity in the face of declining demand for a commodity product. Further, high Exit barriers for the industry imply persistent capacity. Price and reliability form the basis of competition in this industry.

Defining the Steel industry

Students should recognize that steel production is considered an industry (flat rolled, structural, bar) distinctly different from industries that use steel (joists, steel bearings, grinding balls, machine parts, and manufactured buildings). Students may decide to do the five-forces analysis based on the different segments that Nucor operates in.

At the time of the case, Nucor was active in the manufacture of three main product groups: steel rods, wire, and shapes; steel joists used in construction; and steel fasteners. The company had also entered into a joint venture agreement with Kogyo of Japan that took the company into the flat-rolled steel business in 1989.

This venture enabled Nucor to compete directly with the steel majors for the auto and appliance business. The nature of competition in each of these three main areas is discussed below.

Steel. Steel is a commodity product with few opportunities for differentiation, so competition tends to be on the basis of price. The steel industry has been struggling for years because of a number of adverse factors. These include a decline in demand, rising imports, excess manufacturing capacity, and high exit barriers. Demand has been sluggish since 1974 because of slow economic growth, rising energy costs, and the increased use of substitutes such as plastics. Since 1974, low-cost imports have increased to take 25 percent of the U.S. market. In addition, about 33 percent of U.S. capacity was excess to requirements in 1987, and 20 percent of global capacity was excess. The consequence of too much capacity chasing too little demand has been a decade of severe price competition. And this situation has been exacerbated by the high costs that steel majors face when shutting down steel-making capacity (exit barriers).

Steel joists. Nucor makes open-web steel joists that are used primarily as roof support systems in large buildings such as warehouses and stores. The industry is characterized by high competition among many small manufacturers for many small customers. That is, both the buying and selling industries are fragmented. Fragmented industries tend to be characterized by intense price competition, and indeed this is the case in the joist industry, where competition is based on price and delivery performance. For each job, Nucor typically competes with six or seven major competitors. This obviously places strong pressure on prices. Although there are some opportunities for differentiation (Nucor offers engineering support for its customers), they are very limited. Steel joists are essentially a commodity product.

Steel fasteners. Nucor diversified into the steel fastener business in 1986. Steel fasteners are a commodity product with few opportunities for differentiation. Competition is primarily on the basis of price. Because of this, low-cost imports have surged to take 90 percent of the U.S. market.

In each of the business areas in which Nucor operates, the product is essentially a commodity, and price is the main competitive weapon. In order to survive and prosper, therefore, a firm competing in these business areas must try to minimize its operating costs. This suggests that Nucor has little choice but to pursue cost minimization strategy. Meaningful differentiation is not really an option.

2.   **What factors have helped Nucor achieve a low-cost position?**

Nucor has been able to achieve a low cost position due to a number of important factors, including mini-mill technology, vertical integration, a non-union work force, and Nucor's administrative efficiency (its organizational structure, management style, and incentive systems).

- *Mini-mill technology.* Mini-mills use modern electric-arc blast furnace technology and a mix of scrap steel and iron ore to produce low-cost steel. The mini-mill technology was perfected during the late 1960s. Mini-mills are cost-efficient at much lower output levels than fully integrated iron and steel mills, such as those operated by USX and Bethlehem Steel. The availability of low-cost scrap steel that can be used as a raw material is an important element supporting the cost advantage of mini-mills.

- *Vertical integration.* Nucor is a vertically integrated operation. Its steel mills provide the raw materials for its joist and fastener businesses. Having guaranteed internal customers has allowed Nucor to run its mini-mills at full capacity, thereby realizing economies of scale even when the overall level of demand is low. Thus, vertical integration has helped Nucor keep its costs below those of competitors.

- *Non-union work force.* Most mini-mills, including Nucor, have a non-union work force. In contrast, the integrated producers use union labor. Thus, the mini-mills have avoided the problems of high wage rates, poor labor relations, and restrictive working practices that have plagued integrated mills.

- *Administrative efficiency.* Nucor has enhanced its low-cost position through administrative efficiency. It has designed its organizational structure and incentive systems in such a way that cost minimization is constantly stressed within the company. In other words, Nucor has managed to build a distinctive competency in the implementation of a low-cost strategy. The company's competitive advantage lies in its unique organizational structure, management style, and incentive systems:

- The flat organizational structure is decentralized to plants. Self managing work teams are widely used and know-how across plants is shared through extensive use of informal horizontal integrated mechanisms.

- Plants are controlled by plant managers and are profit centers. This increases responsibility, accountability and motivation. Incentive systems are linked to corporate profitability, divisional profitability and output. Peer control in self-managing teams.

- The culture is egalitarian. Employees share the gains and losses, have low cost values, incentivized by money and non-monetary factors.

- The employees are goal-oriented, self-reliant individuals and those that do not fit soon leave.

- Processes such as benchmarking against other mini-mills and customer order system, let customers hold low inventories and enable Nucor to achieve minimal differentiation.

- An early mover in mini-mill technology, the company is a technology innovator and stays on the cutting edge of technology.

- Iverson exhibits many of the attributes of good strategic leadership - eloquence, models desired behavior (low cost), visionary, empowers employees, well connected with employees.

Thus, the case illustrates that how a company implements a strategy is just as important as the strategy it chooses to implement.

3. **How did Nucor's organizational structure help the company achieve a low-cost position?**

A number of key features of Nucor's organizational structure and management style deserve emphasis.

- The small corporate head office of less than 25 people

- The short lines of communication (flat hierarchy with only 4 levels)

- The assignment of responsibility as a profit center to each division

- The practice of setting challenging return-on-assets goals for divisions

- The decentralization of all operating decision responsibilities to divisions

The consequence was that within Nucor each division could be seen as an autonomous, self-contained operation that is accountable for its own profit performance. Each of the steel divisions, for example, had its own sales staff and its own purchasing staff. Although this led to some duplication between divisions, it also had a number of benefits.

First, such decentralization ensured that decisions are made by people close to the facts, rather than by head-office executives who are out of touch with the operating realities. This enabled Nucor's divisions to adapt quickly to the changing demands of the marketplace. Second, decentralization freed head office executives from operating responsibilities and allowed them to concentrate on strategic issues. Third, it eliminated the need for an extensive corporate staff to deal with purchasing, sales, manufacturing, and so on. This helped keep corporate overhead costs to a minimum. Fourth, letting divisional managers run their own operations was a motivator. Managers generally respond favorably to being given greater freedom, and this may increase the effectiveness of their decisions. Fifth, and perhaps most important from the cost perspective, operating autonomy implied that divisional managers had no excuse for poor performance. They were responsible for all the operating decisions that related to their particular business, so they could not blame someone else for poor performance. This was an additional motivating factor, encouraging divisional managers to focus on maximizing operating efficiency and minimizing costs. The practice of setting challenging ROA targets for divisions further encouraged this tendency. Divisional managers could meet these targets only by maximizing operating efficiency. They knew that their performance was visible, and they knew that they could not pass the buck if they failed to meet their goals.

4. **How did Nucor's incentive systems help the company achieve a low-cost position?**

Nucor's incentive systems were designed to motivate both workers and managers to maximize their productivity. They did this by rewarding managers and workers for productive teamwork. Bonuses were not awarded on an individual basis, but on the basis of joint efficiency. Nucor had four basic schemes: one for workers, one for department managers within its divisions (such as managers in sales and manufacturing), one for staff people like accountants, secretaries or engineers and one for senior executives including division managers.

Workers. Pay bonus schemes for workers were tied to output per labor hours. Workers were paid bonuses if the output per labor hour of their plant exceeded estimates based on past performance. This is an example of output control. It promotes teamwork among workers, because the output of the whole plant is being evaluated, rather than that of individuals. Because all must pull their weight for pay bonuses to be achieved, peer pressure among workers ensures that individual shirking is kept to a minimum. At the same time, the incentive scheme encourages workers to strive for constant improvements in productivity. Historic estimates indicate that output per labor hour will increase every time productivity is improved, so workers have to keep increasing their productivity in order to get bonuses.

Department managers. Bonuses for department managers within each division were based on the division's profits. Department managers were paid less than the going rate in their industry, so the bonuses were important. These bonuses promoted teamwork among departments, because the profitability of the whole division rather than the efficiency of any particular department formed the basis for the bonuses. At the same time, the scheme encouraged department managers to try to maximize the effectiveness of their departments. Along with teamwork, this was the best way for them to increase the division's profits.

Division heads. Bonuses for division heads were based on corporate profits. Division managers were also paid less than the going rate in their industry, so bonuses formed an important component of their total salary. As with the bonuses for workers and department heads, the idea was to promote teamwork. The scheme encouraged division managers to (1) maximize the efficiency of their divisions, since that boosts corporate profits, and (2) share ideas for increasing efficiency with other divisions, which also boosts corporate profits. Thus, the bonus scheme had the additional benefit of facilitating communication and cooperation between divisions.

Senior Executives. Senior executives did not have employment contracts and there were no pension or retirement plans available for them. Like the division heads, bonuses were an important part of the salary - base salaries were low and bonuses were tied to the return on equity. This encouraged management to make decisions that raised the return on equity every year and the no frills culture for senior management ensured that all employees shared the good times as well as the bad.

5.   **How did Nucor's management style help the company achieve a low-cost position?**

Nucor's management style fostered a feeling of community within the organization that reinforced its cost-conscious culture and promotes good labor relations. The organization was characterized by good communications between the very top executives and workers on the shop floor. Management had an open-door policy and was receptive to suggestions from workers. Nucor was also characterized by a lack of management perks. There were no executive dining rooms or reserved parking spaces, and fringe benefits were basically the same for all employees. The idea was to promote the feeling that "we are all in this together" rather than an "us and them" attitude—to promote teamwork rather than confrontation. Nucor also had a policy of guaranteeing lifetime employment. Any job reductions were achieved through natural attrition. One consequence of all these factors was to encourage loyalty and commitment in the company's work force. This attitude translated into greater worker productivity, and hence, into lower operating costs.

6.   **Why was Nucor's organizational structure changed in 1999?**

Nucor's initial decentralized structure had been designed to promote within the organization a cost-conscious culture that at the same time placed a premium on teamwork. However, the management felt that the increasing size of the organization warranted a change in structure to better integrate and coordinate the operations of the various divisions. It was expected that a move to a more centralized organizational structure would benefit the company in many ways. For example, centralizing functions such as sales would avoid duplication and keep costs down and the centralization of purchasing would help Nucor achieve greater buying power. It would also help improve communication between division managers and top management so that top management did not lose touch with the rest of the company.

However, centralization of operating functions had the potential to compromise the autonomy and profit accountability of operating divisions. This could destroy the basis for much of Nucor's cost-conscious culture. It would give division managers an alibi for poor performance (they could claim that poor division performance was due to poor sales decisions made at the head office).

7.   **What strategies should Nucor pursue in the future?**

Nucor has a tough challenge ahead of it because of the slow economy and tough conditions in the steel industry. In order to maintain its profitability and competitiveness, the company has to ensure that it continues to maintain its low cost focus. This is critical since Nucor has recently adopted a more centralized structure, which has the potential to increase bureaucratic costs.

The downturn in the steel industry presents an opportunity for Nucor to grasp market share and increase capacity by acquiring other minimills. At a time when a number of steel companies are going bankrupt, Nucor is well positioned to snap up their assets at depressed prices. This consolidation would allow Nucor to become even more competitive versus suppliers. Given that the steel industry in the world is undergoing consolidation (Source: *Wall Street Journal,* April 2001), an increase in capacity will make Nucor competitive should it choose to enter the global market in the near future. Diversification into less cyclical businesses is another option for Nucor, as long as the company "sticks to its knitting" and does not diversify into areas where it has no competencies.

In addition, the company should also continue to maintain its innovative lead by investing in commercialization of new technologies like thin strip casting that could well revolutionize the steel industry by allowing companies to build inexpensive "micro-mills" closer to the markets.

CASE 17

Digital Devices: Current and Future Market Opportunities

SYNOPSIS OF THE CASE

This case describes the paradigm shift in the computer industry from the PC era to the era of the World Wide Web. It is argued that the evolution of computing has—up to now—three distinct eras: the mainframe era, which was overturned by the PC era, which in turn, is in the process to be overtaken by the era of ubiquitous connectivity. Technological trends like the exponential growth in computing power coupled with Internet connectivity and advances in optical communications, wireless data transmission and distributed operating systems are making it possible to achieve persistent connectivity to the Web anytime, anywhere through digital devices as well as the PC.

The case gives an overview and growth rates of the currently utilized digital devices like handheld personal digital assistants, wireless phones, videogame consoles, set-top boxes and other devices. While players in the digital devices industry can broadly be divided into many different segments (hardware providers, operating system providers, application software providers, Internet service providers and Internet server providers), the case focuses on the strategies of companies competing in the operating system segment of the digital device space. Palm, Microsoft and to some extent, Psion, are all in the race for establishing their respective operating systems as the dominant standards for different digital devices.

Since many of the technologies underlying digital devices are still evolving, it is hard to predict who will emerge as the winner. Microsoft, based on its Windows operating system, enjoyed a dominant position in the PC era and was subsequently able to extract economic rents over an extended period of time; i.e., Microsoft enjoyed a sustained competitive advantage. One of the key questions of the case is whether Microsoft will be able to achieve such a dominant position in the unfolding era of ubiquitous computing, i.e., whether its business model based on increasing returns to an installed base is transferable to the world of digital devices. Microsoft's vehicle to accomplish its goal as the "standard" in the world of ubiquitous computing is its Windows CE, an operating system for digital devices. An important question is whether standards in the digital device arena will be as important as they are in the PC arena.

TEACHING OBJECTIVES

This case demonstrates the evolution of computing and its effect on competition and firm performance. It is an excellent case to teach the impact of technological progress (external shocks) on industry and firm performance. In eras of technological discontinuities, new entrants enjoy the advantage over incumbents, i.e., in eras of paradigm shifts we regularly witness the Schumpeterian process of creative destruction. This case demonstrates how one incumbent firm, Microsoft, attempts to weather the storm of creative destruction through its embrace-and-extend strategy. In particular, Microsoft is attempting to transfer its competitive advantage enjoyed in the PC era to the unfolding era of ubiquitous computing. The teaching objectives of this case are as follows:

1. To understand the drivers and timing of technological change.

2. To understand the impact of external, in this case technological, changes on incumbent firms. Technological discontinuities level the competitive playing field; most incumbents have problems to adapt. New entrants regularly have an advantage over incumbents. Is this true in this case?

3. To identify Microsoft's competitive advantage built on the virtuous cycle of the Windows operating system.

4. To understand the importance of standards in technology-driven industries.

5. To discuss whether a competitive advantage enjoyed in one era can be successfully transferred into the next. IBM, for example, was unable to transfer its dominant position in the mainframe era to the PC era. Will Microsoft experience the same fate as the change from the PC era to the era of ubiquitous computing is taking place?

STRATEGIC ISSUES AND DISCUSSION QUESTIONS

1. **Why is the emergence of digital devices happening now? To what extent can the rise of digital devices be viewed as a response to unmet customer needs, to evolutionary changes in the personal computer industry and perceived limitations in the nature of the personal computer?**

    A case can be made that the rise of digital devices is in part a response to the limitations of a general-purpose appliance, such as the personal computer. Specialized appliances (i.e., digital devices) have greater efficacy than general-purpose appliances, since they are optimized by design to their tasks. One can argue that the general purpose PC is an over-engineered and under-optimized device of dubious functional appeal for special tasks. However, so long as the costs of computing power were high—so long as computing power was a scarce resource—the economics of the general purpose PC were very appealing (i.e., the ability to spread the fixed costs of acquiring computing power over many tasks made a general purpose device economically attractive).

    Advances in technology are now changing the relative economics of specialized and digital devices. The cost of computing power continues to plummet. Moreover, the rise of the Web and wireless networks, and the investment now being made in bandwidth-enhancing communications technology, are lowering the costs of connectivity and paving the way for a world of ubiquitous computing. In short, an increase in the supply and reduction in the price of complements (communications bandwidth), coupled with the continuing decline in the costs of computing power, are increasing the performance/price ratio for specialized devices relative to that for the general purpose PC.

2. **Over the next few years, do you think that the way in which people will use digital devices such as the Handspring, Palm, and Windows CE handheld computers will change? How?**

    Historically individuals have bought PDAs and handheld computers for personal information management. These users are beginning to use these devices for mobile web browsing, as a location too (when equipped with a GPS) as well as a communication device. Increasing power of personal digital assistants, greater bandwidth and persistent wireless connectivity is likely to drive forward greater adoption of handheld computers. Specifically, new applications written for digital devices are likely to add more features and increase functionality through value added services. For example, building in GPS functionality could allow for locater services. With advances in mobile computing, handheld computers can be transformed into mobile terminals through which remote information and applications, including Web based data can be accessed and manipulated anytime and anywhere.

    An even more important trend is likely to be widespread adoption of these devices by corporations as an extension of enterprise computing. For example, Palm VII has capabilities that allow it to access data from remote locations—this feature might make it a device of choice for field service technicians who need to access or manipulate client data residing at their corporate offices. Palm has also partnered with many companies to develop applications that allow enterprise databases to be accessed through the Palm platform. Companies like FedEx and retail warehouses can use these devices to access their databases.

3. **Where do handheld computers fit into the broader computing and communications industry? What are the implications of this for the rates of return that can be earned in the handheld segment of the broader industry?**

    Handheld computers are the portals that allow users to access and manipulate data stored remotely on the web. In the near future, most of the data and applications that users need will not reside on the devices themselves, but on the World Wide Web. Value will be added through services (the data and applications) that bring this information to owners of PDAs and smart phones. This implies that while manufacture of PDAs and smart phones could be a commodity business, ownership of the dominant OS could lead to value.

    However, since most communications protocols will be in the public domain (web based), it is unlikely that there will be huge value in the OS. Ultimately, the OS may be invisible to users.

4.   **Does the rise of digital devices represent a potential paradigm shift in the nature of computing? What are the implications of such a paradigm shift for Microsoft?**

This is a potential paradigm shift. It is occurring because of the change in the relative economics of general purpose and specialized devices as discussed above. The paradigm shift is away from the personal computing era, and toward the era of ubiquitous computing. The paradigm shift is being facilitated by the declining costs of computing and communications power.

The implications for Microsoft are potentially enormous. If it occurs, the center of gravity in the computer industry will shift away from the personal computer, and toward specialized devices. This does not mean that the PC will go away, but it does suggest that it will relinquish its role as the growth engine of the industry. For Microsoft to have any hope of continuing to match its growth expectations, it must participate in this new arena.

5.   **Will standards be important in the digital device arena? Why?**

We have standards to ensure that devices work together i.e. to ensure compatibility. In the PC world, standards are required to ensure that hardware, software, and a wide range of peripherals, including printers and modems, all work seamlessly together. Compatibility will remain an important attribute in the digital device arena. The concept of ubiquitous computing relies upon the assumption of common communications standards. Therefore, at some level, standards will be important. The question remains, though, are these standards going to be proprietary or non-proprietary (for example, TCP/IP).

Of particular importance to the players in the industry is the role of operating system (OS) standards. Do digital devices require a common OS, or just a common set of communications protocols? Standards are important if the device has to run many software applications—but by definition, specialized devices will not have to run as many applications as general-purpose devices. On the other hand, at least some devices are designed to run multiple applications (e.g., the various types of PC companion). This suggests a role for standards. The need for an OS standard may also be increased by the need to synchronize data between hand-held digital devices, PCs, and servers.

This suggests that there may be some momentum for the widespread adoption of a single standard. Standardization increases the size of the market for an application, lowers the risks associated with writing that application, increases the supply of applications, and lowers the price of applications. This increases the value of the device to its owner, and drives forward demand for devices. In turn, as the installed base of devices grows, so does the supply of applications. Thus, a positive feedback loop may begin to operate in the industry. Put differently, standardization around a common OS and a common set of communications protocols may be important in order to establish the market for digital devices, to increase the supply of complements (applications) and to grow that market.

6.   **Why was Palm so successful? Why did it continue to be successful through to 2000?**

Palm Pilot was launched in 1996. In 1999, Palm had a 66% share of the worldwide market, and some 75% of PDAs shipped used the palm OS. In the U.S., Palm had around 83% of the market. By 2000, PDAs sales were over $1 billion, up from $150 million in 1996. This success was largely due to the following factors:

- Simplicity and elegance of original design and a focus on basic PIM functionality

- Satisfied an unmet need among consumers.

- Low power consumption.

- Easy synchronization with PC.

- Strong development community (77,000 in 1999).

- Availability of development tools.

- Availability of applications and porting of enterprise applications to run on the Palm.

- Licensing strategy builds Palm community, and elicits the development of more applications in a classic positive feedback loop.

- Continual product improvement, including Palm VII wireless model.
- Continual improvement in value added services through Palm.net

7. Why did Palm's competitor, Handspring, license the Palm OS? What are the advantages and disadvantages for Handspring in using the Palm OS?

The advantages for Handspring from using Palm's OS are:

- Palm OS is already enjoying strong network effect.
- Access to Palm development community.
- Access to Palm users looking for increased functionality but not willing to migrate to a new OS.
- Access to Palm applications.
- Quicker time to market for Handspring product.

The disadvantages can be:

- Handspring could end up in the commodity end of the business (box making). Since the value is in the OS, Palm could capture economic rents.
- To capture value, the Handspring product has to offer significant functionality advantages beyond that already incorporated into the Palm range.

Notwithstanding the disadvantages, without the Palm OS Handspring would have been swimming uphill to attract users. The other option would have been to design their own OS, but they would have lacked installed base, application developers, etc, and the product would have taken longer to develop.

8. What is Microsoft's strategy for establishing the Windows CE as the de facto operating system standard for digital devices? How successful do you think this may be?

Microsoft's strategy

Increase the installed base of devices running CE as rapidly as possible. This can be done through:

- Licensing widely to manufacturers of a diverse array of digital devices.
- Modularizing CE so that it works with a wide array of devices.
- Building in RTOS capabilities as quickly as possible.
- Leveraging the large Windows developer base by utilizing Windows 32 APIs (a critical complement).
- Leveraging synchronization capability between Windows CE and desktop applications.
- Leveraging common GUI environment between Windows CE, CE apps, and familiar desktop environment.
- Designing the product for the early and late majority—not the innovators.

Roadblocks to success

There are impediments to it at work. For a start, there are choices: Java, Java OS, Psion's EPOC, Wind River System's VxWorks and 3 Com's Palm OS. The viability of these choices is enhanced by the fact that key suppliers of complements do not want to see Microsoft dominate the digital device world in the same way as it dominated the desktop world. They do not want Microsoft to extract all of the economic value out of the industry's value chain. Specific examples include TCI (set top boxes) and Symbian (cell phone companies). Symbian is championing Psion's EPOC OS. TCI has let Java in. The point is that the suppliers of hardware complements have choices as to the OS, and they would like to retain bargaining power. In some ways, at this point Microsoft's dominance is working against the company.

Another issue concerns the current limitations of CE – its RTOS capabilities are still suspect its size, relative to embedded system kernels such as VxWorks, works against it. Moreover, 3Com's Palm OS arguably leads the market at this point in time for handheld computers (Exhibit 4).

9. **What is the business model that Microsoft should use to profit from the spread of Windows CE?**

   There are two revenue streams from CE, direct and indirect.

   - Direct: Licensing fees and income from (Microsoft) sales of related apps. The business model is to price Windows CE low and build volume. So long as average costs fall faster than average revenues, margins will balloon. Although the revenue per unit will be significantly lower than for PCs, a potentially huge number of devices could be sold every year, which will translate into an enormous revenue stream.

   - Indirect: Digital devices will connect with servers—and increase demand for server software, such as NT and related apps. Device users will also probably use Web portals to access Web-based databases, and execute transactions. Business Model: Razors and razor blades. Digital devices based on CE, and optimized for use with NT, MSN, etc., are the razor blades. Significant profits can be made on the sale of the related complements.

10. **If digital devices "grow up" to replace the PC, or at least segments of the PC market such as notebooks, what are the implications for Microsoft's core Windows franchise?**

    Microsoft's core Windows franchise is mature. Demand momentum will shift to devices. In the ubiquitous computing view of the world, that core franchise also starts to lose some of its economic value.

CASE 18

Treo: Handspring's Last Stand?[1]

SYNOPSIS OF THE CASE

Handspring, which had fought hard to gain market share in the personal digital assistant (PDA) industry with its line of Handspring Visor PDAs, was now "betting the farm" on a new "smartphone" product, Treo. This was a significant decision for the company because a) smartphones required some different areas of expertise than PDAs, b) the major cellular phone providers such as Nokia, Ericsson, Motorola, and Kyocera, were aggressively entering the smartphone market, meaning that Handspring would have a new range of big, highly efficient and well-established competitors, c) Handspring would be discontinuing its Visor line, and d) the Handspring Visor's key differentiating feature, its Springboard Module, would not be offered on the new Treo smartphone. Handspring's decision to essentially abandon its core product, the Handspring Visor, to develop Treo, probably represents Handspring management's view of where the future of technology is headed. However it also means that Handspring will have to develop new competencies, face new competitors, and may have to write off some of the R&D investment it has put into its Springboard technology.

TEACHING OBJECTIVES

The principal teaching objectives of this case are as follows:

1. To understand the impact of disruptive technology, and the decisions a firm faces about what technology trajectory to follow.

2. To understand the industry environment that Handspring competes in.

3. To understand the internal strengths and weaknesses of the company.

4. To understand and evaluate the corporate, business and functional-level strategies being pursued by Handspring.

STRATEGIC ISSUES AND DISCUSSION QUESTIONS

1. **Why has Handspring decided to move into smartphones?**

    Industry analysts had been predicting that the PDA industry would inevitably be supplanted by the smartphone industry. Students may point out that many of the existing PDA models offered by Palm, Handspring, Compaq and others had begun offering cellular phone capability, but the addition of phone capability to the standard PDA made for an awkward, expensive, and power hungry device. Thus adoption of such models had been slow—instead users tended to carry both a cellular phone and a PDA. The new smartphone concept essentially tackled the problem the other way around: add PDA functionality to a phone. The resulting products were smaller and sleeker, and in general more "phone like."

    Handspring likely felt that smartphones would ultimately displace most PDAs, since the value of having the functionality of both merged into one convenient unit was readily apparent. Since the company's culture and core competencies were in providing technological leadership, its management likely felt that moving into smartphones was necessary in order to maintain a position of technological leadership. Smartphones were also expected to offer higher margins.

---

[1] This teaching note was prepared by Melissa A. Schilling. Adapted by permission.

2.   **How is the smartphone industry different from the PDA industry?**

First, by integrating PDA technology with cellular phones, the smartphone market has the potential to merge the customer bases that currently exist for PDAs and cellular phones. While the majority of existing PDA owners likely have cellular phones, there are probably a great number of people who have cellular phones who do not have PDAs. Thus merging this category may result in a larger and more diverse customer base for Handspring.

Another very significant difference pertains to competition. While computer-oriented companies dominated the PDA industry (e.g., Palm, Compaq, Hewlett Packard, Sony), it is the major cellular phone producers (Nokia, Kyocera, Samsung) that have aggressively targeted the smartphone category. These companies were not only large and well-established, but they also had extensive relationships with wireless service providers who could provide distribution and promotion of the products.

It is worth noting that in the cellular phone industry, handsets were often purchased by the cellular service providers (e.g., Sprint) and then offered at a very low price (or free) to the customer. Profits were made on the charges for the service plans rather than on the handsets. This meant that handset manufacturers often had to negotiate their prices with service providers rather than retailers, and since service providers were fairly consolidated and controlled much of the distribution to the end user, they had significant bargaining power. Furthermore, the fact that handsets were given away by the service providers put enormous price pressure on those handsets that were not sold with a service agreement, and caused the handset margins to decline precipitously. Customers were not inclined to pay a large price for a handset—even one that offered special features—if they knew they could get a reasonable handset for free.

These factors suggested that the smartphone industry might be even more competitive than the PDA industry had been (and students will likely point out that the PDA industry had seen its own share of price wars). However, there was at least one bright side. Looking over the various models of smartphones that had been introduced to the market by 2002 reveals that smartphone producers appeared to favor the Palm operating system over the Microsoft Pocket PC operating system—thus perhaps the move to smartphones would help resolve the operating systems standards battle in favor of Palm, and reduce the threat from competitors such as Compaq and Hewlett Packard (which based their products on Microsoft's operating system).

3.   **What will determine Handspring's success in this new industry? Does it have any sources of sustainable competitive advantage?**

Handspring's strengths going into this new industry are

- Its expertise and credibility as a personal digital assistant manufacturer,

- Its close relationship with Palm, and

- Its positioning as an employee productivity tool. All three of these factors give Palm an advantage in targeting corporate accounts (which would buy the smartphones for their employees) and mobile professionals who would buy the phone individually to improve their productivity and convenience. Handspring's expertise, credibility, and positioning probably did not help it to target the market of people who currently have a cellular phone but not a PDA. However, the close relationship with Palm (Handspring's founder had also founded Palm) might give it an advantage in the future. It might have better or earlier access to upgraded versions of the software, and it might have greater ability to develop applications that work well with the software.

While students will likely point out that Handspring does not have the manufacturing experience or scale of Nokia, Ericsson, Kyocera, etc., this may not matter that much as Handspring outsources all its of its production to Flextronics and Solectron (the instructor may wish to point out that Flextronics and Solectron are the two largest contract manufacturers in the world). Thus Handspring can take advantage of the greater scale and expertise of these dedicated manufacturers.

One key advantage Handspring may possess is pointed out in a quote in the case by John Troyer of Neomar: "I think it's a lot easier to put voice into a PDA than it is to jam a PDA into a phone." If it turned out that PDA companies were able to deliver a better product than phone companies, Handspring was well positioned. While Palm and RIM (Blackberry) were offering products that integrated some phone capabilities, neither were offering a true smartphone at the time of the case, making Handspring the leading PDA company in the smartphone market.

Areas where Handspring is at a marked disadvantage include

- Relationships with service providers

- Expertise in marketing to the mass market,

- Brand image with users who had not previously owned a PDA.

The latter is important to point out: while it may be easy to upgrade a PDA user to a Handspring smartphone because those users are more likely to appreciate Handspring's brand image and functionality, there are many cellular phone users that have relatively little awareness of Handspring, and little ability to discriminate among the PDA functionality offered by the various smartphone models. For these customers, price and battery power are likely to be very important features, which might make the Kyocera (which is less expensive) or the Nokia (which has ten hours of talk time) more attractive.

4. **Why did Handspring decide to discontinue development of its Visor line? Was this a good decision?**

This question raises the discussion to the corporate strategy level: Why has Handspring decided to abandon its Visor line? Students might offer some of the following reasons:

- *It was not making any money anyway*: price competition had chewed away the margins on the PDA models and the Visor was no exception. There may have been no sense in continuing to sink money into its development if it was not yielding profits.

- *Handspring needed to focus on smartphones*: perhaps Handspring wanted to make sure that development effort and expenses were all channeled into smartphones, to increase its likelihood of being able to successfully compete against industry giants like Nokia and Samsung who had much deeper pockets.

- *Handspring wanted to make a credible commitment*: by leaving the Visor line and turning exclusively to smartphones, Handspring was making a credible commitment to its employees, its customers, its alliance partners and its competitors that this was a market it was going to fight for. By putting "its back against a wall" it may have signaled employees that they needed to commit earnestly to the smartphone concept, and it may have prompted existing PDA customers to consider smartphones earlier than they would have otherwise. This move signals to alliance partners (such as service providers and application developers) that Handspring is serious about the smartphone concept and will not back out of the market, and it signals to competitors that it will not be easy to scare Handspring out of the market.

Other students will still argue that Handspring should have retained the Visor line to

- Increase their options

- Support existing customers who may be dismayed that there will be no continued development of Springboard modules for their visors

- Enable further market segmentation (i.e., there may be some activities that are better suited to a traditional PDA model, and development along that path could result in a unique market).

CASE 19

The Home Video Game Industry: From *Pong* to X-Box

SYNOPSIS OF THE CASE

This case depicts the birth and subsequent growth of the (home) video gaming industry. This industry is characterized by boom and bust cycles as well as continued technological innovation. The case begins with a description of the founding of Atari and its initiation of a new industry with the introduction of the video game *Pong* in the early 1970s. Initially designed to be played in arcades, Magnavox was the first to introduce a home version of *Pong* to be played on the TV. By 1976, the industry had attracted some twenty competitors and was now fiercely competitive. Fairchild's innovation of a system that could play more than one game revolutionized the industry. Atari responded with the 2600 System, which featured a console and plug in cartridge format. By 1979, Atari's 2600 System had two-thirds of the U.S. installed base. By 1982, the U.S. industry reached $3 billion in retail sales, and 17 percent of U.S. homes had a video game system. Then, the market collapsed to $100 million by 1985. Subsequently, the case depicts how Nintendo was able to rebuild the industry. The case closes with a description of the technological innovations that led to the introduction of 16-bit, 32-bit, 64-bit and finally 128-bit systems, with different companies innovating the respective technological breakthrough.

TEACHING OBJECTIVES

This case depicts repeated cycles of "creative destruction" as first movers enjoy temporary monopoly rents only to be replaced by competitors. The process of creative destruction in the home video industry is driven by technological innovation and strategic maneuvering. In particular, the case pursues the following teaching objectives:

1. To demonstrate the importance of innovation in creating a new industry (as Atari did).

2. To analyze technological innovation as the driver of industry revolutions.

3. To demonstrate the importance of first-mover advantages in a technology-driven industry.

4. To analyze the industry-life cycles each technology wave is going through with its subsequent impact on competitors.

5. To understand how to "make a market" based on the importance of an installed base (positive returns).

6. To discuss future strategies as the industry is facing continued innovation and threats from the PC as a device to play sophisticated home video games.

STRATEGIC ISSUES AND DISCUSSION QUESTIONS

1. **How did Nintendo successfully recreate the home video game business following the Atari-era boom and bust?**

    Industry began in 1972 with Atari's Pong. By 1979 Atari's 2600 VCS system, which featured a console and plug in cartridge format, had 2/3rds of U.S. installed base. By 1982 the U.S. industry reached $3 billion in retail sales, and 17% of U.S. homes had a video game system. Then, the market collapsed to $100 million by 1985.

    The rapid growth of Atari was due to:

    *   Price for hardware ($200) and cartridges ($25-$30) within reach of many families.

- Availability of hit *arcade* software (Pong, Pac Man, Space Invaders, Asteroids) drove demand. Arcade software with a customer following ported over to home system.

- Compatibility (through expansion modules) helped to build network externalities for all manufacturers (Atari, Mattel, Coleco).

The 1982-85 collapse can be explained by:

- Poor quality software flooding the market. There was no quality control on software development. Consumers got burnt purchasing poor quality products, and it turned them off the market. There was a real quality assurance problem when buying software. Basically anybody could write games to run on Atari generation machines, and so anybody did—including lots of fly by night operators looking to make a quick buck by flooding the market with poor quality games.

- The games did not advance. Two-dimensional simple games dominated the market. The players got bored.

In order to rebuild the industry, Nintendo made the following strategic decisions:

- The positioning strategy of Famicom (Japan) and NEC (U.S.) shifted price/functionality curve to the right based on the following:

  - The product exhibited high functionality in terms of superior graphics and speed.

  - The price was cheap at $100 per unit and helped built a large installed base. It undercut the competition by probably selling below cost to build up installed base.

  - The reason that the hardware was so cheap was that the microprocessors in the cartridges took on a lot of the processing work. In that sense, the hardware was incomplete.

  - In Japan, the Famicom looked more like a toy than a computer in order to generate mass-market appeal and open distribution channels.

  - In the United States the NES was designed to look more like a computer than a toy to create mass-market appeal.

  - Generous payment terms encouraged retailers to experiment with the product in the United States.

- Complementary product (software)

  - Coin-op video game Donkey Kong was already a huge success. When the game was ported over, customer loyalty transferred from arcade games to home video games.

  - Nintendo followed this with a series of other hits developed in-house including Super Mario Brothers (1985), The Legend of Zelda (1987), and Metroid (1987). These games offered a new level and complexity of game play, compared with prior offerings in the industry. They bought leading edge arcade games into the home.

  - Availability of other "quality" games through licensing strategy capitalized on network externalities. Licensees were eager to sign up because Nintendo had rapidly expanded installed base. By 1991 over 100 licensees and 450 titles were available for NES.

- Other Complementary Products

  - The Nintendo Power Magazine and The Wizard (the movie) helped build interest in games and stimulated purchases.

- Quality Control

  - Security chip and encryption technology ensured that only Nintendo approved cartridges could run on the system. This is a significant barrier to imitation. Copyright protection of micro-code embedded in chip is strong. It enables Nintendo to exercise tight control over supply of software and hardware.

- Software/content – licensees were limited in the number of game titles they could release (pushed them to focus on quality).

- Software/content – no excessively violent or sexually suggestive material was allowed. This appealed to the primary buyers—not the kids, but their parents.

- Software/content – minimum order of 30,000 units created incentive for licensees to write good games that will sell. This was the only way to be sure of recouping costs.

- Cartridge quality – licensees were required to place cartridge orders with Nintendo. This enabled Nintendo to maintain control over the quality of cartridges.

- Nintendo's Economic model

  - To make money on cartridge sales which retailed for $40. This is the classic razor and razor blade strategy where you make money on the razor blades (=cartridges) and give away the razor (= hardware) in order to create an installed base that is as large as possible. The transaction is backward loaded because Nintendo made 20% royalties on wholesale price ($30) of cartridges developed by others.

  - Moreover, licensees had to place orders through Nintendo for $14 per cartridge, yet they only cost $6-$8 to manufacture. So Nintendo took a 100% markup.

2. **How was Nintendo able to capture value from the home video game business?**

- Nintendo controlled the valuable asset—hardware and rights to produce games.

- Nintendo had power over retailers because

  - Nintendo limited supply. For example, in 1988 retailers requested 110 million cartridges and market surveys indicated that only 45 million could have been sold, but Nintendo only released 33 million. This drove up the price, and helped avoid the inventory problems experienced by Atari.

  - Retail Price Maintenance (RPM) strategy meant that retailers could not gain a larger share of the pie by discounting. This limited the share and hence power of any one retailer vis-à-vis Nintendo. The RPM strategy was abandoned in 1991 after a consent decree with the Federal Trade Commission.

  - In 1989 Nintendo accounted for 20% of spending on toys in the U.S. This gave them tremendous power.

- Nintendo had power over suppliers

  - Multiple sourcing lowered Nintendo's switching costs.

  - Ricoh (chip supplier) was very dependent on Nintendo.

  - Licensing agreements meant that all cartridge orders had to flow through Nintendo. Thus Nintendo was the gatekeeper.

  - All of the above translated into lower prices in favor of Nintendo.

- Nintendo had Power over Complementors, i.e. suppliers of games since

  - Security chip meant that Nintendo controlled access to the Nintendo compatible game market. It owned and manned the toll gate.

  - Nintendo was the only game in town.

  - Limiting licenses and number of games per licensee created scarcity value. Licensees were willing to pay a high royalty to gain access to a license.

  - In house software and game development expertise further limited dependence on outside developers and increased bargaining power of Nintendo.

- Nintendo lacked direct competitors because

    - Rapid build-up of installed base of hardware and software meant that Nintendo enjoyed positive network externalities. It had effectively pre-empted the competition. It was a monopoly.

3.   **How was Sega able to gain market share from Nintendo?**

Sega launched its 16-bit system in Japan in October 1988, and the United States in 1989. Initial acceptance was slow, but after 1991 sales picked up considerably in the United States. There is no doubt that Sega had some assets that NEC lacked, and its execution was superior. But one can also argue that Nintendo created a window of opportunity.

- Sega's Assets

    - A portfolio of successful arcade games.

    - Customer loyalty from arcade business means crossover potential to the home video market.

- Sega's Strategy

    - Combination of low price, particularly when bundled software is factored in, and enhanced functionality shifted price functionality curve to right. Thus Sega did to Nintendo what Nintendo did to Atari.

    - Low price/functionality helped build installed base.

    - Sega devoted its efforts to in-house game development to seed the market with games.

    - Drawing on its arcade experience, Sega was able to offer a library of "quality" games to solve chicken and egg problem (i.e. to jump start virtuous circle). Games included *Sonic the Hedgehog* and *Altered Beast*.

    - Software developers and retailers were hungry for an alternative to Nintendo.

    - Sega cleverly targeted a different demographic from Nintendo. While Nintendo was aimed at 7-12 year olds, Sega targeted 12-16 year old boys. This demographic had grown up with Nintendo, and now grown out of Nintendo games. They were looking for something more attune to their sensibilities, and Sega's gave it to them. For example, while the version of *Altered Beast* written for Nintendo was sanitized to reduce the violence, the version written for Sega's machine allowed players to rip the heads of their opponents, and added blood and gore.

    - Sega also created a buzz around its machine, with ad messages and the tag line "Sega does what Nintendo don't".

    - The 16-bit machine raised the level of game play, which appealed to users.

    - Even so, early acceptance was slow. It took the 1991 decision to lower price, bundle Sonic the Hedgehog software, and invest heavily in promotions to get the ball rolling.

- Nintendo opened up a window of opportunity for Sega:

    - Nintendo delayed the launch of its 16-bit offering, the Super NES, in the United States in order not to cannibalize its 8-bit product. In retrospect, this was a mistake. Nintendo should have cannibalized itself to stop Sega getting a hold. System was launched in Japan in November 1990, but they held off until September 1991 for the United States launch.

    - By late 1991, 125 games were available for Sega's Genesis while only 25 were available for Nintendo's Super NES. By 1993 Sega still led 320 to 130 game titles.

    - The Super NES was initially priced high compared to Sega.

    - Nintendo was ignoring competitors and focusing on on-line game networks.

Between 1990 and 1994 Nintendo saw its share of the home video market drop from 90% to 40%. Sega went from 5% to 60%.

4. **Evaluate the competitive strategy of 3DO? Given this strategy, how successful do you think 3DO is likely to be?**

    3DO's strategy

    - Capture the missing $17 billion of potential market share. This figure came from saying that since $5 billion spent on movies and $14 billion on video tape rentals, the $7 billion spent on arcade games should translate into $17 billion on home games, not the $3 billion spent in 1991.

    - Offer increased functionality by employing a new technology: 32 bit RISC microprocessor and CD-ROM storage technology as opposed to cartridges. Technology allowed for greater realism and more complex game play/visual and audio-environments.

    - License technology to hardware developers for free.

    - Charge $3 per disk royalty for development of complementary software. No restrictions on software licensees.

    - Thrust: Free hardware licenses should create incentive for multiple companies to enter hardware market. Low royalty rate and promise of technology should encourage software development. This should enable 3DO to rapidly build up an installed base and capture what the company over-optimistically believed would be a huge market of $17 billion.

    The *problems* with the strategy were:

    - 3DO cedes control over initial positioning strategy of both hardware and software. October 1993 launch by Matsushita based on premium price for hardware ($700) and software ($75). Way above comparable technology (Sega). In addition, Matsushita launched through high-end electronics retailers. Arguably should have been low priced machine launched through Toys R Us. Matsushita did better in Japan where it had a great retail network.

    - Another problem is that poor launch strategy can work against adoption of a technology. It becomes an uphill battle.

    - In addition, 3DO is competing against multimedia PCs with CD ROM drives, which are growing very rapidly. General purpose PC might not be as attractive as 3DO design, but its wide utility increases attractiveness.

    - Lack of installed base means that software for 3DO machines is slow in coming to market. Developers will do 16-bit stuff first for Sega and Nintendo, and CR-ROM stuff for multimedia PCs.

    - Also, higher software development costs increases the risk of developing for 3DO, while lack of installed base reduces the return.

    - 3DO has to resort to various maneuvers to try and regain control over marketing (e.g. $3 per disk surcharge placed on developers for marketing expense, giving manufacturers stock if they cut prices)

    Thus, it looks like 3DO is going to be locked out.

5. **Why did the Sony Play Station succeed, while 3DO failed?**

    The Sony PlayStation was based on the same basic technology as 3DO's system—a 32-bit RISC microprocessor and CD ROM storage technology. Yet while 3DO failed, Sony succeeded spectacularly. Reasons for this include:

    - Sony launched its 32-bit CD-ROM base system in fall 1995, two years after 3DO system. It was priced at $300 and offered 55 games in the first four months. In turn, Sega Saturn, a 32-bit machine came out six months earlier, priced at $400 and with only 10 games available at launch.

    - Sony lined up independent software developers.

    - Sony purchased a game development company and used this to develop games in-house (NFL Game Day). It was able to seed the market with games at launch time.

- Sony maintained control of hardware manufacture and positioning strategy.

- Sony had intellectual property from its film and music business that it could and did leverage to games (Sony owned Columbia Pictures).

- Sony targeted a different demographic than either Nintendo or Sega—18 to 34 year old males. These people had once owned Nintendo machines, then grown out of them and moved to Sega. Now they had grown out of Sega and wanted something more compelling. Sony gave it to them with offerings such as *Laura Croft Tomb Raider*, which appealed to the sensibilities of this demographic.

- Sony provided game developers with free software tools that reduced their costs of developing games for the PlayStation.

- Hardware was probably a loss leader. Sony makes profits from $9 royalty per disc. Discs are cheaper to produce than cartridges, although development costs are higher. If volume is there, this will bring down cost of software and expand market.

- Sony worked closely with retailers to find out their needs, and meet them. Retailers were now too dependent on Sega and were again looking for an alternative. Sony was a well-known brand name, and attuned to the needs of its channel.

6. **What drove Microsoft's decision to enter the industry with its X-box offering?**

Both offensive and defensive reasons lay behind Microsoft's entry into the industry.

Offensive Reasons:

- This is a large and growing market with global sales in excess of $10 billion annually.

- Growth in Microsoft's core PC business is slowing down. The PC industry is now mature. Microsoft needs a new growth driver and the home video game industry is one possibility for Microsoft.

- The industry is closely related to Microsoft's existing business. Home video game consoles are nothing more than specialized computers. Just like PCs, they need an operating system to run them, and Microsoft is of course a developer of computer operating systems. In addition, Microsoft has long been a force in the PC gaming industry with offerings such as Flight Simulator and Age of Empires. Entry into the home video game industry is a logical extension of Microsoft's existing software franchise.

- Microsoft can reduce the costs of developing a new home video game system by basing it on Windows technology, which in fact it has done. The operating system for the X-Box is nothing more than a stripped down version of Windows optimized for game playing.

- Because the X-Box is based on Windows technology, there is a huge base of third party developers who have long written applications for Windows (including PC games). These developers can now use that same knowledge base to write games for the X-Box.

- Microsoft has long had a strategy of trying to leverage its Windows technology so that it runs on a wide range of devices. The development of the X-box is consistent with the strategy of having Windows run on any computing device, anywhere and at any time.

- The X-box, like other 128 bit machines, is Internet enabled. Microsoft's vision of the future for gaming includes the possibility of more people playing multiplayer games online. Microsoft wants to ensure that those people use Microsoft technology to access games on the Internet, and one component of doing this is to make sure that the game machine itself is based on Microsoft technology. (Another component is to ensure that the servers on which some games reside, such as role-playing games, are also using Microsoft technology).

Defensive Reasons

- Increasingly, Microsoft sees Sony as a major competitor. Sony has moved into the digital arena with a vengeance, making and selling everything from desktop, laptop, and handheld computers, to cell phones, digital cameras, and game machines. Although some of these offerings use Microsoft software, such as the PCs, others do not—including the Sony PlayStation II, Sony cell phones, and Sony's handheld computers (which use a Palm operating system). Microsoft wants to constrain Sony's quest for digital dominance.

- Microsoft worries that the Sony PlayStation II is a "Trojan Horse" which is designed to gain control of computing in the living room. They reason that ultimately, the PlayStation II might be used not only to play games, but also to browse the web, send and receive e-mail, and engage in online commerce. The last thing Microsoft wants is a company like Sony to dominate this area with non-Microsoft technology. Hence Microsoft launched the X-box in part to try and check the rise of Sony as a digital company.

7. **What lessons can be learned from the history of the home video game industry that could have been used to help launch the Sony PlayStation II and Microsoft's X-Box? Do Microsoft and Sony appear to have learned and applied these lessons?**

The following lessons are key:

- Use a razor and razor blade strategy. Price the hardware at cost and make money on the software. Make sure that you can control the price of the hardware.

- Seed the market with good games to jump start demand for hardware and solve the industry's "chicken and egg" problem and establish a positive feedback loop. The more games out there, the greater the demand for hardware, and the greater the installed base of hardware, the greater the supply of games. Doing this with a new system requires that the hardware company develop some games in-house. It also requires that the company create incentives for third party developers to take the risks of writing games for an unproven system by, for example, offering more favorable royalty rates to game developers that commit early to a system.

- Demand is driven by high performance that brings more compelling game play to consumers. It is also driven by great games. Both must be there for success.

- Make sure that the quality of games is good. Protecting intellectual property rights can do this. Make sure that only approved third party developers are allowed to write games for the market.

- Make it easy for third party developers to write games. Provide them with software tools.

- Cannibalize your own product offering with next generation products, or have your competitors do it for you.

Both Microsoft and Sony seem to have learned these lessons well. Both followed this script closely when introducing their respective offerings.

CASE 20

Microsoft Windows Versus Linux

SYNOPSIS OF THE CASE

This case is concerned with strategies for winning a format war in the computer industry. Microsoft's Windows operating system has emerged as the dominant standard in the PC industry, including desktop computers and servers. However, recently the Linux operating systems has started to make headway in certain segments of the industry. Linux is a free operating system created by a team of self-organized community of developers. This community of computer hobbyists, scattered all over the world, and working without pay, has increased the functionality of Linux to a point where its reliability and features are on par with commercial operating systems. Its low cost and stability makes it an appealing alternative to Microsoft's Windows. As Linux builds momentum, Linux advocates, such as IBM, must decide what strategies to pursue to unseat Microsoft from its dominant position. Microsoft must decide what to do in order to keep the Linux movement in check.

TEACHING OBJECTIVES

The teaching objectives of this case are as follows:

1. To understand the importance of standards in technology-driven industries.

2. To understand the impact of a disruptive technology on incumbent firms.

3. To identify Microsoft's competitive advantage built on the virtuous cycle of the Windows operating system.

4. To examine the relative advantages and disadvantages of Linux vis-à-vis Windows.

5. To study the strategies being used by Linux and IBM to unseat Microsoft from its dominant position in operating systems.

6. To analyze the strategies Microsoft should pursue to prevent Linux from winning the format war.

STRATEGIC ISSUES AND DISCUSSION QUESTIONS

1. **Are their economic reasons why the personal computer market has standardized on a Windows operating system?**

    Network Economics can be used to explain the domination of the Windows operating system on personal computers (PCs). Network economics are said to be present in industries where standards or formats are required to ensure the compatibility of a product with its complements. In such industries, demand for the product is determined by the size of the "network" of complementary products and positive feedback loops tend to be present. The greater the installed base of a format like Windows, the greater the supply of complementary products, such as application software (games, word processors, spreadsheets, financial software) to run on Windows, and the greater the value of Windows to consumers, which tends to reinforce more demand for the operating system. Hence, as the installed base grows, positive feedback loops cause the market to standardize or "lock-in" on a single format.

2. **Is Linux a potentially disruptive technology? What are the advantages of Linux over Microsoft Windows? What are the disadvantages?**

    The Linux operating system is definitely a disruptive technology for Microsoft Windows because it represents a new paradigm for designing software and has the potential for changing the structure of the software industry. Overtime, disruptive technologies can grow in functionality and move into the mainstream markets to challenge incumbents.

Advantages of Linux over Microsoft Windows

- Low Price – The biggest advantage of the Linux operating system is that it is free and is available to anyone under a General Public License (GPL). Some companies (Red Hat, Caldera Systems, VA Linux) bundle Linux with other software programs on a CD, including a graphical user interface, and sell the CDs for a low price.

- Stability – Linux is much more stable than Windows resulting in less downtime, particularly in servers.

- Performance – According to the Transaction Processing Council, Linux is overtaking Windows 2000 in benchmarking tests running database servers.

- Linux can run on older hardware – The ability of Linux to run on aging hardware coupled with its low cost makes it a very attractive operating system for cost conscious companies.

Disadvantages

- Lack of applications – In the desktop as well as the server segments, the number of applications that exist for Windows (Microsoft Office, games, financial software enterprise application etc.) far exceeds the number available for Linux. The total domination of the PC market by Windows helps ensure that future applications continue to be written for Windows by developers.

- Lack of technical support – Since no company owns Linux, there is no technical support available for the operating system. Several companies that distribute Linux for a low price, like Red Hat, Caldera Systems and VA Linux, provide some support to their customers.

- Considered a "technical" system – Linux is not able to shake the image of being a "technical" operating system, much like UNIX, and the average PC user is uncomfortable with the idea of using it, even though a Graphical User Interface (GUI) exists for Linux.

- Complexity and ownership – The open source development paradigm that is built on voluntary cooperation among developers may not scale well to an increasingly complex and bulky code of the new Linux versions. With further growth it may no longer be possible for Torvalds to be the high priest making decisions on which developer's code is incorporated into Linux. In addition, as companies find ways of making profits from a free operating system, the Linux developer community that created the system may demand their share—a fight for ownership could ensue with Linux fragmenting into many incompatible versions.

3. **What are the switching costs that make it difficult for computer users to switch from Windows to Linux? Are these switching costs the same in all market niches, or are their niches where it is easier for Linux to gain market traction?**

    There exist significant switching costs that impact widespread adoption of Linux by Windows users. These costs may not have the same impact in all market niches.

    Enterprise server market

    According to survey by Gartner Group and IDC, the reasons that might make it difficult for users to adopt Linux in the enterprise server market (for enterprise resource planning, customer relationship management, supply chain management etc.) are:

    - A lack of enterprise applications

    - A lack of in-house skills in companies that want to adopt Linux

    - A lack of service and support options

    Application server market

    However, some of the switching costs mentioned above may not be an issue in the application server space. Servers that are used for specific dedicated services (email and messaging, authentication servers, firewall servers, web servers etc.) do have many Linux based applications and open source tools available. Reliability and low cost are the primary considerations driving adoption of Linux servers in this space.

Desktop Market

For Desktop users the costs of switching are the following:

- A very large percentage of applications (Microsoft Office, games etc.) are written for the Desktop Windows software. Linux users are not likely to find many choices in the applications that they can run on their Linux Desktop. In addition, though the Linux operating system is free, the applications themselves are not.

- Users are familiar with the Windows' Graphic User Interface (GUI). Linux does not yet offer any compelling features that Windows does not and hence, users do not have an incentive for learning to navigate the different and less user-friendly Linux GUI.

- There is no service or support for Linux users other than the developer community. Most laptops and PCs are not optimized for Linux and frequent problems may arise when users port Linux on their Desktop. Troubleshooting these problems requires a lot more computer literacy than the average user has.

Other market niches

Linux is finding some acceptance in the educational market. K-12 schools are able to build computer labs for students by using old Intel hardware and installing Linux on it. These labs cost a lot less to build and serve the basic student needs like work processing, spreadsheets, presentation software, email and Web browsing.

Linux can expect to be more successful in price sensitive markets like China and Central and Eastern European countries, which have low PC penetration rates. Since the use of Windows is not as widespread, the costs of adopting Linux are not as high as in PC mature markets like the United States. With Microsoft cracking down on software piracy in developing countries, users may gravitate even more toward Linux. However, a lack of applications is still a hindrance that Linux has to overcome in order to prevent domination of Windows in these markets.

4. **What do you think IBM's motives are in championing Linux?**

IBM has announced investments in Linux software development to the tune of $1 billion. IBM's motive in promoting Linux is to counter competition from both Sun and Microsoft's servers. IBM, which is positioning itself as an e-commerce company, is betting on Linux winning the format war in the server space and if that happens, Linux can then drive sales of IBM's eServer platforms for appliances and mainframes and to give a boost to its consulting and services business.

5. **What strategies is IBM pursuing to establish Linux as a viable alternative to Windows in the market place?**

In order to establish Linux as an alternative to Windows, IBM has put several investments in place. These investments include:

- $1 billion worth of investments in Linux software development, hardware, services, the open source community etc.

- A commitment of 1500 employees to work on Linux based hardware and software development.

- A deal to build the world's largest Linux supercomputer to analyze seismic data.

- Once Linux is ready to offer the same enterprise features that IBM's customers require from its commercial UNIX version (AIX), IBM is willing to discontinue its AIX offerings and replace them with Linux instead.

These investments are critical since they ensure a growing supply of complementary products which when combined with aggressive marketing and advertising might attain the critical mass required to make network effects work in favor of Linux.

6.   **What strategies might Microsoft pursue to check the rise of Linux?**

Microsoft, as the challenged incumbent, has everything to lose if Linux succeeds in establishing a place for itself. Microsoft can and is pursuing a number of strategies to thwart Linux's plans. Specifically, Microsoft could

- Give enterprise customers access to the Windows source code in order to address customers' deployment concerns and to boost customer confidence in the encryption and security features offered by the operating system.

- Increase offerings in the server arena—capitalize on strengths in enterprise application base.

- Try to win back the hearts and minds of the younger community of developers that have been enamored with Linux. Microsoft can do this by distributing the Windows operating system in Universities, colleges and schools.

- Counter Linux's price advantage by offering Windows at a lower price.

- Increase stability of the operating system. Windows 2000 and Windows XP are the right steps in this direction.

- "Overlook" the piracy of Windows software in developing countries in order to establish an installed base in those countries. As noted before, these countries tend to be more price conscious and Microsoft needs to not only protect, but also increase its installed base in these countries.

IBM Global Services: The Professional Computer Services Industry[1]

SYNOPSIS OF THE CASE

This case provides an introduction to the Professional Computer Services industry, the nature of competition in the industry including the players, and existing trends that are creating significant challenges for IBM Global Services (IGS), the world's largest Professional Computer Services provider. IGS supports a wide range of computer hardware and software products and provide services to help customers of all sizes realize the full value of information technology. IBM Global Services provides value through three primary lines of business: Strategic Outsourcing Services, Business Innovation Services and Integrated Technology Services, and has been very successful in increasing its revenue, broadening its range of service offerings, and building its pool of resources through acquisitions and alliances. As a leading provider of Professional Computer Services with more than 136,000 employees worldwide, in 160 countries, IGS markets all its services across these global markets.

While IGS is well positioned in the Professional Computer Services Industry, the company needs to make key strategic decisions to prevent erosion of its leadership status, especially since its recent financial performance has been disappointing. The case closes with Lou Gerstner, the CEO, and IBM executives pondering alternative strategies that could be pursued to take advantage of industry trends, and ensure continued growth and success for IBM Global Services.

TEACHING OBJECTIVES

The main teaching objectives of the case are:

1. To introduce the student to the professional computer services industry, including how it works and the strategic decisions required for success in this industry.

2. To develop specific strategies that will differentiate a company from the competition and enable it to win against specific competitors within the immediate, intermediate, and long-term frames.

3. To critically evaluate alternative courses of action that IBM Global Services can pursue.

4. To make recommendations to the management of IGS regarding future courses of action for the company.

STRATEGIC ISSUES AND DISCUSSION QUESTIONS

1. **What explains the prolonged period of rapid growth in the Professional Computer Services industry?**

    There are four major trends that are driving Professional Computer Services growth and are expected to do so through 2004:

    *   First, enterprises were linking business and Information Technology (IT) strategies as IT moves from the role of a support function to being a business enabler, and as it became clear that Internet technology could differentiate companies in the marketplace. This made businesses critically dependent on the strategic use of IT and Web technology. In particular, business executives were increasingly influencing IT decisions, and Chief Information Officers (CIO's) were more involved in strategic decision making.

    *   Second, this intense and sustained growth had triggered a serious shortage of skilled IT professionals, and this had ignited a war for talent among IT service providers. By 2001, an estimated 800,000 IT positions in

---

[1] Parts of this teaching note were prepared by Robert J. Mockler. Adapted by permission.

the US and Europe were unfilled for lack of qualified candidates, and fewer college graduates were choosing computer sciences.

- Third, services opportunities were expanding beyond the current scope of operations that service providers deliver and almost half (45%) of those opportunities came from Small and Medium Businesses (SMB). SMBs typically have simpler business and IT processes and while they are highly diverse and costly to reach, many, but not all, understand that the Web could enable them to compete with much larger firms on equal footing since everyone was just a click away on the Web. Therefore, SMBs represented a significant opportunity.

- Finally, Internet Technology was becoming pervasive which was driving customers to service providers for their expertise in transforming IT into a competitive advantage. E-commerce was still in its infancy, but its enormous potential compelled many companies to consider how Internet technology could expand and improve their businesses.

2. **What are the opportunities and threats facing IBM Global Services?**

Opportunities

- The increased consumption of computer services by foreign companies both in developed and developing countries, especially in Europe and Asia.

- The growth in the use of computer services by medium and small businesses.

- The explosive growth of the Internet and the continued advances in technology are forcing companies to seek outside help to keep pace with their competition.

- The emerging model of delivery technology and services on an as needed, pay as-you-go basis.

- The growing portion of company spending on Professional Computer Services at both the national and international levels as companies seek to concentrate on their core business and leave IT services to the companies that can do it best.

Threats

- Shortage of computer professionals, including programmers and system designers, impede growth and significantly increase labor costs.

- Outsourcing price war prompted by market share "buying."

- Decreased profits as computer services are viewed as commodities with companies viewing IT services as a utility.

- Increased competition as non-traditional computer services providers enter this segment, i.e. hardware manufacturers (HP).

- Economic down turn causing companies to decrease their overall IT expenditures, including Professional Computer Services.

- Increased competition brought about by the surge of alliances and acquisitions.

3. **Evaluate the competitive position of IBM Global Services. What are the key factors required for success in the Professional Computer Services industry? Compare IBM Global Services and its competitors on each key success factor.**

The rapid evolution of Information Technology was bringing increasing and ever-changing competition into this space, each would-be player hoped to snatch IBM Global Services' marketplace advantage. IBM Global Services faces fierce competition from four prevalent types of competitors:

- Consultants/Systems Integrators (like Accenture, formally Andersen Consulting)

- Full Services Providers (such as EDS and CSC)

- Local/Niche Providers (for example, NTT or ADP)

- Traditional IT Providers (like HP or Oracle, Sybase)

A common trend across all competitors was the focus on e-business. All four competitor types had shifted resources to the development and support of e-business solutions, and all had achieved some level of success. However, with the "dot.com" bust of mid- 2000, success was no longer a guarantee. Therefore, competition in this area was expected to be increasing strongly.

Consultants/Systems Integrators

This competitor type shared IGS' strengths in service offerings in several areas such as the ability to customize services to a specific industry need, provide both business and IT consulting services and the ability to provide a total, end to end solution. However, they had a distinct weakness since they were limited in the services provided, focusing solely on consulting and systems integration. They did not provide outsourcing services, an area that presented significant opportunity. This was especially true because businesses were implementing e-business solutions, and with the emergence of network computing, both were likely to lead to the growth of outsourcing services.

Full Service Providers

IGS fell within this competitor type since they provided a broad range of services. These competitors shared most of IGS' strengths. However, most did not enjoy IGS' strength in size (ability to command markets on a global basis), reputation for quality services, world-class support, same level of R&D investment resulting in industry-leading technologies, and the fact that one of IBM's core businesses was services, along with technology (hardware and software). The latter allowed IGS to be a true, end-to-end service provider and solutions developer.

Local/Niche Providers

This competitor type enjoyed excellent financial results and a strong outlook for future growth. However, this was due to their narrow focus on specific service types, typically computerized transaction processing, data communications, and information services for specific niche markets. They shared several of the strengths of IGS, good industry knowledge, very strong customer knowledge for the industry they supported, both large and SMBs. However, their narrow focus, although a strength, was also a weakness. They did not have the depth of services across multiple industries to be a serious competitor to a giant like IGS. Plus, local/niche providers typically expanded into new services or markets through acquisitions rather than through internal growth. It was believed that continued growth through acquisition for a company in this manner would become increasingly difficult over time, and may ultimately lead to the need for costly restructuring.

Traditional IT Providers

This competitor type shared IGS' strengths in service offerings in several areas such as the ability to customize services to a specific industry need, and the ability to provide a total, end-to-end solution. However, they had a distinct weakness since they were limited in the services provided, they were not major players in the areas of consulting and outsourcing. In addition, many were still deriving most of their revenue from their core businesses, typically hardware or software.

The main factors required for success have been listed in Table 1 for each segment of the Professional Computer Services industry. A comparison of IBM with its major competitor groups has also been provided in the same table. It can easily be seen that IBM is positioned much more advantageously as compared to its competition.

None of the above competitors is able to bring together the unique combination of e-business services, worldwide outsourcing capability and a potential foothold in the Small and Medium business market as could IGS. These factors differentiated IGS from the competition. This combination could be the foundation for capturing the "e-utility" market, the future of computer services.

4. **How would IBM Global Services' competition react to its domination of the market?**

One of the most significant trends in the computer services industry was convergence within the overall computer industry. Companies in diverse areas, computer hardware, software, information services, data communications, telecommunications, were rapidly forming alliances with each other through joint ventures, mergers, and acquisitions. These alliances allowed companies to integrate computer technology products with computer services so that they can offer a greater selection of products and services (services within all three segments). A key objective of these alliances was to remain viable in an increasingly competitive national and international marketplace.

These alliances were designed to ensure the participating firm's competitiveness in the market place by offering business and residential consumers a broader range of high quality products and services. Alliances and acquisitions also offered the ability to increase a company's skilled resources without the need for extensive training of existing or newly hired resources. This strategy also offered the opportunity to increase revenues by acquiring the other company's markets and service offerings.

Therefore, it was clear that the competitive response to IBM Global Services' further development, and possible domination of e-business services, and its expansion of outsourcing services to the European and Asian markets, would be increased alliance and acquisition activity. This would be especially true of the Full Service Providers and Traditional IT Providers.

These larger companies would likely be forming alliances and making acquisitions with smaller, more obscure companies, Local/Niche Providers, and Consulting/Systems Integration Providers.

In addition, EDS stated that it was a strong competitor to IGS' outsourcing leadership. This was based on a strategy of aggressively buying outsourcing market share by over-paying for the infrastructure involved in an outsourcing deal, or underbidding the contracts. Other competitors may follow the lead if EDS is successful, thereby touching off a price war, particularly if IGS is successful in increasing its market share in Europe and Asia. In contrast, it is IGS' position that when putting together an outsourcing deal, it is imperative that they protect the interests of both IGS and the customer. They seek to maintain an acceptable level of profitability while guarding the customer's investment by ensuring IGS' ability to deliver a full range of quality services throughout the life of the contract. That is a win-win philosophy. This is contrasted by EDS' short-term approach of capturing market share, risking profitability, quality and customer satisfaction.

5.   **What are the alternatives confronting IBM Global Services? Evaluate each alternative.**

Alternative 1

IBM Global Services will focus exclusively on e-business solutions leveraging its existing mind share (e-business brand recognition) and research capabilities and reputation for quality. Customer focus will be on large enterprise customers, worldwide, who offer significant opportunity as these customers move through the e-business continuum (from a web presence to supporting all aspects of their business on the web). This customer set is best supported by IGS' existing dedicated sales force. They will seek acquisitions that will build their e-business competency by focusing on premier e-business software and integration providers. Their promotion strategy will focus on e-business to build brand recognition and market share.

This alternative represents a significant change in IBM Global Service's service strategy. The explosive growth of the Internet and the associated demand for e-business services make this alternative appealing. It potentially provides an opportunity for IBM Global Services because it was estimated that over 50% of large companies were still in the early stages of web adoption as of 2000 and were still not leveraging the full power of the Internet for transaction processing and delivery services, which is the basis of e-business. This targeted focus is not likely to dilute IGS resources across multiple service lines, especially custom application development which this alternative would abandon. This is supported by the fact that e-business revenue grew more than 70 percent to approximately $5 billion in 2000, with expected strong growth in subsequent years.

This focus is expected to allow IGS to concentrate resources, thereby addressing the skills shortage issue, and will allow them to win against the competition that does not have the same name recognition with e-business as IGS enjoys.

One drawback of this alternative is that IGS would be losing potential future revenue from traditional professional computer services sources. In addition, often customers contracted for other services contract their existing service provider as they migrate to e-business. Another drawback is that the strategy does not recognize the significant opportunity presented by the Small and Medium Businesses, especially in the area of e-business.

Alternative 2

IBM Global Services will continue to provide a full range of Professional Computer Services in the areas of consulting, systems integration and outsourcing. They will expand their customer focus to include all customer opportunities, worldwide, with a renewed emphasis on the difficult, but potentially profitable small and medium businesses. IGS will leverage the three sales and distribution channels they currently have, dedicated sales force, direct marketing, independent distributors, superior technology and research. They will support this expansion by seeking acquisitions to immediately gain skilled resources. Their promotion strategy will focus on building brand recognition and market share across all service opportunities.

This alternative is primarily one of maintenance with subtle changes in IGS' customers, with an emphasis on Small and Medium Businesses (SMBs) and use of Sales and Distribution to support this customer sector. It is expected to provide an opportunity for IBM Global Services because it was estimated that the global computer services industry would continue growing at a compound annual rate of 11% through 2004. The growing proportion of spending on professional services relative to spending in the information technology market overall, both at the national and international level, also represents a significant opportunity. In addition, maintaining, supporting, and integrating information technology, computer services, and telecommunications in a multi-vendor environment generate a greater demand for computer services, such as consulting or outsourcing. IGS is uniquely suited to address these requirements with its full range of services (consulting, systems integration and outsourcing) making it better than the competition.

IGS' competition does not have the same breadth and depth of services that IGS enjoyed and they all face the increased demands of their customers to provide both customizable, all in one solutions for large customers and at the same time provide standardized solutions at a competitive price.

A major drawback with this strategy is that this is an attempt by IGS to be all things to all customers with this broad range of offerings markets to both large companies and SMBs. Another drawback was the difficulty in supporting SMBs.

Alternative 3

This alternative is a mix of alternatives 1 and 2. According to this alternative, IBM Global Services will provide a full range of Professional Computer Services in the areas of consulting, systems integration and outsourcing with an emphasis on e-business, network computing and the future "network economy." They will expand their customer focus to include all customer opportunities, worldwide, especially Europe and Asia. In particular, they will emphasize on the difficult, but potentially profitable small and medium businesses.

IGS will take advantage of its superior technology and research capabilities across all technology platforms (mainframe, client/server with an emphasis on business) to build upon its current success. It will leverage the three sales and distribution channels they currently have, dedicated sales force, direct marketing and independent distributors. They will support this expansion by seeking acquisitions to immediately gain skilled resources and build their e-business competency by focusing on premier e-business software and integration providers. Their promotion strategy, a multimedia approach, will focus on building brand recognition and market share across all service opportunities.

They will execute acquisitions to support this strategy thereby immediately acquiring skilled resources. They will also execute acquisitions to support this strategy with emphasis on e-business service providers. In order to address the shortage of skilled Information Technology professionals, IGS will implement changes to its management system to include signing bonuses, an aggressively employee stock option plan covering the skill areas it is seeking to attract and retain, and programs to enable resources to realize their business and professional potential.

The opportunity for IBM Global Services because both the Small and Medium Businesses segment as well as e-business services are expected to be growth areas. This strategy would also not limit the targeted services, as did alternative 2. IGS would provide a full range of services from the traditional of client/server and enterprise systems (mainframes), to the emerging e-business, and the future network computing. As noted before, competition is not in a position to offer the full range of services that IGS can.

Drawbacks of this strategy are the same as the drawbacks for alternatives 1 and 2. One drawback is the over-extension of the company's resource to attempt to be all things to all clients. The size of the company has been a weakness before, offering too broad a range of services that could impact negatively IGS' speed in bringing new services to market, plus further the impact of the IT resource shortage. Another drawback is the difficulty in supporting SMBs. In addition, offering such a broad range of services increases the cost required to build and maintain the required skills, central delivery centers, facilities and equipment, especially as they grow their outsourcing presence in Europe and Asia.

6.   What would be your recommendation to the executive team at IBM?

Students may offer different alternatives as recommendations with justifications. Alternative 3 seems to work best for IGS since it has to pay close attention to both, the opportunity in SMBs in the traditional side of the business as well as seek to establish its position as an e-commerce company.

The strategy selected builds a foundation for the future. A future expected to be based on the emerging model of the "network economy" or "e-utility." It accomplishes this by leveraging IBM Global Services' strengths. This strategy uses IGS' e-business brand recognition, converting it into market share. It grows IGS' customer base to include the huge opportunities available within the Small and Medium Business market, and expanding their outsourcing services into the European and Asian markets. This strategy also addresses the problem of attracting and retaining the required skilled resources to ensure the successful execution of this expansion. By doing this, IBM Global Services will differentiate itself from the competition through its extensive e-business service offerings, skills and expertise, outsourcing experience and commitment, and most of all, global reach across all service offerings.

IBM Global Services will be providing a broad range of service choices for companies of all size. They will be in a position to help align their customers' business strategies with industry leading technology solutions, delivering the skills, experience and innovative thinking required. This alternative is better then the other two since it builds upon IGS' strengths, expands its customer base and drives the company toward the future of network computing and the "network economy" or "e-utility." This represented the next major opportunity for IGS, the emerging model of delivering technology and services on an as-needed, pay-as-you-go basis. IGS will be building worldwide data center capacity through its outsourcing expansion, and capturing the Small and Medium Businesses which was expected to be the main drivers for this new model. This was expected to drive a new emerging world economy, calling attention to the distinct economic behaviors that result from global interconnection of information systems.

Information Technology had become a key driver of business success, as a result, CEOs and CIOs were joining forces, working together to build growth strategies in an environment where success depended in a large part on the right combination of IT skills and business acumen. From the boardrooms to the IT departments, executives were realizing the competitive advantage of securing the right third party Professional Computer Services expertise to help align their companies technology with their short and long term business goals. As the world's largest Professional Computer Services provider, IBM Global Services had the knowledge; experience and breadth of capabilities to help companies of all sizes overcome e-business challenges, realize the power of technology and seize new opportunities. This will uniquely position IGS relative to its competition. This strategy brings together the unique combination of e-business services, worldwide outsourcing capability and a foothold in the Small and Medium business market. This combination will be IGS' foundation for capturing the future "e-utility" market.

#	Keys to Success	Weight	IGS	Consultants/ Sys. Integrators 1	Full Service Providers 2	Local/ Niche Providers 3	Traditional IT Providers 4	Compare Weight 1	Compare Weight 2	Compare Weight 3	Compare Weight 4
2	Targeting customer segments with the greatest growth potential through strong market intelligence.	2	Good	Strong	Good	Strong	Good	-	0	-	0
	Large Corporations										
3	Ability to provide a customizable, all-in-one solution.	1	Strong	Strong	Good	Weak	Good	0	+	++	+
4	Demonstrate a proven track record in meeting the specific needs of that customer.	2	Strong	Strong	Strong	Weak	Good	0	0	++	+
	Medium & Small Corporations										
5	Ability to provide standardized solutions at a competitive price.	1	Strong	Good	Good	Strong	Good	+	+	0	+
	Government Institutions										
6	Knowledge of and ability to leverage bureaucracy.	2	?	?	Good	?	?	?	?	?	?
	Non-Profit Organizations										
7	Ability to provide standardized solutions at a competitive price.	3	?	?	?	?	?	?	?	?	?
C.	**Markets**										
1	Maintain and grow market share by servicing diverse markets, geographic and industry specific.	2	Strong	Good	Good	Good	Good	+	+	+	+
D.	**Sales / Distribution**										
1	Control sales costs by applying appropriate sales channel to customer segment.	1	Good	?	?	?	?	?	?	?	?
	Professional Sales Force										
2	Strong industry and technical knowledge.	1	Strong	Good	Good	Good	Weak	+	+	+	++
	Direct Marketing										
3	Extensive network of telemarketing centers.	1	Strong	?	?	?	?	?	?	?	?
4	Internet presence providing catalog of services, purchasing and customer service functions.	1	Good	Good	Good	Weak	Good	0	0	+	0

Competitor Groups · Comparison

Keys to Success	Weight	IGS	Competitor Groups				Comparison			
			Consultants/ Sys. Integrators 1	Full Service Providers 2	Local/ Niche Providers 3	Traditional IT Providers 4	Compare Weight 1	Compare Weight 2	Compare Weight 3	Compare Weight 4
5 Ensure customers have ready access to person when needed.	2	Strong	Weak	Good	?	Good	++	+	?	+
Business Partners										
6 Develop strong relationship with partners through offering wide range of services and offering incentives.	1	Strong	Good	Good	Weak	Good	+	+	++	+
E. Technology Platform										
1 Ability to build new solutions based on current and future technology platforms.	1	Strong	Good	Strong	Strong	Good	+	0	0	+
2 Investment in strong R&D to ensure continuous flow of new services based on emerging technologies.	1	Strong	Good	Good	Good	Good	+	+	+	+
F. Acquisitions & Alliances										
1 Increase skilled resources without extensive training through acquisitions & alliances.	2	Strong	?	?	?	?	?	?	?	?
2 Boost revenue growth through strategic acquisitions & alliances.	2	Strong	?	Good	Good	?	+	0	+	?
3 Increase breadth of service offerings through strategic acquisitions & alliances.	2	Strong	?	Good	Good	?	?	0	+	?
G. Management System										
1. Effective management system and corporate culture to attract and maintain skilled resources.	1	Good	Weak	?	?	?	+	?	?	?

Note: The Compare Weight is the result of comparing the strength of the company under study with the strength of each competitor group. For example, if the company is rated strong and the competitor weak, the rating would be ++. Where the company is strong and the competitor group is strong, the rating would be 0.

CASE 22

SAP and the Evolving Web Software ERP Market

SYNOPSIS OF THE CASE

The case chronicles the inception and growth of SAP as one of the world's leading Enterprise Resource Planning software developer and its subsequent problems with strategy implementation in a highly competitive and uncertain market.

SAP was founded by five IBM engineers to develop cutting edge software to provide companies with a standardized IT platform which would provide these companies with complete information about all aspects of their business processes across functions and divisions, help lower the cost structure, improve responsiveness to the customer and manage business process more efficiently.

SAP grew rapidly to become the market leader in ERP solutions because of its R&D competencies, which resulted in a product far superior to the competition. However, the company faced significant implementation problems because of a lack of a formal organizational structure. By the time it put a centralized, formal structure in place, the environment changed to favor web based ERP software attracting intense competition from other software companies. In the new, dynamic environment, SAP not only had to move quickly to develop competencies in web based ERP software, it also had to change its authority and control structure to suit the new mySAP.com strategy. Whether SAP will be able to maintain its leadership position in the new, dynamic market remains to be seen.

TEACHING OBJECTIVES

The main teaching objectives of this case are as follows:

1. To illustrate the problems encountered in managing a growing entrepreneurial company that requires professional management.

2. To underscore the importance of implementation in strategy making.

3. To understand the web computing environment and how it is changing the rules of the game.

STRATEGIC ISSUES AND DISCUSSION QUESTIONS

1. **What are the main elements of SAP's business-level strategy? What are SAP's main strengths and weaknesses? How did the nature of its culture affect its strategy?**

   In terms of business level strategy SAP followed a focus strategy through a differentiation approach. SAP's Enterprise Resource Management software was the first of its kind and was different from other products in the market in that it provided a state-of-the-art, standardized solution to the business process problems facing companies in many different industries. The solution spanned the entire value chain of a company's operations as opposed to competitor products that focused on specific business process problems. Since SAP's solution was the most comprehensive one available, it was able to charge a premium price for it.

   SAP's' initial focus was on the market niche comprising of the largest multinational companies with revenues in excess of $2.5 billion. This customer segment gained the most from an integration tool like ERP and could afford to pay SAP a premium price for the product. With its 3rd generation ERP solution introduced in the early 1990s, SAP also began to target small and medium companies.

   SAP sought to build its technical competencies through a focus on R&D in order to deliver a superior product as compared to its competitors. In order to develop an installed customer base as quickly as possible, SAP outsourced about 80% of the implementation services required by its clients to external consultants such as IBM, Accenture, and Cap Gemini.

Strengths – SAP's main strengths are:

- A technically superior product as compared to competitors – In particular, the product offered standardized, state-of-the-art features; it spanned many business process problems across a variety of value chain activities and was multilingual. The second generation of the product offered many more modules that could handle not only accounting and finance but also procurement, product development, order tracking and inventory. The software also offered seamless connectivity to databases and communication systems throughout an organization. Every generation of the software offered improvements and a host of features.

- Strong R&D – SAP's product strength was a result of its strong R&D. SAP spent as much as 27% of its revenues on R&D.

Weaknesses – SAP also had a few weaknesses. Specifically these were:

- Sales and marketing – building these competencies took a backseat in the company because of the belief that a superior product would sell itself.

- Consulting – SAP did not consider investment in consulting in installation services as an important component of its strategy and so it began outsourcing 80% of its installation services. As a result, other companies became experts at installing and customizing SAP's software and SAP lost a potential revenue stream. SAP was also not able to keep in close touch with its customers and their needs and problems and lost an opportunity to collect feedback from customers about their experiences with SAP's product.

- Lack of corporate infrastructure – SAP's entrepreneurially minded management team did not have the experience required to build a corporate infrastructure that would allow a smooth implementation of strategies in a rapidly growing company. A lack of infrastructure was one of the main reasons for SAP's subsequent problems.

SAP's choice of strategy was largely influenced by the culture of the company. SAP's culture was based on the engineering mindset of its founders. The values and norms of the company emphasized technical innovation and development of leading edge ERP software as the core goal of the company. The SAP culture underscored the belief that R&D would be the source of competitive advantage and it spent a significant part of its revenues on R&D. This engineering and technical mindset also blinded the management to the importance of strengthening sales and marketing capabilities. The focus on the product led to a neglect of the consulting and training businesses within the company.

2. **What opportunities and threats did SAP encounter in the 1990s? How did it change its strategy in response to those threats?**

Opportunities

- Switching costs – Once ERP software has been enabled for a customer, the nature of the customer's business processes changes significantly and changing over to another ERP software is very difficult, time consuming and expensive. This ensured that companies that had SAP's products running on their systems were less likely to switchover to a different ERP system. The fact that SAP was very successful in penetrating the market with its third generation product, R/3, protected it from the competition.

- Demand – During the early 1990's demand for ERP software grew at an explosive rate. This was an opportunity at the time since there were very few players offering ERP software. Another opportunity was the revenue potential from businesses smaller than SAP's niche market.

Threats

- Development of Internet and Broadband technologies – The effect of these technologies was to make companies view their boundaries differently. While SAP provided software that integrated only the internal business processes of a company, advances in Internet technologies made it possible for companies to interact with their customers and their suppliers in new ways through many different channels, thus creating a need to improve ERP solutions that would account for these new kinds of transactions.

- Growing Web-based software arena where SAP did not have any competencies.

- Increasing competition from clients like Oracle as well as from smaller companies that were earlier niche players in different software application segments wanting to break into the web software business. These companies tried to gain market share by exploiting weaknesses in SAP's software by offering systems that were more easily customizable, or had a lower cost than SAP software.

- Slackening demand in the late 1990s – Due to the complexity of the software and the fact that about 80% of the software was still standardized, created problems for SAP. First, customers did not like to change their business processes to suit SAP's "best practices". Second, complexity of the software made it difficult and expensive to install and most businesses were reluctant to pay the high costs. This fact coupled with availability of comparative products at lower prices led to a slackening of demand for SAP's solutions.

Change in strategy

- Client base – Realizing the potential of small business clients, SAP ensured that its third generation ERP software, R/3, could not only be customized for multiple industry needs, but could also be configured to suit the needs of small customers. Thus, its strategy shifted to that of differentiation.

- Product design – Open architecture was one of the most important changes SAP made to the product design. An open architecture allowed SAP's software to be used with any kind of software or hardware that the company was using. In addition, prior to R/3, SAP offered a standardized system and customers had to change their business processes in order to be compatible with SAP's "best practice" solutions. To avoid the resultant implementation problems, SAP introduced some customization capabilities with the launch of R/3 that allowed customers to change 20% of SAP's software to work with their existing systems. This made it quicker and easier for companies to learn about and implement the new SAP system and SAP was able to target a wider range of customers.

3. **What major implementation problems arose in SAP over time? Why do you think it experienced these problems?**

SAP's implementation problems were largely due to the decisions it made regarding its organizational structure and human resource management. More specifically,

- In the early 1990s, SAP had decentralized its marketing, sales and installation services to foreign subsidiaries, while keeping R&D centralized. The rationale was to make regional subsidiaries responsible for all installation, training and customization of software to meet the needs of customers in that region. This led to problems as the subsidiaries followed inconsistent policies regarding pricing of products, responding to customer complaints and training of consultants. These inconsistent procedures resulted in poor customer responsiveness, poorly trained consultants and a lack of organizational learning between its subsidiaries.

- In addition, SAP did not invest in development of its employees. Its human resource management was outsourced, there was no reward system and employees did not have well-defined career paths. The result was that SAP began losing its key people to the competition.

SAP's decentralization strategy was a reflection of its entrepreneurial roots—delegation of control to lower levels and empowering subsidiaries had created an open culture that spurred innovation, risk taking through trial and error and motivated, hard working employees who worked well in teams. However, the company's approach was also a very informal one and it did not translate well to SAP's rapidly increasing size.

SAP's culture valued innovation and technical superiority of the product and neglected all other aspects of managing a company. The value created by a superior product was being dissipated since the company did not have any means of assigning people to their tasks and integrating the activities of different functions and subsidiaries. It needed to put a formal structure in place to implement its strategies effectively and create a sustainable competitive advantage.

4. **Why did competition increase in the ERP industry in the mid 1990s and beyond?**

During the mid 1990s the opportunities presented by the ERP industry were enormous. The emergence of web based software technology made it easy for many small software companies to enter the ERP market and they chose to take advantage of the opportunity that existed in this market.

New software companies that operated in niche segments like intranets, supply chain management, customer relationship management, and website hosting and development started to expand into SAP's territory by providing modules that competed with parts of SAP's R/3 ERP solution.

Moreover, the weak economy in 2000 and 2001 also led to software companies moving outside of their traditional areas in order to survive.

5. **How has SAP responded to the threat of new competition, what is its new strategy? How successful do you think it will be in the future?**

SAP's response to the threat of new competitors was manifested in mySAP, a comprehensive e-commerce platform. The main elements of SAP's mySAP.com strategy are:

- Making mySAP an online portal and provide a total solutions ERP package instead of ERP components. Part of this package would be a range of products like Supply Chain Management and Customer Relationship Management solutions. The platform would allow customers to customize SAP software to their needs.

- Providing a platform scalable and flexible would ensure SAP's product offerings expand over time as technological development makes new applications possible.

- Focusing on lowering prices of SAP's software to make it more attractive against the competition. SAP has also tried to break up its modules into smaller pieces, so that it is easy for the customers to pick modules that they need.

- Making SAP software compatible with as many operating systems (Microsoft NT, Sun's Java and Unix) and web based application software from different software makers. This was done in keeping with the "open architecture concept".

- Alliances and Acquisitions – In order to bring new mySAP products to market quickly, SAP chose to partner with companies with which it had mutual synergies. For example it formed an alliance with Commerce One, a B2B marketplace software provider, to share common resources and development costs and enter the B2B e-commerce market. It also joined hands with IBM to develop a product Lifecycle Management software in order to capture a base of manufacturing companies. SAP acquired Top Tier Software in 2001, to gain access to its iViews technology that further enabled SAP's open systems architecture by allowing customers to seamlessly integrate SAP and non-SAP platforms. SAP's also entered the web hosting and maintenance services market through a partnership with Yahoo.

With its mySAP.com platform, SAP has certainly moved in the right direction. However, it faces significant challenges—Microsoft and Oracle pose a formidable challenge to its software; it has to convince the small and medium businesses that its software is easy and inexpensive to install and use; another challenge is to convert non-SAP users to mySAP.com. However, a plus point is that ERP in general is not going to fade away—organizations that have had successful ERP implementations have seen the positive results. SAP is the market leader and in spite of the intense competition, as long as it keeps innovating and adding new features to its software, it can potentially enjoy a sustainable competitive advantage.

6. **Why is Microsoft emerging as a potential threat to SAP?**

Microsoft's is emerging as a potential threat to SAP because of its decision to compete in the small and medium ERP web software segment. Microsoft has already bought two companies to augment its offerings in the segment and has broad competencies in software development that allow it to mobilize the resources required to develop web based ERP solutions relatively quickly. Microsoft's move into Small and Medium Enterprise ERP software puts it on the path to direct competition with SAP and Oracle.

7. **How did SAP change its structure to help support its changes in strategy?**

The mySAP initiative had led to an increase in overhead costs and SAP's centralization strategy adopted in the mid-1990s had made SAP slow to respond to the fast changing web-software ERP environment. In order to be more responsive to the customer, SAP started to move back toward a decentralized organizational structure by allowing employees to manage problems where and when they arise. In conjunction with the above change, SAP also implemented its own applications software in order to integrate its different divisions. This was intended to help prevent problems that decentralization might pose.

In order to make the software development process faster, SAP divided its central German team into the following three groups:

- A team to develop new products and features.

- A team to refine and update all its functions in existing products.

- A team to work on making SAP software easier to install.

In 2000, SAP centralized its global marketing operations at its U.S. subsidiary so that co-ordination across all mySAP product groups, and across all world regions could take place without wasting time and resources.

MySAP product lines were split into groups of related products and each group was treated as a profit center. A large part of the engineering development work was done inside the mySAP product group so that the sales persons and the engineers were able to work together and design a product closely matching customer needs.

Globally, SAP divided its operations into 3 main world regions: Europe, Asia/Pacific and the Americas. This made it easy to co-ordinate the marketing and training efforts, to manage relationships with consulting companies, to transfer knowledge and information between countries, and serve national markets better.

SAP currently has a loose matrix form structure that helps them be responsive to the customer, boost efficiency, achieve greater market penetration and increase internal flexibility.

CASE 23

Iridium: Communication for the New Millennium[1]

SYNOPSIS OF THE CASE

Iridium began in 1987 as a project conceived by three Motorola engineers. Their proposal was to build a global satellite telecommunication system that would enable individuals to call from anywhere on earth, at any time. The project's price tag would be $5 billion. The project inspired sufficient confidence of public and institutional investors to raise initial funding, so Motorola spun it off as a separate company that would then use Motorola as its primary contractor for developing and constructing the system. The potential customers that stood to gain the most from the service were those that worked in remote locations such as those employed in mining, oil exploration, etc. However Motorola was counting on also attracting the mass market to the product (particularly business travelers) in order to generate enough volume to make the service viable.

The satellites were launched in May of 1998. However, by April of 1999 the service had only attracted 10,230 voice customers and 2,000 pager customers. The handsets were bulky and expensive, and the service charges were considerably higher than those for terrestrial cellular systems, making it hard to attract mass market customers. Worse still, two other satellite service companies were launched at almost the exact same time as Iridium, making it extremely difficult for any of the companies to secure a critical mass of customers. By the summer of 1999, it was clear revenue goals were not going to be met and the company was in trouble.

TEACHING OBJECTIVES

The teaching objectives of this case are as follows:

1. Exploring the roles of network externalities, minimum efficient scale, industry analysis, strategic positioning, first mover advantages (and disadvantages), and project valuation methods.

2. Consider such topics as real options, and alternative methods of finance and governance for new projects.

STRATEGIC ISSUES AND DISCUSSION QUESTIONS

External Analysis

*   Existing Rivalry

    The global satellite voice market consisted of only a few players: Iridium, Globalstar, and ICO Global. Each had large initial capital investments ($2.2 billion for Globalstar, $3.5 billion for ICO Global, and $5 billion for Iridium). Each sold satellite voice service and attempted to differentiate their products through different types of service plans, resulting effectively in their competing almost purely on price. They were also essentially competing against terrestrial cellular service providers, since by 1999 terrestrial cellular service provided more than adequate global coverage for the average wireless voice customer. Though none of the companies met their revenue goals, huge capital investments made them reluctant to exit the industry.

*   Threat of Entry

    It was not easy for a company to enter the global voice arena. Each of the companies had major backers (such as Motorola, Lockheed Martin, Loral Space System, Qualcomm, and NEC) that had long been involved in the space and/or telecommunications industries. The tremendous development costs would

---

[1] This teaching note was prepared by Melissa A. Schilling. Adapted by permission.

require a potential entrant to endure major losses in the early stages of the company. Additionally, licenses to operate such a satellite system would have to be approved by countries all over the world, prolonging the development stage further.

- Bargaining Power of Buyers

Customers in this industry can be broken into 2 segments, telecommunication service providers, and individual end users. Cellular service providers were consolidated into large regional and national players that would have significant bargaining power due to their size, and ability to tap their large installed bases. Providers such as Sprint also marketed their own terrestrial-based wireless services. Due to the differences in the technologies and the huge development costs involved, there was almost no threat of a cellular service provider backwardly integrating into its own satellite service. However, a cellular service provider could opt to not offer satellite service at all.

End users could be segmented into two primary groups, the specialized industry workers and the international business travelers. International business travelers could use other substitutes such as traditional cellular service. Workers in specialized industries had few choices if their isolated workplaces required the use of satellite phones. However, these people made up only 3% of the workforce in the U.S. (there is no data in the case to determine what percentage of the global population works in remote areas). Once a customer had chosen a satellite phone service, they faced high switching costs due to the price of the handsets.

- Bargaining Power of Suppliers

Iridium's primary supplier was Motorola, who supplied satellite and gateway hardware through the operating contracts. Motorola would have had tremendous bargaining power over Iridium, but it was also very vested in the success of the project due to its ownership share. Both Motorola and Kyocera supplied handsets to the company. Since the handsets had to be designed to work with the system, Iridium and its suppliers faced major switching costs. Iridium's reliance on only a few suppliers backfired when Kyocera was unable to deliver quality phones.

- Threat of Substitutes

GSM-based cellular phones posed a very credible (and much less costly) substitute. Although service was not available globally, the GSM system had been implemented in almost all major cities, and in more than 100 countries. Assuming that international business travelers primarily conducted their business in major cities, a GSM phone would be sufficient to keep them in touch with the home office at a much lower price per minute. The rapid growth of coverage for these phones posed a major threat to the satellite service. Since GSM phones were much more affordable, satellite phones only appealed to the select individuals requiring telecommunications in remote areas.

- Other Factors

A primary issue driving the success and failure of the satellite phone systems was the role of network externalities. The larger the installed base of phones, the more useful (and less expensive) they would be. The value of a global satellite service increased with the number of users it connected, and the development and operating costs could be amortized over a larger customer base, enabling the companies to decrease their prices. Furthermore, if a company attracted more subscribers, it would also attract complementary goods providers that develop handsets and pagers, leading to better technology, more innovative products, and lower prices. Thus if a company could obtain a significant initial installed base, it should reap increasing returns to size. Unfortunately, getting that initial installed base proved much more difficult than had been expected. Had the service been launched much earlier—before terrestrial cellular service had secured abundant global coverage—the perceived value of the service would have been far greater, and would likely have attracted many more customers. Unfortunately, by 1999, cellular service had considerable global coverage.

Additionally, had only one company been launched to provide global satellite service, it may have been able to attract more customers both because the market share would not have been fragmented among different companies, and because there might have been less customer ambiguity about which service to adopt. Unfortunately, with three major companies targeting the market at the same time, it was almost inevitable that none would be able to achieve minimum efficient scale. Each of companies invested in the development and launch of their own satellite systems, dramatically ramping up the development costs that the industry would need to recoup.

Finally, advanced though Iridium's satellite system was, it was only able to handle 1100 simultaneous calls, which suggests that had the system been successful in attracting customers it would have required scaling up at some point. Furthermore, the satellites had a life span of only 5 years, at which point they would have to be replaced. This suggests the ongoing cost of operation was to be substantial.

Financial Analysis

At the time of the case, Iridium and rivals were operating at net losses. Iridium's current ratio of .20 indicates that the company was in immediate danger of bankruptcy if it was unable to secure additional credit. Although all three of the companies were showing a loss in 1998, Iridium's is by far the greatest at $1.7 billion, over five times its loss of $293 million in the previous year.

The financial data in the case also reveals that even if Iridium's subscription rates had been strong, it would have had trouble breaking even. According to exhibit 7, with a $5 billion dollar cost for the satellite system, the company needed to make almost $3 million a *day* just to recoup its development costs! If we assume that Iridium hoped to recoup its initial $5 billion in development expenses prior to replacing the satellites at the end of 2002, then using Iridium's original forecasts, the company would have had to net $756 dollars (after operating expenses) per customer, per year, just to break even on the development costs ($5 billion /(160+796+1259+1852+2547).

1. **What are the benefits of Iridium's technology? Limitations?**

   Benefits:
   - Could provide service *anywhere*

   Limitations:
   - Bulky, expensive handsets
   - System could only handle 1100 simultaneous calls
   - Satellites have lifespan of only 5 years

2. **Was Motorola's decision to spin Iridium off as a separate company a good one?**

   Motorola's decision to spin off Iridium was a *crucial* one. Setting up Iridium as a separate entity enabled it to take a gamble on a very risky new technology. If the project had been successful, Motorola would have been well positioned to capture profits both from its share in the company and its service contracts to the company. However, in the event of the project's failure, Motorola was shielded from incurring the company's debt or tarnished image.

3. **What were Iridium's target markets? Were they appropriate? Was the potential market not big enough, or was it not adequately penetrated? What factors facilitated/hindered the market penetration of the system?**

   Iridium needed to target the mass market to secure sufficient volume, but its pricing and the bulkiness of its handsets limited it to the remote worker market. One can thus argue the second question two ways. If the target market it considered to be strictly the remote worker market, it was probably not big enough to sustain the company. If the target market was the mass market, it was not adequately penetrated. To penetrate the mass market Iridium would have probably needed to charge a price comparable to that of terrestrial cellular service rates. Hopefully the global satellite coverage would have provided enough of a differentiating feature that it could have attracted shares away from terrestrial providers and subsequently had enough volume to reap a profit even at lower prices. However, it's important to remember that its system capacity at the time of the case was probably not adequate to have serviced the mass market effectively even if the company had deployed this strategy.

4. **What competitors and substitutes did Iridium face? How did the relevant cost and price factors compare? (e.g., development costs, variable costs, price to consumers, etc.)**

    Students can use the data in the case to create a table comparing the costs and price of the services offered by the different companies. What's more important is to get the students to realize that the real competition here did not come from Globalstar or ICO, but from terrestrial-based cellular providers.

5. **What strengths and advantages did Motorola/Iridium have in developing and deploying this technology? Was the relationship/tie-in with Motorola an advantage or constraint?**

    Motorola was an industry leader in the telecommunication industry. It provided technological expertise, and the significant credibility required to attract investors. Students may point out that Iridium was very reliant upon Motorola and may see this a weakness, but others will likely point out that it is somewhat of a fiction to think of them as separate entities—in many ways Iridium was simply a Motorola project.

6. **Was the satellite phone system a bad project choice? Could Iridium have done anything differently?**

    This is probably the most interesting issue of the case. Students should be encouraged to consider whether they would be attracted to a phone that could operate from anywhere, at anytime. Most will agree that this is an alluring idea. At the time the project was proposed (1987), this kind of service also offered an even greater advantage over terrestrial cellular service than it does today. Terrestrial cellular service coverage was much spottier then, and the lack of multi-band phones meant that the different cellular standards (e.g., GSM, CDMA, TDMA, etc.) were incompatible. A phone with worldwide capability would have had an enormous advantage—especially for business travelers. However, as cellular coverage increased and phones were adapted to operate on multiple phone standards, the differentiating features of satellite service were diminished.

    Based on the development costs of the project and the subscription forecasts, it is hard to see how any discounted cash flow analysis would have rendered a positive value for this project. However, it could also be argued that discounted cash flow analysis would inadequately capture some of the value of this project, such as establishing technological leadership in the telecommunications arena, developing greater expertise in satellite network systems (which might eventually be used for a multitude of purposes beyond telecommunications), developing future satellite platforms that were much lower in cost, etc. Thus Motorola might have seen this project as a "real option" on future investment opportunities.

POSTSCRIPT

Iridium LLC shut down service in March 2000 after being unable to find a buyer for the Iridium System. The $5 billion satellites would be de-orbited, allowing them to plunge into the earth's atmosphere to disintegrate[2]. As a consequence, Rune Gjeldnesand Torry Larsen, a Nordic team that were attempting to be the first people to ski from Russia to Canada while hauling sledges, would be stranded in the arctic without a means to contact the outside world. But through a strange turn of events, Iridium would arise from the ashes. In September of 2001, Dan Colussy, an aviation-industry veteran with no connection to the original company purchased the company's name and assets for $25 million at its bankruptcy hearing. Now rid of all of the debt incurred in its development efforts, the company was in a position to offer its service at a much cheaper rate, and it was estimated that it would need to secure only 63,000 users to turn a profit![3]

[2] 2000. Flaming End for Satellites. *BBC News.*
[3] Caluza, M. 2001. Iridium struggles into a higher orbit. *Upside,* 13(9):29.

Exhibit 1 – Iridium's Organization Structure (Geographic Structure)

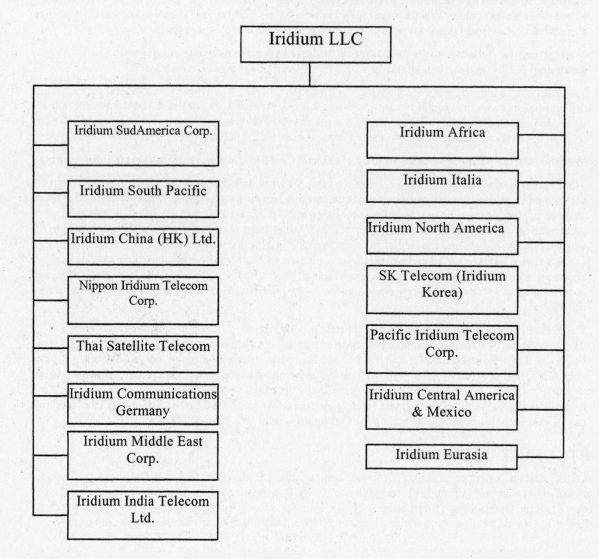

CASE 24

A Hundred-Year War: Coke vs. Pepsi, 1890s-1990s

SYNOPSIS OF THE CASE

This case looks at the evolution of competition in the soft drink industry from the industry's inception to the present day. The central theme in the case is the development of industry structure and competitive strategy. The case begins by exploring the structure of the industry with particular reference to the rise of the franchised bottler system. The case then looks at the early rise of Coke and Pepsi to a position of dominance within the industry. The main focus of the case however, is on the Cola wars, which the case identifies as beginning in the 1950s, accelerating in the 1970s, and reaching a crescendo in the 80s and the 90s. The case also contains an appendix, which profiles some of the smaller soft drink companies, and particularly the Seven-Up company.

TEACHING OBJECTIVES

This case can be used to illustrate issues related to industry structure, the relationship between competitive strategy and industry structure, and vertical integration. It works best when positioned toward the end of the first half of a strategic management course, since the main themes deal with the material covered in the first half of the text. At the same time, the vertical integration issues raised by the case provide a nice bridge to the second half of a strategic management course. The case works extremely well when used as the basis for an instructor-led class discussion. At the same time, it can also be used as the basis for a written report. It is perhaps one of the most straightforward Harvard cases to teach, and the average undergraduate class should have no problem grasping the main issues. The specific teaching objectives of the case are as follows:

1. Provide students with an opportunity to analyze the competitive structure of the soft-drink industry

2. Illustrate the importance of first-mover advantages in explaining the establishment and persistence of competitive advantage

3. Explore the evolution of business level strategy in a concentrated industry dominated by two major players

4. Discuss the link between the management of vertical relations and competitive strategy

STRATEGIC ISSUES AND DISCUSSION QUESTIONS

1. **The soft drink industry evolved with a franchised bottler system. For most of the industry's history the concentrate producers nurtured and preserved this system. Why?**

   The best way to start answering this question is to map out the main features of the franchised bottler system on the board. Briefly, the main features are as follows:

   • There is an exclusive bottler in each area or territory.

   • Bottlers are given franchises in perpetuity.

   • Bottlers are prohibited from marketing competing brands. Thus, a Coke bottler cannot bottle Pepsi. (This arrangement technically violates antitrust norms, and it required a special act of Congress to adopt it.)

   • There are territorial restrictions on bottler expansion. Thus, a Coke bottler in one area cannot start to compete head-to-head with a neighboring Coke bottler.

   Concentrate producers have nurtured this setup, primarily because it benefits them in a number of ways:

- The arrangement raises entry barriers into the industry. Bottlers are a major distribution channel. Potential competitors to Coke and Pepsi are shut out of this channel by the prohibition against carrying competing brands.

- Bottlers absorb the risks associated with heavy capital investments and new technological developments. Bottling is a capital-intensive process. Moreover, innovations in packaging have increased the rate of obsolescence of bottling lines. The franchise system means that bottlers bear these expenses and associated risks, not the concentrate producers.

- The high fixed costs associated with bottling create the maximum incentive for bottlers to build volume in order to amortize those costs. In other words, the incentive structure of the arrangement favors the concentrate producers, who want the bottlers to be aggressive in pushing their products.

- The concentrate producers still retain control over the valuable asset—the concentrate. Thus, the concentrate producers are in a very powerful bargaining position vis-à-vis the bottlers.

Hence the franchise setup enables concentrate producers to build entry barriers and to capture rents, without requiring them to become involved in a capital-intensive production process where there is a high risk of technological obsolescence. However, it is important to understand that while the structure of the arrangement does give bottlers an incentive to build volume, this arrangement does impose some costs on the concentrate producers, although for most of the industry's history these costs have been relatively minor compared to the benefits. Specifically:

- The concentrate producers are not in direct control of point-of-sale marketing. The bottlers control this.

- The concentrate producers must pursue bottlers to add products and packaging. Despite their bargaining power, they cannot dictate terms to the bottlers with regard to new products and packaging.

- Bottlers might get lazy or inefficient—particularly given that bottlers are granted franchises "in perpetuity."

Thus the concentrate producers do not have complete control over the bottlers.

2. **During the 1980s both Coke and Pepsi began to acquire bottlers. Why?**

As noted in the case, both Coca-Cola and Pepsi started purchasing bottlers in the 1980s—integrating forward into bottling and distribution. Given the advantages of the franchised system articulated above, this development can only be explained by a shift in the benefit-cost equation with regard to franchising versus vertical integration. What appears to have occurred is that as the end market became more competitive due to the intensification of the cola wars, and as the rate of new product introductions has increased, both Pepsi and Coke felt the need for greater control over bottlers. Controlling bottlers enabled both companies to ensure that bottlers adopt new products, new packaging, and aggressive point of sale marketing.

A second reason for the forward shift into bottling is that the structure of the bottling industry itself changed in the 1980s. Most significantly, multiple franchise owners started to purchase more bottlers. By doing so, they started to change the bargaining power between bottlers and concentrate producers (multiple franchise bottlers are more powerful than single franchise bottlers). The forward integration into bottling and distribution by concentrate producers may in part have been an attempt to stop this trend from going too far.

3. **Why did Coca-Cola dominate the soft drink industry by the end of World War II?**

The quick answer is that Coke was a classic first mover. Coke pioneered most of the industry's practices, and earned large returns by doing so. More precisely:

- Coke pioneered the franchising system.

- Coke introduced the first open-top coolers and vending machines.

- Coke pioneered life-style advertising.

- Coke used World War II to expand overseas.

As a result, by the end of World War II Coke outsold Pepsi by ten to one and dominated the industry.

4. **How was Pepsi able to come back from near bankruptcy and gain market share at the expense of Coke from the 1950s to 1975?**

The case suggests that from the early 1950s onward Pepsi was very much the innovator in the industry. Consider:

- Under Alfred Steel, in 1950 Pepsi focused on "beating Coke" (an early example of strategic intent).

- Pepsi encouraged bottlers to sell through newly emerging supermarkets where entry barriers were lowest and where Coke did not initially have a large presence.

- Pepsi introduced several new bottle sizes.

- In the early 1970s Pepsi increased its concentrate price and invested the proceeds in marketing.

While all of these factors help explain Pepsi's rise, none of them really get at the central issue, which was that Pepsi gained share because Coke did not respond! Coke seemed asleep—it let Pepsi take the initiative. One reason for this may have been that Coke was focused overseas. By the early 1970s Coke believed that the domestic market was mature and saw most future growth coming from overseas operations. As the dominant company, Coke may also have been risk averse: Coke's large share made it risky to follow Pepsi.

5. **During the 1950s, 1960s, and early 1970s, being a concentrate producer yielded high returns. Why was this the case?**

This question calls for students to analyze the competitive structure of the soft-drink industry during the 1950–1975 period. It sets the scene for a discussion of competitive changes in the industry since the intensification of competition that followed the cola wars. The basic points to make are as follow:

Entry Barriers: Entry barriers into the industry were enormous due to

- Franchise bottler system

- High brand loyalty enjoyed by Coke and Pepsi

- Economies of scale in advertising enjoyed by incumbents

Buyer Power: For most of the 1950–75 period the primary buyers of concentrate were bottlers. For reasons already explained above, the bottlers were at a bargaining power disadvantage vis-à-vis the concentrate producers. The concentrate producers owned the valuable asset in the industry, the concentrate. In addition, the concentrate amounted to a small percentage of the bottlers' total costs, which reduced their incentive to bargain intensively. Moreover, the bottlers faced very high switching costs; they could not walk away from a franchise agreement without suffering a major loss.

In addition to selling to the bottlers, the concentrate producers also sold concentrate to the fountain market. Fountain outlets charge a very high mark-up on soft drinks—indeed, that is how many fast-food operations make their money—so they had little incentive to bargain for lower concentrate prices.

Substitutes: Although there were and still are many substitutes for soft drinks, enormous brand loyalty enjoyed by Pepsi and Coke limited the impact of substitutes.

Supplier Power: During this time period the concentrate producers had no major suppliers.

Rivalry: As a result of the above conditions, the rivalry in the industry was not intense. The high entry barriers kept potential competitors locked out of the industry even when returns were high. The weak bargaining power of bottlers and fountain outlets allowed the concentrate producers to capture all of the rents derived from concentrate. The lack of strong suppliers and substitutes also worked to the concentrate producers' advantage. In addition:

- Primary demand continued to expand during this period.

- Competition was on the basis of product differentiation rather than price.

- The limited number of major players reduced the potential for price competition: there were relatively few potential "spoilers" in the industry.

- The low fixed costs meant an absence of exit barriers.

Summary: The soft-drink industry during this time period had all of the characteristics required for the generation of high returns.

6. **How did the national launch of the Pepsi challenge in 1977 change the nature of competition in the industry?**

In 1977 Pepsi went nationwide with the Pepsi challenge, a blind taste test that indicated that 58 percent of consumers preferred Pepsi to Coke. The Pepsi challenge was a head-on attack on Coke. Pepsi chose a hard-to-imitate basis for attack—taste. This represented a shift from the more abstract competition based on life-style advertising that had characterized the previous two decades. The challenge woke Coke up. Coke responded in the only way open to it at that time—by cutting prices—and Pepsi had to follow. As a result, by 1981 price discounting had become an industry norm. Operating margins followed prices down. Thus, the *short-term* result of the Pepsi challenge was to increase price competition, erode brand loyalties, and depress returns for both Coke and Pepsi, but particularly for Pepsi.

One point worth emphasizing here is how the competitive actions of one company can depress returns in an industry that has all of the characteristics necessary for high returns. Most importantly, the Pepsi challenge helped erode brand loyalty in the industry—by clearly showing that brand loyalty was often based on perception—and let the genie of price discounting out of the proverbial bottle.

7. **In retrospect, did the Pepsi challenge and the competition that followed it benefit or harm Pepsi and Coke?**

Students might initially answer this question by stating that the price competition and widespread discounting that followed the Pepsi challenge harmed both companies. There is some truth to this. After all, by 1982–84 margins had declined significantly from their levels a decade earlier (see Exhibit 3). However, the question deserves closer examination. By the late 1980s margins were on the rise again, as was Pepsi and Coke's share of the U.S. market (see Exhibits 1–3). The following points are worth noting:

- There has been genuine product innovation since 1977, which seems to have played a role in expanding primary demand. Against all expectations, primary demand for colas continued to grow during the 1980s in the United States.

- The price and advertising war between Pepsi and Coke seems to have played a part in expanding primary demand.

- Colas sharply increased their share of total soft-drink sales during the 1980s.

- There has been a decline in the market share accounted for by smaller players in the industry (e.g., Seven-Up).

- The intense competition between Pepsi and Coke has substantially reduced the risk of entry into the industry by potential competitors. The product proliferation undertaken by Pepsi and Coke has had the effect of closing most gaps in the market. The only company to try to enter, Philip Morris, which purchased Seven-Up, failed miserably in its attempt to expand Seven-Up's market share.

- By the end of the 1980s there were signs that price discounting was beginning to moderate and there was a shift back to life-style advertising.

In sum, although the short-run impact of the Pepsi challenge seemed negative, in the long run the increased competition that followed the challenge seemed to boost primary demand and increase profit margins, probably because of the economies of scale available given the virtual doubling of unit volume sales that occurred between 1975 and 1990. The message: increased competition is not always a bad thing.

The one big worry that Pepsi and Coke still have, however, is that a slowdown in the growth rate of industry demand might lead to more intense price competition in the future. If this happens, profit margins in the United States might once more head downward.

8. **During the 1990s Coca-Cola gained market share back from Pepsi, and was significantly more profitable. Why?**

   Coca-Cola gained market share from Pepsi in the 1990s as a result of some strategic initiatives undertaken by its management in the 1980s and 1990s. More specifically:

   - Coca-Cola introduced a large number of product innovations. One of the extensions of the Coke brand name, Diet Coke, was a phenomenal success in the market. Diet Coke and the other brand extensions of Coke (Cherry Coke, Caffeine-free Coke etc.) were able to wrest back market share from Pepsi's brand extensions.

   - While Pepsi diversified into restaurants and snack food business, Coca-Cola decided to concentrate on its soft drink business and sold off most of its non-soft drink businesses.

   - Coca-Cola improved its profit margins by creating a highly efficient bottling infrastructure. While Pepsi used owned and operated its bottling plants, Coca-Cola acquired bottlers that were not performing well and organized them under an independent subsidiary, Coca-Cola Enterprises (CCE). CCE was then spun-off to the public while Coca-Cola retained 49% stake in the company, giving it a lot of power over decision making in CCE. Coca-Cola uses CCE to acquire and consolidate bottlers, renegotiate contracts and do away with redundant distribution. CCE has invested in mega facilities with high volume production lines, increased automation and boasts massive warehouse and delivery capabilities, resulting in lower costs.

9. **Why do you think Coca-Cola holds such a dominant position over Pepsi in the international marketplace?**

   Coca-Cola has enjoyed a dominant position in the international markets since World War II and has steadily expanded its international operations over the years. Historically, for Coca-Cola, international sales have always been by far the biggest component of its total sales. Some of the reasons that explain Coca-Cola's success in international markets are:

   - Coca-Cola enjoyed significant first mover advantages in a large number of markets since World War II. Pepsi, on the other hand, did not internationalize until the 1980s. This gave Coca-Cola time to build its brand as well as a distribution network in different countries.

   - Coca-Cola appointed the large and experienced bottlers in foreign markets as anchor bottlers. This strategy allowed it to enter new markets and set up a distribution network relatively quickly. Retaining minority interests in the anchor bottlers also gave Coca-Cola significant influence over their management. In addition, contracts with bottlers overseas were not granted in "perpetuity", but for period of 3-10 years without any renewal guarantee. This increased Coca-Cola's bargaining power with the bottlers and allowed it more control over concentrate prices.

   - Coca-Cola entered countries that had low soft drink consumption but high potential. Thus, Coca-Cola ensured growth for its brands in the new markets.

CASE 25

Wal-Mart Stores, Inc.: Strategies for Dominance in the New Millennium[1]

SYNOPSIS OF THE CASE

Wal-Mart Stores Inc., in 2000, with corporate headquarters in Bentonville, Arkansas, was not only the nation's largest discount department store chain, but also had surpassed Sears, Roebuck, and Company as the largest retail organization in sales volume in the United States. It was also considered the largest retailer in the world. The firm operated stores under a variety of names and retail formats including: Wal-Mart, discount department stores; Sam's Clubs, wholesale and retail membership warehouses; and Supercenters, large combination general merchandise and grocery stores. In the international division, it operated stores in Canada, Mexico, Argentina, Brazil, Germany, United Kingdom, Puerto Rico, South Korea and China. The McLane Company, a support division with over 36,000 customers, was the nation's largest distributor of food and merchandise to convenience stores and selected Wal-Marts, Sam's Clubs, and Supercenters.

A major concern was Wal-Mart's spectacular growth and the dominance of the firm in the market. The firm was perceived to be in the accelerated development or growth stage of institutional life cycle in which sales increased rapidly, profits were high, new stores were opened, existing stores were being refurbished, the product line was being reevaluated, service offerings were upgraded, automation was introduced to store operation, and better management controls were developed. What makes this situation unique is that the discount department store industry was perceived as being at maturity. It faced increased competition, leveling of sales, moderate profits by surviving firms, over-stored markets, and more complex operational problems than previously.

Senior management, including the new CEO, Lee Scott, felt that the firm could continue to maintain its blistering growth pace by "outmaneuvering the competition with innovative retailing concepts."

TEACHING OBJECTIVES

The teaching objectives of this case are as follows:

1.   To show what role leadership plays in establishing strategy and creating a distinctive corporate culture.

2.   To emphasize the need to identify market segments and then to design an appropriate retailing mix to meet customer needs and wants.

3.   To show what role customer responsiveness and innovation play in building and sustaining a competitive advantage.

4.   To demonstrate the importance of developing a strategy that will allow the firm to survive and continue to grow domestically and internationally in a dynamic—and perhaps more hostile—environment.

5.   To use financial analysis of a high-yield performance organization to evaluate its strategy.

STRATEGIC ISSUES AND DISCUSSION QUESTIONS

1.   **Identify and evaluate the strategies that Wal-Mart pursued to maintain its cost-leadership position.**

Wal-Mart pursued the following strategies to maintain its cost-leadership position:

*   The development of a human relations/human resource based corporate culture linked to the satisfaction of consumer needs and wants in the marketplace. The team spirit, employee involvement

---

[1] This teaching note was prepared by James W. Camerius. Adapted by permission.

in company affairs, local hiring, employee recognition awards, employees as "associates," training programs, Saturday morning meetings, stock ownership and profit sharing programs are part of this plan.

- Market segmentation/market target/marketing positioning strategy of operating a discount store in small communities, offering brand name merchandise at "everyday low prices" and offering friendly service.

- The strategically preemptive location of stores in small towns helps Wal-Mart gain first mover advantage and capture the local markets. In addition, Wal-Mart is able to get higher margins and reduced promotion advertising costs from being the only discounter in a small town. Other cost advantages of locating in small towns are a non-unionized employee force and cheaper real estate.

- Market dominance strategy of first opening a distribution center, dominating a market area with Wal-Mart stores and then growing by expanding in contiguous trading areas. The resultant Hub and Spoke distribution system that allows several stores to be serviced by a single distribution center reduces costs through sorting and consolidation and leads to greater efficiency in logistics.

- An inventory control system that links stores with distribution centers and the staff at corporate headquarters. This enables managers to learn immediately what merchandise is moving slowly, and thus avoids overstocking and deep discounting leading to high revenues and lower inventory costs.

- Wal-Mart's powerful position with vendors also helps it to get a good deal on merchandising costs by negotiating on prices, promotion allowances and continuity of supply.

- Offering a wide variety of general merchandise to the customer in 36 different departments with specialty centers at some locations.

- Developing a competitive differential advantage by being able to "strike a delicate balance needed to convince customers that [Wal-Mart] prices were low without making people feel that its stores were too cheap." People greeters, paper sacks, warm colors, wide aisles were considered part of this strategy.

- Liberal refund and exchange policies were part of a "Satisfaction Guaranteed" program.

- Corporate programs like developing new retail formats like Sam's Club, and Supercenters.

- Programs to emphasize contemporary social issues like the Buy American Program and Green Marketing.

2. **Evaluate Wal-Mart's competitive environment.**

Industry analysts had labeled the 1990s as an era of economic uncertainty for retailers. There were mergers and acquisitions by domestic and foreign firms, failures, restructuring, and discontinued operations. Serving of debt became a major issue. Many of the largest retail organizations either suffered sales decline or posted marginal sales gains. The United States had passed through a recession in the business cycle and returned to prosperity. Students can be asked how this turbulent external environment affects retailing activity in the marketplace.

The following issues could be discussed in a review of the competitive environment: (1) Intra industry competition, Wal-Mart compared to other discount department stores like Kmart, Target, Shopko or Ames. (2) Inter industry competition, Wal-Mart compared to department stores like Macy's, Dillard's, Dayton-Hudson, or any of the Federated Department Stores, Inc. divisions; and (3) Cross industry competition, Wal-Mart compared with specialty retailers like The Gap, Tandy, Limited Express, and Sound Warehouse.

Wal-Mart competes with retail firms operating supermarkets, department-like specialty stores, and other mass merchandise organizations like Toys 'R' Us as "category killers," which have potential to dominate a merchandise line in a single category at such low prices that the competition might be destroyed.

3. **Discuss the importance of changes in the external environment to an organization like Wal-Mart.**

A number of changes had taken place in the external environment of Wal-Mart. The country was in an economic recession. Despite the fact that the company continued to grow in terms of sales volume, profitability, and physical size, the discount department store industry was perceived to be in the maturity stage of the institutional life cycle. It experienced sales increases at a decreasing rate, which is a characteristic of the maturity stage of retail institutional life cycle.

In terms of market served, the Wal-Mart focus was on small towns and cities. One question that might be explored is the acceptability of the firm in other market areas like suburban and inner city. An industry analyst had questioned, "Will Wal-Mart take over the world?" with respect to Wal-Mart's international strategy. The price sensitive shopper seemed to be everywhere. Wal-Mart continued to expand in contiguous trading areas and into larger urban areas such as Dallas and Phoenix as well as internationally.

4.   **What conclusions can be drawn from a review of Wal-Mart's financial performance over the decade of the 1980s? From this review, what can you conclude about the financial future of the firm?**

Data is available in the case to derive the performance measures of (1) asset turnover, (2) profit margin, and (3) financial leverage, i.e., debt management. Data in the case can also be used to measure the liquidity of the organization. The strategic profit model, as shown below with normative ratios, is a useful vehicle for analyzing the financial performance of firms of this type. Figures are considered normative for in-store retailing and as such provide a base for comparison.

$$\frac{\text{Net Profit}}{\text{Net Sales}} \quad x \quad \frac{\text{Net Sales}}{\text{Total Assets}} \quad = \quad \frac{\text{Net Profit}}{\text{Total Assets}} \quad x \quad \frac{\text{Total Assets}}{\text{Net Worth}} \quad = \quad \frac{\text{Net Profit}}{\text{Net Worth}}$$

3-5%	3-4 X	8-10%	1.5-2.5 X	15-20%
Profit Margin	Asset Turnover	Return on Assets	Financial Leverage	Return on Net Worth

Strategic profit model ratios for Wal-Mart Stores, Inc., for the years 1999-1996, are reviewed below:

Year	Profit Margin (%)		Asset Turnover (x)		Return on Assets (%)		Financial Leverage (x)		Return on Net Worth (%)
1999	3.20	x	2.35	=	7.6	x	2.72	=	20.8
1998	3.20	x	2.75	=	8.9	x	2.37	=	21.0
1997	2.90	x	2.60	=	8.5	x	2.45	=	19.8
1996	2.90	x	2.65	=	7.9	x	2.31	=	19.2

In a financial profile of leading retailers developed in the Distribution Research Program at the University of Oklahoma, strategic profit model ratios for discount department stores revealed the following results in a recent study: profit margin 2.6 percent; asset turnover 2.5 percent; return on assets 6.5 percent; leverage 2.6 percent; and return on net worth 16.8 percent. This indicates that Wal-Mart Stores is a high performance retailer with return on net worth significantly greater than the industry average and other normative figures. Return on Assets is also higher than the industry average.

5.   **Speculate on how much impact the "absence" of Sam Walton had on the forward momentum of the organization. What steps have been or should be taken by management to continue Sam Walton's formula for success?**

The case points out that much of the forward momentum at Wal-Mart had come from the entrepreneurial spirit of Sam Walton. He was the Chairman of the board and corporate representative for the immediate future. When approached on the departure of Mr. Walton, David Glass, new president and CEO, suggests: "There's no transition to make because this company is so sound and so universally accepted. As for the future, there's more opportunity ahead of us than behind us."

A number of programs might be introduced to perpetuate the enthusiastic and exciting leadership that Sam Walton brought to the organization:

- Capture Walton's philosophy in any way possible: on film, in books, in articles, in a painting to hang in every store

- Introduce leadership programs which would emphasize continuing the Walton philosophy in the company

- Develop Walton as a symbol or idea as opposed to an individual

- Perpetuate in the firm all of the ideas that Walton stood for: like his homespun humor, life style, or morality

- Continue to encourage the human relations and human resource bottom up style of management in the firm

In this question the instructor may wish to introduce the concept of "organizational culture" by discussing or assigning library research on other corporate/leadership scenarios like Henry Ford, F. W. Woolworth, Marshall Field, Richard W. Sears, and more recently like Eugene Ferkauf at E. J. Korvette discount stores; Mary Kay Ash at Mary Kay Cosmetics; and Richard M. Devos and Jay Van Andel of Amway. Harry Cunningham was credited as providing much leadership in the growth stage of Kmart.

6. **Is Wal-Mart's competitive advantage imitable?**

The main sources of competitive advantage, or core competencies are:

- Rural locations – Due to preemption Wal-Mart has a reasonably secure advantage here.

- The company's distribution and inventory control system – This is imitable, but Wal-Mart is a leader that stays one step ahead of the competition.

- The company's culture, structure, and incentive systems – These may be difficult to imitate, since established enterprises find it difficult to change their culture. So imitation by established competitors, while theoretically possible, is unlikely.

The point is that while ultimately anything is imitable, in many ways Wal-Mart does have a very strong competitive position that is protected by high barriers to imitation.

7. **What are the challenges facing Wal-Mart in the New Millennium?**

The greatest challenge for Wal-Mart is to maintain its tremendous growth. The company is now focusing more and more on international markets (See Exhibit 5). However, internationally too, Wal-Mart is expected to encounter competition from local retailers such as Carrefour in France and Karstadt in Germany. In addition, it will be a challenge to transfer the unique Wal-Mart culture to foreign lands and to train local employees in the Wal-Mart way. Other challenges Wal-Mart is facing include:

- Unionization in a number of its U.S. stores. This may be a threat to the unique Wal-Mart culture.

- Competition from Web-based enterprises. As of early 2000, Wal-Mart had only a poorly defined Web presence. They have improved their website significantly since then but they still have to contend with stiff competition online.

- Foreign competition is entering the global market place.

- Resistance from rural communities to Wal-Mart's "intrusion."

8. **What recommendations do you have for CEO Lee Scott?**

Lee Scott should continue with a diversification strategy in the domestic market and an expansion strategy in international markets.

Domestic market:

- Leverage competencies into complementary business and services to increase one-stop-shopping at traditional stores.

- Create synergies between Walmart.com and traditional stores' customer service.

- Develop an urban penetration system, i.e., grow grocery/supercenter and neighborhood market business.

- Continue to use emergent, opportunistic strategy: "Try a lot of things and keep what works."

Global markets:

- Pursue expansion through targeted acquisition and joint ventures. In particular, focus on areas where the majority of people have a steady income, reliable transportation infrastructure exists, and the capacity to support many stores close to distribution centers is given.

- Implement a transnational strategy to address cost pressures and local responsiveness simultaneously.

- Maximize advantage of technological expertise.

CASE 26

Wal-Mart's Mexican Adventure

SYNOPSIS OF THE CASE

Strengthened by a unique culture and armed with the industry's state of the art information system that powers a unique hub and spoke distribution system, Wal-Mart entered the Mexican market. It perceived that continued growth in the United States market was no longer possible and took advantage of the free trade environment to be created by NAFTA.

The strategy originally adopted by Wal-Mart was to begin a joint venture with the discount and grocery store giant, Cifra. Problems became apparent very early. Wal-Mart encountered transportation problems, poor merchandise selection, and government interference. In the mid-1990s, the collapse of the Mexican Peso hit Wal-Mart hard, because it meant that the goods imported from the United States were more expensive.

During the market slump, Wal-Mart built its market share and began to invest heavily in Mexico. It improved the distribution problems, sourced more products from Mexico, and changed its mix of products to appeal to the Mexican market. Soon, Wal-Mart had improved its cost structure and repositioned all of its Mexican stores to operate under the strategy of Every Day Low Pricing. Surging volume in early 2000 was an indication that Wal-Mart had finally hit it big to control most of the Mexican market.

TEACHING OBJECTIVES

The teaching objectives for this case are as follows:

1.   To understand the strategies that may be used while entering international markets.

2.   To illustrate potential problems confronted by a company when entering a foreign country.

3.   To understand how to create value in a foreign venture.

4.   To appreciate the operational culture of one of America's great retail firms.

STRATEGIC ISSUES AND DISCUSSION QUESTIONS

1.   **Why did Mexico make such a good proving ground for Wal-Mart's foreign expansion strategy?**

     First, the logistics of dealing with a foreign neighbor nearby, connected by land, was a great opportunity to utilize Wal-Mart's hub and spoke distribution system. Second, the nature of the retail system in Mexico, with many mom and pop stores located in non-major retail areas with no other major competitors was advantageous to Wal-Mart's retail strategy. The higher cost structure of the mom and pop stores enabled a discounter like Wal-Mart to gain market share and get higher margins on its products. Finally, Wal-Mart's operating efficiency, as illustrated by its state of the art information system, made the operation of a foreign entity more efficient and less costly.

2.   **What is the source of Wal-Mart's competitive advantage? What barriers did Wal-Mart have to overcome in transferring its competencies to Mexico?**

     Wal-Mart's competitive advantage lies in three areas. First, it's unique hub and spoke distribution system allows it to rapidly replenish stock and keep floor space for selling to a minimum. That means that less store space is devoted to holding inventory and more space is devoted to selling. Second, its information system allows it to quickly register a sale and replace inventory so that major selling items are always available and out of stock occurrences are virtually non-existent. Third, its unique culture of involving employees in decision making and generous profit sharing and stock ownership plans empower employees and managers to do their best for the company, thereby improving employee turnover and lowering costs.

However, these core competencies were not easily transferable to a different country—a number of missteps by Wal-Mart and a different external environment and customer base prevented a smooth transfer. First, high tariff structures between Mexico and the United States in the pre-NAFTA days led to a situation where Wal-Mart was pricing its products sold in Mexico 15-20% higher than at a Wal-Mart store in Texas that was merely 2 hours away. This made customers in Mexico extremely unhappy. Second, poor infrastructure, crowded roads and a lack of agreements with suppliers prevented Wal-Mart from duplicating its unique distribution system in Mexico, leading to reduced margins. Third, Wal-Mart initially stocked products that were popular in the United States, but were not used much in Mexico and this led to inventory build-up for certain products. Fourth, Wal-Mart ran into bureaucratic problems with inspectors in Mexico regarding its product labeling and that led to higher costs. Fifth, the devaluation of the Peso in 1994 not only led to a significant drop in consumer spending, it also increased the cost of importing goods from the United States.

However, Wal-Mart quickly learned from its mistakes and as the Mexican economy improved and beneficial effects of the NAFTA agreement started to kick-in, Wal-Mart was able to expand successfully in Mexico.

3. **How did Wal-Mart create value in the Mexican market?**

Wal-Mart created value through a combination of the following:

- A rapid replacement distribution system – Wal-Mart was able to take advantage of low labor costs, agreements with local and U.S. based trucking companies to make its distribution centers more cost effective.

- A product-mix that was attractive to the Mexican consumers.

- By leveraging its huge purchasing power with suppliers – Wal-Mart was able to source more merchandise locally from suppliers that set up base in Mexico to take advantage of the lower production costs. In addition, as Wal-Mart's operations grew in Mexico, it was able to negotiate better deals with suppliers.

All of the above resulted in lower costs and lower prices. When Wal-Mart repositioned its stores to implement an Every Day Low Pricing strategy, the results were significant. Mexican consumers could now purchase products that they needed at prices that were affordable and competitive.

4. **Despite some early setbacks, Wal-Mart has apparently been successful in Mexico. In contrast, some other United States retailers pulled out of the country in the aftermath of the 1994 peso crisis. What do you think distinguishes Wal-Mart from those companies?**

In addition to operational efficiencies already discussed, Wal-Mart brought an administrative tenacity to its Mexican operations that few other firms could match. When the peso was devalued and economic turmoil threatened businesses, Wal-Mart did not close stores but rather saw the economic downturn as an opportunity to build its market share. It opened an efficient distribution center in Mexico city and used it to reduce inventory and operating costs. It also struck a partnership with a Mexican trucking company to improve delivery and distribution.

5. **"If Wal-Mart can succeed in Mexico, it can probably succeed in most other countries." Discuss this statement. Is it correct?**

While Wal-Mart's operational excellence is virtually unparalleled, it is difficult to assume that the circumstances that allowed it to profit in Mexico could be duplicate in other countries. The product-mix necessary to stock Mexican stores was only moderately different from that used in stores in the United States. NAFTA gave Wal-Mart an advantage with the free flow of goods into the country, and the culture of Mexico was not resistant to the empowerment culture within Wal-Mart that allowed managers and employees to make decisions for the good of the company. Other countries may not accept that culture so readily, and the duplication of the success factors may be more difficult. Still, given the enormous commitment that Wal-Mart management makes to new ventures, and its successful track record, it may be a mistake to underestimate their resolve should they choose to expand aggressively beyond North America.

CASE 27

Kmart Corporation: Seeking Customer Acceptance and Preference[1]

SYNOPSIS OF THE CASE

In 2000, Kmart Corporation was one of the world's largest mass merchandise retailers. After several years of restructuring, it was composed largely of general merchandise businesses in the form of Kmart discount department stores, Big Kmart stores and large combination stores called Super Kmart Centers in all 50 states of the United States as well as Puerto Rico, the U.S. Virgin Islands and Guam. Measured in sales volume, it was the third largest retailer and the second largest discount department store chain in the United States.

On June 1, 2000, the search for the new chairman and chief executive officer was over. Charles C. Conaway was selected to fill the position. Floyd Hall, the retiring chairman, president, and chief executive officer of Kmart Corporation since June of 1995, was not pleased with Kmart's financial results reported in the fiscal first quarter of 2000. He was very optimistic, however, about the company's future. He was convinced that the new corporate strategies that he had recently introduced would revitalize Kmart's core business, its 2,171 discount department stores, and put the company on the road to recovery. Industry analysts had noted that Kmart had posted 15 straight quarters of profit increases that Floyd Hall felt signaled a turnaround at the discount chain. Industry analysts, however, suggested that much of K-Mart's recent growth may have reflected the strength of the consumer economy rather than acceptance of the company's new retail strategies. Conaway was expected to provide new direction for the firm.

Kmart had put heavy emphasis on the planning function. Management perceived the role of corporate planning to be "making decisions now to improve performance tomorrow." Kmart had been very successful in the area of strategic planning in the past. Management felt that strategic planning used intelligently by management would be the key to corporate growth in the future.

TEACHING OBJECTIVES

The teaching objectives of this case are as follows:

1. It is an excellent case to demonstrate the importance of strategic planning.

2. It can be used to differentiate between strategic, administrative, and operational planning.

3. It dramatizes the importance of adjusting to a changing multi-dimensional external environment.

4. It emphasizes the need to identify target markets and then to design an appropriate retailing mix to meet consumer needs and wants.

5. It can be used to show how a potentially high yield performance retailer adjusts to change.

6. To provide a discussion basis for the question of how Kmart competes with Wal-Mart and other mass merchandisers like Sears and Target (Dayton Hudson) in the area of price leadership.

STRATEGIC ISSUES AND DISCUSSION QUESTIONS

1. **Evaluate the strategies that Kmart has introduced as part of its renewal program of the 1990s. How much impact did these strategies have in the competitive environment as the firm sought to maintain its position and grow in the future?**

---

[1] This teaching note was prepared by James W. Camerius. Adapted by permission.

This case dramatically demonstrates the importance of strategic planning in a firm with a track record of sales and asset growth. Class discussion may begin by asking the class to discuss the following statement: "Planning has primacy over the other functions and is a necessity for all organizations in the 1990s and into the 21st century."

Kmart's concept focused on slowing the tempo of physical expansion and concentrated instead on a greater return on investment in existing stores. Six key strategies were developed for the 1990s. They included (1) accelerated store expansion and refurbishing, (2) capitalizing of dominant lifestyle departments, (3) centralized merchandising, (4) more capital investment in retail automation, (5) an aggressive and focused advertising program, and (6) growth through new specialty retail formats.

Strategy can be defined as a decisive allocation of resources to an intended course of action. It can be a long-run, time-phased plan to achieve the following goals: (1) a high rate of return of investment and/or (2) a market position so advantageous that competition can retaliate only over an extended time interval and at a prohibition cost. What Kmart needed was something more dramatic than the incremental approaches of the past. The 1990 marketing program might be called an "inside-out" approach to planning. Top management used the company's experience in the marketplace to determine what the organization was exceptionally good at and then designed a program to exploit that ability or resource. While there are merits to this approach, it is not a decisive allocation of resources to a major course of action; i.e., it is not a strategy. The firm, although strengthened and revitalized after self-examination, remained vulnerable to newer types of retail organizations that potentially could emerge as surprise elements and threaten its future. In addition, existing retail leader Wal-Mart is a major competitive threat to Kmart.

2.   **How much importance is placed on the planning function at Kmart? What are some constraints that are likely to decrease its effect on the development of the organization?**

Kmart had a reasonably formal planning organization. It involved a constant evaluation of what was happening in the marketplace, what the competition was doing, and what kinds of opportunities were available. The organization provided for a Director of Planning and Research who reported directly to the Chief Executive Officer. A planning group made up of individuals representing a number of functional areas of the organization aided and assisted the Director of Planning and Research. As noted in the case, management recognized the need to emphasize planning, since it felt it was not going to grow with the traditional Kmart format forever.

There are several constraints that hinder "innovative competition" as part of the planning process: (1) traditional trade practices, (2) limited goals and expectations, (3) deeply entrenched patterns of behavior within the firm, (4) the pressures of other firms within the channel of distribution to maintain the status quo, and (5) efforts to cultivate an identified market segment to the neglect of others.

3.   **Why do you think strategic planning is important to an organization like Kmart?**

It is generally agreed that planning involves such activities as (1) developing the objectives and goals for a company, (2) projecting economic conditions that will affect the firm's future, (3) formulating alternative courses of action to reach identified goals, (4) analyzing the consequences of identified alternatives, (5) deciding which strategies are most feasible in light of limited corporate resources, and (6) devising methods for measuring progress toward a intended goal when a strategy has been chosen.

Kmart developed a corporate culture that was accustomed to challenges. Management was obligated to find ways to expand that energy. With the discount department store industry at maturity, management would have to recognize that it would have to decide where it wanted to go and how it was going to get there. It had to make major commitments in the present to continue its high-yield performance mandate in the future.

4.   **How does strategic planning fit into the management process at Kmart?**

The chairman of the board, as chief executive officer (CEO), is the primary planner of the organization. Management had recognized that the director of planning and research and his "group" are only advisory in nature and in a staff position. They function much the same as an in-house consulting group.

Recognition of the need for planning is a key phrase here. Management felt that corporate planning at Kmart was the result of executives, primarily the senior executives, recognizing change and getting others to recognize that nothing is good forever. Good planning, it was noted, is making decisions now to improve performance tomorrow.

5. **Discuss the importance of changes in the external environment. How much impact do they have on strategic plans in retail firms like Kmart?**

The external forces confronting the retail enterprises are typically identified as (1) the technological environment, (2) behavior of channel members, (3) behavior of consumers, (4) behavior of competitors, (5) the legal environment, and (6) the socioeconomic environment. New forms of retailing generally emerge as a response to changing environmental factors. As the environment changes, retail organizations must change to survive and to prosper. An analysis of three retailers indicates Wal-Mart, Target (Dayton Hudson), and Sears have learned to do things better than Kmart. The analysis is shown in Exhibit 1 in the case. Sears, Roebuck and Company was formerly the nation's largest retailer in sales volume. It also should be noted that Sears' figures were historically inflated by catalogue sales and insurance subsidiaries.

6. **What conclusions can be drawn from a review of Kmart's financial performance in the period 1990-1999?**

The strategic profit model shown in Exhibit TN 1 is a useful vehicle for analyzing the financial performance of retail firms like Kmart. It dramatizes the performance imperative in retail organizations, as companies attempt to maximize their return on net worth. Net income for Kmart as a percent of net worth has varied from a high of a defensible 17.4 percent in 1986 to a low in the minus figures for 1993, 1995, and 1996. Major variations are not shown for the early 1970s and early 1980s in the case. In earlier years, sales increased each year as Kmart increased its share of the market. In later years, sales have shown decreases primarily because of stores closures and asset disposition. Strategic profit model ratios for Kmart Corporation for selected years, 1990-1999, are shown in Exhibit TN 2.

Kmart is an organization that emphasizes margin management with price as an appeal. Profit margin has continued to be low with defensible asset turnover. The basic conclusions that can be drawn from the review are

- Kmart is a potentially high yield performance firm that has not increased its return on net worth substantially over the past years.

- Kmart sales volume performance is mixed.

- Kmart has used margin management, asset management, and financial management to dramatize the principle areas of decision making.

7. **What new directions are needed to position Kmart to meet the challenges of the next 20 years? Review the alternative strategies that Kmart might implement in order to be successful.**

Management must regularly ask itself: (1) Where are we now? (2) Where do we want to go? and (3) How do we get there? Strategic planning that is risk oriented has to emerge as a central corporate concern and be the primary responsibility of senior management. The role of looking ahead at Kmart widens management's perspectives and dramatizes the necessity for continually evaluating the organization.

A summary of Kmart's recent strategies reveals that management planned to upgrade and remodel its Kmart stores while aggressively diversifying into membership clubs, bookstores, home improvement centers and warehouse stores. In some sectors it has been highly criticized for this attempt to revitalize a maturing company. Louis W. Stern of the Marketing Science Institute suggests, "Kmart's real ace in the hole is a warehouse technology—they buy goods in huge quantities at good prices and deliver value.... Once you begin to deviate from that core activity," he continued, "you have to begin to wonder." Kmart reemphasized its core retailing strategy in the late 1990s following the divestiture of eleven non-core and peripheral businesses.

High yield performance retailers in the 1990s were found primarily in the following four categories: (1) off-price retail outlets, (2) broad-line mass merchandising, (3) specialized mass merchandising and (4) positioned specialty stores. Kmart is dominant as a broad-line mass merchandiser in the discount department store field. The case suggests reviewing alternative approaches for future strategies with emphasis upon planning, positioning, and technology.

Exhibit TN 1

Strategic Profit Model with Normative Ratios After Taxes:

| Net Profit | x | Net Sales | = | Net Profit | x | Total Assets | = | Net Profit |
Net Sales		Total Assets		Total Assets		Net Worth		Net Worth
3-5%		3-4 (x)		8-10%		1.5-2.5 (x)		15-20%

Exhibit TN 2

Kmart Selected Strategic Profit Model Ratios, 1988-1997

Year	(%)		(x)		(%)		(x)		(%)
1988	2.0	x	2.3	=	6.0	x	2.4	=	14.4
1989	1.1	x	2.3	=	2.5	x	2.6	=	6.5
1990	2.0	x	2.3	=	5.0	x	2.58	=	12.9
1991	2.0	x	2.1	=	5.0	x	2.32	=	11.6
1992	2.5	x	2.0	=	5.0	x	2.51	=	12.6
1993	(0.8)	x	2.0	=	(1.6)	x	2.87	=	(4.6)
1994	0.9	x	2.0	=	1.7	x	2.82	=	4.8
1995	(1.8)	x	2.1	=	(3.8)	x	2.85	=	(10.8)
1996	(0.7)	x	2.2	=	(1.5)	x	2.32	=	(3.5)
1997	0.7	x	2.4	=	1.8	x	2.10	=	3.78

CASE 28

Tosco and the New Millennium

SYNOPSIS OF THE CASE

This case describes how Tosco, a company that developed oil shale reserves all over the world, grew and diversified into the oil and gas refining industry. Over a ten-year period ranging from 1990-2000, it underwent rapid growth and went from a struggling company to the third largest oil refinery in the United States and one of the top 8 sellers of retail gasoline in the country.

From 1990 onwards, Tosco took advantage of the restructuring and consolidation taking place in the oil and gas industry and grew through acquisitions. In the next 10 years, Tosco was able to compete effectively against the largest players in the oil and gas industry. Tosco was also able to establish operations in 31 states on both the east and the west coast of the United States and was able to enter international markets using its acquisitions strategy. In 2000, its annual revenues were $25 billion. Tosco's strengths clearly lie in "buying assets at a reasonable price, reorganizing them and running them at a profit".

TEACHING OBJECTIVES

The main teaching objectives of this case are as follows:

1.   To analyze the dynamics and structure of the oil and gas industry.

2.   To illustrate how rapid growth is possible in mature industries.

3.   To critically evaluate the growth strategy and its inherent risks.

STRATEGIC ISSUES AND DISCUSSION QUESTIONS

1.   **Describe the competitive structure of the oil and gas industry in the 1990s.**

In the 1980s, falling prices of crude oil and overcapacity created consolidation and restructuring in the early 1990s in the oil and gas industry in general as well as in the refining and marketing segment in which Tosco operated. As a result, the refining and marketing segment had been characterized by a lot of changes in the last decade, as the major energy companies began divesting their refining and marketing assets. Independent companies like Tosco took advantage of availability of surplus assets at discounted prices and the 1990s saw a large number of assets change hands. The refining and marketing sector consists of three sub-segments:

- Refineries – The refining industry has many players, including independent companies as well as integrated energy companies. This was a result of the redistribution of refining assets throughout the last decade. This industry seems to be a mature industry offering limited growth opportunities. There are significant entry barriers in the industry because of its capital-intensive nature, technologically complex equipment, sensitivity to the fluctuation in prices of crude oil, and its margins can be severely affected by 'mandated' expenses imposed by environmental regulatory authorities.

- Gas Retail – Gas retail is dominated largely by major integrated energy players and very few independent companies are present in this sector. However, the independents companies seem to be gaining market share. This sector is also very capital intensive and technologically sophisticated, and raises the barriers to entry.

- Convenience Stores Industry – These are convenience stores that sell merchandise as well as gasoline. This sector also suffers from overcapacity.

Overall, all three segments of the refining and marketing industry have seen intense competition and a rise in the number of independent companies. The future is expected to bring more consolidation. There is also the possibility that retailers/grocers like Safeway and Wal-Mart might enter the retail gasoline sector, intensifying the competition further. The outlook for the industry looks promising in the near future because domestic demand in the United States is expected to be greater than the refinery capacity and prices for oil and gas are expected to go up.

2.   **What was the growth strategy followed by Tosco?**

Tosco has primarily grown through acquisitions. Since 1990, it has acquired operations in refineries, retail gasoline marketing business and the convenience store industry. The refining and gas retail industry was dominated by large players and new entrants faced significant barriers to entry. Acquisitions were the only way that Tosco could have acquired the resources and capabilities required to establish market presence and generate profits to compete successfully against the incumbents.

More specifically, the strategy was to buy refinery and gas retail assets at prices that were lower than the replacement values, restructure them and then operate them at as low a cost as possible. Tosco was thus able to achieve the economies of scale required to enter the industry.

Economies of location were another important factor in refining – buying crude oil from a single geographic location helped keep operating costs down and increased production output. Instead of a concentration strategy, Tosco followed a strategy of geographic expansion. It acquired assets in more than one location so that it could affect margins through being more flexible in choosing a source of supply. Flexibility in choosing supply sources also improved margins because each refinery was able to produce the highest margin product mix. The effect of this strategy was significant given that companies like Tosco are extremely dependent on fluctuations of crude oil prices.

Tosco was also not shy of selling off units that it was not able to operate profitably. It sold its Avon refinery to UDS after being bitten by negative press and losses from the refinery.

3.   **Critically evaluate Tosco's growth strategy and the inherent risks it represents.**

Overall, Tosco seems to have done well by following a growth strategy through acquisitions. The risks inherent in an acquisition strategy are that often, acquiring companies fail to add value to their acquisitions and instead dissipate value because they overestimate the economic benefits from the acquisitions, or fail to screen acquisitions targets carefully, or even pay too much for the acquisitions.

Tosco seems to have avoided all the pitfalls:

- The company's position in the refining and marketing sector is very strong where it competes with the largest integrated energy majors. It is the 7th largest company in retail gas marketing in the United States, has the 3rd largest capacity in refining, and is the largest company owning convenience stores in the country.

- It has selected the locations of its refineries carefully so as to benefit from the proximity to its primary retail markets.

- It has been able to achieve economies of scale and has one of the highest capacity utilizations as compared to the other leading refining firms. Hence it is able to keep its costs down.

- Tosco has purchased all its assets at a discounted price and has successfully restructured them to improve margins. It sold the operations that were not performing well.

One issue of concern to Tosco should be its debt situation—its financial leverage is very high and they might need to lower it in order to have a healthier balance sheet.

4.   **What are the future growth prospects for Tosco in this industry?**

Given the industry environment, the near term prospects for Tosco look positive since demand for oil and gas in the United States is higher than the supply. However, in the long term, as the industry consolidates and matures further, Tosco may have to identify other growth strategies in order to sustain its rapid growth. There are two viable options for Tosco in the future:

- It may venture into upstream activities like production and exploration of oil to consolidate and strengthen its position.

- It may merge with another company in order to accelerate and sustain profitable growth within the refining and marketing industry.

Students may come up with other options that might make strategic sense.

POSTSCRIPT

Philips Petroleum Company acquired Tosco in 2001 in a $7 billion stock deal. This deal created the second largest refiner in the United States with total revenues of $50 billion. Later, in the same year Philips and Conoco announced a merger to create the 3rd largest oil company in the country and the 6th largest global integrated oil company (Source: CNN Money, February and November, 2001).

CASE 29

The Evolution of the Air Express Industry, 1973-2002

SYNOPSIS OF THE CASE

This case describes the evolution of competition in the air express industry from the industry's creation by Federal Express in 1973 to 2002. The case begins by describing how Federal Express essentially created the industry with a major innovation in the way small packages were transported by air (the hub-and-spoke system). This innovation enabled Federal Express to offer next-day delivery for small packages at a time when other companies took two to three days to make a delivery.

Next, the industry's development in the aftermath of deregulation in 1977 is examined. The story in the early 1980s was one of rapid growth and new entry by a number of companies, including, most significantly, UPS and Airborne Express. Because of this new entry and the commodity nature of the product, significant price competition developed in the industry during this period. The case then describes the consolidation of the industry between 1987 and 1996 and pricing and product trends over this period. The case has a detailed discussion of the race to globalize the air express industry—a process that is just getting under way but promises to revolutionize the international airfreight business. It closes with the main trends that have characterized the industry in the last five years. From 1997 to 2002, the top three players have concentrated on building their logistics services, ground networks and hubs, and have bundled service offerings to business customers. Although the weak economy in 2001 and 2002 has not led to another round of price wars, it may lead to further consolidation in the industry.

TEACHING OBJECTIVES

This is an excellent case for illustrating the power of Porter's five forces model and for discussing how competitive forces change as an industry evolves. The case works well both as a basis for classroom discussion or as a basis for a written report. The case is designed to be used in conjunction with the Airborne Express case, although it can be studied on its own. Its main teaching objectives are as follows:

1. To familiarize the students with the dynamics of industry competition and the techniques of industry analysis. Porter's five forces model, discussed in Chapter 2 of the text, can be applied to the material contained in this case.

2. To show students how competitive structure changes as an industry evolves. The U.S. air express industry has gone through clearly defined growth and shakeout stages and is now becoming mature.

STRATEGIC ISSUES AND DISCUSSION QUESTIONS

1. **How true is it to say that "Federal Express pulled off one of the greatest marketing scams in the industry by making people believe that they absolutely, positively had to have something right away"? (This comment by an industry observer was made with reference to Federal Express's creation of the industry.)**

    This is an interesting question to open discussion with, since it gets right to the heart of the consumer needs that this industry is trying to satisfy. The real issue is, how vital is next-day delivery to many consumers? Clearly, for some customers it is a necessity. This is true for the manufacturers of high-value, low-weight products that rely on next-day delivery to support their just-in-time systems. It is also true for those customers of air express companies who genuinely need next-day delivery to better serve their own clients (for example, many high-value, low-weight replacement parts for computers are delivered by air). For these customers it is not true to say that Fed Ex pulled off a marketing scam. Fed Ex and its competitors are satisfying a genuine need.

On the other hand, many business customers use next-day delivery simply because it is available; they could get by without it. For these customers next-day delivery is a convenience product, a luxury. In a sense, Fed Ex did pull off a marketing scam in these cases, since the need that is being served is something of an artificial creation.

The distinction between those customers for whom the product is a necessity and those for whom it is a luxury is important. The greater the number for whom it is a luxury, the more vulnerable the industry is to a severe recession. When corporate and personal incomes fall, the first things that get cut are the luxuries.

2.   **Why, despite rapid growth, was the air express industry characterized by low returns during much of the 1980s?**

The best way to answer this question is to use Porter's five forces model to analyze competitive intensity in the industry. The picture that emerges is one of an industry in which the structural conditions made intense price competition the rule during much of the 1980s.

New Entry

This industry has three main entry barriers:

- High capital costs involved in establishing nationwide air and ground networks.

- Brand loyalty and name recognition enjoyed by established companies, particularly Federal Express.

- Access to landing slots in congested airport hubs.

Despite these significant entry barriers, during the early 1980s six major companies entered the industry, including Airborne Express, Emery, Purolator, and UPS. This illustrates an important point: although high entry barriers reduce the probability of entry, they do not eliminate it.

Five of the six new entrants were freight forwarders (Airborne Express, Emery, Purolator). These companies already had ground delivery networks and had historically relied on established passenger and all-cargo airlines to deliver their freight in two to three days. The decline in cargo carrying by passenger airlines, along with the threat to their business from Federal Express's next-day service, meant that these companies had to enter the air express industry or go out of business. This gave them an incentive to bear the high capital costs of setting up an air network. The other new entrant, UPS, also had an established ground network. In addition, it was a cash-rich operation that could afford to bear the costs of entry.

It is notable that no firm from outside the general transportation industry entered the air express market. All of the new entrants had ground networks and a reputation in the industry. This helped them circumvent the otherwise substantial barriers to entry.

Rivalry

With regard to rivalry, four main factors are of note. First, the air express service is a commodity-type product. Differentiation is difficult, except on the "reliability of next-day service" dimension. This in itself makes price competition more likely and nonprice competition relatively ineffective, thereby increasing the danger of a price war.

Second, the industry was consolidated enough for the competitive actions of one firm to directly affect other firms. Such interdependence is characteristic of oligopolies and can result in a price war. In the air express industry, discounting by UPS after its entry in 1982 immediately cut into the market share of other air express companies. They were forced to respond in the only way they could, by cutting their own prices. UPS responded by making further cuts, and so the industry slid into a price war.

Third, because of new entry, there was a significant increase in carrying capacity in the industry between 1979 and 1982. This rapid increase far outstripped even the rapid growth in demand. The emergence of some excess capacity was an additional factor that helped spark a price war, which in turn depressed margins.

Fourth, the firms that entered the industry in the early 1980s faced high exit barriers from (a) high fixed costs and (b) the need to maintain extensive national coverage. Both of these factors made it all but impossible for troubled firms to incrementally cut their capacity. Thus excess capacity persisted, prolonging the price war.

Buyer Power

The major consumers of air express services are corporations. Corporations have significant buyer power for the following reasons:

- Their costs of switching among air express companies are low.

- They are significant customers that can use their leverage to bargain down prices.

- They banded together, further increasing their bargaining power.

As a result, major corporations were in a position to play air express operators off against each other. They have used this ability to demand deep discounts, further squeezing profits out of the industry.

Supplier Power

One of the major variable cost elements in operating an air express operation is the cost of aviation fuel. Although the worldwide oil glut led to relatively low fuel prices during the late 1980s and early 1990s, any disruption in the world oil supply will raise fuel prices and squeeze profits out of the industry. This didn't occur during the 1980s (because of a growing oil glut), but it did occur in the aftermath of the invasion of Kuwait by Iraq, cutting the margins of air express operators in half.

Substitutes

There are three viable substitutes for air express services:

- Fax machines (for small documents and letters).

- Electronic document transmission over the Internet.

- Second-day delivery and surface mail.

Fax machines undoubtedly slowed down the growth rate in the air express industry and exacerbated the excess capacity problem. The existence of lower-cost second-day and surface mail delivery services reduces the ability of air express operators to raise their prices too high (otherwise customers will simply shift to this less expensive substitute). While the Internet was not a big factor in the 1980s, it is rapidly becoming one.

3. **Why did competitive intensity moderate and prices rise during 1988–1989?**

The quick answer is that the structural conditions in the industry became more favorable. There was no new entry after 1982. All the likely entrants came in during the 1979–1982 period. Barriers to entry remain high, making further entry unlikely. This may change, however, if the rule prohibiting foreign companies from owning more than 25 percent of a U.S. airline is changed (the air express operators are classed as airlines). If this happens, TNT and DHL may enter the U.S. domestic market (they already handle express freight into and out of the United States).

As a result of the price war, there was a shakeout and the industry consolidated. By 1988 only three major players were left—Fed Ex, Airborne, and UPS. This solved the excess capacity problem and facilitated the emergence of what looks like tacit price collusion, with UPS taking on the role of price leader. In January 1989 and February 1990 UPS announced price increases. On both occasions the other players in the industry quickly followed suit.

4. **What do you think will happen in the industry if the U.S. economy enters a deep recession?**

This is an industry that has never been tested during a serious recession. Even the 1990–1991 recession was relatively minor by historic standards. The underlying structural conditions of the industry suggest that if a serious recession occurs profit margins will plunge for these reasons:

- As this product is a luxury for a significant proportion of customers, it is likely to be avoided in a recession; consumers will switch to less expensive substitutes such as ground delivery and second-day delivery.

- Those customers that do not switch to substitutes will demand deeper discounts.

- Excess capacity may emerge as demand drops.

- Because of all of the above, a reemergence of serious price competition is likely. The commodity nature of the product, the power of buyers, and the interdependence that is characteristic of a consolidated industry suggest that this could be serious.

The weak economic conditions of 2001 have led to a 7.6% decline in the number of packages shipped by air domestically. Estimates for 2002 are expected to increase by only 3%. However, the recessionary conditions did not lead to a price war among the air express industry players – in fact the prices were increased moderately to make up for increased fuel costs. However, all of the above concerns remain valid if economic conditions do not improve.

5.   **What form do you think the competitive structure of the global air express industry will take during the next decade?**

If unhindered by governmental constraints (a big "if"), the global industry is likely to develop along lines very similar to those in the United States. Demand growth may take off as the globalization of competition and markets in a wide variety of industries increases demand for the services of international air express operations. Considerations of logistics and cost suggest that competitive advantage will go to those companies that own integrated air and ground operations and that operate a hub-and-spoke system capable of knitting together the three main advanced economic regions of the world—North America, Western Europe, and the Asian Pacific Rim countries. As in the United States, all of these factors point to the eventual emergence of a consolidated industry protected by high barriers to entry. However, as in the United States, the commodity nature of the product suggests that price competition will always be important and may periodically become intense, particularly during the inevitable shakeout period.

6.   **To what degree do first-mover advantages form the basis of Federal Express's competitive position in the air express industry? Given this, how vulnerable is Federal Express to renewed price competition?**

Federal Express pioneered many of the practices in the industry. It was the first company to operate an integrated ground and air network, to establish a hub-and-spoke system, and to introduce package-tracking systems. All of these innovations gave Federal Express a tremendous reputation with the general public. When people think of express mail, they think of Federal Express. This reputation forms the basis of much of the company's first-mover advantage.

However, because of the commodity nature of the product, Federal Express is in no position to use its reputation as the basis for charging higher prices. Major corporate customers are hard-nosed and prepared to play off Federal Express against other air express companies when demanding discounts. Moreover, relative to Airborne Express (and perhaps UPS), Federal Express has a high cost structure because of (a) the cost of serving small customers and (b) the cost of serving the debt taken on to finance its global operation, including the cost of acquiring Flying Tiger. All of this suggests that Federal Express is vulnerable to intense price competition.

7.   **How vulnerable is UPS to intense price competition?**

Not very vulnerable. UPS is a profitable, well-run company with low debt and an enormous ground operation that can be used to subsidize its air express operation in times of difficulty. Of all the air express companies, by virtue of its size and financial strength, UPS is best equipped to survive a price war in the air express operations. Indeed, it was UPS that (deliberately) initiated the last price war in the industry. It could do so again.

CASE 30

Airborne Express in 2002

SYNOPSIS OF THE CASE

Airborne Express is the third largest company in the U.S. air express industry; it is also the low-cost player. The case focuses on the strengths and weaknesses of Airborne Express, its business-level strategy, and its strategy for building a global business. The case offers a detailed view of a company that has been forced by adverse circumstances to become very efficient. The theme that runs through the case is that everything that Airborne Express does can be viewed as an attempt to reduce costs and boost productivity while maintaining an excellent service.

The case opens with a brief review of the history of the company. It discusses the main features of Airborne Express's operations, including the "nuts and bolts" of its domestic and international delivery systems. Next, the case reviews Airborne Express's strategy—both in the domestic market and with regard to international expansion—and examines the company's organizational structure, control systems, and culture. The case closes with the text of an interview that the case author conducted with Airborne Express's CEO, Robert Cline.

TEACHING OBJECTIVES

This is a very good case for illustrating the company wide effort needed for a firm to become a low-cost player. The case works well as a basis for class discussion or for a written report. Its main teaching objectives are as follows:

1. To familiarize students with the strategic and organizational characteristics of a company that has successfully pursued a low-cost/focus business-level strategy. This fits in with the discussion contained in Chapters 3 through 6 of the text, as well as with the material on implementation.

2. To explore the concepts of distinctive competencies and barriers to imitation as they apply to Airborne Express. This complements material covered in Chapter 3 of the text.

3. To examine the pros and cons of using strategic alliances to expand overseas. This complements the material on strategic alliances contained in Chapter 8 of the text.

STRATEGIC ISSUES AND DISCUSSION QUESTIONS

1. **According to Porter's framework, what generic strategy is Airborne Express pursuing? Is this a sound strategy in the context of the air express industry?**

    Airborne Express is pursuing a focus/low-cost strategy. The company focuses on serving the needs of high-volume corporate customers, and it aims to be the lowest-cost company serving this particular segment.

    This strategy makes very good sense in the context of the air express industry (see Case 29 Teaching Notes, on the air express industry). This is an industry where the product is essentially a commodity, differentiation is difficult, and price is the main competitive weapon. Substantial buyer power and the closeness of viable substitutes such as fax and second-day surface delivery imply constant downward pressure on prices. To survive and prosper in this industry, a company has to have a low-cost structure.

    The strategy of focusing on large corporate customers is consistent with this environment. By focusing on large accounts, Airborne can utilize its ground capacity more effectively. On the average, Airborne delivery drivers drop off and pick up far more packages per stop than do the drivers of companies that focus on serving smaller accounts and individual customers (Federal Express and UPS). This helps boost productivity and lower costs, enabling Airborne to make a profit at a price that would imply losses for UPS or Federal Express.

2.   **What are the strengths of Airborne Express? Does it have a distinctive competency? If so, where does it lie? Is this competency imitable?**

Airborne has a number of strengths, all of which contribute to the company's ability to offer a low-cost but very reliable service to its customers.

- The strategy of focusing on corporate accounts is a strength, since it leads to better capacity utilization and lower costs.

- The patented innovation of C-containers to hold packages represents a strength. C-containers fit through the passenger doors of aircraft, doing away with the need to install expensive cargo doors in aircraft. In addition, they can be easily maneuvered by small conveyor belts and individuals, and this convenience does away with the need to invest in expensive cargo-loading equipment. Thus the innovation lowers costs.

- Airborne's practice of buying used aircraft, converting them to its own specifications, and doing its own maintenance represents further strengths. It is less expensive to buy used aircraft and convert them than to buy new aircraft. It is also less expensive to do maintenance in-house. Thus both practices lower costs. Airborne installs state-of-the-art electronic equipment in its aircraft. Although expensive up front, it increases reliability. (Airborne's aircraft can land in thick fog.)

- The company's incentive systems are designed to reward employees for meeting the twin goals of high productivity and high reliability.

- Airborne's national and international tracking systems are the best in the industry. they enable Airborne to tell customers at a moment's notice where their packages are in the system. This helps improve reliability and build brand loyalty. The same information systems help Airborne to manage its billing systems efficiently, thereby lowering costs.

- The longevity of the top-management team is a clear strength. Most of its members have worked together for fifteen to twenty years. They are very knowledgeable about the industry and the company. Any personal problems were resolved years ago. There is a lack of political infighting, which helps create an environment for effective top-management decision-making.

- Airborne is the only air express company to own its own airport (the major hub at Wilmington, Ohio). Thus Airborne is less vulnerable to problems arising from airport congestion than other air express operations. This contributes to the smooth running of its operation and further increases reliability.

- The company's attempts to diversify its product offering by moving into logistics services represents a significant strength, since this is a less price-sensitive segment of the air express business.

As can be seen, Airborne's strengths are significant. Indeed, the organization-wide focus on productivity, low cost, and high reliability does seem to constitute something of a distinctive competency. Because of this Airborne has a lower cost structure than any of its rivals. Moreover, this is a distinctive competency that its two major competitors, UPS and Federal Express, could imitate only with difficulty. Eventually any distinctive competency can be imitated, and there is no reason why Federal Express and UPS could not ultimately do many of the things that Airborne does. However, for UPS and Federal Express to imitate Airborne, they would have to abandon their broad market coverage and adopt a similar focused strategy. This would be difficult since they would have to write off years of investments in serving smaller customers, to say nothing of the dislocation such a strategic change would cause in their respective organizations. Thus inertia at UPS and Federal Express makes it unlikely that they will imitate Airborne Express anytime soon.

3.   **What are Airborne Express's weaknesses?**

The truth is that Airborne has few major weaknesses. This is a very well run operation. The main weakness is a lack of financial strength. Years of tight margins have left the company with few cash reserves. However, the alliance with Mitsui, along with the financial resources it brings, makes this weakness look less serious. Nevertheless, it is an important constraint on the company's ability to finance growth (overseas, for example) or to survive a prolonged price war should another occur.

4. **Is Airborne's strategy of using strategic alliances to expand overseas wise? What are the pros and cons of this strategy?**

    Airborne's global strategy involves two main steps. First, the company enters into alliances with foreign ground operations (such as Panther Express in Japan). Second, Airborne buys cargo space from other airlines (both passenger and cargo) to get its packages overseas. The pros of this strategy are as follows:

    *   Airborne does not have to invest in aircraft to fly overseas (there are no fixed costs). Since there is currently no international demand that would be required if Airborne were to fly its own aircraft overseas at full capacity, this makes good sense. (Both UPS and Federal Express are flying half-empty aircraft on transoceanic routes and losing money in the process.)

    *   There is currently plenty of spare cargo capacity in the holds of transoceanic passenger flights.

    *   Foreign partners bring local knowledge to the operation and can help with market access.

    *   There is no need to invest in an overseas ground network.

    *   Thus the strategy is a low-cost way of expanding overseas. Airborne refers to the strategy as a variable-cost strategy; there are no fixed costs.

    On the other hand, it has some drawbacks:

    *   Airborne lacks the tight control over aircraft schedules and foreign ground networks that might be required to run a tight ship. Since reliability (in terms of ability to deliver a package on time) is a key issue in the industry, this could present Airborne with a problem in the future.

    *   Airborne risks having its packages pushed to the back of aircraft, further damaging reliability. JAL, one of Airborne's main carriers on the trans-Pacific route, has just entered into an alliance with DHL to establish a global express network. Thus Airborne may find that when space is tight JAL will assign Airborne's packages a lower priority than DHL's.

    If the international business picks up (as many predict it will) and transoceanic capacity becomes tight, Airborne could lose out to companies such as Federal Express and UPS. At that point in time it might pay Airborne to start flying its own aircraft overseas. For the present, however, it makes good sense to stick to the current variable-cost strategy. Other reasons aside, Airborne doesn't have the financial resources required to absorb the kind of losses that Federal Express and UPS have had to bear while pioneering their transoceanic routes.

5. **Is Airborne's strategy of trying to diversify its product offering to include logistics services for clients wise?**

    Absolutely. The document business is a low-margin commodity-type business in which buyers have a lot of power. Moreover, it is increasingly threatened by the growth of the Internet as a medium for the electronic transmission of documents. Logistics services—managing the just-in-time inventory systems of clients and helping coordinate their global logistics—promise higher margins for three reasons:

    *   Such services are a necessity for many cost-conscious clients and therefore are unlikely to be cut in a recession.

    *   If Airborne can develop a firm-specific skill in handling this kind of business, it may be able to charge a premium price.

    *   Buyer power is reduced because making such systems work requires a much closer link between the air express operator and its client. This raises switching costs to the buyers and limits their ability to play off air express companies against each other.

6. **If you were CEO of Airborne, what would your strategy be?**

    The economics of the air express industry are extremely unfavorable for the players in the industry. In order to be successful, the CEO of Airborne might consider taking steps that could potentially alter the economics of the industry. The key strategy that can be pursued in addition to diversification into logistics services is further investment in Ground Delivery Services (GDS). Increased differentiation through value added logistics services help raise switching costs as explained in question 6. Offering Ground Delivery Service—a lower priced service meant for less time sensitive packages—is another area that has the potential to grow, especially in a weak economy when corporate as well as individual customers concentrate on cutting costs. GDS is an important service to offer because it allows Airborne to support their logistics services and be able to offer customers bundled products, which, help raise switching costs and reduce buyer power even further. Airborne's existing ground infrastructure, tracking systems and other assets lower the initial costs of adding the service and puts Airborne on par with its competitors, Fed Ex and UPS, who are already offering this service.

CASE 31

Blockbuster in 2002

SYNOPSIS OF THE CASE

This case charts the growth of the very successful Blockbuster Entertainment Corporation, the largest global video store chain. The case starts by looking at the reasons for the success of Blockbuster's original concept for a video superstore. It then examines how Wayne Huizenga, the entrepreneur who made Waste Management a $6 billion company, helped the company grow and establish itself as the only national video superstore. The case highlights the sources of competitive advantage, and it highlights how a company can develop a simultaneous low-cost and differentiation business-level strategy. Then it examines how Blockbuster diversified to counter the threat from new technologies like videos-on-demand (which may threaten Blockbuster's core video-rental business) and to exploit its own distinctive competencies in new entertainment businesses.

The case then recounts how Blockbuster was bought by Viacom, and how in 1996 its performance plummeted because of a number of related factors. Attempts to turn around Blockbuster are then described and the case goes on to look at how radical changes in its functional-, business-, global-, and corporate-level strategies were necessary to turn around the company's performance and shows students how value is created by the fit between all levels of strategy.

TEACHING OBJECTIVES

The main teaching objectives of this case are as follows:

1. To illustrate how an entrepreneur with a vision of a new way of delivering a product to customers founds a company.

2. To chart how a company develops a set of distinctive competencies that allow it to achieve a low cost/differentiation advantage and to outperform its competitors.

3. To illustrate the way a retail chain store grows, and how chaining, franchising, and horizontal merger work to consolidate a fragmented industry.

4. To show how global expansion is an extension of a company's domestic strategy and how it allows a company to create more value.

5. To give students the opportunity to understand how the different levels of strategy fit together, and how achieving this fit and a fit with organizational structure are key to competitive advantage.

6. To show how changes in the environment such as the emergence of new technologies or new competition can quickly erode the source of a company's competitive advantage and require shifts in strategic direction.

This is a good case to use either after the chapters on business-level strategy or at the end of the lectures on strategy, to illustrate how strategy emerges in a company over time. The Blockbuster name is very familiar to students, and the video-rental business is easy to understand; they can appreciate the issues involved in establishing a new business. It is a good vehicle for introducing students to the way strategy develops over time. Although Blockbuster was initially successful, strategic problems arose for the company because of competition from new video store chains and new technologies. The case recounts Blockbuster's takeover by Viacom, its problems and then the development of new competitive strategies that have helped to restore its profitability. After analyzing the Blockbuster case, it is useful to then analyze the Viacom case to clarify the link between business- and corporate-level strategy (See synopsis of Viacom case for more details).

STRATEGIC ISSUES AND DISCUSSION QUESTIONS

1.   What gap in the video-rental market did David Cook discover and how did he fill it?

In the early 1980s, the number of VCRs in peoples' homes was expanding rapidly and many small video-rental stores offering a limited selection were opening. Many of them rented X-rated movies, and parents with children, the largest segment of the video market, were reluctant to take their children there. David Cook, the founder of Blockbuster Entertainment, was searching for a new business opportunity and realized that there was an opportunity in the video-rental market for a new kind of store, one that would appeal to families and could satisfy their needs in a different way. In 1985 he opened his first Blockbuster video store based on several concepts.

First, he decided that the stores should be very prominent they should be freestanding, in good locations, and brightly lit with lots of parking to encourage families to come in and browse. Second, he offered three-day rentals for three dollars and made sure his stores were full of titles that appealed to families. Each one carries a large selection of seven thousand to thirteen thousand titles that are clearly categorized and there are many sections devoted specifically to children. Third, Cook targeted the two largest customer groups, adults from eighteen to forty-five and children from six to twelve, and adopted a marketing campaign for the family-viewing audience. Blockbuster does not offer X-rated movies. Finally, he pioneered the development of software using laser-bar code scanners that read information from both the tape and from the customer's membership card. This improved customer service and led to shorter checkout times.

His new video-store concept was a smash hit. The combination of a huge selection of tapes, fast checkout, three-day rental, and a family-oriented atmosphere gave the organization a competitive advantage. Every store he opened was immediately successful and each store grossed $70 to 80 thousand a month. Soon he franchised his concept and took his company public, where it became one of the hundred fastest-growing companies in Fortune 500. Its stock price continually hits record highs. In 1992 it opened its three thousandth national and its thousandth international store, and intends to double this number by 1995.

2.   What key strengths did David Cook develop in his company that made it so successful?

The success of David Cook's video superstore concept was based on developing functional strengths in three main areas: store management and operations, distribution, and sales and marketing. First, he created a store operations function to devise the most efficient way of managing each video store's activities. For example, the store operations department developed a state-of-the-art video checkout procedure that minimized customers' time in line for service. This allowed the company to track its customers and discover their preferences so that it could better serve their needs. The department also devised the best store layout for arranging videotapes to maximize the ease with which customers could make their selections. In every store managers and employers learned these skills from experienced operations personnel.

Second, Cook created a very efficient distribution function to manage the flow of videotapes from Blockbuster's warehouse to the video stores so that new releases would be available to customers in the shortest possible time. Moreover, the distribution department developed the capabilities for transferring videos between stores so that they could be rapidly moved from a store where they were not renting to one where they were.

Third, Cook developed a sophisticated sales and marketing department to target families with children, and he designed marketing campaigns to attract them into the stores. For example, the marketing department started a Blockbuster kids program that created Blockbuster characters to appeal to children and a Kidprint program to imprint on a videotape a child's name, height, and address for identification purposes.

By creating these distinctive competencies, Cook was able to outperform his main competitors, the mom and pop stores. In these stores, owners and part-time staff perform all functions and do not develop the distinctive competencies that are possible when a company owns a chain of thousands of stores.

3.   How did these distinctive competencies provide Blockbuster with a competitive advantage?

The three building blocks of competitive advantage are efficiency, quality of customer service, and innovation.

Efficiency. Cook's new system gave Blockbuster a low-cost advantage in many areas. First, his new distribution system lowered the costs of equipping and servicing the different video stores. Second, Blockbuster's size allowed it to negotiate discounts for prerecorded videotapes. Third, the company's skills in store operations and management gave it an advantage in reducing store management costs.

Quality of customer service. For a service organization like Blockbuster, improving the quality of customer service is key to competitive success. Quality means increasing the reliability with which customers receive the product, and Blockbuster imitated McDonald's in developing systems that resulted in customers receiving quick and consistent service. For example, its checkout procedure reduced customers' waits at busy times. The store layout and distribution system both helped to increase the quality of customer service.

Innovation. Cook innovated the entire video superstore concept. His functional innovations all contributed to the company's success and it became the company to imitate. As discussed below, one issue facing Blockbuster now is the increasing sophistication of local mom and pop stores, which are copying Blockbuster's efficient checkout procedures. This may threaten Blockbuster's ability to increase its market share except by taking over its competitors.

In short, Blockbuster's distinctive competencies provided it with a competitive advantage that it used to become the dominant competitor in the marketplace.

4. **What generic, competitive business-level strategy did Blockbuster use to become the leading competitor in the video-rental business?**

Blockbuster used its distinctive competencies to develop both a low-cost and a differentiation business-level strategy. On the differentiation dimension it used its distinctive competencies in marketing to establish a national reputation and to differentiate its products by, for example, its three-day three dollar rental policy. Also, store location in dense population areas and unique store layout contributed to its national identity. In the video-rental business, where all the stores are selling essentially the same product, store location is a critical factor, because customers will tend to go to the nearest one, providing it carries what they want. Thus, Blockbuster's ability to strategically locate its stores was a critical factor in allowing it to develop its differentiated appeal. Finally, its unique checkout procedure, which allowed it to monitor the tastes and preferences of its customers, helped give it a differentiation advantage.

On the low-cost dimension, Blockbuster developed a low-cost competitive advantage from its strengths in store management and distribution and also by carefully targeting the largest market segments.

5. **How did Blockbuster manage the industry environment over time to support and develop its business-level strategy?**

Blockbuster entered a fragmented industry, composed of a large number of mom and pop stores. Wayne Huizenga, who took control of Blockbuster from David Cook, took Blockbuster national using the strategies of chaining, franchising, and horizontal merger to consolidate the fragmented industry. It began to open many company-owned stores in large urban markets and at the same time it sold the rights to franchise its store concept to entrepreneurs in other urban areas. It used the revenues from franchising to build its own stores and to take over rival chains. The speed of its expansion was partly the result of its need to exploit first-mover advantages, because many of its strengths could be imitated. Thus, it was very important to build a national base as soon as possible, and Blockbuster succeeded well.

By 1993 Blockbuster had gained only 15 percent of the video-rental market, which was still very fragmented, and it was attempting to reach 25-30 percent in three to five years. To achieve this ambitious goal, it needed to continue its program of take over and horizontal merger and pursue a market penetration strategy, which involved a cluster strategy: opening stores in urban areas to surround competitors and to attract their customers. National advertising also helped its market penetration strategy. However, its smaller rivals are now stronger and more resistant to the Blockbuster challenge because they have imitated its product and pricing strategies as well as the size and layout of its stores. (The next case, Video Concepts, Inc., focuses on these issues and shows students what the Blockbuster challenge means for a small video store chain.)

6. **How did Blockbuster use its strengths at the business level to exploit new opportunities, counter threats, and develop its corporate-level strategy?**

    In an effort to use its distinctive competencies to exploit new opportunities and to counter threats from new technology, Blockbuster has embarked on a program of (1) global expansion, (2) vertical integration, and (3) diversification.

    Global expansion. Blockbuster is attempting to exploit its strengths throughout the world, and particularly in Europe and Japan. In the United Kingdom, it now owns over a thousand video stores and in Japan it has a joint venture with a Japanese company to franchise Blockbuster. It is using the same strategy of chaining, franchising, and horizontal merger that it used in the United States to obtain a foothold in a foreign market. Here Blockbuster is following the lead of companies such as Toys R Us and McDonalds.

    Vertical Integration. Blockbuster has also vertically integrated backward to take control over movie libraries and to develop the ability to produce its own movies. It entered into agreements with Spelling Entertainment and Republic Pictures to take control over their movie libraries, and is seeking new ventures with companies like Viacom to secure a foothold in the production end of the business. In pursing movie production, Blockbuster is going a long way from its core business of video rental, but apparently it believes that to compete with giants like Time Warner and Paramount in a changing technological environment, it needs control of its inputs.

    Diversification. Blockbuster has also embarked on a program of related diversification by expanding into the music retailing business. The company applied its distinctive competencies in store management and marketing to create a new national chain of Blockbuster Music stores. Opportunities for exploiting synergies and for sharing skills and resources between its video business and the music business are possible. For example, its 50 million video customers can be given discount certificates for tapes and CDs in its music stores. Similarly, it can share its skills in store operations and distribution between different store chains.

7. **What structure did Blockbuster use to manage its corporate-level strategy?**

    To manage its ambitious program of global expansion and diversification Blockbuster adopted a multidivisional structure in 1993. It created seven different divisions: domestic home video, international home video, music retailing, international music retailing, new technology ventures, and other entertainment ventures.

8. **After Viacom acquired Blockbuster in 1996 what developing problems came together to cause its profitability and stock price to plunge?**

    Competitors. Although Blockbuster was the industry leader and had a strong brand name by 1996 competition was growing in the industry. The video-rental industry was consolidating and large aggressive regional competitors emerged which imitated Blockbuster's competencies, such as its number and range of videos, its three-day product and pricing policies, and checkout procedures.

    Movie Studios. Increasingly the movie studios began to realize that they could make more money by selling tapes directly to customers, and the price of tapes began to fall. This eroded Blockbuster's buying power, all video chains could acquire tapes at a lower cost. This change in strategy by the movie studios choked off growth in Blockbuster's revenues, and indeed reduced them, it signaled an important change in industry competition

    New technology. Another major perceived threat was the development of new technology, particularly video-on-demand systems through the Internet and using broadband technology that would bypass and outdate the local video store. In the future, with a video-on-demand system, customers will be able to watch a video of their choice by going on the internet or telephoning the local cable company to ask for a video to be downloaded over the cable or telephone lines to their television set. With no video to pick up or return to a store, the systems would have enormous advantages, particularly for new releases.

    Although publicly, before the merger with Viacom Huizenga shrugged off the threat from new technology, arguing that video-on-demand and other new technologies will be more expensive than video rental and cannot offer customers the same range of options, he clearly saw it as a major threat. Blockbuster tried to counter this threat by establishing agreements with telephone or cable companies to use its local stores as the warehouse for these movies. However, it faced competition here from companies like TCI and Time Warner, which also had the capability to act as video warehouses and it met little success. Blockbuster failure to become the "video warehouse" that controls the system hurt the company seriously and after Blockbuster's merger with Viacom caused a fall in Blockbuster's revenues which ruined Viacom's stock price.

Risky Diversification. Moreover, it is clear that Huizenga entered the music business and also into the production of movies and television programs to diversify to counter this threat. However, diversification into the music business is risky because the music industry is characterized by intense competition among the major retail chains and profit margins have been low. Similarly, producing hit movies or shows is a very risky business and there is intense competition among the major studios for new talent.

9.   **What steps did Redstone, Field's and Antioco take to turnaround Blockbuster's declining performance?**

Redstone searched for a CEO who could solve its problems, and since revenues were not growing it seemed he would have to try to reduce the chains cost structure. He hired William Fields, and IT expert and senior manager from cost leader Wal-Mart to revitalize Blockbusters video and music chain businesses. Field's put in place an ambitious IT strategy, involving building a new national IT distribution infrastructure to reduce costs. He also tried to increase revenues by having each video store sell a wider range of entertainment products such as books, comics, CDs, candy, computer, and multimedia products. Given that this would cannibalize sales from Blockbuster Music stores one idea was to open new mega-entertainment stores that could offer a wide range of entertainment products. However, the success of such stores had yet to be demonstrated because of intense competition in these parts of the entertainment retail business. Meanwhile, Blockbuster's video rental revenues were still flat or falling.

And, despite Field's objections, Redstone decided to scale back expansion plans and cut planned new store openings to try to improve its financial picture. In fact, as described in the Viacom case, Viacom's stock price plunged in 1996 on fears over the future profitability of its Blockbuster division and analysts were waiting to see if Viacom could turn the division, for which it had paid $8.4 billion so it could buy Paramount, around.

Viacom's mounting problems, and Field's IT orientation was not changing Blockbuster or Viacom fast enough for Redstone's liking. Field's strategy would not bring the fast turnaround he wanted. In 1997, he fired Fields and brought in a new CEO John Antioco, who had engineered a turnaround in Taco Bell.

Antioco had a new vision for how to develop a strategy for Blockbuster that would restore its profitability. Antioco's strategy was rather than try to boost revenues by offering more kinds of products in Blockbuster stores or developing new music stores, find a way to drive up revenues from video sales. He proposed a revolutionary new competitive strategy in the mature video rental market. He proposed that Blockbuster would share rental revenues of new movie rentals with major movie studios, each taking a proportion of all revenues generated from each new movie rental. In return, Blockbuster would pay only $8 for new movie tapes, reducing a major source of its high cost structure, which would allow it to purchase many more copies of the same movie. In turn, with more copies of a movie on the shelf when it was released—the peak time for generating video rental revenues—there would always be tapes in stock for customers to rent so revenues would increase. Moreover, Blockbuster would be able to guarantee the tape was in stock and this would lessen the appeal of video-on-demand which also could offer this new service.

This strategy was enormously successful, it was a positive sum game for Blockbuster and the movie studios, Blockbuster's revenues and profits soared, and so did Viacom's stock price. It was now clear that the chain could be profitable and that the threat from pay per view and broadband would materialize far slower than analysts had once thought. Blockbuster once more became an important generator of cash flow, indeed its market share increased from less than 30% to over 40% in the next five years and it went from being a thorn in Viacom's empire to one of its jewels since it once more became a major cash generator.

The other side of Antioco's strategy was to abandon attempts to develop entertainment mega-stores, and indeed to abandon the low-profit music business. He sold off the Blockbuster music chain in 1998 to Wherehouse entertainment. However, realizing as Field's had done the need to expand product offerings in each Blockbuster store, the question became to find the right product mix. He started with a strategic alliance with Citibank to place the latter's computer terminals in Blockbuster stores. More video games were stocked, and stores were allowed to customize their tapes to appeal to the needs of local customers. Another major step came in 1999 when it became obvious that DVDs were the medium of the future and Blockbuster began to increase the percentage of DVD's it carried in its stores and to rent DVD players. Globally, Antioco realized the importance of maintaining and developing Blockbuster's global strengths and put in motion a global expansion plan that led to its entry into many new countries, especially in Central and South America. One major advantage of this was that when demand for new tapes dropped inside the US they could be introduced in other countries so that a steady stream of revenues from global rentals would be obtained over time helping to contribute to Blockbuster's bottom line.

In 1989, its state of the art new 820,000 distribution center opened in Kinney Texas to help move tapes around stores in the US and globally and to make the best use of its expensive inventory, still its biggest cost of doing business. Blockbuster also introduced the "Blockbuster Rewards Program" to encourage more frequent rentals and build customer returns and revenues.

10. **How was Blockbuster positioned by 1999 to deal with the future?**

Redstone took advantage of Blockbuster's turnaround to sell 20% of Blockbuster stock in 1999 to create a "tracking stock" that would allow investors to evaluate Viacom's and Blockbuster's performance separately. Then, it was up to Antioco to demonstrate how well Blockbuster could perform in a changing environment.

Antioco and his managers continued to forge strategic alliances to build Blockbuster's revenue streams. He formed an alliance with DirecTV to distribute its satellite dishes that allow for pay per view. This was a strategic move designed to keep Blockbuster in the running to become the "video warehouse" of the future, and would add to Blockbuster revenues since it would also receive a share of the pay per view rentals DirecTV customers order. DirecTV gains access to Blockbuster's huge 40 million database on regular video rental customers allowing it to better target its marketing. In 2000, Blockbuster formed an agreement that would allow it to digitally stream MGM's recent and old movie to customers something again directed at keeping its digital options open in an uncertain environment.

In 2001, the explosive growth in demand for DVDs led to yet another major change in strategy. Blockbuster abandoned its strategy of customization of tapes by store, shipped its excess inventory abroad, and began to increase the percentage of DVDs on its shelves. Unlike in the case of tapes, no revenue sharing agreement was announced with the movie studios, probably because there were rumors that its tape revenue-sharing deal was being increasingly viewed as anti-competitive, and a similar DVD arrangement might only increase its market share at the expanse of smaller chains. Also, why would movie studios wish to offer it low prices when this would only contribute to its market strength? They would be creating a powerful buyer since Blockbuster already had over a 40% market share by 2001.

Indeed, in August 2001 five major movie studios (including Paramount) joined together to announce plans to bypass powerful middlemen like Blockbuster and HBO and offer their own PPV service of new release movies directly to customers. In 2002, this was still a specialized service, however, which was mainly aimed at downloading movies to PCs for people on the move. It is still unclear how this technology will emerge in the future and what role if any Blockbuster will play in it.

To reduce the risk of future lost revenue streams from movie rental, Blockbuster began to increase its presence in the $30 billion a year video game industry. It began to stock increasing numbers of tapes for the Sony Playstation II, Microsoft game cube, and Nintendo X-box, and rent machines to generate revenues from this growing segment of the market. It is strange it did not do this earlier, for customers ability to try out video games before purchase is a major element in their purchase decisions and Blockbuster was well positioned to take advantage of this. In 2002, it began to offer a monthly rental fee for unlimited video game use to drive demand. This move was successful and resulted in a lucrative stream of revenue, especially as it complements video rentals and DVDs. Today, the whole family can go into a Blockbuster store and each member rent or buy those products that most appeal to them. This has allowed Blockbuster to gain an increase share of booming sales of DVDs. Finally, the lawsuit brought by smaller chains claiming the revenue sharing agreement was anticompetitive dismissed in 2002 because all chains can now participate in the revenue sharing agreement.

Thus, Blockbuster's product mix has changed to suit changing market conditions, and with its cost structure under control the chain is being run to generate cash flow and profit, and to position itself for future competition in the video rental and video game industry as technology unfolds over time. The ability of customers to physically enter the store, and scan the merchandise, and test it by renting it out would seem to be a definite source of competitive advantage in the future as the store can 'showcase' new movie and game developments. At the same time, there will always be a market for watching older, specialized, or foreign movies, and Blockbuster's strategy of reducing its stock of these may backfire. It would seem there should be a way of allowing it to stock these older titles at the same time as it increases its holdings of new DVDs and video games. However, it is now much quicker to respond to customers changing demands than it has been in the past, and it is competing in the segments that offer the highest revenue potential.

Thus, the future of Blockbuster seems bright indeed, if it can change its product mix to suit changes in customer demands and changes in technology. It is in a strong competitive position and its stock price has risen to reflect this. The case strong demonstrates how managers must carefully monitor their environments and forge strategies to convert potential threats into opportunities.

CASE 32

Video Concepts, Inc.

SYNOPSIS OF THE CASE

This case chronicles how Chad Rowan, an entrepreneur who had invested his life savings in opening a series of video stores in Lexington, Kentucky, suddenly confronted a situation in which Blockbuster opened a video store across the road from his principal store. The case discusses the tactics he used to deal with Blockbuster's challenge and vividly reveals how much competitive power Blockbuster wields by virtue of its distinctive competencies in marketing and purchasing. Although Rowan can fend off Blockbuster's power and remain profitable, unless he can find a new way to compete against Blockbuster, he cannot increase his stores' revenue to be able to profit adequately to support himself and to reinvest in the business.

The case ends with Rowan's deliberations, in which he considers, for example, exiting the market, selling off his tape inventory, and finding a new venture. Another option is to fight back by increasing the price of tape rental to $2.49 to provide him with the needed extra revenue. However, Rowan is afraid this action might alienate his customers, who might then turn to Blockbuster. Although that is not stated in the case, he did increase prices but lost no customers at all.

The case vividly captures the dynamics of industry competition and the way a large company such as Blockbuster can affect the nature of industry competition and consolidate a fragmented industry. With Video Concepts gone, Blockbuster would have had a virtual monopoly in the Lexington area because Rowan himself had driven many smaller video stores out of business. However, the case also shows that small companies can compete effectively if they imitate the industry leader and develop core competencies of their own.

TEACHING OBJECTIVES

This is an excellent case to use after the Blockbuster case to drive home the message that competition is a cutthroat business and that competitive advantage is a relative concept. Big fish such as Video Concepts can drive out little fish, smaller mom-and-pop stores with limited selection; however, even big fish are driven out by bigger fish that stay in a shoal and work together, and the economies of scale that Blockbuster's chain of video stores provides give it the means to swallow up smaller competitors.

The principal teaching objectives of this case are as follows:

1. To illustrate the fragility of competitive advantage.

2. To show how a successful competitor such as Blockbuster can dominate and control the nature of industry competition.

3. To show the perils faced by an entrepreneur when confronted with the challenge from an aggressive competitor.

STRATEGIC ISSUES AND DISCUSSION QUESTIONS

1. **What was Chad Brown's original strategy for Video Concepts, and what distinctive competencies did he try to develop?**

    Recognizing the need to offer a product superior to that provided by several mom-and-pop video stores in the Lexington market, Rowan tried to create a differentiation strategy for his stores based on several factors:

    - *Number of videotapes carried.* His first store began with 500 videos, his second store had 5,000, and his third store had enough space for 12,000.

- *The way the videos were marketed.* To attract customers, he used innovative marketing techniques, such as home delivery, a free rental after ten rentals, and selling soft drinks and popcorn with videos.

- *Number of stores.* Recognizing that the best way to attract more customers was to offer convenient locations, he opened three video stores in the busiest shopping centers.

- *Efficient checkout procedures.* Like Blockbuster, he installed quick checkout systems to reduce checkout time and allow him to keep track of his inventory and the number of times each tape was used. In addition, the system allowed him to discover when the popularity of a video peaked, so that he could sell it while it was still popular. This is very important, since a video store frequently purchases multiple copies of a video but only needs two or three when the demand for the title decreases. If the excess copies are not sold at the right time, a store is left with expensive unnecessary inventory, and funds are not available to buy new tapes.

- *Targeted marketing.* Rowan targeted specific market segments, such as high schools, and then developed advertising promotions tailored for them.

2.   **How did Rowan's strategy help Video Concepts manage the competitive industry environment before Blockbuster's arrival?**

When Rowan started his first video store, he faced competition from seventeen small mom-and-pop video stores. His differentiation strategy allowed him to attract customers from these stores, and, in response (although that is not explicitly stated in the case), they reduced their rental prices to compete with Video Concepts. Rowan was then forced to reduce his price to $1.99 to match their prices and protect his market share. This strategy paid off, however, for by the summer of 1991, four years after his original store opened, only six of the original seventeen stores remained. We can surmise that Rowan's strategy had driven several of the stores out of the market.

Thus Video Concepts was firmly in control of the Lexington market, and we are told at the beginning of the case that Rowan was contemplating moving into other small towns to pursue the same kind of differentiation strategy. He was poised to create a regional video store chain that would provide him with the ability to increase his revenues and achieve economies of scale.

3.   **How did the entry of Blockbuster affect Video Concepts' competitive advantage, and what steps did Rowan take to fight back?**

Blockbuster's entry into the Lexington market changed the rules of the competitive game. From being the big fish, Video Concepts now turned into the little fish because of all of Blockbuster's competitive advantages discussed in the last case. Chief among them are Blockbuster's purchasing and marketing advantages. Blockbuster can buy tapes at a much lower cost than Video Concepts, and it also has the advantage of a national-brand reputation. Besides, on entering a new market, a Blockbuster store can call upon all the resources of the national chain, such as support for its grand opening campaign of more than $150,000 for the Lexington store.

Video Concepts' revenues fell 25 percent for two months after Blockbuster's Lexington opening, but then they started to climb up slowly to pre-opening levels. To fight back, Rowan introduced several marketing programs, including rent-one, get-one-free on slow nights, and a low-priced, targeted marketing campaign to bring back and retain customers.

Nevertheless, Blockbuster became the market leader, with estimated revenues of $700,000 a year compared with Video Concepts' $466,000. However, one reason for the difference in revenues was not the number of customers but rental price, since Blockbuster charged $3 for a two-day rental compared with Video Concepts' $1.99 for a one-day rental. Dividing revenue by rental price (and ignoring other sources of income), Blockbuster generated approximately 233,000 rentals per year, while Video Concepts generated 234,000. Thus, each of the stores is comparable according to number of rentals, and the two are tied in the Lexington market.

4.   **What problems is Rowan experiencing in the short term, and what strategy would you recommend that he adopt to respond to Blockbuster's challenge?**

Rowan's primary short-run problem is that his lower revenues, as compared with Blockbuster's, are not generating sufficient income. Blockbuster's competitive challenge makes it unlikely that he will be able to increase his share of the Lexington market and expand into other towns as originally planned. Moreover, the promotions that he is launching to compete with Blockbuster are also reducing net earnings. His central problem is that he is in a no-growth business, with all prospect of expansion checked by Blockbuster's competitive challenge.

The options he faces are:

- To find a way to raise revenues without reducing profits or

- To exit the market.

Possible exits include selling the store as a going enterprise (which might be difficult, given the strength of Blockbuster's challenge), or selling his tape inventory to one of the specialized companies that handle such sales and cutting his losses.

Since he has already tried increased marketing, the only remaining method of fighting back seems to be to raise the price of tape rentals to $2.49, a lower price than Blockbuster's, but only for a one-day rental. Such an increase would boost revenues by 20 percent with no attendant rise in costs, thus increasing net earnings substantially and perhaps providing the needed returns. Students will have different opinions on Rowan's strategies, but after long thought and advice from the case authors, this is the strategy he adopted. He found that customers were unaffected by the increase in price. Customers in the Lexington market were relatively price insensitive; they were more interested in having the tape in stock, or a wide selection of tapes, and good customer service than they were in the rental price. The number of rentals remained steady, and Rowan's revenues increased by almost 20 percent.

At this point a subsidiary question can be asked about the long-term potential of the Video Concepts store for Rowan even if the higher price strategy is adopted. Will it be worth his while in the long run to manage the business, given its potential return? For example, even if revenues increase, the balance sheet shows that Rowan will still be making only a modest income in view of the loans he has to pay off and the possible future investment he will need to make to remain viable. Perhaps he should first raise prices to show an improved balance sheet and then try to find a prospective buyer for his store. He could then invest his money in a more profitable venture. Alternatively, he could hire a manager for the store and find a new way to employ his talents to increase his income.

Students will have many different opinions on the future of Video Concepts, especially given potential future competition from cable companies and cellular technology, which will allow customers to call up videos through their television sets, thus possibly making video stores obsolete. However, students will quickly grasp the realities of competition if this case is used immediately following the Blockbuster case.

CASE 33

AOL Time Warner: Creating a Colossus

SYNOPSIS OF THE CASE

This case details the rapid growth of America Online (AOL), the challenges it faced along the way, the strategies it employed to deal with those challenges to become the world's largest provider of commercial online services, and its subsequent merger with Time Warner.

In 2000, AOL and Time Warner, the publishing giant, announced the merger of the two companies to create the largest media company in the world. The merger, which was valued at $156 billion, was the largest in history and was expected to revolutionize the media industry. The case discusses the aftermath of the merger—how the expected synergies from the merger are still to be realized and how the company's ambitious plans have fallen by the wayside. In 2001, the merged company was forced to take a one-time charge of $54 billion to reflect the real value of the firm in the market, and it has not been able to meet its earnings targets and faces significant challenges going forward. The problems it faces include stiff competition, lack of bargaining power against cable companies and rising debt. There is a lot of uncertainty about the future strategy of the company and a big question mark regarding its return to profitability.

TEACHING OBJECTIVES

The AOL case illustrates the problems created by managing rapid growth in a highly competitive business where rapid technological change is altering the competitive playing field on an almost daily basis. The teaching objectives of the case are as follows:

1. To analyze the competitive structure of a newly emerging industry characterized by explosive growth and rapid technological change.

2. To illustrate the problem that can arise when an entrepreneurial company has to manage rapid growth.

3. To understand the power of pricing, and its relationship to demand.

4. To critically evaluate the merits of the merger between Time Warner and AOL

5. To debate how AOL Time Warner should position itself in the industry in order to establish and maintain a long-term competitive position.

STRATEGIC ISSUES AND DISCUSSION QUESTIONS

1. **Following AOL's decision to move to a flat rate pricing scheme, demand for AOL's service ballooned. What does this tell you about AOL's service, and demand for its product?**

   Demand was price elastic. The move shifted the industry price/functionality curve to the right. AOL ended up offering a product that was priced at a level similar to that offered by ISPs, but offered substantially more functionality. Differentiation at a low price led to a surge in demand. The point to bear in mind is that for many Americans, AOL was the Internet. The news media frenzy that followed the August 1996 blackout at AOL proved this.

2. **What business model did AOL move to under Pittman? What were the strategic implications of this model for AOL's strategy?**

   Under Pittman, revenues were to come from four sources—subscription fees, advertising revenues, commissions on e-commerce transactions executed via AOL, and "rents" charged to content providers *and* on-line retailers.

Essentially, Pittman's thrust was twofold. First, grow AOL's subscriber base as quickly as possible, and second, leverage those subscribers. The greater the subscriber base, the greater the advertising fees, commissions, and rents that AOL can charge.

The key, therefore, from a strategy perspective is to grow the subscriber base as rapidly as possible. The more subscribers AOL has, the greater its bargaining power relative to advertisers and complementors (the providers of e-commerce services), and the greater the economic rents that it can extract from these providers. Put differently, AOL's task is to create the most valuable real estate in cyberspace, and to extract economic rent from those that want to utilize that real estate.

AOL charges a rent of at least $250,000 to retailers. In addition, the advance on commissions that AOL has extracted is a sure sign of its bargaining power. For example, it extracted $100 million from Tele-Save holdings in advances on commissions. By the spring of 1999, AOL had a $1.3 billion revenue backlog under its current agreements with e-commerce entities.

3.   **How does AOL's quest for bandwidth fit into the company's strategy?**

As noted in the case, AOL needs the bandwidth. It will need it even more in the future as rich data flows start to dominate the Web (streaming audio and video). Microsoft has outmaneuvered AOL with its investments in cable companies, but satellite could give AOL a way back in, since most Web data flows one way, i.e., downstream. (Satellites offer high bandwidth download, but not upload).

The "AOL anywhere" thrust of the company drives its quest for bandwidth. It is a recognition that the world is moving towards a profusion of digital devices, and that users must be able to access AOL through any device, smart phone, handheld, or PC, if the service is to have value.

4.   **By 2000, who were AOL's primary competitors? What potential advantages, if any, did they have over AOL? What advantages did AOL have over them?**

AOL's primary competitors in 2000 were the Portals like Yahoo and Internet service and software providers like MSN. The nature of competition in the industry was changing—in order to gain a competitive advantage, a company not only had to provide access to the Internet, but also bundle this access with a host of other services (email, news and other media content, chat and bulletin board facilities etc.). While AOL was in a position to offer any bundle of services that its competitors could, AOL had a key asset that it's competitors lacked—access to a 22 million strong subscriber base as compared to MSN's 3 million. This access to customers' eyeballs gave AOL a competitive advantage over its competitors.

5.   **What was he primary strategic rationale for the AOL-Time Warner merger? How was it expected to benefit both parties?**

The strategic rationale underlying the merger of AOL and Time Warner was the expectation of distribution, content, operating and venture synergies that the combined company would realize.

Distribution synergies – As noted in the case, AOL had been largely shut out of the cable TV market, thus limiting its ability to offer high-speed internet service to its users. The merger was expected to feed AOL's need for bandwidth and allow it to integrate forward into distribution of its content over Time Warner's cable TV systems.

Content Synergies – Further, the merger would allow AOL to improve the quality of content offered to its online subscribers by giving them access to Time Warner's entire range of rich content including magazines and news service. Thus, AOL could add value to its service and justify its premium pricing.

Operating synergies – The merged company expected to achieve operational efficiency by integrating the sales and back office functions of Time Warner and AOL and by cross selling and cross-advertising products to their combined base of 100 million subscribers. This was expected to result in substantial cost savings (approximately $1 billion).

Venture synergies – The potential existed for creating new businesses by combining the strengths of the two companies. As the largest music company in the world, the combined entity would be able to combat the threat of peer-to-peer distributed file sharing technology being pioneered by Napster. The merger would likely initiate advances in digitalization and digital distribution of film and books.

6.   **Evaluate the early experience with the merger? Has it worked? Could it work in the future?**

Once the merger went through, AOL Time Warner showed very strong results for the first half of 2001. In the first quarter of 2001, the company posted a 20% increase, ahead of targets, in EBTIDA earnings, the AOL unit posted a 10% growth in online ad revenues in spite of a weaker advertising market, and other divisions of AOL Time Warner, particularly the Filmed Entertainment division, also did very well.

The latter half of 2001 did not present as rosy a picture for the future of the merger. The overall performance in 2001 was a much lower EBITDA of $7.43 billion against revenues of $38.2 billion, against targets of $11 billion and $40 billion respectively. The stock price fell from its peak of $56.60 to $32.10.

The year 2002 has been even worse. The company took a one-time charge of $54 billion against earnings to write down the goodwill due to the merger and drastically reduced its forecasts for the coming year.

The reasons for this dismal performance from the company were manifold. First, as the United States economy entered a recession in 2001, the advertising spending of most companies fell through the floor. This has impacted AOL unit's revenue from advertising negatively, as the ad contracts that expired were not renewed. Second, the subscription growth slowed down and while the overall base of subscribers increased in 2002, the company added 40% less subscribers in 2002 than in the corresponding period in 2001. Third, AOL Time Warner has not yet been able to resolve its broadband problem. AOL Time Warner has no bargaining power with cable operators who want a share in AOL's advertising revenues generated from the broadband business as well as control over customers, and this conflict over who controls the relationship with the customers is preventing AOL Time Warner from striking deals with cable operators.

Clearly, the merger, which was overvalued to begin with, is not working with little to look forward to. Customers who switch to cable broadband offerings often end up canceling their AOL membership because AOL Time Warner is not adding compelling value to packaging and delivering content.

7.   **What are the main strategic issues that AOL Time Warner must grapple with in mid 2002?**

The biggest strategic issue confronting AOL Time Warner in mid-2002 is the broadband challenge. With broadband going mainstream, AOL Time Warner is likely to be left behind as its competitors such as MSN and Earthlink strike deals with cable and telephone companies, and advertise their broadband offerings aggressively. With customers clamoring for broadband access so that they can download music and video from the Internet, AOL Time Warner is steadily losing its dial-up subscribers to the competition and is likely to lose more unless they put together a comprehensive broadband solution that allows them to effectively distribute Time Warner's entire array of entertainment and media content through the Internet. As a start in the right direction, the company has bought AT&T's stake in Time Warner Entertainment that allows it to offer broadband to 10 million households served by AT&T and Comcast (Source: AT&T Comcast press releases, August 2002). However, there is still no guarantee that customers will rush to buy AOL's service.

The AOL unit, which is the largest unit in the company, is not performing as expected—it has seen decreasing subscriber growth, diminishing ad revenue and faces stiff competition from high-speed Internet providers. The issue confronting AOL Time Warner management is how to make the AOL unit profitable.

A spate of management changes has introduced uncertainty about the future direction and strategy of the company. Bob Pittman, the architect of AOL's strategy prior to the merger, has resigned (Source: Business Week Online Special, July 19, 2002).

The company also has a high level of debt (close to $30 billion), due to its commitment to buy a) Bertelsmann's stake in AOL (Europe), and b) AT&T's stake in Time Warner Entertainment. This could mean a higher cost of financing for the company if it needed to raise more cash to buy smaller cable TV providers.

The first step for AOL Time Warner is to realize that cable companies control broadband access, and therefore they also control the customer. The company has to accept this lack of bargaining power with cable companies, pay cable companies for the bandwidth and try and capture as much subscriber base as it can by offering a bundle of services that enhances membership experience.

CASE 34

The Viacom Empire

SYNOPSIS OF THE CASE

This case can be used alone or it can be used after the Blockbuster Entertainment and Video Concepts cases as a way of showing students the relationship between business- and corporate-level strategy. It could then be followed by the AOL TimeWarner case to show students the full implications of what is happening in the volatile entertainment industry today.

The case focuses on the development of Viacom, one of the three biggest entertainment companies in the U.S., from its origin as a small cable television company to the entertainment giant it is today. The growth of Viacom is a case study in how managers can use mergers and acquisitions to pursue a strategy of related diversification but it also shows how obtaining the potential synergies from this strategy is not an automatic process. The case ends in the spring of 2002 when Viacom has now built a broad based platform of assets that seem ready to finally deliver the sustained profitability that the company has sought for over a decade.

TEACHING OBJECTIVES

The main teaching objectives of this case are as follows:

1.   To chart the rise of a giant corporation by acquisition and merger.

2.   To show how managers can develop a differentiation business-level strategy by making key acquisitions.

3.   To show the nature of the benefits or synergies associated with a strategy of related diversification and why they are difficult to achieve.

4.   To show strategic leadership in action.

This case provides an excellent illustration of the way strategy evolves over time as managers seek to develop a competitive advantage and find the most profitable opportunities for growth. As previously mentioned, it is best used after the Blockbuster case has been covered to show how one company's business-level strategy becomes another company's corporate-level strategy. It provides a graphic account of the uncertainty and ambiguity in the strategy making process and how managers must move quickly to take advantage of opportunities that arise. However, it also demonstrates the difficulties associated with obtaining synergies from related diversification, no matter how skilled the management team.

STRATEGIC ISSUES AND DISCUSSION QUESTIONS

1.   **How did Viacom's businesses activities evolved until 1996? What business-level strategy(ies) did it use to obtain a competitive advantage?**

Viacom began as a company that both syndicated the rights to previously run television series to television stations and which was one of the early pioneers of cable TV service in the U.S. Since it had virtually a monopoly over both its television series and its cable customers it was very profitable and its managers had plenty of funds for expansion. However, in the late 1970s, Viacom's managers seeing the profitability associated with popular television reruns, decided that Viacom should go into the actual production of television series to capture more profits. This venture didn't work as the big motion picture studios and the big three TV networks still had most of the creative talent locked up. So, Viacom's managers pushed the cable TV side of their business and Viacom emerged as one of the biggest cable TV systems in the U.S. Given their interests in cable television, in 1976 Viacom also established the ShowTime movie cable channel to compete with the very successful HBO. ShowTime could be distributed to Viacom's cable customers, as well as nationally, so there seemed to be a natural fit between these two businesses.

In the early 1980s, Viacom's managers decided again that in a regulated cable TV environment most profit could be made through providing cable content (because they could not charge a high price for cable TV service). They began to search around for opportunities to enter the content or "entertainment software" side of the business and in 1985, the opportunity came along when Warner Communications (now a division of Time Warner) in desperate need of cash to finance its growing cable TV operations agreed to sell Viacom its MTV networks which included MTV and Nickelodeon. Viacom moved quickly to revamp both these channels to increase their appeal to customers and thus increase their advertising revenues. The advantage of owning cable channels is that a company can make money from both advertisers on the channels, and by selling the rights to carry these channels to cable companies which need to offer customers a broad range of channels.

Thus, Viacom's strategy was to be a major player in both the software or content side of the entertainment business in providing programming through its TV channels and in providing a medium--cable TV--to send that content to its customers. In terms of business-level strategy its strategy was differentiation: providing viewers with unique programming content, and of course with cable TV it was also providing customers with a unique product since most people do not have a choice of cable companies to buy from.

2.   **Why did Sumner Redstone take over Viacom?**

Viacom's differentiation strategy ran into problems in 1986 when the company found itself with a cash flow problem. To establish a cable TV infrastructure, to start Showtime, and to buy the MTV networks Viacom took on $2 billion of debt. Between March 1985 and March 1986 Viacom lost 300,000 subscribers which significantly reduced its cash flow and when it found it hard to service its debt it became a takeover target.

Sumner Redstone, who operated a movie theater screen empire and is credited with developing the multiplex or multi-theater concept, was waiting in the wings. Redstone understood Viacom's strategy and recognized the potential of cable channels in the rapidly developing cable TV industry. He also feared for the future growth in movie theater revenues given the proliferation of pay movie channels and was on the lookout for an opportunity to diversify his entertainment interests. He launched a takeover battle for Viacom and after a fight bought it for about $3.4 billion in March 1986.

Many analysts thought that Redstone had paid too much for Viacom but he went to work to raise the value of its businesses. He focused on differentiating the MTV channels and making them even more unique and different. This strategy worked and as their viewing audience increased so did revenues. To turn Viacom around he hired Frank Biondi, the ex-CEO of Viacom and sold 20% of Showtime to TCI cable, another major cable TV company, to help increase Showtime's subscriber base. Then, Redstone was aided by a fortuitous event. Congress deregulated cable TV prices allowing Viacom and the other major cable companies to increase their prices and the value of cable TV franchises exploded. To reduce Viacom's debt, Redstone now sold off some of Viacom's cable TV franchises as he also realized that providing the entertainment content, rather than providing the medium to bring it to the consumer, would create the most value for Viacom in the future.

3.   **Why did Redstone think that a merger with Paramount could add value to Viacom's core businesses? After the merger with Paramount what corporate-level strategy was Viacom pursuing?**

Realizing that Viacom's future lay in providing innovative new programming that it could then use on its TV channels, Redstone went in search of companies that could provide Viacom with the skills to produce it. He began to court Paramount because it possessed a major movie studio, television production division, and publishing and multimedia interests with its Simon and Schuster division (see the list of Viacom's businesses in the case). Redstone realized the potential synergies that could be realized if Paramount's resources and Viacom's Showtime channel and MTV movie channels were brought together. Redstone also realized that many new TV channels could be developed to exploit Paramount's rich library of movies and television programs. The number of cable channels was proliferating in the 1980s and has continued to do so ever since.

Thus, Redstone's rationale for acquiring Paramount was based on the argument that many potential synergies existed between Viacom's and Paramount's different entertainment businesses. The acquisition would allow Viacom to pursue a strategy of related diversification.

4.   **Why did Sumner Redstone want to merge with Blockbuster Video Corp.? How did the merger with Blockbuster affect Viacom's corporate-level strategy?**

The rational for the merger with Blockbuster Video was far more convoluted. As described in the case, after Redstone made his bid for Paramount a vicious takeover battle ensued with Barry Diller, the Chairman of QVC, another entertainment company. In order to acquire the financing necessary for the takeover, Redstone was eventually forced to agree to a merger with Blockbuster. On the plus side, as described in the Blockbuster case, Blockbuster was doing extremely well at this time and had huge cash flow that could fund both Viacom's debt and expensive acquisitions and growth plans. Moreover, in taking over the major outlet for the distribution of movies on videocassette, the Blockbuster merger would allow Viacom to vertically integrate forwards into the distribution, rental and sales of movies. There were possible synergies available to. For example, a huge Blockbuster advertising campaign could be timed to coincide with the release of a Paramount movie on video. Thus, the merger might bolster Viacom's related diversification strategy. Additionally, Blockbuster owned a majority stake in Spelling entertainment, also a major provider of television programming and movies, although the studios activities overlapped somewhat with Paramount's programming division.

On the downside, however, the acquisition would be very expensive and would increase Viacom's debt. Moreover, such a merger had not been contemplated until Redstone was desperate to acquire the financing to buy Paramount. In addition, there was another major threat facing Blockbuster that is described in the Blockbuster case: the looming threat that the video rental business would be swept away by the fast growth of pay per view movies and digital, satellite, and wireless cable television which bring new movies direct to consumers in their own homes. This threat was increasing even as negotiations were taking place but a merger with Blockbuster was the price that Redstone had to pay for Paramount.

In the event, the merger with both companies did go through and Viacom gained full ownership of Paramount and Blockbuster in 1994. The rich and extensive businesses owned by Viacom in 1994 are listed in the case.

5.   **What major challenges and problems faced Redstone and his managers as they attempted to manage Viacom's diverse array of businesses to create new value for shareholders in 1996?**

a.   Viacom had many valuable assets such as its cable channels, movie studio, television studios, cable TV system, television and radio stations, and publishing division. Perhaps Viacom's managers' most important challenge is to engineer or obtain synergies from cooperative business ventures between its different business units. On paper, the number of potential synergies is enormous. The case talks about how Viacom established a new network channel, the United Paramount Network (UPN) to take advantage of Paramount's extensive movies library; and about how MTV and Paramount cooperated to make Beavis and Butthead movies, while Simon and Schuster developed a line of Beavis and Butthead books to take advantage of this opportunity.

On paper, there seems to be an endless possible stream of synergies to take advantage of, synergies that can only increase as the managers of the different Viacom units become more familiar with each other and with each other's operations.

However, the case discusses how in 1996 Viacom's stock plunged because its managers found it hard to realize enough synergies to justify the acquisitions and service the company's huge debt. In 1996, it was not clear whether this was because Viacom has the wrong management team in place, because these synergies just weren't there to be obtained, or whether achieving them was simply a matter of time. Redstone, however, had to take quick action. **The discussion of this issue is an important aspect of analyzing this case and students should be asked to list examples of the kinds of synergies that could be achieved based on their knowledge of the company's businesses.**

b.   Another enormous challenge for Viacom's managers in 1996 was to build Viacom's franchise abroad and promote its entertainment products. While MTV already had a global presence and reached 250 million households in over 74 countries, and Paramount and Blockbuster have some global presence, many of Viacom's other business divisions did not. Viacom needed to have over half its revenues coming from its foreign operations in the future if it was to really exploit the potential of its brand names. Also, Viacom should be on the lookout for foreign entertainment products that it can distribute on its U.S. networks such as new hit series and new music trends. Analysts criticized Viacom's managers for their lack of attention to the global market place but this may be simply a matter of time as its managers move to take advantage of the opportunities available.

c.   A major challenge for Redstone was to reduce debt. While many assets have been sold off, in 1996, plans for the sale of Viacom's cable TV system to TCI for $1.6 billion were on hold. Also, Viacom did attempt to sell Spelling Entertainment for $1 billion but then withdrew the studio after it could not find a buyer at this price. (Spellings television series production business overlaps with Viacom's).

d.   Another challenge facing Blockbuster's managers comes from the changes occurring in the entertainment industry itself, particularly, in the technology being used to transmit entertainment content. The case describes how the growth in wireless and satellite cable systems has posed major problems for Blockbuster. Also, how the introduction of new CD's capable of both playing and recording movies will make the videocassette tape out of date, ultimately rendering Blockbusters stock of videotapes less valuable. In the future, perhaps Blockbuster can start to export these tapes to poorer countries in which the VCR is still the main medium for the transmission of movies.

e.   Another challenge from the environment is the rapid consolidation of the entertainment industry brought about in part because of the emergence of Viacom as a major force in the industry. Since the merger, Disney has merged with Capital Cities/ABC and in 1996 Times Warner was trying to merge with Turner to extend the reach of their entertainment franchises. One immediate result of all this competition was an increase in the number of movies each movie studio produced in 1996 and a corresponding increase in the number of expensive flops which hurt Viacom along with the other major entertainment companies.

f.   Another challenges came from trying to change the culture of Viacom's mew divisions and to install Redstone's "frugal or economical" way of developing innovative new software content. Also, the need to find the right balance between centralized authority and decentralized authority to make best use of the company's resources.

As noted in the case, Sumner Redstone has a hands-on management style and actively gets involved in all aspects of Viacom's business. The case relates how, in 1996, he fired his CEO, Frank Biondi, because that executive has a "hands off" decentralized management style and believes in letting his subordinates take responsibility for their actions. Redstone felt this style would not be sufficient to create the synergies Viacom needs and solve the pressing problems that it faces. Since Bind's ousting, Redstone has moved to take closer control of Paramount to try to increase its performance.

Another aspect of Redstone's management style is his constant push to keep costs down. Since taking over at Viacom, he has made cost control one of the central aspects of his strategy, and in the free spending entertainment industry this is an unusual approach. Given increased competition in the industry, the need to reduce costs is coming to the fore. This aspect of his management style, and his policy of hiring executives who seem to share his frugal style of operating is likely to prove beneficial to Viacom in the future.

6.   **What kind of structure does Viacom have, why does Viacom use it, and what are the potential problems associated with its for Viacom?**

As Exhibit 1 shows Viacom operates with a multidivisional structure. Each division, Paramount, Simon and Schuster, Blockbuster, etc., has its own set of divisional managers who are responsible for making the best use of divisional resources. A potential problem that may be emerging for Viacom is that each division is pursuing its own interests and not making the necessary efforts to integrate with the other divisions to produce the synergies that Viacom is depending on to fuel its future growth. Top managers may need to use more complex integrating mechanisms such as integrating roles to promote new joint product opportunities. They might also want to consider the formation of some high-powered product teams composed of members of all relevant divisions to take responsibility for the development of new kinds of innovative software products.

7.   **What steps did Sumner Redstone take in and after 1996, to turnaround the performance of its Blockbuster division?**

In 1996, Redstone fired his CEO Frank Biondi, believing he did not have the hands on skills necessary to reduce Viacom's cost structure. The future of the Blockbuster division became a major problems because since the merger, its revenues were flat because of the challenge from new chains of video stores, and because of competition from pay per view TV on wired and wireless and satellite cable TV. It was not helping to service Viacom's huge debt. In spring of 1996 Viacom's stock plunged because the synergies from its Paramount and Blockbuster mergers have not been forthcoming quickly enough and investors fled the stock.

Redstone hired William Fields, a low-cost Wal-Mart IT expert to take over Blockbuster and lower its cost structure and debt, essentially going from a differentiation to a low-cost or low-cost/differentiation strategy. Redstone himself became more closely involved in Paramount and its other divisions and worked there to lower costs. Fields strategy was to expand the range of Blockbuster's products including software, candy, comics, and so on to generate increased revenues. Also, Fields planned to expand the number of its entertainment superstores so that they sell books, CDs, and multimedia products.

Viacom's mounting problems, and Field's IT orientation was not changing Blockbuster or Viacom fast enough for Redstone's liking. Field's new strategy would not bring the fast turnaround he wanted. In 1997, he fired Fields and brought in a new CEO John Antioco who had a new vision for how to develop a strategy for Blockbuster that would restore its profitability.

Antioco's strategy was visionary. Rather than try to boost revenues by offering more kinds of products in Blockbuster stores or developing new music stores, Antioco sold off all music stores and found a new solution to drive up revenues. He proposed a revolutionary new competitive strategy in the mature video rental market of *sharing* rental revenues with major movie studios. In return, Blockbuster would pay far less for the movie tapes—only their cost price $8—so reducing the major reason for its high cost structure. At the same time, this new strategy would allow it to buy many more copies of a new title when a new movie was released to the rental market, the key time for generating video rental revenues—there would always be a copy of the new title in stock for customers to rent.

This strategy was enormously successful, it was a positive sum game for Blockbuster and the movie studios, Blockbuster's revenues, profits, and market share soared, and so did Viacom's stock price. It was now clear that the chain could be profitable and that the threat from pay per view and broadband would materialize far slower than analysts had once thought. Blockbuster once more became an important generator of cash flow.

8. **What steps did Redstone take to manage Viacom's problems and achieve the promise of its other extensive entertainment assets?**

Outside the Blockbuster division, Redstone's strategy was to speed up the process of developing synergies and reducing Viacom's cost structure, at a time when the costs of making movies and TV programming was soaring.

While he had some success progress was slow, and in 1999 he hired Mel Karmazin, a former head of CBS, as Viacom's Chief operating Officer, and together they worked to get the most out of the company's assets. Karmazin was known for his knack of picking and developing hit programming, and known for getting the most out of people and resources. Karmazin also understood the importance of generating and building advertising revenue, and he worked on the strategy of offering potential advertisers special pricing if they would advertise across Viacom properties, such as UPN, MTV, and so on. Essentially, the goal was to taker advantage of the Viacom Empire to generate advertising synergies from being able to bundle advertising time across distribution channels. The case relates how P&G became one of the first companies to try this idea and it has become successful. Viacom created a separate division to manage its cross-organization marketing efforts and its advertising revenues did increase, although it like all companies suffered because of the recession and the aftermath of September 11.

Redstone has also watched Disney swallow ABC, and although that merger had not proved very profitable, he was aware that he lacked access to one of the traditional "Big Three" major networks. In 1999, an opportunity arose to fill this gap in Viacom's product line when CBS, which had also been experiencing declining profits, also realized it needed to become part of a "bigger empire." CBS had just bought Infinity radio broadcasting as part of its strategy to broaden its media properties and Viacom had no radio stations. CBS had also just bought King World productions that syndicated shows like Jeopardy and Oprah Winfrey.

For Viacom, access to CBS would also provide it with high quality news and sports coverage, something it could use across all its many TV properties. CBS also could produce TV programming for all of Viacom's divisions. Moreover, access to a major network would increase the value of Viacom's advertising package to large companies such as P&G which would now see their name and products leveraged across TV, movie, and radio stations capable of reaching every demographic segment in the US—something very important as niche marketing was becoming increasingly important.

Thus there many potential synergies to be obtained and a merger looked attractive.

Viacom and CBS merged in 2000 through a stock swap that did not increase Viacom's debt. Now, all of Karmazin's attention was on managing its new empire of properties to share and leverage competencies across all its divisions. Perhaps the company was now big enough to achieve the sustained profitability that had eluded it?

To help ensure this in 2001, in yet another move to make the company the "Number 1 advertising platform in the world" Viacom acquired the Black Entertainment Television Network (BET). BET also had a substantial global presence, and this represented another major aspect of the company's strategy. To leverage its programming across the world and drive up its global revenues. Indeed, Viacom began to allow the development of increasing amounts of locally produced programming, and hit shows introduced in other parts of the world were quickly transferred to other countries, including the US. These moves pushed up Viacom's revenue streams at a time when advertising revenues fell after September 11.

Given Redstone's expensive acquisitions, but frugal operating methods, the push was on to use the companies' resources as efficiently and effectively as possible. In the 2000s, Viacom has merged and pruned its operations, integrating Paramount's and CBS programming operations, for example, and finding the best was to connect skills and competencies across divisions to reap most value. Making low budget movies also became a major priority and cooperation between MTV, Nickelodeon, and Paramount became common.

By 2002 Viacom seemed to be well positioned. The degree to which its advertising revenues grow in the 2000s if the economy recovers will demonstrate the success of Redstone and Karmazin's strategy. However, its collection of properties is second to none, and its potential seems as high if not higher that its main rivals DisneyABC and AOLTimeWarner.

CASE 35

Monsanto (A): Building a Life Sciences Company

SYNOPSIS OF THE CASE

This case depicts Monsanto's 30-year transformation from a commodity chemicals company to a dynamic, R&D intensive life sciences company with a focus in agricultural products and human pharmaceuticals. It details Monsanto's successes and failures in its transformation history. Much of this transformation was accomplished through mergers and acquisitions. For example, Monsanto acquired the pharmaceutical company Searle in 1985. However, transforming Monsanto into a life science company did not come cheap as Monsanto's CEO Shapiro is confronted with an $8.2 billion debt load, a debt to equity ratio of 1.25, and with an annual interest rate bill of $360 million. In addition, Monsanto is experiencing growing opposition to its genetically engineered agricultural products in the United States and in particular in the EU.

Analysts are concerned whether Monsanto would be in a position to deliver its promised return of equity of over 20 percent consistently year after year. In particular, they worry that the company lacked the resources to grow its business given Monsanto's debt load. In particular, analysts were concerned whether Monsanto could exploit Searle's promising research pipeline given its relatively weak sales presence. An intended merger with American Home Products was seen as a solution to this problem, but the merger failed in 1998. Now Monsanto's management decided to 'go it alone.' Can they pull it off?

TEACHING OBJECTIVES

This case emphasizes the issue of corporate development and thus fits particularly well with Chapter 10 of the text. In addition, the case also fits with Chapters 2–9. The teaching objectives of this case are as follows:

1. Understanding the issues of the industry life cycle and how to deal with declining industries.

2. Understanding the challenges a company faces when it decides to leave its core business and transform itself into a 'new company.'

3. Understanding the impact of technological innovation on your business.

4. How to place options on emerging technologies.

5. How to pursue a mergers and acquisitions strategy to accelerate its transformation.

6. How to manage the regulatory processes, e.g., EPA and FDA.

7. How to price and distribute innovative products.

8. How to manage non-economic stakeholders that put pressure on the company's new business lines.

STRATEGIC ISSUES AND DISCUSSION QUESTIONS

1. **How would you describe the competitive economics of Monsanto's business in the 1970s? What does this description suggest about the outlook for the company at that time?**

    The competitive economics of Monsanto's business in the 1970s can be described as follows:

    *   Monsanto was a manufacturer of high volume commodity chemical products. This is a capital intensive low margin business.

    *   Most of Monsanto's products were at late stage in the evolutionary S-curve.

- Increase in raw material prices due to OPEC price increases put pressure on Monsanto's margins. This situation was compounded by difficult economic environment and weak demand.

Outlook for the company: Difficult to earn economic rents in a business where products are commodities and margins are being squeezed from the demand *and* supply side.

2. **Trace the evolution of technology strategy at Monsanto. Think through the advantages, disadvantages and risks associated with the various approaches that were used to build world class skills in life science research at Monsanto.**

Stage 1: The Genesis of Life Sciences at Monsanto: Jaworski's skunk works.

- The catalyst: Cohen-Boyer's 1973 discovery of recombinant DNA (r-DNA) technology.

- Jaworski immediately saw the opportunities that might flow from applying recombinant DNA technology to plants and animals.

- Bottom up process driven by a scientist. Could this have been driven by management? Probably not! Most managers would not have grasped the significance of the r-DNA breakthrough.

- Focus was on understanding cell biology. Long term goal was to produce herbicide resistant crops. Jaworski had no idea how to achieve this at this point. First step was to do the basic science.

- Hanley agreed to what was in essence a side bet at Monsanto.

Advantages

- Bottom up science driven approach.

- Jaworski's team had considerable freedom.

- Necessary first step to enter the field?

Disadvantages

- Underfunded and vulnerable to being cut (35 scientists). This was a skunk works project. Hanley and Monsanto had other irons in the fire at the time (e.g., producing Silicon for semi-conductor chips).

- No big strategic commitment. Lacked the critical mass.

- Evidence that Monsanto was not (yet) committed to biotechnology was the failure to invest in Genentech. However, Genentech's early success opened the eyes of Monsanto's management and led to Stage 2.

Stage 2: Big Science: Schneiderman's era: Building Core Skills.

Part I: The Internal Effort

- In 1979 Hanley hires Schneiderman and decides to commit big funds to the biotechnology effort. Why is this important?

- Schneiderman is a world class expert in biological sciences.

- Schneiderman brings academic legitimacy to the effort. This is key in attracting young talent.

- Schneiderman was attracted by the scale of resources offered by Monsanto: over $100 million a year compared to $8 million at UC-Irvine.

- Jaworski was given free rein to hire top young talent.

- Monsanto builds Life Sciences Center. By 1990, it has 250 laboratories and 900 research scientists. One of the largest private biotechnology research efforts in the world. Replicates university atmosphere in a private setting.

- The Goal: Understanding the basic science and building knowledge. Advances and practical applications would flow from this. Besides, these have been in the crosshairs since the early days in plant science. The problem is that one cannot develop applications until one understands the basic science.

Part II: Alliances: Monsanto cannot do it all alone. Why not?

- Progress in science is not a straight line.

- Discoveries are often serendipitous.

- Impossible to monopolize the discovery process.

- Need to leverage the efforts of others.

- Need a window into advances in academia.

- Thus, Monsanto created the links with Washington University and Genentech. Many others followed.

Strategic Focus of Effort in Stage II

- *Strategic Focus of Monsanto's Effort:* If we understand the basic science of cell biology and recombinant DNA, where are the applications? Answer: any living thing, plant, animal and human.

- *Should Monsanto focus on just one area?* Not necessarily. The game plan here is to build core skills and then leverage them across different areas of the life sciences.

- *Does this not represent a lack of focus?* Perhaps, but think about the nature of the discovery process. Progress in science is not a straight line. Discoveries are often serendipitous. Do not shut out possible avenues too early. Keep your options open. There is an option value to maintaining flexibility.

Advantages

- Need to build basic skills since they are the bedrock for applications. Applications will follow the basic science.

- Required to value (price) the advances of others.

- Internal skills enhance Monsanto's ability to understand and absorb the advances of others (absorptive capacity).

- Alliances leverage limited financial resources. Raise the ratio of knowledge acquired per dollar spent of research. Reduce the risk associated with R&D. Concentrated R&D spending is much more risky, if we accept that the probability of breakthroughs is somewhat random.

Disadvantages

- Alliances can lead to leakage of knowledge to others.

- Opportunism and malperformance are problems.

- Monsanto's experience with Harvard University is instructive. What was meant to be an open window proved to be a closed door.

- Minimize these problems by designing governance structure to harmonize incentives and limit possibility of malperformance. Look at agreement between Monsanto and Washington University:

  - Individual faculty members are free to publish their work.

  - Washington University holds patents.

  - Monsanto has exclusive marketing rights, more specifically, right of first refusal.

  - Funding decided by a committee that is balanced (4 x 4). All are scientists. This is not about business people telling scientists what to do.

3. **What decision process did Monsanto go through when considering whether to build a life sciences business?**

Monsanto's decision process to build a life sciences business was not a systematic one. This is a clear example of a strategy that emerged due to a combination of individual action (Jaworski) and external stimulus (Genentech). This would probably not have occurred had not Jaworski pushed it. It was clearly an emergent strategy. Is this necessarily bad? No. Particularly in technology, it is unreasonable to expect top management to know how the world of science is evolving (not even scientists know it ex ante!). The critical point is that Monsanto was prepared to make side bets on an ill-defined emerging field, and then to up those bets once the field began to crystallize.

4. **One could argue that scientific talent was the most critical resource that Monsanto needed to access in order to develop its life sciences business. What did Monsanto have on its side in the competition for scarce talent? What factors were working against the company? How did it overcome some of these factors?**

Monsanto had tremendous resources that attracted scientists. Their research budget at Monsanto was often ten times higher that what they had at universities. In addition, Monsanto had built the largest private research campus in the world, imitating a university environment. Also, Schneiderman and Needleman had strong academic reputations in the life science field, which attracted many young researchers to Monsanto. In addition, a position at Monsanto was more secure (and probably offering a higher salary and more benefits) than one at biotechnology start-up.

Working against the company were its bureaucratic and stodgy image, compared to Genentech, Amgen, and a host of other hot start-ups. Nor did a position at Monsanto carry the status of a position at renowned research universities like the University of Washington, for example. Academic positions were still the first place of choice for many scientists. Nor did Monsanto offer the stock option grants that one could get at a biotech startup.

The company overcame these factors by taking a number of steps:

- Hiring world class scientists to lead its program.
- Building a campus like research facility.
- Building close ties with academic institutions.
- Allowing hires the opportunity to undertake ten-year projects. Monsanto was willing to take the long view, and to invest time and money in research projects. For researchers who are continually having to fight for resources, this was a huge benefit.

5. **What was the logic for the Searle acquisition? How did the acquisition add value to Monsanto's life science program?**

Biotechnology can be applied to plant, animal, and human products. As an outgrowth of its research, Monsanto had developed techniques and identified products that had applications in the human population. Due to its existing businesses, Monsanto had some knowledge of the regulatory process and distribution channels for agricultural products. This was not true of human pharmaceuticals. To execute in the human area however, Monsanto needed regulatory skills and a marketing and distribution machine. Searle brought this in addition to an interesting, and some would say under appreciated, product pipeline.

6. **What was Needleman's strategy for drug development at Searle? Does this strategy make sense for a company like Monsanto? Why or why not?**

Needleman's strategy was focused on maximizing the potential return to R&D dollars, and minimizing the risks:

- Monsanto was still a small player in human pharmacology compared to Merck or Pfizer.
- Needleman focused Monsanto's R&D money on three therapeutic areas: arthritis, oncology, and cardiovascular. These were diseases associated with aging. Needleman was looking at the demographics of the United States, and figuring out that the best return per R&D dollar lay in these areas due to the aging baby boom.

- Submit drugs to killer experiments early on (e.g., Cox-2 in toothache). This is an attempt to reduce the risks and expenses associated with sticking with questionable drugs through phase II and III trials.

7. **What is the value proposition to farmers of Monsanto's Roundup Ready and Bt seeds? Does Monsanto's pricing strategy make sense given this value proposition? What special problems does Monsanto face in trying to sell to farmers?**

Roundup Ready seeds reduced costs and increased yields. It also reduces need for deep tillage, which helps check soil erosion. Bt seeds eliminate or reduce use of insecticides. Again, it serves to reduce costs and boost yields.

Pricing strategy included a separate technology fee. Why this rather than bundled into the price of the product? An attempt to signal to farmers that this was a different kind of product, produced by technology, with major benefits to farmers. Farmers are inherently conservative. The pricing strategy was designed to focus their attention on the unique aspects of Monsanto's products. Also the technology fee was a way of making sure that Monsanto got its fair return, since the price of seeds was controlled by distributors. It is a licensing fee. The fee reflects Monsanto's view of the economic rent.

8. **Outline Monsanto's business model for Roundup Ready seeds and its Roundup products. What is the basic strategy here and how might it lead to economic profits?**

Monsanto is trying to boost its earnings in two ways. First, by capturing economic rents from Roundup Ready seeds through its technology fee. Second, by boosting sales of Roundup. The tie-in sales requirement implies that farmers who use Roundup Ready seeds must also use Roundup. In other words, Monsanto is trying to make profit on both the razors and the razor blades. The agreement with Zeneca means that even when farmers do not use Roundup, and use a competitor's glyphospate instead, Monsanto still receives a significant licensing fee.

Roundup patent expires September 2000. To maintain its dominant position in this market segment, Monsanto is cutting prices and boosting investment in capacity. The objective is to increase sales and capture significant scale economies, making it difficult for second movers to enter the market given the company's price/cost advantage. Monsanto has found from other markets that demand for the product is price elastic (e.g., in Canada, a 34 percent cut in price led to a 685 percent surge in volume sales). Monsanto is also entering into agreements to supply glyphospate to other producers, thereby strengthening its scale advantage.

Roundup Ultra is an attempt to solidify its position by extending the Roundup patent, although the efficacy of this tactic is somewhat limited since it is the patent on glyphospate that is the key issue here.

9. **Why has Monsanto been vertically integrating forward into the seed corn industry? What is the strategic rationale for such a move?**

The strategic rationale for vertically integrating into the seed corn industry is gaining control over a "delivery vehicle" and distribution channels. Seed is the delivery vehicle for desirable traits. Bt or Roundup resistance is just one of a number of desirable traits. Monsanto needed to match its traits with the best seed traits out there in order to create real value. Thus, Monsanto needed control over seed companies to do this.

If Monsanto does not gain control over its delivery vehicle and distribution channel, what might happen? Seed companies might favor the traits of Monsanto's rivals, such as Du Pont and Novartis. It is about relative bargaining power. Gaining control over seed companies ensures that they do not capture the rents in the value chain, and that Monsanto can get its traits to market. It also makes sure that Monsanto's traits get to market quickly. This strategy is about locking up downstream value creation activities.

10. **Evaluate Monsanto's launch strategy for its Cox-2 inhibitor. Does the strategy make sense? Why?**

Monsanto's goal in its launch strategy for its Cox-2 inhibitor was to capture first-mover advantages given Merck's rival product. Monsanto's launch strategy was based on the following elements:

- Partnership with Pfizer (one of best sales forces in business).

- Once patients use a product, and if it works, they are reluctant to switch. Thus, capture customers and benefit from non-trivial switching costs.

- Mass distribution of patient starter kits to 45,000 physicians and pharmacies. Targeting of physicians who prescribed NSAIDs.

- Relatively low price ($2.42 per day).

- Massive direct sales effort.

- $100 million direct advertising campaign—pull through demand.

- Result: Second fastest sales ramp-up in history (only Pfizer's Viagra experienced a strong ramp-up).

11. **Comment on the opposition of groups such as EU consumers and Rifkin's organization to Monsanto's genetically engineered products. Are these groups latter day Luddites, or do they have a point? How should Monsanto deal with the opposition from such groups?**

There are certainly Luddite elements to the antiMonsanto movement. For example, opposition to BST came from farmers who were afraid of overproduction. They used fear of the unknown as a weapon to block the product. In the EU, the common agricultural policy implies over-production in some sectors. Genetically engineered seeds might make this worse. Thus, farmers oppose additional over-production. Politicians and food manufacturers have jumped on the bandwagon. Still, there are uncertainties here. Super bugs may be the result of genetic engineering. You start off an arms race. Monsanto needs to address the concerns of its non-economic stakeholders.

CASE 36

Monsanto (B): Merger and Rebirth

SYNOPSIS OF THE CASE

This case is about the acquisition and spin-off of Monsanto by Pharmacia. The two companies announced a merger, valued at $27 billion, in 1999. Pharmacia expected to gain new blockbuster drugs to drive its growth and saw the Searle's division of Monsanto as a means to achieve this growth and compete in the global pharmaceutical companies. Monsanto was plagued by a huge debt and the environmental suits against the company were making it hard for the company to find a buyer until Pharmacia came along. The agricultural biotechnology business of Monsanto was spun off under the Monsanto name within a year, leaving behind a pure pharmaceutical entity with Pharmacia. The new Monsanto has a momentous task ahead. How can it counter environmental concerns about genetically engineered crops and grow the agricultural biotechnology business?

TEACHING OBJECTIVES

This case is meant to be used as a supplement for Case 35 (Monsanto (A)) and applies well to the discussion on acquisitions in Chapter 10. The main teaching objectives of this case are as follows:

1. To underscore the importance of acquisitions as a driver of growth.

2. To study how a company undergoes transition from a commodity business to offering value added solutions.

3. To illustrate how environmental consciousness can create an adverse impact on a company's operations.

STRATEGIC ISSUES AND DISCUSSION QUESTIONS

1. **What was the rationale behind the merger between Pharmacia and Monsanto?**

    Pharmacia was a small player that wanted to compete in the global pharmaceutical marketplace and did not have the resources to do so. It needed quick access to a pipeline of potential blockbuster drugs, and marketing and R&D operations on a larger scale. Monsanto had a blockbuster arthritis drug (Celebrex), its Searle unit had a number of prescription drugs under development and it could support the development, marketing, and sales expenses required to discover new pharmaceutical drugs. All these resources made Monsanto an attractive buy for Pharmacia.

    Monsanto also stood to benefit from the merger because it had accumulated huge debt and because of environmental lawsuits and protests against its genetically modified seeds, sales as well as the stock price were headed south.

    Thus, the merger was an opportunity for both companies as Monsanto needed a buyer to bail it out of its financial trouble and Pharmacia was looking for easy access to resources for further growth.

2. **Evaluate Pharmacia's decision to spin-off Monsanto.**

    Pharmacia's decision to spin-off the agriculture business was a strategically sound decision. Pharmacia realized the problems that Monsanto's agriculture unit could create for the merged company. It was a controversial division that had attracted a lot of negative publicity from environmental activists and was the focus of many lawsuits. Moreover, it might have distracted Pharmacia from focusing on its core business, which was pharmaceuticals and not agriculture. An added factor might have been that agriculture does not deliver the high margins that the prescription pharmaceutical business does.

3.   **What are the main challenges that the new Monsanto faces?**

The new Monsanto is a focused agricultural biotechnology company. Ever since the spin-off from Pharmacia, the company has managed to reduce costs, scaled back spending on R&D to focus on a limited number of products and has largely contained its large debt. In the year 2001, the company actually saw an overall increase in its revenues and profits despite a slow economy. However, Monsanto is in a transition phase and is confronted with a number of challenges:

- The consumers, environmental activists as well as the investors are not hopeful about the future of the agricultural biotechnology industry. Monsanto has spent a lot of money of building competencies and assets in agricultural biotechnology and this aversion could spell grave times ahead for the company.

- Many countries in the world have imposed regulations on genetically modified seeds and foodstuffs. A Brazilian court has in fact banned the sale of Monsanto's genetically engineered soybeans in Brazil. Since Brazil is Monsanto's largest export market and the focus of significant expansion plans involving genetically engineered seeds, this ban is a discouraging development for the company. The effect of such regulations could spread to the U.S. market since farmers who sell their crops abroad will be affected and may stop buying genetically altered seeds from Monsanto.

- The U.S. patent on Monsanto's cash cow product, Roundup, expired in 2000. Roundup contributed to about 45% of the company's revenue. The 20% annual growth in Roundup is expected to slow down to about 5%. In addition, availability of substitutes for Roundup and the slowing economy are likely to drive the prices of Roundup down, affecting Monsanto's revenues and margins. The company needs to develop another blockbuster product like Roundup in the near future in order to be profitable.

- Monsanto's customer base is comprised of farmers—a group that does not like paying high prices for seeds and are likely to continuously drive prices down.

4.   **Why is Monsanto's strategy going forward?**

Monsanto's goal is to provide integrated solutions in seeds, biotechnology and agricultural chemistry. It is moving away from the low margin commodity agricultural products to high value seeds and genomics. On one hand this seems to be risky given the popular fears about genetically altered foodstuffs. However, it is the only viable strategy in the long run if the company can dispel concerns about the health effects of its products. A recent report by United Nations supporting biotechnology crops and outlining the benefits of such crops for the world's poor and hungry is likely to help the company's image management efforts. Also encouraging is the fact that the Environmental Protection agency has approved the use of genetically modified corn seed for another seven years and the use of these seeds by farmers is going up. However, foreign markets regulations still pose a challenge for the company and its success in winning regulatory approval in these markets is likely to determine its survival.

CASE 37

Eli Lilly & Company: The Global Pharmaceutical Industry[1]

SYNOPSIS OF THE CASE

The industry under study is the pharmaceutical industry, a segment of the overall healthcare industry. It involves the research, development, manufacture and marketing of pharmaceutical products for human patients and animal health and also includes the production of medical devices. Pharmaceutical products consist of those produced for prescription as well as over-the-counter sales. Firms in this industry participate to some degree in one or more of these sectors with their specific focus being part of a unique strategic plan. Drugs produced for prescription sales must be approved by some government regulatory body depending on the geographical market in which they are intended to be marketed. With research, discovery and regulatory approval, it normally takes ten to fifteen years before a drug will actually arrive on the market. Scientific advancement has allowed drug researchers to direct their studies toward specific maladies whereas in the past discovery was largely due to chance. The projected growth for the industry is substantial due to an aging of the world population and a largely untreated percentage of the population. The U.S. market boasted the largest growth for several decades and while this trend is continuing, growth in other markets is expected due to untreated populations.

Eli Lilly & Company is considered to be one of the major pharmaceutical firms in the world. In terms of sales, it is usually listed in the top ten to fifteen firms. Changing dynamics in the pharmaceutical industry have included, the dominance of managed care in the U.S. market causing doubt about future growth, changing dynamics outside the U.S. due to deregulation and a tendency for firms to join forces in the way of mergers and acquisitions due to the staggering costs of research and development. In light of these issues and their own internal issues including the impending expiration of their blockbuster drug, Prozac, Lilly was exploring strategic decisions in order to maintain their status and earnings growth. Areas examined included possible expansion into other production sectors including generic, over-the-counter drugs, or different therapeutic areas (did the company need to adjust them to concentrate on the highest growth areas?), merging possibilities, and finally geographical markets.

TEACHING OBJECTIVES

The teaching objectives of the case are:

1. To provide an example of how a company identifies and reacts to opportunities and threats.

2. To gain a better understanding of the complex pharmaceutical industry.

3. To provide an opportunity to analyze competitive market situations, develop alternative strategies, and make decisions.

4. Enable students to practice developing specific strategic strategies that will win against specific competitors.

STRATEGIC ISSUES AND DISCUSSION QUESTIONS

1. **Describe the structure of the pharmaceutical industry.**

    Pharmaceutical manufacturers research, develop, manufacture and market pharmaceutical products and medical devices that are targeted to various types of buyers. Pharmaceutical medicines are grouped into those that must be prescribed by a physician, ethical products and those that are sold over-the-counter (OTC). This case study focuses primarily on ethical products, however, since many companies manufacture

[1] Parts of this teaching note were prepared by Robert J. Mockler. Adapted by permission.

both types of pharmaceuticals as part of their businesses portfolios, OTC product discussions must be included.

The pharmaceutical industry targets its products worldwide to different types of customers who can range from individual patients to governments depending on the geographical market as well as the product itself.

The individual patient's role began to change in the mid-1990s when companies began to use direct-to-consumer (DTC) advertising for ethical products. Whereas in the past with ethical products the individual patient did not have much say in the product decision, in the late 1990s, individuals were now requesting certain brand name medicines from their doctors. In terms of therapeutic areas and classes, it was important for pharmaceutical firms to recognize which conditions would be prominent in the future in order to target those maladies. The worldwide trend of an aging population put certain conditions at the top of this list including heart disease, stroke, arthritis, cancer, depression, impotence, osteoporosis and Alzheimer's disease.

Large-scale purchasers such as hospitals and managed care companies buy ethical products in large quantities are therefore benefit from price discounting. This was especially prevalent in the U.S. market where managed care patients were responsible for 65 percent of the prescriptions filled by pharmacies by mid-1998.

The other major purchaser of pharmaceutical products is government. In the U.S., this is represented by the Medicare and Medicaid government health programs. In countries outside the U.S. with socialized pharmaceutical benefit programs, governments have much more influence in the industry in general since they are major purchasers and have an interest in keeping health care costs down. In many cases, there are price controls, contracts between pharmaceutical companies and governments and covert agreements involved. This makes it more difficult for foreign players to succeed in these markets.

2.   **What are the major industry trends, including opportunities and threats?**

- The pharmaceutical industry is growing by leaps and bounds due to a largely untreated world population, especially in developing countries and countries whose markets opened up in the 1990s, as well as the demographic trend of an aging population. This leaves large amounts of territory either untreated or still uncharted. It was predicted that, like other industries, companies needed to keep their eyes open for expansion into new and less regulated markets. Projected worldwide growth is 6 to 7 percent with growth rates varying among geographical markets for the years.

- Research and Development is considered to be the lifeblood of the industry, however costs to bring a new drug to market from the time of its discovery more than doubled between 1990 and 1998. It was estimated that the cost to bring a drug to market in 1998 was between $350 and $500 million. Those companies able to spend at least 15 percent of earnings on R&D were considered to be in a healthy position as long as earnings growth followed similar pattern, that is, R&D spending growth rates should not exceed earnings growth rates in order to avoid pressure on profits.

- The U.S. market is the most attractive on the globe now because of high historical rates of growth and rates of 10 percent predicted for the years 1998–2002 by the IMS. There are those who feel that this prediction is overly optimistic as the U.S. healthcare market is forever becoming more dominated by managed care and effected by the encroachment of generic drug products.

- Direct-to-consumer advertising had been on the rise since the mid-1990s starting in the U.S. market, but was also being utilized in Europe to a lesser degree. Companies found it to be very effective especially with the increasing development of lifestyle improvement drugs. Companies who concentrated some of their R&D efforts toward these types of drugs would be participating in a growing market that included drugs to fight impotence and baldness.

- Generic companies definitely had their place in the market with strongholds in the U.S., UK and Germany. Generic versions of patented products were getting a lot of attention with the expected expiration of 120 patented molecules representing $15 billion in sales. Generic companies were also showing some aggression by starting legal action against branded producers stating that patent protection was turning into anti-competitive and monopolistic practices.

- Regulatory bodies around the globe (including the U.S., Europe and Japan) were in the midst of trying to streamline and harmonize drug regulatory and approval practices. This would have the eventual effect of streamlining the drug approval process for drug companies who at the end of the 1990s had to apply for regulatory approval in each country for which a drug was to be sold. During this time however, these efforts were apparent, but actual goals had not necessarily been reached. It was still necessary for drug companies to either establish alliances in foreign countries in order to overcome entrance barriers or have a means to relationship build with foreign governments.

- In response to the ever-escalating costs of R&D, drug companies were looking for alternative therapeutic benefits for drugs already on the market. One example was a medication originally approved for depression was found to be an effective smoking cessation treatment.

- The use of joint ventures and alliances had been around for many years in an industry where R&D alliances with biotechnology firms or agreements with university scientists could bode well for companies in this research-intensive industry. Biotechnology had become a strong force in the research end of the business as genetics research was increasingly used to develop therapeutic compounds. Alliances with foreign entities were commonly used to allow a host country easier access to foreign markets.

- The extreme form of joint venture, mergers and acquisitions was the most prevalent strategy in the 1990s, another response to the high cost of R&D. This also allowed companies to participate in economies of scale, which would have the effect of producing strong profit margins and buying time between drug discoveries. Thus, for some, it was argued that size was important. It was a strategy specialty of European firms to find an American partner through whom they could participate in the strong U.S. market.

3. **What are the critical factors affecting success?**

In terms of customers, it has become more important to have good company image in the eyes of individual patients who are now affected by DTC advertising. Traditionally, it was always essential to "look good" in the eyes of the customer who in the past were more often physicians, pharmacies and hospitals. Although this is still very important, as physicians, pharmacists and hospitals are part of the selling chain, the ultimate customer, the patient, is now the target of advertisement. Having strong sales people, who are sometimes called detail people, is important for the success of a firm. They represent the firm to hospitals, pharmacies, doctors, managed care companies, and at times, governments. The tactics they use to well represent a company include providing samples and literature as well as sales skills Trade journal advertising is a method for companies to communicate about products to medical people and others concerned within the industry.

As with many industries, management and the organization of a firms will dictate success or otherwise. To have clear objectives, including clearly identifying the sectors of the business in which a firm will participate i.e., OTC drugs versus ethical drugs, specific therapeutic areas targeted, medical devices, and/or animal health care. Companies with clearly defined objectives were more successful during the 1990s and the trend was to focus objectives. Organizational structure is important for the health of the company. Some pharmaceutical firms took major steps in re-organizing their firms in order to have people who performed the research on a particular drug, bring the drug through development and also participate in the marketing of the drug. It was important that after a drug was developed, it was not just dropped into another executive's lap to carry out other aspects of its production. Size of a firm is also considered to be crucial since firms with a larger capital base are able to donate more resources to research and development, one reason for the merger craze.

In terms of OTC products, since in reality they are a consumer good, brand recognition and customer loyalty are cited to be of prime importance. For branded drugs, a company which focuses its efforts on top-selling therapeutic areas is destined for more success. The difficulty is in the development of a drug which requires at least 10 years. Firms have to anticipate what future demand will be. Life style drugs are in great demand and have gained recognition during the 1990s. Firms which recognized this trend and continue to approach this sector as one offering growth potential is a key to success. Patent protection on drugs is imperative to protect a company's earnings; it is a necessary, but not always a sufficient prerequisite. Patent protection is not necessarily a given in certain geographical markets like China. As difficult as it is to achieve, a company which has a few top-selling products, another way of saying a good portfolio, has more insurance against earnings loss, therefore, this is a key to success. A varied therapeutic mix is also a key to success which makes a stronger case for strong R&D. Companies which can offer a variety of products to large purchasers allow that particular customer a type of one-stop-shopping.

The prescription drugs themselves must be easy to use. Of particular importance to drug producers is the fact that making a given drug easier to use is a way to extend its patent and therefore a key to success. Brand recognition for ethical products is more important now because of DTC advertising, but it has always been important for recognition of quality in the industry as there are often several products on the market for the same illness. Another key to success related to products is the ability of a company to optimize the sales potential of a given drug due to the astronomical cost of R&D; that is a company should always look for new ways to market a drug, or ways to improve on it including such things as dosage or the further elimination of side effects. The product efficacy cannot be overlooked for obvious reasons and thus is a key to success. Some drugs have failed because they actually have not provided the benefit for which they were intended. Similarly, a drug which is not safe cannot be put on the market, however, there have been many cases where drugs are taken off the market due to problematic side effects.

Drug prices are affected by efficacy as well as the geographic market in which they are being sold. Prices in the U.S. tend to be high, as there is less pricing intervention by the government and therefore having a strong presence in this market is a key to success. Conversely, companies doing business in the U.S. will be affected by the trend for managed care health coverage which translates to pricing discounts for drug companies, thus a key to success for companies is deriving a lower portion of the earnings from managed care. Lastly, with regard to pricing, companies whose products are first on the market and thus have no competition at least for a period of perhaps six months, will have more freedom regarding price level.

Since generic products are considered to be the culprits in pilfering profits away from drug companies, generic production as part of business portfolios is a key to success. Similarly, production of medical devices and animal health products are additional ways companies can protect earnings when drug portfolios are weak.

Strong research and development is a essential in this business—the lifeblood—as stated by many industry participants and observers. A strong pipeline indicates a positive future profit scenario and thus is a key to success. Alliances with biotechnology firms are a key to success since this genetic research is considered to be a major area in drug design. Likewise the ability to carry out research with university scientists is important in the discovery of new compounds. The ability of companies to produce new compounds is at the heart of drug production and the ability of a company to accomplish this relatively quickly are both keys to success. Companies may look carefully at their rate of research growth compared to the rate of sales growth. A key to success is the latter being greater than the former. Technology investment is a key to success since by its nature, pharmaceutical development is considered a high-tech business and requires the latest developments in the sciences and information technology. Lastly, larger companies are usually able to devote a greater absolute amount of earnings to R&D and this is then considered a key to success.

Within the U.S., Pharmaceutical Benefits Management companies are now part of the distribution chain and some pharmaceutical companies have purchased them as units of their business. They are considered to be a profitable participant in the business and therefore a key to success. Since wholesalers distribute 70 percent of the prescription drugs in America, strong relationships with them is a key to success.

Within the areas of sales and promotion, effective DTC as well as OTC advertising are keys to success. DTC advertising gained in importance in the U.S. in the mid-1990s and was changing the dynamics of the industry, therefore it is a key to success. A widely distributed sales force is also a key to success since it helps firms to stay competitive globally.

In the U.S., keys to success are considered effectiveness with the FDA since they are the approval body as well as strong wholesaler relationships and alliances with U.S. companies for research and development or marketing. The presence of manufacturing and R&D facilities in this geographical market is important for distribution purposes. Since the U.S. market is the fast-growing market, the presence of operations in general is a key to success.

In Europe, again relationships with regulatory bodies in specific countries or the EMEA are important, as they are the regulatory body governing the approval of new drugs. Ties with the government(s) in Europe are very important since government are basically the largest consumers of pharmaceuticals. As in the U.S., alliances between companies are important for research and development purposes. In order to reach these markets more easily, retaining manufacturing and R&D facilities are also keys to success.

In Southeast Asia and China, an ability to manage relationships with governments and regulatory agencies are keys to success as within these markets, the pharmaceutical industry is heavily regulated with high barriers to entry. It was important for countries to have a presence in this area because of the growth prospects at the end of the 1990s. An ability to create alliances was a key to success in order to enter these markets. Around the globe there was the greater trend of deregulation in the 1990s, which was prevalent in these markets especially. This created opportunities in selected markets, but also created uncertainty. Again, the presence of a company's manufacturing and R&D facilities in these countries would enhance a company's opportunity for success.

Other geographical markets offered opportunity as well such as in Africa and Australia. As with the other markets ties with the government and regulatory bodies, alliances, manufacturing and R&D facilities were also keys to success.

Company size was a key to success at the end of the 1990s principally because of the emphasis on R&D and marketing capability and reach.

Lastly, if a company's earnings were not concentrated heavily around just one drug, the company's earnings were considered to be less at risk, thus earnings spread over several strong products was considered a key to success.

4. **Do a comparative evaluation of Eli Lilly and other players in the pharmaceutical industry.**

The pharmaceutical industry was noted to be a high growth industry at the end of the 1990s due to an aging world population and companies tending toward largeness in order to devote significant spending to R&D and realization of economies of scale. Certain health conditions were identified as being those on which companies should focus, that is health problems common to older people. With advances in biotechnology and information technology, researchers were now able to pinpoint research toward specific health conditions. Drug discovery was no longer largely a product of chance. Focus on well-defined objectives and areas of strength was also important since the chances of having success with a particular drug were greater if company's could be come specialized in particular areas. Conversely, diversification would have the effect of protecting profits when top-selling drugs were threatened with generic encroachment or patent expirations or even competition from other firms in the same therapeutic area with different drug compounds. Diversification into too many therapeutic areas was deemed to be a poor approach, but diversification into animal health products, medical device manufacturing or OTC drugs were common areas of concentration outside of pharmaceutical ethical products. One could recognize these different strategies by noting the different business unit portfolios across the industry.

Since Lilly's restructuring in the early to mid-1990s implemented by Sidney Taurel through which the blockbuster anti-depressant Prozac emerged, the company had been considered a very strong player in the market with sold earnings growth during the second half of the 1990s. The equity capitalization growth of the company bore witness to the company's success. Earnings per share increased a very respectable 21 percent compared to Pfizer's 13 percent. The main objective of the reorganization was to focus the company around pharmaceutical strengths which resulted in five therapeutic areas on which they chose to concentrate. Prozac's success allowed the company to pour large amounts of funds into further R&D which produced new drugs having limited success. Zyprexa, the anti-psychotic medication was the company's next most profitable drug having sold $1.4 during 1998 after having been on the world market for one year. Prozac appeared to be the backbone of the company's strength now and as the patent expiration was approaching with generic firms foaming at the mouth as well as other anti-depressants experiencing success. Lilly could only try to protect Prozac's patent for so long and even then other companies were producing anti-depressants making inroads into this market. Their other strong areas were insulin-production for which one of their competitors was the leading-insulin producer in the world. Anti-infectives comprised another significant portion of sales but were decreasing due to generic competition and competition from foreign competitors.

5. **How is Eli Lilly positioned in the pharmaceutical industry?**

The Company. Eli Lilly and Company is a research-based, global pharmaceutical company which conducts research, develops, and market ethical products in the following therapeutic areas: neuroscience, endocrinology, oncology, cardiovascular disease, infectious disease and women's health. The company also develops and sells animal health products and maintains alliances with U.S. and foreign firms for the development and marketing of drugs.

Products. In the above therapeutic areas, Lilly's top products include Prozac, an anti-depressive, Zyprexa, an anti-psychotic. Three of the company's newest products were developed in 1997 and 1998 and include ReoPro, a cardiovascular agent, Gemzar, a cancer treatment, and Evista, a treatment for osteoporosis. Other significant drug treatments (determined by percentage of sales) include anti-infectives as well as insulins. The company is desperately trying to protect its earnings on the blockbuster drug Prozac whose patents will expire in 2001 and 2003. Its efforts are being met with limited success. In a lawsuit filed by Barr Laboratories, a producer of generic drugs, Lilly won the right to exclusively market Prozac until patent expiration, however this represented a partial decision and appeals had been filed. In addition, initial earnings reports in early 1999 showed lower sales of Prozac by 4 percent. Other drugs in Lilly's portfolio had performed well.

Distribution. Within the U.S., Lilly uses 200 independent wholesale distributing outlets. The company's principal concern is that their customers—physicians, pharmacies, hospitals, and health care professionals—have immediate access to their products. Four primary wholesalers were responsible for 55 percent of the company's sales within the U.S. Outside of the U.S., sales representatives are primarily responsible for distribution.

Alliances. As with many pharmaceutical firms, Lilly uses strategic alliances to perform research and development. In 1998 they were involved in one particular strategic alliance with Sepracor, a company which specializes in removing side effects from drugs already on the market, which attracted the attention of the FTC. Lilly's agreement with Sepracor involved researching a new form of Prozac in order to retain exclusive rights to the product patents. In general, Lilly along with many firms in the industry concentrated on strategic alliances and joint ventures in order to maximize R&D efforts.

Research and Development. Lilly's level of expenditure on R&D was approximately 16 percent of earnings in 1997 which was in line with the 16-18 percent considered a high standard in the industry. In 1998, the company's R&D costs had increased 27 percent due to increased efforts in this area as well as increased R&D external collaborations.

6. **What are the different alternatives available to the new CEO, Sidney Taurel, in order to provide a strategic direction for Eli Lilly in the new millennium?**

Alternative I: The objective of Eli Lilly is to continue their research and development efforts using joint venture and alliances in the development of researched-based pharmaceuticals only, but to narrow their focus to less than the five therapeutic areas. With less spending on research and development, the company could acquire a generic subsidiary, a strategy to allow them to alleviate completely the idea of patent infringement by generic firms, the greatest threat to profits industry-wide. They would continue to develop and market pharmaceuticals in current geographical markets to hospitals, managed-care organizations in the U.S., governments, physicians and individual patients.

Alternative II: The objective of Eli Lilly is to merge with another research-based firm which has some compatible products in its portfolio but allows Lilly to also expand their therapeutic mix. If they could link perhaps with a European firm, they would be able to better participate in the European market in time for hopeful deregulation. This would protect Lilly from becoming too small a fish in an ever-expanding pond due to the merger craze of the 1990s. Consistent with "size matters," they would not loose their position in an industry of larger and larger-sized firms. This would also allow them to increase their marketing muscle in Europe and in other markets, an important consideration in the industry at the shift to a new millennium.

Alternative III: The objective of Eli Lilly is to retain their core competencies in terms of therapeutic mix, but to add to their product line, OTC products. This would likely entail the purchase of a division of a consumer products firm which already has established brands and customer loyalty. In this way, Lilly could protect future earnings and loss of patents by working in another business while also creating synergies.

7.   **Evaluate the strengths and weaknesses of each of the three alternatives and recommend a course of action for Sidney Taurel.**

Alternative I: In this scenario, Lilly would focus itself even more and narrow the therapeutic areas in which they do R&D, manufacturing and marketing. They could accomplish this by selling off a part of the firm which focuses on these areas and purchase a generic firm as a subsidiary. They could specifically sell off and eliminate areas which are not necessarily profitable such as the anti-infectives area in which sales have been dropping and where other firms are basically doing it better. With these funds, they would then purchase a generic subsidiary. With the addition of generics Lilly is eliminating from their business operations one of the greatest threats to profitability among ethical pharmaceutical producers. Lilly would save the company a lot of headaches without generic companies breathing down their neck, in terms of moving in when patents are due to expire. Additionally, this would eliminate lawsuits brought against the company by generic firms desiring approval to copy patented drugs and crying anti-competitiveness on the part of therapeutic companies.

This would also protect the company's image since they may appear as not just a company selling high-priced prescription drugs, but one which has the consumer in mind and is not only concerned with profits. Business moves such as the alliance with Sepracor only make Lilly look like a profit-hungry pharmaceutical firm. Even though Prozac would be re-marketed with less side effects, the company will have much to gain if the FTC deems the arrangement appropriate. However from the perspective of their customers, it might not put them in a positive light.

 Lilly would have to acquire this company as a subsidiary in order to keep the business completely separate and to ensure that innovation on the part of the core company would not suffer. It would be a logical addition to their business since manufacturing processes would not have to be adjusted, only labeling. In addition, in terms of selling and distribution, at least in the U.S., with emphasis on managed care and large-scale purchases, drug profits are being squeezed and thus being able to offer generics after patents expired would be an attractive means to satisfy these purchasers. In addition, in certain markets, generic prices would be attractive to price-sensitive governments outside the U.S. market. This type of business portfolio would also allow Lilly to maximize the potential of each drug developed without having to scramble to find ways to protect patents through the re-marketing of a drug to produce less side effects or in terms of finding other therapeutic uses for the drug. Essentially, this would alleviate the company of a lot of profit pressure.

If Lilly took this approach, they might lose their incentive to be productive in terms of research and development. One of the company's strengths is their focus on core competencies which was the result of the mid-1990s reorganization. Drug companies who stand to reap high rewards at the development of new compounds are those which pump that money into more R&D. Lilly has already proven that it can produce a reasonably good pipeline and this only happened when they sharpened their focus. Generics are a lower profit margin business when compared to ethical pharmaceuticals. It may be worthwhile to note that among the top competitors in terms of sales, none of them produces generics. Lilly is not a generics firm.

Alternative II: In this scenario, Lilly will merge with or even acquire another research-based firm which does R&D for some compatible products, but which would add some established R&D efforts as well as products to Lilly's product portfolio, essentially expanding their therapeutic mix. In 1998-1999, the industry saw several European firms merging or looking to merge especially with American partners. In the case of an acquisition, U.S. equity prices have been high and it would be advantageous to target an acquisition for this reason outside the U.S. For example, European firms are ripe to merge with U.S. companies in order to enter the U.S. market. Lilly could take advantage of this merger environment and thus increase the company's size and reach in an industry where firms are enlarging and optimum size appears to be changing. In general, global consolidation in this industry can protect future earnings through cost-cutting which in turn gives companies more time for development of new drugs enhancing a company's portfolio. Lastly, it enhances a company's research and development prospects and expands its global market reach.

Europe also appears to be attractive because of the swifter passage of drugs through the approval process—this is perhaps one of the greatest advantages of operating in Europe as a key to success involves a drug's time to market. This aspect of the business will be crucial to the company's future success in light of the Prozac situation. Europe has also been said to be strong in the area of R&D thus providing Lilly with talent required in new drug discovery.

Another supporting argument toward a merger with regard to Prozac involves the loss of sales which would likely be followed by lesser R&D expenditure, thus limiting Lilly's ability to develop new drugs, the backbone of a strong pharmaceuticals company. The addition of more muscle in the way of a merger could address this problem, and in addition, allow them to participate in greater economies of scale, another essential ingredient.

A key to success involves size, but also the ability to address current and future ailments as well as lifestyle improvement drugs. With the increased size of a merged company, Lilly would have the ability to target these areas with a greater base of assets. They would also be in a position to expand into new markets from outside the U.S.

If Lilly merges with another research-based company, they risk the possibility of moving toward an unsuccessful venture. Lilly management, which had already streamlined their R&D direction, does not need to complicate the matter by adding a merger partner. There was a reason for the failure of three mergers in 1998 one of which appeared to be incompatibility of practices between the firms involved. Yes, global mergers at the end of the 1990s were on the rise even amidst diversity existing between firms from different countries, however, the pharmaceutical industry has more to tangle with in terms of getting products to market, especially when it comes to regulatory requirements. Lilly could continue to use its current R&D capability, but look to improve its efficiency in bringing drugs to market. This would involve staying with the company's core competencies and using present resources and ever-improving technological innovation, to improve in this area. The company would also have to stay on top of trends in the areas of treatment so as to target the most appropriate therapeutic areas. The company has already proven that they have the ability to address current patient needs.

Alternative 3: In alternative three, Lilly continues its current efforts in the five main therapeutic areas, but also moves into the area of OTC products by acquiring some known name brands, a key to success in this particular sector. This could entail purchasing a particular division of a consumer products company. In this way, Lilly is not touching it's efforts in pharmaceuticals—this business unit would not in any way be altered from its current form—and by purchasing known brands, it can benefit by marketing already established names. With the added area of consumer products, Lilly is insuring the company against swings in earnings due to gaps in the company's pipeline of drugs. Since U.S. drug companies cannot expect the U.S. market to continue to demonstrate strong growth, they have to devise ways to achieve growth beyond the U.S. market. If Lilly participates in OTC production and selling beyond the U.S., they will be ready to enter deregulated drug markets in Europe, China and other geographical areas with high barriers to entry.

Another aspect of marketing in the U.S. involves changes in the U.S. pharmaceuticals market, namely, the pressure put on drug prices by large purchasers. The era of automatically high ethical drug prices appeared to be finishing in the 1990s due to a dominance of managed care companies purchasing drugs. Alternatively, even though consumer products carry lower margins, ethical products also appear to be heading in this direction. So, again, the two types of products appear to have more in common than in previous years.

Lilly will have to keep the ethical and OTC business units completely separate in order to avoid slacking in terms of R&D. In addition, if one looks at one of Lilly's top competitors, Pfizer, this company is ahead of Lilly in terms of sales. Revenues from prescription drugs are on par with Lilly, but they have the added insurance of consumer products (OTC) medicines with strong brand names. With the success of Viagra and other drugs developed by Pfizer, the prospect of achieving success in both businesses is evident; Pfizer was able to develop this blockbuster drug in their pharmaceuticals division, boasts a formidable pipeline and markets OTC drugs as well.

A second advantage of moving into OTC products is the aspect of selling in overseas markets. Over-the counter products are regulated less, thus successful selling of them would be less subject to difficult governmental and regulatory hurdles when marketing abroad. OTC drugs are a compatible product in terms of production. They would also be a logical added business unit in terms of moving a drug beyond the patent expiration. Changing a drug to OTC status is a common method of combating lost sales due to patent expiration and most OTC drugs had their start as ethical products.

Another advantage is the emphasis on advertising and promotion for OTC drugs. With the increase in DTC advertising for ethical products, pharmaceutical firms have had to direct more attention and resources to this area of business and this trend is sure to continue in the U.S. as well as enter into overseas markets. Thus, advertising is now a required ingredient for participation in both these types of businesses which will bode well for companies who participate in both in both sectors. There may be a type of economies of scale within the area of advertising now that ethical producers must also use product promotion.

With Lilly's restructuring in the mid-1990s, their status in the industry changed as sales grew with the blockbuster Prozac. Lilly's earnings per share in 1997 had grown 21 percent compared to Pfizer's 13 percent. However, one of Lilly's greatest weaknesses is the fact that this growth is represented by the strength of a single drug whereas companies such as Pfizer have several top-selling drugs with a strong pipeline to back them up, not to mention highly recognizable consumer products brands. Thus, for Pfizer, this appears to be a good combination of compatible business units.

Lilly, under the direction of the ex-CEO, Mr. Randall Tobias, had proven that the company is capable of developing at least one top-selling prescription drug in the 1990s post restructuring. However, beyond Prozac, it has not proven that it can smoothly make the transition from one blockbuster to the next, that is if and when there is a next. Other strategy ideas have worked to the company's detriment such as the purchasing of a PBM company. However, the time is running out on Prozac and the company must devise a way of shielding itself from potentially great earnings loss which would catapult Lilly from its position as one of the top pharmaceutical firms in terms of sales.

ELI LILLY & COMPANY DECISION CHART

	ALTERNATIVES		
	ONE	**TWO**	**THREE**
ORGANIZATION/ STRUCTURE	Acquire generic subsidiary	Lilly merges with R&D firm	Lilly operates alone using JV and alliances
PRODUCTS	Add generics to previous mix of research-based pharmaceuticals	Researched-based pharmaceuticals only	Researched-based pharmaceuticals + OTC (Branded products)
THERAPEUTIC AREAS	Subset of alternative three	Expand therapeutic mix (see Alternative 3)	Neuroscience, endocrinology, oncology, cardiovascular disease, infectious diseases, women's health
MARKETS	U.S., Europe, Asia	U.S. + concentrated efforts in specific markets	Forays into special markets with barriers to entry, but high-growth potential
CUSTOMERS	Hospitals, Managed-care, Governments, Physicians, Individual patients		Add individual patients of OTC products

CASE 38

Kikkoman Corporation in the Mid-1990s: Market Maturity, Diversification, and Globalization[1]

SYNOPSIS OF THE CASE

This case profiles Kikkoman Corporation, the oldest continuous enterprise among the two hundred largest industrial firms in Japan during the mid-1990s. It provides opportunity to examine the various strategic phases in the company's history as a backdrop to the challenges the company faced in the mid-1990s. Specifically, Kikkoman faced maturing markets for its most important product, soy sauce (or shoyu), an increasing need to diversify its product line, and continuing impetus for expanding into new country markets.

The first major section of the case examines Kikkoman's strategic evolution in Japan from its beginnings in the early 1600s through the mid-1990s. The case traces the evolution of the shoyu industry in Japan as well as the Mogi family company's changes in response to the industry changes through the early 20th Century. In the early 20th Century Kikkoman Corporation took on a new form of organization, introduced modern management practices, and developed the relationship between the company and its community. The section also briefly describes Kikkoman's early internationalization efforts.

The second section of the case examines how Kikkoman managed the U.S. market from immediately after WWII until the mid-1990s. The company's post-WWII entry into the U.S. market followed the classic evolutionary pattern—first exporting into the U.S. market, then establishing a market organization, and finally building a plant. The case describes these strategic moves with a special emphasis on the manufacturing plant in Walworth, Wisconsin. In addition, the case gives insight into how the company manages its U.S. facility.

The third section summarizes recent moves by U.S. competitors and the challenges confronting the company in the US market. The final section of the case overviews the company's mid-1990's international position and outlines its vision and current challenges.

TEACHING OBJECTIVES

A major objective of the case is to provide an opportunity for class participants to examine the skills and knowledge of a traditional, family owned Japanese firm that enabled it to become an early successful international player. In particular the case provides opportunity for examining the firm's entry into the United States, the largest and most sophisticated consumer market in the world. The teaching objectives of this case are as follows:

1. To understand the development of family traditions, values, and culture that lead to successful business venturing.

2. To examine the factors impacting industry consolidation and the role of a specific firm in that consolidation.

3. To examine factors which encourage international activity.

4. To study the traditional model for increasing more intensive international activities.

5. To develop an understanding of how to transfer competitive advantages in a home country market into the international arena.

6. To illustrate strategic and tactical choices made by a company when entering a new market (i.e., undertaking a "foreign invasion" of new territory).

---

[1] This teaching note is based on a teaching note by Marilyn L. Taylor.

STRATEGIC ISSUES AND DISCUSSION QUESTIONS

1. **Evaluate Kikkoman's development of key success factors or various competitive advantages. How has the firm managed to remain successful over such an extended period of time?**

   Tracking Kikkoman's development of its success factors is essentially a study in ascertaining how the company invested in the development of competitive advantages that have kept them in the forefront of competition in their niche, i.e. soy sauce manufacture and distribution. As implied in the case, these various competences formed at least temporary barriers to competition, however the barriers were typically eroded with time. Kikkoman Corporation took advantage of first mover advantage (or nearly so) in Japan on a number of instances, for example, in advertising, in building a modern large-scale plant, and in entering the U.S. market. However, each of these barriers to entry was surmounted by competitors in time. The lesson is that no competitive advantage lasts forever (unless, of course, the company owns a unique resource) The analysis of the evolution of the success factors profile is essentially an analysis based on the resource-based viewpoint (RBV).

   An alternate conceptual framework is presented by Porter's value chain, which focuses, as do all resource-based frameworks, on the internal competences of the firm. The often used Strengths and Weaknesses (SWs) in SWOT analyses reflect the basic RBV or Porter's value chain approach. A full exploration of the SWs, the competitive advantages, or the components of the value chain will explore: a) the evolution of the strengths and b) the strategic implications of the same.

   The activities begun by the various Mogi family members and joined later by the Takanashi families, became the Noda Shoyu Company and, since WWII, the Kikkoman Corporation. The company has continually augmented its skill set since inception. Kikkoman Corp., its precursory companies, and the previous activities undertaken by family members were often first moves in the market (e.g., advertising in Japan in the 19th Century and the U.S. Walworth plant as the first Japanese FDI after WWII). Competitors have clearly emulated company moves.

   From the very beginning this family has emphasized quality in it's basic product i.e. Shoyu. The founder obviously was a courageous, resourceful and energetic matriach. This set of qualities is reflected in much of the company/family's history through almost four centuries. The location on the Edo River provided access to Japan's largest market, i.e. Tokyo. As the city grew, the family continued to find ways of aggressively developing niches in that market. As the family grew, so did their various talents. The early strategy of the family can be described as backward vertical integration, that is various family members learned various skills, such as barrel making, that otherwise would have been undertaken by other firms. Obviously the family grew large enough to enable the development of this variety of skills. Only in 1918, almost 300 years after inception did the various family enterprises join together into the combined firm called Noda Shoyu Co. As implied in the case, the impact of WWI created a competitive situation that encouraged family interests to join forces.

   Perhaps the most intriguing is the emphasis on R&D that has led to a line of sophisticated products which students might not readily associate with the humble soy sauce that sits on the grocery store shelf. The early initiation of R&D activities demonstrates the family commitment to the future vitality of its enterprise. R&D activities made a tremendous impact on process technology as well as caused a proliferation in the set of products. The firm appears to have become more efficient in the production of its base product and has continuously added to its product line.

   The marketing activities, and especially the development of the brand name are important to note. Kikkoman as a brand has enjoyed an international recognition for over 100 years. The aggressive brand recognition efforts intended to differentiate the product began in the early 1800's when Mogi Saheiji received the shogunate's recognition for the family premier brand. Students should note that the aggressive promotion of the brand through multiple tactics. The family created a high quality product with a recognized brand name. Mogi Saheiji in particular added value through brand development. He avoided competitive pressures by creating brand loyalty. Brand recognition led to higher demand and greater market share. Under these favorable conditions, the company could demand a higher price and thus obtain a higher margin resulting in greater profits. These were in turn used to invest in the company's aggressive strategies, including R&D activities as well as plant and facilities modernization.

The company's development of international experience goes back to the late 17th century—in short, this company has been practicing international strategies for three hundred years. Through its import activities the company gradually developed knowledge and experience in dealing with foreign governments and unfamiliar customs and business practices. The company also used its relationships with food export/import agents to learn about foreign markets.

The family's development of resources and skills has proved invaluable in the international marketplace. The ready adoption of new technologies led to breweries with economies of scale and thus to absolute lower advantages. The process technology advances could be transferred into the other companies that the company acquired (e.g. other shoyu companies, the Del Monte product lines).

Beginning in 1918 the Noda Shoyu Company also increasingly improved its managerial systems and skill by organizing into a single enterprise with coordinated decision-making. When the individual breweries formed the manufacturer's association, only marketing and procurement functions were coordinated. All internal functions were independent. Under the new organization formed in 1918, all other functions of the company were consolidated within the corporate structure. Some decisions were deliberately made at the top management level while others were delegated to the managers of specific product lines or company activities. Such coordination in decision making allowed management to determine and implement corporate strategies without being caught up in time-consuming day-to-day minutiae. This ability stands them in good stead even today with far flung Kikkoman enterprises. For example, similar patterns can be identified in how the firm manages the U.S. operations, especially in the Walworth plant.

The company also learnt how to manage its relationships with its employees, community and various other public entities. The long 1927-28 labor strike was not financially crippling for the company. However, it gave impetus to activities to build strong identity between the employees and the company. After the strike, the Noda Shoyu Company began a deliberate program to rebuild its relationship with Noda city and its public image. The program included carefully selected acts of corporate philanthropy. The company learned that it is important to nurture its relationships with its employees and the local community and developed policies and programs to support those relationships.

The company also developed its community relations expertise through its heavy involvement in the city of Noda. The careful attention to "nemawashi" or root tending is an example of risk management. In Noda Kikkoman worked at being a good citizen in order to diminish the work force propensity to strike. The company invested in health facilities and education for Noda citizens. Such investment helped provide a steady stream of educated and healthy workers. Other investments in cultural and civic aspects of Noda assured a social system in which families thrived and good workers wanted to stay in the area. Thus the company and community became mutually supporting systems.

These community skills stood the company in good stead as it entered the Walworth area in the 1970s. The company's entry into Walworth and its continuing activities in the immediate region and beyond, reflect how thoroughly those skills have become embedded in the very fabric of the company.

The skill sets of Kikkoman Corporation have certainly evolved. The pattern of evolution suggests a company that understands the need to continually enhance and augment its skill sets even as it transfers them across country boundaries and product applications. However, whether the company will be able to evolve quickly enough to remain competitive in the ever-quickening pace of change in the food industry is open to question.

The company financials reflect the above strengths. In it's fourth century of operation, Kikkoman has a strong balance sheet with shareholder's equity remaining consistently at about 40% of the capitalization structure. The company has remained consistently profitable over the last seven years.

2.   **What factors led to industry consolidation in Japan? How did the company respond to consolidation and in what ways did the company contribute to industry consolidation?**

Students will quickly identify that Shoyu manufacturing or brewing apparently occurred at the family unit level during Japan's agriculturally based history. Shoyu obviously became a critical condiment, much like ketchup in the United States. In Japan each family would have a particular "recipe". As the country became urbanized, it was natural that some farm families, including the Mogi clan, would reach out to serve the urban markets.

The case clearly depicts the extreme fragmentation of the industry during the 17th century and the factors that led to industry consolidation. Most important to the consolidation was probably the development of a national transportation system, i.e. the railroad. Prior to that Shoyu remained very local in distribution. Noda Shoyu traveled to Edo City (Tokyo) by water route, not unlike the canal system in the United States during the 18th and 19th centuries. The railway system opened the possibility of a regional, even national brand information dissemination and product distribution. Visitors to Tokyo were exposed to Kikkoman's distinctive labeling and the company's promotional activities. Thus demand was initiated in other parts of the country when travelers returned home, perhaps with a bottle of Kikkoman from Tokyo. Although Shoyu use overall did not appear to rise, the demand for Noda Shoyu could and did.

Students might point out the development of the strong tonya or wholesaling system to serve the Edo/Tokyo market. For example, the wholesalers had control even over final pricing. The alternatives available to counteract tonya strength were coopting (e.g., as in marriage alliance) or, as depicted in the case, bypassing the tonya entirely. By coalescing into a manufacturers association, the Noda Shoyu strengthened their upstream bargaining power. Having at least one member within the wholesalers' alliance provided information valuable in negotiations. Differentiating through brand strategy efforts further strengthened the Noda Shoyu in negotiations. The promotional efforts heightened the visibility of the Kikkoman brand.

The shoyu business was an easy entry business even in the 19th century. With 14,000 known brewers, oversupply was a serious problem. The formation of the Noda Shoyu Brewers' Association demonstrates the family's reaction to counteract these forces. Their initial objectives were to cut costs through purchasing raw materials in volume and standardizing wages. They also agreed to limit the quantity of Shoyu sent to the Tokyo market. However, internal operations remained under the control of individual family branches and the state of production facilities and their costs of production must have varied widely.

When consumer taste preference shifted to the Tokyo style shoyu produced by eastern Japanese brewers, Noda Shoyu Brewers' association allowed the extended family to make considerable investment in one of the first R&D labs in Japan. The R&D efforts specifically investigated shoyu brewing and fermenting processes, improved shoyu quality, and gave impetus to the shoyu fermenting process mechanization. Various members of the clan adopted the newest technological advances. These efforts ultimately put the company in the forefront of the learning curve in this industry with greatest economies of scale, and continuing ability to improve and advertise quality. The changes in shoyu brewing processes, from small-batch, brewmaster-controlled craft to a large batch, mechanized fermentation process and subsequently to a continuous batch process upped the entry barriers into the industry.

The evolution of Kikkoman Corporation itself, including its origins as independent small family enterprises, the move to an association, the families' organization of their facilities and assets into a privately held company, and its subsequent move to public status, all parallel the increasing economies of scale required to compete and the industry consolidation that necessarily accompanied these changes. Additional evidence is provided by the company's press for increased integration of operations, the pre-WWII acquisition of other firms, and the declining number of firms in the industry.

3.   **Evaluate the firm's various phases of international activity.**

The evolution of Noda Shoyu's international activities follows a typical four-stage pattern for penetrating a country market:

Stage 1: Import/export activities

Stage 2: Alliances for packaging & production

Stage 3: Marketing offices

Stage 4: Manufacturing facilities

The company entered each stage seeking distinct advantages. Importing raw materials gave the company access to higher quality raw materials and thus continued building the quality image that had been the firm's hallmark since its inception. Exporting gave the company additional outlet for their shoyu and allowed them to take advantage of economies of scale and thus lower production costs as technology changed. The company followed the export-marketing-manufacturing pattern twice, before WWII and again after the war.

Thus, Kikkoman Corp. built its knowledge base and expertise in each market before making sequentially heavier investments in the next stage.

Students may be quick to point out the early moves to manufacture in such diverse locations as Korea, Manchuria, Indonesia and the United States. The company appears to be a significant risk taker from its inception. Its moves after WWII into the U.S. market appear tame in retrospect.

It is important that students note that the company's original export market was people who typically used shoyu, not individuals whom the company had to persuade de nova. Thus, the original markets outside Japan were either other Asian peoples or Japanese people living in other countries. Further, the company initially relied on third parties, that is, agents who were familiar with the markets into which the goods were imported. The discussion should point out the importance of such agents in organizational learning process.

Students might also point out that in the U.S. marketing activities initially took place in territories nearest to Japan and where there was greater concentration of people of Asian origin, namely Hawaii and California. The manufacturing facility, in contrast, was located near the source of raw materials.

Kikkoman is not a "stateless corporation". Rather, Kikkoman Corp. is clearly a Japanese firm that has adapted itself in terms of marketing to a majority of the world's countries and has slowly made its presence known through direct foreign investment in manufacturing facilities. Neither does the company aggressively pursue strategic alliances as is so common with other MNCs (Multi National Corporation). The firm chooses to absorb alliance activities internally. If the activity is not purchased (e.g. the purchase of Del Monte operations in Asia and the PTC alliance followed by purchase), the company will start the activity de nova (e.g. Kikkoman's evolution in the US since the Leslie Salt partnership and the Walworth plant).

4. **Evaluate the attractiveness of the U.S. market for entry in the mid and late 1960's.**

Factors that might have affected Kikkoman's decision to invest in the United States market were related to marketing, barriers to trade, costs and investment climate. More specifically,

- Marketing Factors – The US market size was sufficient and showed promising growth, and Kikkoman had some experience with the complex distribution system in the United States.

- Barriers to Trade – At the time the Walworth plant opened, there was no embargo on soybean exports to Japan.

- Cost Factors – The Walworth location placed the company near sources of supply (soybeans, wheat, salt). Labor was cheaper in Walworth, transportation costs were low, Walworth was strategically located to address the entire U.S. market.

- Investment Climate – Post WWII United States was economically and politically stable.

- Other factors – The strength of having an aggressive U.S. trained MBA in the person of Yuzaburo Mogi who came into significant positions in the company no doubt contributed to the company's ability to react in the US market in a timely fashion.

In summary, the US market provided a stable growing set of opportunities for Kikkoman Corp. Given the company's strengths, i.e. aggressive marketers, efficient producers, and long history in international markets, the entry into the U.S. market was very appropriate.

5. **Evaluate the firm's strategic and operational choices in entering the U.S. market in the post WWII period.**

Only after WWII did non-traditional users begin using shoyu. These were veterans and other individuals who had traveled or lived in Japan. The company realized that the traditional markets would not provide significant growth opportunities in the WWII period and its programs to penetrate non-traditional markets were diverse and aggressive. The case notes the argument that unlike other non-U.S. food manufacturers and marketers, Kikkoman sold a non-modified product in the US market. The argument is weakened when one realizes that the company has sought application in different foods and recipes than in Japan. However, the company had already begun the process of "westernizing" soy sauce in its home market.

One important set of the company's skills is its ability to manage a large far flung enterprise with apparently strong controls from corporate headquarters, yet with the employees feeling that they have an impact on the choices that are made. The case describes consensus decision making in Walworth facility where three of the five top managers are Japanese. Clearly, neither corporate executives nor local workers in Walworth expect to attain the most senior positions in the United States in the near future. The questions might well arise, thus, whether the company truly practices what it preaches and what is an appropriate pattern for a geographically dispersed firm.

It has been suggested that Japanese MNCs internationalize because of three factors:

- General intensification of international competition among MNCs and the consequent need to deepen their involvement in key oversees markets.

- Changes in production techniques and technological developments that paralleled changes in consumer and industrial demand, leading to shortening of product cycles and an increased need to locate production in foreign markets

- A revolution in information technologies that facilitated the transfer abroad of top-level management and coordination functions.

In the case of Kikkoman the forces that have acted on the company may be somewhat different. The company has been an aggressive marketer throughout much of its history. During the post WWII period the GI occupation forces in Japan became familiar with soy sauce. They took the acquired taste back home. An extension beyond Japan would appear "natural" when a former customer moved offshore. The second factor mentioned above does apply in the sense that the company sought more volume in order to take advantage of economies of scale.

Companies can be identified as belonging in one or more of three categories:

- Resource seekers that are after natural or human resources

- Market seekers, an orientation that is enhanced if the government closes or restricts market access

- Efficiency seekers, firms that drive for the most economical sources of production

In this topology Kikkoman's approach to the U.S. market was driven by all three. The company strove to be near the source of soybeans and wheat that it imported heavily from the United States. Finally the company's drive for efficiency for production was realized in Walworth. The case does give only general observation regarding U.S. labor costs, but general observation suggests that the U.S. labor costs have decreased relative to those in Japan in recent years. Further, the hourly cost of labor in Walworth is modest at the stated wage level of a little over $10.00 per hour.

6. **What was the status of Kikkoman's operations in the U.S., European, and Asian markets in the mid-1990's.**

United States

The market size was sufficient though growth was slower and dependent on new product introductions. Kikkoman's traditional customer base (people of Asian descent) was growing. Barriers to trade between Japan and United States change over time depending on market conditions. Kikkoman expanded in the Walworth location but did not build other manufacturing plants and the investment climate was stable both politically and economically.

Europe

The size of the market appeared to be sufficient with attractive prospects for growth. Kikkoman plans to spur primary demand for soy sauce and take advantage of opportunities in soy based foods. Significant barriers to trade exist for non-European companies. The company has invested in restaurants in Germany and owns a distribution facility in UK. Kikkoman supported the European market from its Singapore plant. The investment climate in Europe was relatively stable both politically and economically.

Asia

By mid 90s, the Asian markets seemed ripe for expansion. Kikkoman had opened a plant in Singapore in 1987 and planned on opening another one in China. However, the investment climate offered low stability politically and economically in general, but this varied from country to country.

In summary, although the US market may remain the strongest and most stable, Europe offers more growth opportunities with little more risk (in the western European countries at least). Some parts of Asia (e.g. China) may offer significant more growth opportunities, but they also offer greater risks due to instability.

7. **What challenges do you foresee for Kikkoman, especially in the U.S. market, and how should the company respond?**

Kikkoman's major challenges can be seen in the slow growth of its consolidated sales and decreased asset turnover. From 1989 through 1995, sales growth ranged from a decrease of 4% (1992–93) to a high of a 5% increase (1990–91) and has been about 2% overall. Margins have held in recent years at about 4% - not too bad for a food company. The company's slipping shoyu market share in Japan poses an issue. How much effort should the company exert to maintain its base product in its home market? There is no ready answer to this dilemma. Clearly the growth in parent company revenues have come in the "Food" product lines with food growing at 8–13% over the 1994–1996 time period and the other lines growing at an even lower rate. Further, profits are greater outside Japan with overseas margins being more than twice the domestic.

Another aspect of the U.S. market is that until recently the country had the highest per capita and family income in the world. Kikkoman's choices in the higher income maturing markets form an important model. In the United States the company began by importing its base products to customers to whom the product was a staple. Later marketing efforts were aimed at higher margin products. Finally the company diversified the product line to fit the emerging trends of the specific market. The later phase has included sauces and other easy to prepare, flavorful and natural food substances in the United States. There is no guarantee that other markets will evolve with same patterns as the United States. However it is clear that Kikkoman has learned to assimilate market information and adapt the company's product development and marketing efforts to market changes. The current stagnation in growth underscores the difficulty of undertaking these changes fast enough in mature food markets to make a difference in the performance of such a large company.

Beyond the United States and Japan, the company has many opportunities. By the mid-1990's Kikkoman operated in 90 countries. With Soy sauce Kikkoman has a global strategy, i.e. the company offers the same product through out the world. With its broad product line the company has the ability to tailor its offering mix in any one country. Students might note the reduction in number of products. Presumably Kikkoman plans to "cherry pick", i.e. concentrate on its higher end margin products and/or decrease the costs of inventory control. Does this decrease in product line breadth suggest a greater emphasis on a global rather than a multi-domestic strategy, or is it a cost containment tactic? Either explanation is possible.

Success in a mature market like the U.S. poses significant challenges. The company chose a differentiation strategy long ago. Its current brands are well known in various markets. In the US students will recognize Del Monte and Kikkoman. One could debate the extent of additional effort that the company should invest in branding. Product innovations especially in mature markets like the United States are quickly copied and competition often reduces to cost/price. Kikkoman appears well positioned on a cost basis in soya sauce. Whether it is well-positioned on cost in the remainder of its product line remains open to question.

Kikkoman basically has the following six choices:

Extent of Offering (→)	Constrained Offering	Existing Offering	Expanded Offering
Existing Markets	Strategy #1	Strategy #2	Strategy #3
New Markets	Strategy #6	Strategy #5	Strategy #4

The question of which strategy to apply to any particular market will need to take into consideration a number of factors including the company's current position, emerging trends, and likely competitor moves. For example, if the company determines that higher margins can be obtained through new products, it may choose Strategies #3, or #4. i.e. an expanded offering. Market choices must be predicated on buying power. For example China is expected to be a market that will open up significantly in terms of buying power.

What Kikkoman actually seems to be doing is adopting a set of combination strategies. The company has constrained its offering by reducing the breadth of its product line (Strategies #1 & #6). At the same time it emphasizes R&D. The company's R&D niche is high-technology products such as the heat resistant luciferase and its application in a testing kit for microorganisms. The latter product is clearly a product line diversification related to its identity as a Food company. Kikkoman also clearly focuses its skills in developing new products, e.g. sauces that enhance the flavor of easy-to-prepare meals. These strategies are #3 and #4.

The company already distributes its food products in 90 countries, a fairly widespread marketing presence in the global community. The issues appear to be a) what new markets to enter, b) what markets to press in more aggressively and c) in what countries to make direct investment in the form of plant and equipment. In a class with good representation from other countries, there may be lively discussion about the appeal Kikkoman may have in a particular market, how to enter the market (e.g. what the distribution channels are like), how to aggressively pursue a market (e.g. product offering including portion size, packaging, advertising, including point-of-sale, etc).

Ongoing changes in taste preferences should portend well for Kikkoman soy sauce. Although the Kikkoman soy sauce has remained the same, the company has continually put its soy sauce to new uses in all of the markets it serves, both geographically as well as based on consumer/institutional markets. The firm is innovative in its application and adaptation in the use of its base product as well as its marketing efforts. Perhaps, more important Kikkoman is a long way down the learning curve compared to its competitors.

There are competitive moves that need to be monitored. The case points out that three competitors from Japan built U.S. plants in the late 1980's and the early 1990's. Students may debate whether the market is growing rapidly enough to absorb the increased capacity. The company must also consider product life cycle issues. Canned oriental entries had fallen out with the American consumers while sauces were "in". How long could sales of sauces grow at above 10% was a significant question.

A major issue for any firm operating a branch office or activity is locus of control. The home office must determine how closely to be involved in monitoring and decision making at the local level. Some organizations use hierarchy and chain of command as methods and means of operation to evaluate performance at the local level. Other organizations use price/profit and the results of operations to evaluate performance. Kikkoman appears to use a combination. Yet, there is evidence that the satisfaction at the local level is very genuine and that the company is a good corporate citizen in Walworth, in the state of Wisconsin and indeed in the United States.

In short, the company's skill set is superb. Many of the skills date from the company's inception—dedication to continuing quality and process improvement, for example. The company has been on the forefront on any issues among which are R&D, community relations, and localization of management. In spite of its age and size, the company appears nimble. The case can help students develop an appreciation for the superior strategies pursued by a "foreign" competitor whose base is a fairly "humble" product.

POSTSCRIPT

Kikkoman opened a plant in Folsom in 1998, since the United States market for soy sauce was growing at 10% annually and represented a significant opportunity for the company. Kikkoman also opened a plant in Europe (Netherlands) in 1997 (Source: Knight-Ridder, various dates).

CASE 39

CenturyTel in a Bear Hug[1]

SYNOPSIS OF THE CASE

This case gives an overview of the telecommunications industry, which encompasses the movement of voice, video and data over long as well as short distances. The economic recession has hit the telecommunications industry extremely hard and it faces extreme consolidation pressures. The case describes the trends and future outlook for the industry, and the challenges facing the management at CenturyTel as they consider how to win the hostile takeover bid from AllTel.

CenturyTel's CEO Glen Post faces the prospect of fending off a bear hug. Although CenturyTel has made an open offer to sell its wireless division, it had not intended to sell the entire firm. In July 2001, AllTel (AT), in an effort to force the sale of CenturyTel announced a public bid for the purchase of the competitor. The asking price was $43 per share or 0.6934 shares of AllTel stock for each share of CenturyTel stock. Glen Post, CEO of CenturyTel (CTL) and managers of the firm are optimistic about the firm's future performance while the investment manager is more conservative in expectations. He asks the analysts with the firm to determine the value of the firm and of the wireless division. Then the analysts must determine whether to sell the wireless division or the entire firm. The group must decide how to counter the bear hug since CTL believes that the offer of $43 per share currently on the table sorely undervalues the firm.

TEACHING OBJECTIVES

The main teaching objectives of the case are:

1. To illustrate how one might analyze an acquisition decision strategically.

2. To understand environmental, technological and competitive factors as well as internal managerial and financial factors at play in a hostile buyout offer.

3. To understand the role of the Board of Directors in acquisitions/buyouts.

4. To gain an appreciation for environmental factors affecting telecommunications service providers.

STRATEGIC ISSUES AND DISCUSSION QUESTIONS

1. **What are the threats and opportunities facing telecommunications service providers?**

    The global telecommunications industry is going through one of its worst phases. Telecommunications service providers are struggling to survive amid overcapacity and lowered earnings and valuations.

    There are significant threats facing firms in this sector. Specifically,

    - Overcapacity in the industry outweighs demand and the situation is not expected to improve in the near future. Companies built large capacity in the hope that explosive growth in Internet traffic would drive demand in the coming years, but their projections regarding Internet traffic growth have fallen far short of the rosy projections.

    - There is intense price based competition as a result of the overcapacity. This can cause companies with huge debts to go bankrupt if prices continue to tumble.

---

[1] Parts of this teaching note are based on a teaching note by Lawrence R. Jauch.

- Local and long-distance voice sectors of the industry are in decline and are not likely to grow again. According to some industry players, telecommunications companies might offer voice services free of cost in the near future.

- The rate of wireless subscriptions is increasing, but at a declining rate. Wireless Internet is far from becoming a reality and is not likely to show growth for some time to come.

- New technologies like wireless phones, emails, instant messaging and cable modems, are taking away traffic from the old telephone networks. There is also greater convergence of telephone service and email, and technologies like Voice over Internet, voice based chatting facilities and instant messaging, provide alternatives to regular telephone technology.

However, there exist some opportunities as well:

- The 1996 Telecommunications Act has authorized a new federal and state Universal Service Fund to support eligible carriers in rural areas in order to promote universal service. The effect of this act is to negatively impact ILECs (Incumbent Local Exchange Carriers) and positively impact companies like CTL.

- Some segments of the market such as data from Internet Services and network management still remain healthy. These represent only a small portion of the telecommunications market, but their long-term prospects are encouraging.

- New Technologies and the convergence of services may also be regarded as an opportunity because of the cost and efficiency benefits they offer.

- Competition in the rural and suburban markets has not yet developed and the Baby Bells may divest their stakes in these markets, leaving the field open for companies focusing on rural and suburban areas.

- The attacks of September 11, 2001, may cause consumers to think of cell phones as a necessity—the wireless growth rate may go up by 30% because of this. Since the attacks people have also started to substitute video conferencing for business travel.

2.   **What is the situation facing CTL? What are the strengths and weaknesses of CTL and of the opposition?**

CenturyTel (CTL)

CenturyTel (CTL), the rural telecommunications giant, faces the prospect of a "bear hug"—an unsolicited public takeover bid—from AllTel (AT). AT has offered $8.75 billion to buy CTL—at a 40% premium over CTL's actual market price. CTL is resisting the takeover bid and has sued AT to prevent it from promoting the unsolicited bid.

CTL is the 8th largest local-exchange carrier and cellular operator in United States. It provides phone services in rural areas, suburbs and small towns in 21 states including Arkansas, Washington, Missouri, Michigan, Louisiana and Colorado, and cellular services in 6 states. Other services offered by CTL are cable TV, long-distance, Internet access and business data services and security monitoring. CTL aspires to become the leading provider of integrated communications services to rural areas and smaller cities in the United States with a primary focus on wireless and telephone services. CTL also plans to penetrate vertical services such as caller ID and voice mail and provide customers with additional services such as long-distance, Internet, DSL and data.

CTL's key strength is its access to local switches. It has been growing for several years primarily through its acquisitions telephone assets of Verizon and PTI and through expansion of services.

CTL's primary weakness is its wireless business because it does not yet have any agreements with wireless carriers to provide roaming services even though CTL has targeted roaming service revenues. It does not have the infrastructure to have a national presence in wireless, hence it is missing out on capturing business customers that require nationwide wireless.

Another weakness of CTL is its high debt. In an industry where price wars are squeezing margins for companies, a high debt situation may create problems for its long-term survival.

AllTel (AT)

AT aims to become a dominant rural communications carrier. It has the 2nd largest Incumbent Local Exchange Carrier (ILEC) operation in the United States and it is trying to expand into providing Competitive Local Exchange Carrier (CLEC) services outside its ILEC areas.

AT's strength is its wireless business. It has several agreements in place with companies such as Bell Atlantic, GTE and Vodafone to offer its customers national coverage with no roaming or toll charges. It has strong cash flows that it can use to fund its CLEC services.

Its primary weakness is that it does not have access to local switches.

3. **What would be the advantages and disadvantages of the acquisition of the wireless segment or acquisition of the entire firm from CenturyTel's view and from AllTel's perspective?**

Acquisition of the Wireless segment

For CTL, the sale of its wireless division is advantageous because the company is weak in the area, the wireless business has been declining and the proceeds from the sale are likely to increase the company's liquidity and enable it to maintain a healthy balance sheet. It can also use the funds generated by the sale in order to buy rural switches from other companies. The company has been looking to sell off the business for some time and this is an opportunity for it to focus on its wireline assets. A disadvantage of selling just the wireless business for CTL may be an adverse tax impact on the company, but company executives believe that they can avoid the tax penalty. Selling the wireless business alone implies that CTL will no longer offer a bundled service to its customers. This may be a disadvantage for CTL since bundled services offer the simplicity of a single bill to the consumer. If another competitor in the same region offers a bundle of services, CTL's customers may no longer stay with CTL.

By buying CTL's wireless business AT can augment its wireless network and add more customers at an attractive price. However, this is not as attractive a deal for AT as buying CTL as a whole because AT's long term plans are to provide rural communications in both wireless and wireline segments.

Acquisition of the entire company by AT

Acquisition of CTL offers substantial strategic benefits for both companies. The combination of both companies has synergies because their wireline and wireless businesses are complementary and the expanded scale and scope can potentially create new opportunities for the merged company. By combining their customer base and revenues, AT and CTL can emerge into a "communications powerhouse." In addition there are cost synergies to be expected from combining operations.

It could also greatly benefit rural customers, who would get more services, and cellular phone users might end up with lower roaming fees.

There are no apparent disadvantages of the acquisition for AT. For CTL, the buyout may also be a win-win situation, but the management at CTL believes that the offer is too low and does not reflect the correct valuation for CTL's business. In such a case, the disadvantage to CTL shareholders may be that they receive less compensation for their shares. Another disadvantage for CTL may be that its community relations might be jeopardized if the merged company does not share its current community oriented values. In addition, CTL's management may also not get meaningful roles in the new company and there can be staff reductions as a result of the consolidation.

To sum up, from the point of view of AT, buying CTL as a whole is a better decision, and for CTL, selling their wireless division seems to be a better decision.

4. **How successful is the 'bear hug' likely to be? Give reasons for your answer. What role does the Board of Directors play in the takeover battle?**

A 'bear hug' requires that the Board of Directors of a company receiving the 'bear hug' give serious consideration to the offer in order to provide the best returns for shareholders. AllTel is trying to pressurize an unwilling Board at CTL by directing its public relations efforts at institutional shareholders, hoping that the investors will influence the Board to make a decision in favor of the takeover. However, this hostile bid is not likely to go through because of the takeover defense mechanisms that are in place at CTL.

According to American Lawyer (October 2001), CTL has instituted a "Poison Pill" defense that allows its shareholders to buy back shares of the company at a discounted price in case of a hostile takeover. CTL also has a 'staggered board" in place which makes sure that only a few of the board members are up for elections each year, thus making it hard for the acquiring company to takeover CTL through a proxy fight. This is an example of a "shark repellent" strategy. CTL also has a voting structure that gives the management and employees at CTL a disproportionate amount of voting power as compared to their holdings in the company.

Therefore, if AT is not able to persuade a significant number of CTL shareholders that selling CTL provides for adequate returns for them, then AT's takeover bid cannot succeed. AT might have to be satisfied with the CTL's wireless division, if that option is still made available to them.

POSTSCRIPT

In March 2002, AllTel and CenturyTel reached an agreement on a merger deal in which Alltel will acquire CenturyTel's wireless business for US$1.65 billion in cash (Source: *Wireless NewsFactor*, March 2002).

CASE 40

Whirlpool Corporation's Global Strategy

SYNOPSIS OF THE CASE

This case describes the expansion of Whirlpool into the global home appliances market, the problems it encountered and its restructuring efforts.

In 1989, Whirlpool Corporation, the largest manufacturer of household appliances in the United States, decided to focus on building a global presence in the home appliance industry. In order to achieve its objective, it expanded into markets like India, China, Latin America and Europe through a combination of joint ventures and acquisitions.

By about 1995, Whirlpool's international operations began to exhibit signs of deterioration. Instead of a growth in profits, the next two years saw disappointing results from Whirlpool's overseas markets. Losses accumulated to a point where Whirlpool was forced to announce a restructuring of its activities in these markets.

The case illustrates the pitfalls a company can encounter when expanding into global markets. Whirlpool has a long way to go before it is able to produce significant yields from its global markets and this has caused critics to question the wisdom of its aggressive international strategy.

TEACHING OBJECTIVES

The primary teaching objectives of the case are:

1. To understand the nature of competition in the global home appliance industry.

2. To illustrate how a company develops and implements a global strategy.

3. To demonstrate the effect of country specific economic and environmental factors on company success in a global industry.

4. To understand the pitfalls of expanding into emerging markets in developing countries.

STRATEGIC ISSUES AND DISCUSSION QUESTIONS

1. **What was the structure of the home appliances industry in the United States in the 1990s?**

    The home appliances industry is a capital-intensive industry that is typically classified into four categories—laundry, refrigeration, cooking and other appliances. With over 70% of the households in the United States owning washers and 100% owning refrigerators and cookers, this industry showed little growth prospects in the 1990s and the consolidation in the 1980s has led to fierce competition between four dominant firms. The resultant pressure on margins has prompted companies in the industry to reduce costs and enhance productivity and scale in manufacturing. Firms have tried to improve their product quality as well as the rate of product innovation in order to wrest market share from each other.

2. **How was the appliances industry in Asia, Europe and Latin America different from the United States industry?**

    *   Asia – The Asian market for appliances was expected to achieve growth rates of 10-12% annually throughout the 1990s. The industry was extremely fragmented and was dominated by Japanese, Korean and Taiwanese manufacturers. The Asian markets tended to demand smaller, portable and easy to operate appliances and the demand for appliances varied a lot from country to country. The greatest growth in demand was expected from China and India.

- Europe – The European appliances market had undergone a wave of consolidation like in the United States and was dominated by five companies by 1995. Most manufacturers customized their products for specific countries since product preferences were different for different countries. This was also a mature market with limited growth opportunities.

- Latin America – This was an attractive market with good growth prospects particularly since most countries in the region seemed to be economically stable.

Overall, the appliances industry in Europe, Asia and Latin America was different from the market in United States because of the nature of the demand. Consumer preferences differed by country and region and companies operating in these countries had to be locally responsive to succeed.

3. **Why did Whirlpool choose to expand globally?**

Whirlpool's decision to globalize was a result of a downward pressure on profits, intense competition and limited growth prospects in United States. Whirlpool expected that entry into emerging markets would help its revenues as well as its profits. In addition, Whirlpool's competitors in the United States had begun internationalizing their operations and Whirlpool did not want to wait until they entrenched themselves in the new markets.

Whirlpool's management also believed that globalization was the route to sustainable competitive advantage in the appliance industry since the company would be able to leverage its capabilities in the United States market to other countries.

4. **What was Whirlpool's global strategy? Was it an appropriate strategy to pursue? Why or why not?**

Whirlpool adopted a global strategy with a focus on standardization. A purely global strategy is one where the product being sold is the same in all countries, and control is centralized with little decision-making authority at the local level. By locating production, marketing and R&D in a few favorable locations, by centralizing control with little decision-making authority at the local level, and by producing a standard product, a company can exploit experience curve effects and location economies to reduce costs.

Whirlpool's strategy was to standardize on a common platform for each of its products and add on the different features required by different markets in regional manufacturing centers. Thus, the common platform would define the technological heart of the product and this would not vary from one market to another. Whirlpool hoped to save on design and component costs by following this strategy.

The global strategy was not the most appropriate one to pursue for the appliance industry. On one hand the global appliance industry has some elements of a global industry. For example, products like refrigerators, microwaves, washers and cookers are sold in every country without any functional differences, economies of scale are an important success factor and the industry is largely consolidated in most markets.

However, there also existed significant pressures for local responsiveness (requiring local production and distribution with an emphasis on product customization based on regional and country specific preferences) in this industry. Most companies operating in Asia, Europe and Latin America tended to compete on a local basis in each region. In addition, the nature of competition in the industry did not preclude small competitors from being profitable. Hence the appliance industry cannot be classified as a purely global industry and it did not make sense for Whirlpool to follow a purely global strategy.

5. **What was Whirlpool's experience in Asia, Europe and Latin America? Why did it fail to generate profits?**

Whirlpool's experiences with implementing its strategy in different markets were varied. More specifically:

- Asia – Whirlpool mainly focused on India and China and established joint ventures with local companies. This entry strategy was soon followed by acquisitions.

    By 1997, Whirlpool was making losses in Asia. In China, overcapacity and increased competition from Chinese companies led to saturation of the market within 2 years. This saturation came four years too soon by Whirlpool's projections. Whirlpool also overestimated the demand in the Chinese market. These conditions coupled with low quality products, and a lack of strong distribution and communications infrastructure created further problems for Whirlpool. The Indian market also suffered a similar fate due to overcapacity and a demand that was much lower than expected.

- Europe – Between 1989-1991, Whirlpool bought a majority stake in a Dutch firm, Philips, in order to gain a 20% share of the $20 billion market by 2000. In the belief that Europe and United States were very similar markets, Whirlpool intended to replicate its successful U.S. strategies in Europe and take advantage of the consolidation pressures facing Europe. Whirlpool followed a brand segmentation strategy by positioning products in the high-end, middle range and lower end value segments. It also created centralized distribution centers and focused on increasing operational efficiency. It regularly rotated managers between its United States and European offices.

  The early 1990s proved to be successful years for Whirlpool—sales and profits increased and costs went down. However, other competitors began to imitate Whirlpool and increased their operational efficiency, cut costs and doubled their output. This changed the nature of competition in the industry away from operational efficiency to product innovation. Established players thus became more powerful, rivalry intensified and new entrants entered the market. Whirlpool was not able to build barriers to imitation for its strategies in Europe and the result was an erosion of its market share, falling sales in spite of restructuring and layoffs, and rising costs. Whirlpool also expanded to Eastern Europe but sales in the market were disappointing.

- Latin America – Whirlpool entered the Latin American markets, primarily Brazil, Argentina and Chile, through taking up equity positions in local companies with high market share, brand recognition and brand loyalty. Whirlpool considered Brazil to be a high growth market and by 1997, it made large investments in the country. Initial sales and profits (up to 1995) were encouraging.

  However, by 1998, interest rates in the industry had quadrupled from their 1997 levels, the Brazilian currency depreciated and the economy started to slide downwards. In addition, consumers reacted to the economic problems by a reduction in spending and the result was 25% lower sales for Whirlpool.

Overall, Whirlpool did not succeed in achieving its objective of becoming the leader in the global appliance industry primarily because of inadequate market research, which led to a failure to understand the nature of the appliance industry in other countries (the company overestimated demand and ignored pressures for local responsiveness). The company was too ambitious and expanded too fast into all the markets simultaneously. The company did not pursue strategies that were inimitable and thus, the strategies failed to give it a competitive advantage.

CASE 41

"You Push the Button, We Do The Rest": From Silver Halide to Infoimaging at Eastman Kodak

SYNOPSIS OF THE CASE

The Kodak case chronicles the events that have occurred in the Kodak company up to 2002. It is about the continuing problems that Kodak has been experiencing in its core photographic business. It also chronicles the way the company changed its strategy and structure to try to recapture market share in the photographic products industry and to enter new digital markets that would provide it with long-term potential in the future. First, the case focuses on analyzing how changes in industry competition and the emergence of new industries threatened Kodak's competitive position in the photographic imaging industry, an industry it had so long dominated. There follows an analysis of how Kodak dealt with the problems in the industry and how it is attempting to enter new industries to exploit its skills in new areas. The analysis here centers on whether Kodak is really creating value through its acquisitions or is really pursuing growth without profitability.

Next appears an in-depth discussion of strategy-structure linkages at Kodak and an examination of how Kodak's former CEO, Colby Chandler, attempted to decentralize Kodak's decision making and to encourage a more entrepreneurial style in the individual product divisions. He also tried to curtail costs by massively reducing the work force and introducing control systems to improve manufacturing efficiency.

Then, the case examines the efforts of first, George Fisher and then Daniel Carp both to reduce its debt and cost structure while at the same time promoting its pipline of new profitable digital products. The case ends with the question of whether Carp will be able to find ways of changing Kodak's strategy and structure to create value and restore it to its traditionally high levels of profitability and return on investment or whether, instead, the takeover threat will increase.

TEACHING OBJECTIVES

The main teaching objectives of this case are as follows:

1. Illustrate how changes in the competitive environment of the imaging industry, and the emergence of new industries with substitute products, can threaten even large, successful companies.

2. Discuss how Kodak embarked on a policy of diversification into new industries, product development, and further vertical integration in the photographic business to counter these environmental threats.

3. Examine the pros and cons of these strategies and determine whether value and synergies were obtained from diversification.

4. Demonstrate the role and importance of matching strategy and structure in helping a company respond to environmental threats and correct the weaknesses that led to these threats in the first place.

Because the company is a household name, the Kodak case provokes a high level of interest and debate among students. Currently, Kodak is performing better, and the case provides an excellent opportunity to have students do some library research and update it to see how Kodak is dong today.

The case is appropriate to use after the chapter on strategy and structure so that students can understand the practical advantages and disadvantages of pursuing a strategy of vertical integration and/or diversification. It also exposes the hazards of pursuing a global strategy when efficient foreign competitors attack your market.

STRATEGIC ISSUES AND DISCUSSION QUESTIONS

The overriding issue in the case is how Kodak should position itself for future growth and profitability, given increased competition in the photographic imaging market, and in industries such as electronic imaging, information systems, pharmaceuticals, and chemicals, where Kodak has made many acquisitions to obtain an industry presence. Its profitability has been declining steadily as Fuji in film and paper products, Canon in photocopiers, and IBM and Hewlett-Packard in office information systems have penetrated the various industries in which Kodak competes.

Traditionally, Kodak pursued a strategy of vertical integration and was dominant in each of the phases of the photographic business: chemical and film production, cameras, and developing and printing. However, its conservative style and industry dominance led it to underestimate the potential threat from foreign firms, and it failed to understand the limitations of staying inside one business. Kodak counterattacked by extending its control in its domestic photographic operations (by increasing its control over film processing, for example), and it also entered new businesses to find ways to expand profitably. These new businesses were marginally related in some way to its existing operations; most involve the application of Kodak's strengths in chemicals or imaging sciences. However, some businesses such as its battery and plastics ventures were new and are not related to the company's existing businesses. Here the links are weaker.

The best ways to analyze the case is to start by looking at Kodak's history and then analyze the strengths and weaknesses of its existing strategy. The following questions can help focus the discussion and analysis for students.

1. **How did Kodak's corporate strategy change over time? How did the strengths and weakness of Kodak change as its strategy changed over time?**

    Traditionally, Kodak was a vertically integrated company that manufactured the chemicals necessary to produce film, produced film and cameras, and then provided the chemicals and processing equipment to develop and print film. Being involved in all aspects of the production chain was a primary cause of its profitability: it was able to achieve all the advantage of vertical integration.

    *   Its huge production volumes allowed it to achieve huge economies of scale.

    *   As its own supplier of chemicals, it was able to avoid the costs of buying from suppliers and to internalize the value added at all stages of the production process.

    *   It was able to maintain the quality of its products by its control of all the stages of the production process. This allowed it to pursue a strategy of differentiation.

    *   Its broad-ranging activities allowed it to establish a well-known brand name, and it could protect its image and reputation because it controlled all the stages of production.

    *   It was the expert in silver-halide-based photographic products and spent large amounts on R&D.

    Its established reputation and brand name in the United States made the next step in Kodak's corporate strategy obvious: global expansion. Kodak was able to take its core skills and apply them in almost every country in the world. It established a worldwide network of manufacturing plants and set up wholly owned foreign subsidiaries to produce chemicals and film products abroad. It thus protected its technology, and its foreign subsidiaries (such as Kodak Pathe in France) made major technological breakthroughs in film production that were transferred back to the United States. Kodak consolidated its hold on the world market and established a worldwide reputation for quality products. This strategy also added to its profitability and helped overcome the limit to growth posed by vertical integration.

    Kodak's strategy stopped there and the company made few attempts to depart from this corporate strategy. Management became content to operate what was now a huge global corporation. However, there were weaknesses associated with this strategy.

    By concentrating on one business, even though on a global basis, the company was missing out on opportunities to apply its core skills elsewhere. Kodak was global by the 1960s, and after this point it lost the entrepreneurial spirit; it became too involved in managing its existing businesses to sense profitable opportunities elsewhere. Moreover, it failed to control the costs of its existing operations and became a high-cost manufacturer compared to competitors such as Fuji.

Kodak's very success led it to develop a conservative, centralized management style where managers were more concerned with protecting Kodak's and their position in existing markets than with seeking out opportunities elsewhere. Decision making slowed down, and R&D became confined to silver halide photography. Kodak made little attempt to internally venture or to expand its skills elsewhere. Why should it? It was exploiting its protected position in the film business and making high profits.

With its protected position and high level of vertical integration (Kodak was really a fully integrated company), its manufacturing plants became protected from outside competition, and Kodak's manufacturing costs slowly started to rise to offset economies of scale.

Also, Kodak became slow to introduce new products and improve quality, and it let opportunities like instant photography and xerography slip by because it was adopting a product-oriented, not a consumer-oriented, business definition: silver halide film processing. Also, it failed to develop 35mm cameras even when it had the opportunity to do so. There was a slowing of R&D and marketing, Kodak did not protect its differentiation advantage, and its costs were rising.

Kodak was tied to the fortunes of one industry, and in this industry it was not protecting its competitive position.

2.   **In what ways did the environment affect Kodak during this period?**

Kodak was in a very weak position when the environment changed and foreign firms such as Fuji attacked its existing markets. There were a number of threats that Kodak experienced:

- A mature photographic market. Sales were increasing only 5% a year, and Kodak had 80 percent of the market. Slow growth would hurt profitability.

- Increases in foreign competition in film processing and cameras, and increases in film processing competition from new, fast-developing film operators such as Fox photo that used other than Kodak chemicals and paper.

- Growth in substitute products from new industries that offered different ways of recording images and memories, Kodak's major business. Electronic imaging was a particularly important threat.

- Increases in competition from substitute products.

- More powerful customers who could now choose which product to purchase.

- Increases in rivalry from existing film suppliers such as Fuji, which quickly became a major player.

The environment became more hostile on all fronts, and Kodak was facing a number of internal problems that were the product of its long dominance in the industry. It was this combination of increased environmental threats and increased internal weaknesses that occasioned Kodak's declining profitability. The issue facing Kodak was how to reverse this trend and find a successful new strategy.

3.   **How did Kodak change its strategy to respond to the changes in the photographic imaging market?**

First, Kodak attempted to improve its position in existing businesses by improving its products and by entering into strategic alliances with foreign manufacturers to sell their products under the Kodak name to fill gaps in its product line. It also took over Fox photo, the quick photo developing chain to increase its control of the processing end of the market and then entered into an agreement with Fuqua Industries to form a joint venture, Qualex Inc., to manage the resulting nationwide chain of film laboratories. This also protected the market for its paper and chemical products, which had been increasingly threatened by low-cost manufacturers. Now all the laboratories used Kodak products. Thus Kodak's competitive moves were designed to strengthen its core business by pursuing a strategy of vertical integration.

4.   **What other changes in corporate strategy did Kodak make to strengthen its position?**

The strategy of vertical integration makes perfect sense from a strategic point of view; it is with the movement to diversification that Kodak's problems began. Essentially Kodak was cash rich: its photographic products division was a cash cow. However, with its declining profitability it was a target for raiders, and new ways had to be found to expand its sphere of operations and use up its cash resources.

Hence Kodak embarked on a strategy of diversification, with the aim of finding new growth opportunities to reduce its dependence on the photographic industry while increasing long-run profitability.

What Kodak did was to enter businesses that were marginally related to its existing businesses by virtue of some connection to Kodak's core business, photographic products. For example, Kodak has always produced film for X-rays, so it saw an opportunity to develop products in medical imaging techniques, which are logical product extensions. Kodak also supplied itself with chemicals for its film operations, so being involved in both medical imaging and chemicals made entry into the pharmaceuticals industry seem like related diversification. This was the strategy Kodak pursued with its biotechnology ventures and then with the purchase of Sterling Drugs. However, did pharmaceuticals add value to Kodak? So far, the answer is no. This move was an example of unrelated (not related) diversification and conglomerate growth, despite Chandler's claim of "logical synergies."

A similar story can be told in the nature of Kodak's other acquisitions. Kodak was in the imaging business and was trying to become the leader in electronic imaging, so what could be more logical than entry into the information systems business, which for Kodak was primarily oriented around business systems? Accordingly, Kodak purchased floppy disc manufacturers and information system software companies to try to build a presence in this area. Again, however, it had no knowledge of these businesses, and the financial figures given in the case show the results of this venture.

Kodak's, then, was really a strategy of unrelated diversification. It is difficult to see any synergies in the relationships between its different operating groups. Although it is true that they could all use the Kodak name, there was little opportunity for transferring skills or sharing functions between divisions.

5. **How did these changes in strategy affect Kodak's performance?**

Two problems arose from this change in strategy. First, as we have noted, Kodak had no core skills or strengths in these new businesses and hence was not in a position to exploit opportunities in the new markets. Second, Kodak was entering markets where strong competitors existed so that it encountered intense competition, which also drove down revenues. In chemicals, for example, and in office systems, there are very strong foreign firms in markets Kodak was entering. Even in imaging Kodak did not have its own way, as Fuji film counterattacked, built new capacity in Europe, and engaged in intense advertising to build market share in the United States. Competition depressed prices and helped contribute to the poor results for all its business operating groups, as shown in Exhibit 2.

Thus its strategy of diversification to date has not been successful. What Whitmore can do to change the situation remains to be seen. Probably Kodak will divest itself of many of the peripheral businesses it has entered and make new acquisitions to strengthen its presence in those it has already entered. For example, given its purchase of Sterling Drug, Upjohn would seem to be a very complementary acquisition. However, a total reassessment of its portfolio is needed to avoid a takeover threat. (Kodak has in fact divested all these peripheral businesses as your students will find out from research.)

6. **How did Kodak change its structure and control systems to respond to a hostile environmental threats and internal weaknesses?**

In addition to revising its strategy, Kodak responded to threats from the environment by altering its structure, control systems, and managerial style. Kodak had become very centralized over the years, and major decisions were being made increasingly by managers at the top of the organization. Entrepreneurship was stifled by a culture that was conservative and risk-averse; managers were afraid to rock the boat to promote product development. The effect of these factors was to slow the company's response to changes in the environment, and one reason why the threats emerged was weakness in the company's structure. Chandler decided to reorganize the company to deal with these problems.

First, he reorganized the divisional structure of the corporation, and eventually four divisions or strategic business units emerged to handle the company's businesses: the imaging (photographic) division, the information systems division, the health group, and the Eastman chemical division. Each division (or what Kodak called an operating group) contained broadly similar businesses. Then, inside each SBU, each business was organized as a profit center and was controlled by a manager who was evaluated on bottom-line performance. The result was the decentralization of decision making to lower levels in the organization. For example, in the imaging group, which contained photographic and information products and accounted for 80 percent of Kodak's sales, 18 individual businesses were identified and given all the functional resources necessary to compete in the new environment. Kodak also changed its control systems to emphasize efficiency and productivity. New operating and expense budgets were introduced to reduce costs, and managers were evaluated on measures of both efficiency and quality.

Kodak reorganized its global operating structure to reduce costs. It streamlined its worldwide operations by reducing the number of its foreign manufacturing operations, concentrating production in countries with either low labor costs or good geographic location. It also consolidated its expensive R&D operations to reduce costs. These changes led to $55 million in productivity savings.

Kodak changed its structure and control systems to try to reduce costs. Over the years Kodak had become a high-cost manufacturer, and it paid little attention to ways to cut costs through altering its internal procedures. This became crucial in view of competition from Fuji, and Kodak closed down manufacturing facilities and embarked on new form of output control, measuring waste and taking like measures to try to improve productivity. This increased use of behavior control and output control was linked to reward at all levels in the organization. Compensation was now based much more on meeting output goals. Decentralization had not succeeded in increasing motivation, and Kodak realized that in its new ventures, as well as in its existing operations, it needed to relate pay to performance.

Another significant part of Kodak's attempt to reduce costs was reduction in its work force; it achieved savings of over $1 billion per year from this strategy by the end of the 1980s. Over 20 percent of the work force has been terminated, and employment is continuing to fall as the company streamlines its operations and reduces levels in the hierarchy via its new policy of decentralization. This winnowing also affected the culture of the company: many young managers were promoted to handle the new business, while many older, conservative employees retired or were transferred sideways. Finally, Kodak created a "new venture" board with the aim of encouraging internal venturing and is seeking to develop new products through extensions from its existing skills in R&D.

The new structure was designed to match Kodak's new strategy of aggressive competition in existing photographic markets with quick response to Fuji and competitors. The new SBU structure enables Kodak to assimilate new acquisitions into the Kodak family quickly and provides for the integration and transfer of R&D or marketing skills. Also, the decentralized management style allows managers in acquired companies the autonomy to develop their businesses inside the Kodak umbrella. Finally, the SBU structure permits Kodak to operate vertical integration and to effect related and unrelated diversification simultaneously.

However, there have been problems in managing the new structure, and Kodak has increasingly formed joint ventures to handle some of its new ventures because of problems that arose in managing them internally. It has also closed down many units or sold them off because of management problems. It has had great difficulty in becoming more entrepreneurial, and many of its internal ventures have been discounted. The constant downsizing has damaged morale among the work force; it is difficult to be innovative if the prospect of being laid off is in your mind. In 1990, Kodak announced a "tin parachute" scheme whereby if it was taken over, employees would receive substantial severance pay and other benefits. It hoped this would raise morale as well as discourage raiders.

7. **What was George Fisher's new strategy for Kodak? Did he succeed in turning it around its performance?**

Kay Whitmore, who replaced Chandler, was an insider who could not make the hard decisions necessary to stem Kodak's losses. He was soon replaced by George Fisher, the former CEO of Motorola, who had had enormous success it revitalizing that company's product line. Fisher immediately began to reverse Chandler's diversification strategy, he sold off Sterling drugs, and closed down the health division to reduce Kodak's massive debt, saving only health imaging. He also decided that the chemicals division no longer was important to what Fisher viewed as Kodak's digital future, and it was spun off as a separate company. In the information systems group Fisher decided to focus on document imaging through photocopiers, commercial inkjet printers, and commercial digital imaging, and he sold off all the other businesses that did not fit this theme.

These moves boosted Kodak's stock price in the short term, but he was till left with the problem of what to do in the core photographic product imaging group. Here Kodak still lagged its major competitors in innovation and technological advances; it had no special competencies in this area, yet this was clearly where the future lay. Fisher began to massively increase funding for digital projects. To speed product development he created 14 autonomous business units based up on serving the needs of different customers. While this gave more autonomy to the divisions, it also raised costs and he probably would have been better off in focusing down to less than 10 different groups.

In the silver halide business, the company came under increasing competition from Fuji which opened a low-cost state of the art manufacturing plant in the U.S. and Europe and through 1995-1997Fuji lowered its prices and began a price war to raise its market share, snatching away the Wal-Mart account in the process. Kodak's market share fell 4%, which cost the company $125 million in lost revenues and profits—profits it needed to fund its debt and invest in digital technology.

The problem was that Kodak did not have the internal technological competences to warrant its investment in all the new digital technologies. Fisher would have been better off to massively downscale the company's activities and focus on reducing its global cost structure to make Kodak a money-making machine for shareholders. However, it still viewed itself as a technological powerhouse and Fisher was probably not the right person to lead the company into the future.

Kodak continued to decline steadily through the 1990s, and by late 1998 it was clear that Fishers days as CEO were numbered. In fact, another Kodak insider, Daniel Carp had been steadily building his power base in the organization and by 1997 he was already in charge of Kodak's global digital and applied imaging businesses, which were seen as the key to the future.

In 1997 Kodak took a controlling stake in Chinon the Japanese photographic products company that had been making its digital cameras and scanners and began an aggressive global push to build its global market share. In 1998, it began to emerge as the cost leader in the digital camera business with new models offering great clarity for the price and it also began to enter the world of digital image editing kiosks which allowed consumers to scan, edit, share and print their digital pictures and it also formed an alliance with AOL for an exclusive online service "You've Got pictures." Under Carp, Kodak was making easy to use digital cameras, however, the price of digital cameras began to fall dramatically as competition increased so this was not building profitability. Furthermore, digital cameras did not use silver halide film so this did not boost Kodak's film sales.

8.   **How did Kodak's strategy change under Carp?**

Recognizing that Carp was Kodak's best hope for major recovery, in 1999 he was named CEO and he increased the push to introduce advanced digital products in all of Kodak's divisions including entry into making full color active matrix organic electroluminescent (OEL) displays which was one of the many competing technologies to be used for digital devices in the future.

Between 1998 and 2000 Kodak's profits and stock price recovered somewhat, however, this was not because Carp had implanted in Kodak some new competence in digital technology but because the price war with Fuji had ended as both companies realized they were losing more than they were gaining by their fight for market share. Kodak was still stuck in the middle between differentiation and low cost, and the huge digital development costs were offsetting profit increases from its sale of film so profits were not increasing. It did introduce some very popular new digital cameras that sold in the millions, however, this cannibalized film sales, and while it argued consumers would still need to buy Kodak paper to print their photographs it was becoming clear that they were printing fewer photographs, preferring to share images by disc, and over digital devices ranging from computers to PDA's. How great was the profit in digital imaging, especially when competitors like Sony and Canon were coming with constant improvements and companies like Microsoft were introducing new "tablet" computers that could show digital images and be connected to digital cameras.

On the photofinishing end, Kodak strived hard to develop its own advanced digital photofinishing kiosks to put in retail and drug stores throughout the US and world to lead in this lucrative business. However, Fuji was developing its own advanced kiosks and it was not clear in 2002 which company would become the leader. At the same time the shift to digital imaging led to the bankruptcy of Kodak's Fox photo photofinishing chain which could no longer compete, and one major customer Kmart entered Chapter 11. The digital kiosk business is potential very profitable and HP is also a major contender here, if Kodak loses here then it will be hard for it to claim a real digital presence, especially as its online ventures have not proved successful, there are so many software programs that allow customers to edit and share their photographs it is not clear there is a market here at all.

In 2001, Carp realized that Kodak simply had to reduce its cost structure. Very belatedly he announced a major reorganization of Kodak's businesses to give it a sharper focus on products and customers. Essentially, as the case relates, he once again returned Kodak to focus on four major product groups on a global basis to reduce overhead costs and speed the introduction of new products to the market—the photography group (both digital and chemical), commercial imaging, health imaging, and the components group to handle the OEL optics business on which Carp put high hopes. Kodak also began another major round of layoffs to cut costs.

9. **What do you think of Kodak's future prospects? Would you buy shares in this firm? Why or why not?**

Kodak is once again at a turning point. Its strategy under Fisher or Carp has not succeeded, and although digital revenues have increased, the increase represents growth without profitability. It faces intense competition in its product markets and even its core business is under threat because of the time it has taken Kodak to get its costs under control. Future growth in profitability will have to come from increased revenue generation, and it is not clear where this revenue will come from. It seems increasingly likely that Kodak may be taken over.

Its film business is a major generator of cash but its high cost structure has reduced profitability and its continuing efforts to fund digital product development is showing little sign of showing sustained growth.

CASE 42

Restructuring Exide

SYNOPSIS OF THE CASE

When faced with financial trouble, Exide Corporation decided to fix the trouble by bringing in Robert Lutz, a former Chrysler executive and an ex-Marine with a kick-down-the-doors management style. As the new CEO, Lutz decided to make a number of autocratic decisions to stop the red ink. He quickly pulled out of an unprofitable supply agreement, introduced new products, settled legal suits and replaced the entire board of directors. Additionally, he closed plants while at the same time completing a major acquisition of GNB technologies. But by far his biggest problem was to deal with an organizational structure that featured country anonymity and paid big bonuses to country executives for reaching operational objectives, often at the expense of subsidiaries operating in other countries.

Although Lutz had asked for a series of corporate retreats to solve the organizational problem, it became clear that the retreats would not propose the solution he favored. Lutz soon announced that he had unilaterally decided to replace the geographic organization with global business units, causing several country managers to defect. Lutz promoted one country manager, Albrecht Leuschner to head of a global business unit. Compounding the problem was GNB technologies with its charismatic leader Mitchell Bergman. When Lutz amended the restructuring of the company into business units to give Bergman a key role, a turf war threatened between Leuschner and Bergman.

TEACHING OBJECTIVES

This case pursues the following teaching objectives:

1.   To provide an understanding of the complexity of organizational structures on the success of international businesses.

2.   To demonstrate how autocratic decisions can breed trouble and resentment within an international firm.

3.   Become more aware of the key role that an organizational structure plays in the successful functioning of international business.

STRATEGIC ISSUES AND DISCUSSION QUESTIONS

1.   **What kind of industry environment does Exide operate in? Is it a global industry, a multi-domestic industry, or something in between? What are the pressures for local representatives in the industry? What are the pressures for globalization?**

The industrial environment for Exide is extremely complex. Although it operates in the broad areas of industrial and automotive segments, Exide has many different types of customers: the manufacturers of fork lifts, golf carts, wheel chairs, electric floor cleaning equipment, telecommunications equipment, businesses that use standby batteries and the users of lift-trucks. The automotive area includes automobile manufacturers and huge aftermarket distributors like Wal-Mart and K-Mart. Because of the diversity of these types of customers, Exide's industrial environment can best be described as something between global and multi-domestic. It can be described as global in that Exide deals with customers like Ford and Mack trucks, but it is more multi-domestic in nature when dealing with the European Battery market. Consequently, the pressures of dealing with the complexities of so many different market segments demand that it will be very locally responsive. However, although some configurations and model needs vary widely, a battery is still an item that can affect great economies of scale, especially when reducing the cost of acquiring lead, a major ingredient.

2.   **How might a structure based on geography (country subsidies) result in inefficiencies at Exide?**

Lutz inherited a geography based organizational structure that had as many as 10 different country organizations. Each country organization had its own brands, manufacturing facilities, distribution systems, profit goals and incentives. This type of a structure can potentially lead to inefficiencies because it may require separate manufacturing facilities in order to be locally responsive for certain regions of the globe. Those separate facilities would result in the duplication of manufacturing operations and a significant increase in manufacturing costs. Additionally, a geographic structure might require separate geographic subsidiaries to compete with each other for business from areas where no geographic turf ownership has been decided.

3.   **What are the potential benefits to Exide from moving from a geographic structure based on country organization to a product structure based on global business units? What are the potential drawbacks to such a structure?**

Lutz restructured Exide to an organization with global business units along distinct product lines, where each product unit was responsible for strategic and operational product decisions with country managers coordinating sales and distribution activities. By moving from a geographic structure to a product structure, Exide was able to eliminate much duplication in the manufacturing process and to close ineffective and unprofitable manufacturing locations. It also eliminated the internal competition between business units competing for businesses with the same customer.

A product structure could potentially lead to problems if it turns out the different geographic regions have different requirements within the same product line. There may be increased communication and coordination problems when product teams are dispersed all over the world.

4.   **Following the GNB acquisition, Lutz again changed the structure of Exide, at least on the industrial side of the organization. Why did he do this? Do you think this was a wise move, or might it create additional problems in the future?**

Lutz changed the structure for Exide's industrial business yet again and moved from a product structure to a regional one with a European business each for network power and industrial motive power, and a North American business for industrial batteries. The apparent reason was that Lutz wished to retrain Bregman, an executive for whom he had great respect. By offering Bregman a position of authority and power, it was likely that Bregman would stay on after the acquisition. The wisdom in that approach would directly depend on the effectiveness of Bregman and whether his corporate contributions will be enough to offset the harm that will result from Lutz restructuring the restructured organization. Whether Bregman can make those contributions still remains to be seen.

The new structure may not be a wise move because regional profitability pressures can cause the company to fall back into competition between firm subsidiaries for a third market. Signs of the threat can be seen in the plans each regional executive has for the China market. Moreover, Lutz has certainly shown that his mandate of a geographic organization, a decree that caused considerable tumult within the executive ranks, was not as ironclad as he first described, and that concessions could be made. Other executives may resent may resent the concessions made to Bregman when they had to toe the line and if they do, the move is likely to cause major internal strife.

CASE 43

First Greyhound, Then Greyhound Dial, Then Dial: What Will Happen in 2002?

SYNOPSIS OF THE CASE

For most of the 1980s and 1990s under John Teets, its chairman, president, and chief executive officer, the Dial Corporation's stock price has stagnated because he was unable to increase its profitability by turning around its businesses. In large part the problem Teets faces is that his predecessor pursued an unrestrained strategy of unrelated diversification and bought businesses that all turned out to be unprofitable. Teets spent six years trying to turn these businesses around, failed, finally divested them, and for the next six years tried to develop a strong new corporate portfolio by making acquisitions to strengthen each of the company's four main operating groups: bus manufacturing, consumer products, financial services, and other services. Even though the company was still a conglomerate, inside each group Teets bought related businesses and pursued a niche strategy to find product areas that were profitable and recession proof. This strategy also did not pay off, and in 1999 Teets decided to split the company into two halves to realize value for stockholders and at this point he retired. The case then recounts the attempts of two new CEOs to turn what remained of Dial around and restore profitability, although as was true in 1980, the best future for this company and its shareholders appears to be that it is dismembered and its business sold to the highest bidder.

TEACHING OBJECTIVES

The main teaching objectives of this case are as follows:

1.   Illustrate how corporate strategy changes over time in an organization, and illustrate the rationale, and lack of rationale, behind a corporation's growth path over time.

2.   Show how a company can lose sight of its core business in the pursuit of diversification.

3.   Illustrate the pitfalls of unrestrained unrelated diversification.

4.   Illustrate how changes in the macro-environment can have disastrous effects on a firm's strategy and how these effects are out of the control of the managers of a corporation.

STRATEGIC ISSUES AND DISCUSSION QUESTIONS

The bulk of the case is an account of Greyhound or Greyhound Dial's acquisitions and divestitures over time, the rationale for such acquisitions, and an analysis of the major changes in the environment that caused Greyhound problems as its portfolio was growing and changing. Before analyzing the material strategically, it is helpful to understand the critical incidents in Greyhound Dial's growth over time.

1.   **What were the critical incidents in Greyhound's growth and development over time?**

The company was formed in 1914 in Hibbing, Minnesota, to carry miners to work at the Mesabi Iron Range. By 1966, when Gerald Trautman became Greyhound's CEO, the company's route system spanned the continental United States and Canada, and there were few remaining opportunities to expand. Although Greyhound had become the world's largest bus carrier, it was highly dependent on fluctuating business cycles in its single-industry business.

In order to balance its dependence on its intercity bus business, Trautman determined that the company should diversify into unrelated businesses. Using bus revenues, he quickly acquired more than thirty companies to operate under the umbrella of the newly formed Greyhound Holding Company. Many of these acquisitions proved troublesome and were later divested; however, others were retained and became important operations for Greyhound. This same pattern of acquisitions and divestitures was to continue until Trautman turned over the driver's seat to John Teets at the end of 1981.

To understand Greyhound's strategy, we have to examine the variety and unrelatedness of Greyhound's diverse holdings. Although it was not Trautman's intention to get out of the bus business, by the end of his tenure more than 70 percent of Greyhound's revenues were to come from nontransportation sources. To Trautman's credit, his strategy of unrelated diversification was effective in lessening Greyhound's historical reliance on its bus business and in providing an avenue for further expansion in the face of a saturated and declining industry.

Nevertheless, Trautman's strategy was to be both helpful and detrimental to his successor. It was helpful because when problems arose in the bus business Greyhound was able to draw on other sources of revenue. However, the businesses Trautman acquired had their own problems, and Greyhound's inexperienced management at times aggravated them. Moreover, in focusing on these new acquisitions, Greyhound neglected its bus lines.

In 1978 Greyhound learned that it had serious problems in its bus operations, including inadequate maintenance of its buses and terminals, filthy conditions for customers, and poor security. Poor employee morale and declining ridership had resulted. Responding immediately, Trautman fired the president of Greyhound Lines and spent $60 million to successfully address these problems.

As soon as Teets had resolved the problems at Greyhound Lines, OPEC raised the price of oil, bus ridership soared, and profits jumped 150 percent, even after accounting for the cost of rehabilitating the bus business. Trautman was overjoyed with the money that his buses were making. Moreover, the tightening of the money supply by the Federal Reserve had caused the prime rate to jump to close to 20 percent, and Greyhound's interest-sensitive financial services businesses became highly profitable, accounting for the majority of Greyhound's net income.

In spite of the beneficial effects of OPEC's actions and the interest-rate-generated profits of the Financial Services Group, Trautman had serious problems at Armour Foods. They occurred as a result of mismanagement, obsolete plants and equipment, and noncompetitive labor costs. They began in 1979, when Greyhound attempted to make Armour's traditional production orientation more market focused and succeeded only in alienating its profitable private-label canned meats customers, in raising costs, and in immediately losing money on $2 billion in sales. Again, Trautman fired the management team responsible. He then reversed the marketing orientation, promoted John Teets from an affiliated restaurant operation in the Food Services Group to CEO of Armour Foods, and began to close obsolete plants to cut overhead. Teets threatened the meat packers' union with more plant closings if they did not accept an immediate wage cut. After a bitter strike, concessions were obtained. By these means and by achieving more efficient operations, it looked as though Armour had bought itself some time. In the process, Teets had impressed Trautman, who recommended that Teets succeed him as Greyhound's CEO.

Just as Teets was made CEO, at the height of Greyhound's revenues and net income, the bus and airline industries were deregulated. This generated cutthroat competition among bus carriers. Air fares dropped so low that airlines offered to exchange bus tickets for airline tickets at no additional cost. Also at about this time, OPEC's grip on oil prices was loosened and the public began to drive more. Consequently bus ridership began a sharp decline that was to continue for the next several years. Furthermore, Armour's high labor costs still adversely affected its competitiveness, even though Teets had recently won concessions. Moreover, Greyhound Lines was to learn that it was woefully unprepared to compete as a low-cost provider of bus service in a deregulated market. Its routes were overrun by competitors as its riders deserted the industry leader in droves. Teets realized that it was not advantageous to be the market leader in an industry that was in sharp decline.

In 1982, in spite of the problems that Teets anticipated, Greyhound's securities outperformed the Dow Jones Industrial average by 20 percent, even though its net income fell from $138 million in 1981 to $103 million, largely as a result of problems at Armour. The stock market apparently approved of what Teets was attempting to do with Greyhound.

Teets's goal was to create a company that would earn 15 percent on its equity, and stock analysts like Teets even though he was to find this objective difficult to reach. Nevertheless, he sold ten businesses during 1982 and made secret plans to sell Armour Foods.

In 1983 Teets sold Armour to ConAgra and trimmed $2.3 billion from Greyhound's sales. However, he did not stop with Armour. He sold ten more businesses in 1983. He also fought a bitter forty-seven-day strike with the bus drivers' Amalgamated Transit Union, which cost the company $25 million in lost fares. Fortunately, he won concessions amounting to 15 percent of wages and benefits.

By 1984, net income rose 19 percent to $125 million, but Greyhound Lines lost $1 million, despite wage concessions. It had become apparent that Teets was going to have to either make Greyhound Lines a low-cost provider of bus transportation or withdraw from the bus business. During his tenure he had already sold $300 million in assets, and only twenty-two operating units remained.

In 1985 Teets paid $264 million for the consumer products division of Purex Industries. This acquisition was acknowledged as providing Greyhound with the opportunity to use its sales force from Dial, a division Teets held back from the sale of Amour, to market the new line of products it had acquired from Purex.

Greyhound's ties to its history made it difficult to think of disposing of its bus business. However, between 1983 and 1986 Greyhound Lines lost $35 million, and in the face of renewed labor unrest it was sold in 1987 to an investor group in Dallas, Texas. Also in 1978, after attempting to sell Verex and failing, Teets announced that Greyhound was discontinuing its operations.

By 1986 Teets had created a company that was half the size it was when he took it over five years earlier. Nevertheless, he felt that he had created a company that was leaner, less leveraged, and better able to compete in the future. He has yet to be successful, in achieving his stated objective of 15 percent ROI. (Refer to exhibits in the text.

2.   **What was the underlying corporate strategy behind the development of Greyhound's portfolio of investments up to Teet's appointment as CEO? Was Trautman correct to pursue this strategy? What were the advantages and pitfalls of this strategy?**

Greyhound's initial strategy was concentration on a single business. Until 1957, Greyhound proceeded to develop bus routes and to acquire many small bus companies in order to build a nationwide route structure. In doing so, at the business level it moved from being a focused regional carrier to a nationwide differentiator, and the blue running dog logo emerged as a household name. There were extensive economies of scale associated with this strategy as the company's costs fell with each new acquisition.

At the same time, Greyhound was pursuing vertical integration: it started to manufacture buses and bus parts for its own use and for other bus companies. Finally, with its American route structure complete, it embarked on limited global expansion into Canada with the development of a transcontinental Canadian bus operation.

These ventures were very successful, and Greyhound was the pre-eminent nationwide bus carrier. Its operations proved very profitable and generated considerable cash for investment purposes. However, since there were now few opportunities for growth in the bus transportation industry, Greyhound could no longer pursue its strategy profitably. Increased global expansion was not really an option since the transportation needs of foreign countries depend on a whole host of factors. Also, most countries' bus services are under the control of the state.

In this situation, Greyhound's management decided on a policy of diversification outside the bus business. In acquiring Boothe Leasing, a financial services company, it was engaging in unrelated diversification. Gerry Trautman was appointed to spearhead the diversification effort, and under him the company enlarged its portfolio. First, Trautman bought transportation-related businesses. However, the acquisitions were in the airline industry, in the cruise business, and in providing food for travelers, and many were only marginally related to Greyhound's core bus business. Other acquisitions were intended to build Greyhound's strengths in bus manufacturing and in specialty bus service (sightseeing tours) and thus were related to Greyhound's businesses.

In making acquisitions Trautman claimed to be looking for synergies in the acquisitions; however, many acquisitions were simply the result of a desire to diversify the corporation. He also claimed that entering businesses that were not subject to the same economic downturns as the bus business would provide counter cyclical revenues, hence stabilizing Greyhound's revenue stream.

The lack of a real rationale behind the diversification program became clear when Trautman took over the Armour Corporation, apparently because the two companies shared some board members who proposed a friendly takeover. There was little acquisition screening done or any consideration of the place of the new businesses in Greyhound's portfolio. Armour contained a cash cow division producing the best-selling deodorant soap, but its food group even then was at best a question mark, and at worst a dog. The acquisition might therefore increase Greyhound's revenues, but it was not clear it would increase its profitability. Nevertheless, it paved the whole future for Greyhound, because now Greyhound had added a consumer products group to its portfolio, and this group would become the core of the company's future.

There were several pitfalls associated with the acquisitions Trautman made during his tenure as CEO:

a.   He built the portfolio but obtained only growth, not improved profitability.

b.   In entering new industries, he was entering businesses in which Greyhound had no previous experience and where the corporate center could not direct operations. All business-level strategy decisions had to be delegated to divisional or group management, with the result that the corporate center became increasingly remote from the problems confronting the divisions.

c.   The industries and macro-environments in these new industries were unlike those of the bus business. The new businesses had their own economic cycles and their own kinds of competition. This situation increased the corporate center's problems in evaluating divisional performance and potential.

d.   While all these acquisitions were being made, the bus business was essentially left to manage itself: the corporate center lost interest in it. The result was that problems in the bus business, particularly those of inefficiency and high costs, multiplied, and investment in the bus business was being curtailed because all surplus cash was being spent in acquiring new companies.

Thus, Trautman's expansionist policies were setting the scene for Greyhound's future problems. Although he always argued that the growth in Greyhound's income stream proved the soundness of his acquisition policies, Greyhound's bus business only contributed 27 percent to corporate revenues in 1981, as opposed to nearly 100 percent when Trautman took over.

3.   **What environmental factors affected Greyhound's businesses? Could anything have been done to control for environmental factors? In what ways did they distort the picture of Greyhound's performance?**

The environmental factors that affected Greyhound's businesses first improved corporate performance and then revealed the weaknesses in the portfolio. First, in the financial services group, the high interest rates of the early 1980s artificially inflated the profits of this group, which contributed substantially to corporate performance. When interest rates fell and the financial system was deregulated, the weaknesses of the financial services group became clear, and the businesses started to drain Greyhound's profits.

In the bus group, the fact that Greyhound had become an inefficient high-cost carrier was disguised for a period by the oil crisis and the subsequent huge increase in demand for bus travel that high oil prices generated. However, as soon as prices fell, cheap gas and the deregulation of the bus industry increased Greyhound's competition on all fronts and the weakness in Greyhound's former core business was felt.

Finally, there were major problems with Armour, which simply could not match competitors' prices because of its high cost structure. With an outmoded plant, outmoded equipment, and high labor costs, the food group had turned into a dog and was also draining profits.

Thus environmental changes precipitated the crisis facing Greyhound. They revealed the intrinsic weaknesses in the portfolio, and there was little that management could have done to counter their effect except not to enter into the business in the first place. The fact that corporate management was so remote from the operating groups compounded the problems because it always intervened too late to minimize the effects.

4.   **What did Teets do to change Greyhound's corporate strategy and financial position? Analyze the rationale behind this strategy. Did he succeed?**

With these environmental problems facing his businesses, Teets knew he had to restructure Greyhound's portfolio and provide a rationale for owning its collection of businesses. He decided to reverse the strategy of unrestrained unrelated diversification and concentrate corporate resources in a few key businesses. He set as a corporate goal a 15 percent ROE for Greyhound's portfolio. To prevent a corporate raider from splitting up and selling off the portfolio, Teets (1) embarked on a divestiture strategy to eliminate poor performers and raise cash for future acquisitions, and (2) started an acquisition strategy to strengthen Greyhound in its remaining four operating areas.

- Divestitures

First he sold Armour Foods, realizing that it was always going to be a high-cost business. Then he sold a collection of other businesses from all the various business groups to raise cash and trim the portfolio. The bus business was the next casualty: Teets sold it for $350 million. However, the company maintained a 22.5 percent stake in the business, as well as its Canadian bus operations. Then, with the performance of the financial group continuing to decline, Teets sold the Greyhound Capital Corporation and liquidated Verex's reinsurance business after he failed to find a buyer. This was very expensive for the company.

This restructuring cut revenues by half but also left the company with a lower ROE than when Teets took over from Trautman, excluding returns from the sale of assets. Even after the divestitures a 15 percent ROE was not achieved. Teets then turned his attention to positioning Greyhound Dial's core businesses.

- Acquisitions

The sell-off provided Teets with the extra cash he needed to fund further acquisitions in the four major product areas. He began making related acquisitions to strengthen the company's operating positions. Thus he pursued related diversification inside each operating group while the corporation as a whole was pursuing unrelated diversification. In the consumer product group he had bought Purex industries in 1985 to achieve a fit with the Dial unit. He believed there were considerable synergies to be obtained from sharing Purex and Dial's sales and marketing resources and that these would improve the company's market position in the consumer products business, which was now the star performer. So he concentrated on product development in the Dial unit and on further acquisitions. Beginning in 1987, products such as Lunch Buckets and Dial antibacterial soap were introduced using Dial's newfound marketing skills. This was very successful and helped increase revenues. He then acquired the Borax brand name of cleaning products, and in 1990 bought Breck hair products, a unit that also needed good marketing to turn it around. By now revenues of Dial were over $1 billion a year and it was the flagship business.

In the service group Teets embarked on a program of acquisitions to strengthen the company's food operations. Already involved in contract feeding, it now entered airline catering with the purchase of Dobbs. Teets then extended and consolidated other areas of the service group's operations. For example, he strengthened the money-order business by taking over Republic Money Orders. In bus manufacturing he enlarged the size of operations by taking over General Motors' bus-making business. Teet's strategy seemed successful: revenues and profits rose in 1988 and 1989.

When analysts argued that the company was still much too diversified and that further rationalization was necessary, he argued that it was following a niching strategy and focusing on profitable product areas where competition was low. He also argued that the company was recession proof. Just when the real test of his strategy was coming in 1990, Greyhound Bus Lines went bankrupt. This affected the bus manufacturing business and forced a $100-million loss provision. Dial's stock started to plunge in 1990 after it reported a loss, Teet's strategy was still a failure. In the early 1990s, even Dial's principal niche products began to perform poorly as it began to experience increased competition from its larger rivals. Dial's Purex bleach business started to lose money and was shut down in 1995. To try to increase profits, Teets began to pursue an across-the board cost-cutting strategy; it included almost halving the Dial soap divisions marketing budget! This move was disastrous because Procter & Gamble and Unilever were waiting in the wings to boost their sales of deodorant soaps. Dial lost considerable market share and P&G also began to target Purex washing powder. Previously P&G had not sought to compete in the low end of the market, however the success of Purex led it to bring out its own brand Ultra Bonus, targeted directly at Purex and Dial had to cut prices by 10% to fight back.

Many of its other businesses came under attack. Its successful Lunch Buckets line of microwavable foods was closed down after it was imitated by other major food companies such as Campbell and Heinz. Its cruise business was closed down after Walt Disney decided (mistakenly) to start its own cruise line. Its airline food business suffered when airlines, to keep prices low, began to offer customers less expensive or no meals. Ands as airports increasingly allowed fast food chains to open in airports.

Teet's strategy was not working, and the niches were not safe from competitors attack. Dial was simply a weak player in many of its businesses because it either lacked a low-cost or a differentiation advantage or lost them because of poor management, as in the case of Dial Soap, where the attempt to make a differentiators pursue a low-cost strategy resulted in that division becoming stuck in the middle.

5.   **Why did Dial break up into two different companies? Was this good for shareholders? For Teets and his managers?**

Teets became desperate to find a successful strategy. Noting the number of company ies that were splitting apart in the 1990s to focus on core businesses, he decided to split Dial into two different companies—consumer products, which would still be called Dial, and services, which would be called Viad. As related in the case, he tried to justify this by arguing that, as each business would be free to pursue its own interests, it would find profitable new growth opportunities. By allowing each part to operate separately better decision could be made and managers could focus on their own businesses and make acquisitions and follow strategies that would maximize value and stock price. He did not explain what these opportunities would be, however. Moreover, another justification for the breakup of Dial was that the performance of one set of businesses would no longer affect the performance of the other set allowing its stock price to be more fairly valued.

Critics argued, however, that there would now be two sets of possible ineffective managers at the helm, costs would increase, and that it would be better to sell off all the pieces to other more efficiently run companies, there was no rationale for having two smaller and more inefficient companies. Analysts came to realize that this was one last desperate attempt by Teets to keep control of the company and, led by Michael Price, began to demand that Dial sell off its profitable businesses and give the money to shareholders.

Obviously Teets wanted none of this, and despite the efforts of his critics, Teets pushed through the split of businesses and in 1996 Viad Corp., consisting of its remaining financial, catering, and exhibition businesses was split off. This stock subsequently performed very well, and Dial shareholders who kept their Viad shares have been rewarded. However, part of its success was that Teets essentially saddled Dial with over $500 million of debt that was really incurred by Viad, thus distorting the real value creating potential of both companies. By allowing Viad to operate from a strong initial position, its success was guaranteed and one wonders how many of Dial's top managers bought large holdings of this stock after its spin-off when prices were low.

6.   **What happened to Dial under its new CEO's Jozoff and then Baum? What strategies did they pursue?**

In 1996, Teets helped to recruit Malcolm Jozoff, a senior Procter & Gamble executive to head what was now a consumer products company, albeit one which still sold canned beef and shampoo. As a former executive of P&G, a company whose claim to fame is its ability to continually develop new and improved products, Jozoff was a strong believer in product differentiation. So, he proceeded to put in place a differentiation strategy across all of Dial's businesses. This proved to be a total disaster. While it is true that Dial soap is a differentiated product, its other products such as Purex were bought for their low cost. To improve and promote Purex, he entered into a high cost agreement with a German company for their stain fighting technology and then raised Purex's price by a few dollars a pack and sales plunged. He entered the home dry cleaning market and bought two higher end personal care products companies to take Dial up market. He also bought the Plusbelle hair care business from Revlon, a company unknown in the US but a leader in Argentina!

Jozoff's strategy was a disaster for Dial, he raised its cost structure, and its high prices soon turned its customers off and revenues started to fall. While he did set in motion a strategy to improve Dial soap, something that was entirely justified given its brand image, with new fragrances and formulations, problems emerged here too. It turned out that Dial had stuffed the channels with its old soap product and even when its new improved soaps came out in 1999 retailers would not sell it until they had sold the old stuff so P&G and Unilever gained more market share at Dial's expense.

Overall the Dial Corporation was once again brought to its knees. Any shareholders who had sold their Viad stock were now in deep trouble as its price plunged. Jozoff was replaced by Herbert Baum, one of Dial's directors and former CEO of Quaker State in 2000. Baum was known for his ability to manage a company's cost structure, in the canned oil and soup business profitability revolves around being able to control costs at the margin. When a member of the board, he had questioned Jozoff's strategy of simply raising Purex's price, why not introduce a premium Purex product he had argued and broaden its product line?

Now given Dial's deteriorating position he had to move fast to save the company. Baum reorganized the company according to product group—personal cleansing, washing powders, air fresheners, food products, and international and for the first time made product managers accountable for their own inventory management and profit! Now under-performing brands could be recognized and corrective measure taken, the company had more control of its strategy. In the Dial business he pumped money into advertising to reverse its fall in market share and protect the "cash cow." In washing powders he abandoned the differentiation strategy and went back to a low cost one, also withdrawing from the home dry cleaning market and abandoning many projects in progress to reduce costs. He sold off the upscale personal care companies and used proceeds to reduce debt. These moves quickly brought Dial's revenue and cost structure back into balance and indeed in 2002 it announced increased revenue estimates and its stock surged from its low of $12.

The question though is should Dial remain an independent company or should it be broken up and sold to the highest bidders for each of its product lines? Baum and Dial's board announced it was receptive to takeover proposals but in the Fall of 2002 it was not clear how to realize the value of Dial's assets separately, and Baum was continuing to manage the company's turnaround successfully.